Fifth Edition

W9-APR-273

ORGANIZATION DEVELOPMENT

Behavioral Science Interventions for Organization Improvement

Wendell L. French
University of Washington

Cecil H. Bell, Jr.
University of Washington

Prentice Hall, Englewood Cliffs, NJ 07632

Library of Congress Cataloging-in-Publication Data

French, Wendell L.
    Organization development : behavioral science interventions for
organization improvement / Wendell L. French, Cecil H. Bell, Jr. —
5th ed.
        p.   cm.
    Includes bibliographical references and index.
    ISBN 0–13–009374–2
    1. Organizational change.   I. Bell, Cecil.   II. Title.
HD58.8.F76   1995
658.4'06—dc20
                                                            94–27132
                                                            CIP

Acquisitions editor   *Natalie Anderson*
Production editor   *Maureen Wilson*
Cover designer   *Robert Farrar-Wagner*
Buyer   *Herb Klein*
Editorial assistant   *Diane Peirano*

© 1995, 1990, 1984, 1978, 1973 by Prentice-Hall, Inc.
A Simon & Schuster Company
Englewood Cliffs, New Jersey 07632

All rights reserved. No part of this book may be
reproduced, in any form or by any means,
without permission in writing from the publisher.

Printed in the United States of America

10 9 8 7 6 5 4 3 2

ISBN 0-13-009374-2

Prentice-Hall International (UK) Limited, *London*
Prentice-Hall of Australia Pty. Limited, *Sydney*
Prentice-Hall Canada Inc., *Toronto*
Prentice-Hall Hispanoamericana, S.A., *Mexico*
Prentice-Hall of India Private Limited, *New Delhi*
Prentice-Hall of Japan, Inc., *Tokyo*
Simon & Schuster Asia Pte. Ltd., *Singapore*
Editora Prentice-Hall do Brasil, Ltda., *Rio de Janeiro*

To
MARJORIE
and
DIANNE and MY MOTHER and FATHER

CONTENTS

v

PREFACE

Organization development is the applied behavioral science discipline dedicated to improving organizations and the people in them through the use of the theory and practice of planned change. Organizations face multiple challenges and threats today—threats to effectiveness, efficiency, and profitability; challenges from turbulent environments, increased competition, and changing customer demands; and the constant challenge to maintain congruence among organizational dimensions such as strategy, culture, and processes. Keeping organizations healthy and viable in today's world is a daunting task.

Individuals in organizations likewise face multiple challenges—finding satisfaction in and through work, fighting obsolescence of one's knowledge and skills, finding dignity and purpose in pursuit of organizational goals, and achieving human connectedness and community in the workplace. Simple survival—continuing to have an adequate job—is a major challenge today as people face layoffs and cutbacks. Although new jobs are being created, old jobs are being destroyed at an accelerating pace. "Knowledge" work is replacing "muscle" work. (Job losses from layoffs and furloughs in large firms in the United States were averaging over 50,000 *per month* in the first eight months of 1993.[1]) In summary, organizations and the individuals in them face an enormously demanding present and future.

Are there any strategies and technologies available to help people and organizations cope, adapt, survive, and even prosper in these vexing times? Fortunately, the answer is "yes." A variety of solutions exists, and organization development (OD) is one of them. *Basically, organization development is a process for teaching people how to solve problems, take advantage of opportunities, and learn how to do that better and better over time.* OD focuses on issues related to the "human side" of the organization by finding ways to increase the effectiveness of individuals, teams, and the organization's human and social processes.

As the term suggests, organization development is about developing (improving) organizations. But it is also about developing individuals. This dual focus is a unique strength of OD. We began the Preface of the first edition of this book as follows: "This book is about an exciting and profound idea and about the growing body of knowledge related to that idea. The idea is this: it is possible for the people within an organization collaboratively to manage the culture of that organization in such a way that the goals and purposes of the organization are attained at the same time that human values of individuals within the organization are furthered." OD programs energize the talents of organization members in the pursuit of their own self-interests in making the organization more successful and making their quality of working life more satisfying. OD channels the intelligence, experience, and creativity of organization members in systematic, participative programs in which the members themselves find solutions to their most pressing challenges. This is a powerful formula for change. Ingredients for the formula came from behavioral science theory and practice and were applied in a trial-and-error fashion until today there is a coherent improvement strategy called organization development.

Organization development is a relatively recent invention. It started in the late 1950s when behavioral scientists steeped in the lore and technology of group dynamics attempted to apply that knowledge to improve team functioning and intergroup relations in organizations. Early returns were encouraging, and attention was soon directed toward other human and social processes in organizations such as the design of work tasks, organization structure, conflict resolution, strategy formulation and implementation, and the like. The field of OD grew rapidly in the 1970s and 1980s with thousands of organizations in the private and public sectors utilizing the theory and methods of OD with great success. Today organization development represents one of the best strategies for coping with the rampant changes occurring in the marketplace and society. We predict that organization development will be a preferred improvement strategy well into the next century.

This book is about organization development. It tells the story of what OD is, how it works, its values, its change techniques (called interventions), and what the future of OD might be. The first edition of the book appeared in 1973, and revisions were published in 1978, 1984, and

1990. Along with domestic editions, the book has been published in the German, Spanish, Italian, and Finnish languages as well as in an international English-language edition. We have always attempted to present a concise but complete exposition of the theory, practice, and research related to organization development in the belief that leaders, students, and OD practitioners can use these concepts to make their lives and their organizations better. This edition continues that tradition.

ORGANIZATION OF THE BOOK

Chapters 1–8 provide an overview of OD and its changing context. Sequentially, the reader is provided with illustrations of OD efforts; definitions of OD; a history of OD; its underlying values, assumptions, and beliefs; its theoretical and research foundations; managing the OD process; the history and utility of action research; and an overview of OD interventions.

Chapters 9–13 describe interventions in some detail. Chapters 9 and 10 detail OD interventions of importance to teams and to intergroup and interpersonal relationships. Chapter 11 describes interventions that involve the entire organization, including "getting the whole system in the room." Chapter 12 focuses on structural (or "technostructural") interventions, including work redesign, sociotechnical systems (STS), self-managed teams, parallel learning structures, total quality management (TQM), and large-scale systems change. Included is a discussion of reengineering. Chapter 13 focuses on training interventions of relevance to OD.

Chapters 14–16 deal with a number of issues in OD consulting. Chapter 14 looks at issues in consultant-client relationships, including ethical matters. Chapter 15 focuses on the ramifications of an OD effort, including its relationship to human resources management policies and practices. Chapter 16 deals with the sensitive issue of power and politics in OD.

The book ends with Chapters 17 and 18 on OD research and the future of OD. Together they provide a very positive, optimistic conclusion to the volume, as well as a number of challenges.

ADDED FEATURES

This edition is a major revision. While the basic fundamentals remain, we emphasize the changing paradigms in management and OD theory and describe several new and important interventions. Further, the discussion is set in the rapidly changing context of globalization, intensified competition and collaboration, and high interest in such matters as total quality management (TQM) and large-scale organizational change. Following are some of the added highlights of individual chapters:

Chapter 1: "The Field of Organization Development" presents a brief overview of the field. In addition, Chapter 1 presents new illustrations of OD interventions from a variety of settings.

Chapter 2: "Definitions of Organization Development" presents a number of definitions from leading practitioners and theorists, modifying our earlier definition to include terms like *visioning, empowerment,* and *learning processes.*

Chapter 3: "A History of Organization Development," an already widely-quoted chapter, adds the contribution of another early OD pioneer, Eva Schindler-Rainman. Added is an up-to-date statement from an executive of TRW Space & Electronics Group—the location of one of the most long-lived OD efforts in the world—on the current status of OD in that corporation. This chapter also presents second-generation OD and the rapidly changing context of OD.

Chapter 4: "Values, Assumptions, and Beliefs in OD" adds a chronology of management thought and the results of a survey of OD practitioners on values in OD.

Chapter 5: "Foundations of Organization Development" presents new material on models and theories of planned change, and on systems theory, as well as concepts on participation and empowerment, teams and teamwork, and parallel learning structures.

Chapter 6: "Managing the OD Process" describes phases in OD programs; presents tables on diagnosis, that is, what to look for and where to look; and examines the action component and process management components of OD efforts.

Chapter 7: "Action Research and Organization Development" supplements an historical account of different versions of action research with new, contemporary forms.

Chapter 8: "OD Interventions—An Overview" lists a number of additional contemporary interventions and concepts, including organizational transformation and large-scale systems change.

Chapter 9: "Team Interventions" adds material on the characteristics of high-performance teams and describes additional interventions, including the interdependency exercise, the appreciations-and-concerns exercise, appreciative inquiry, and visioning.

Chapter 10: "Intergroup and Third-Party Peacemaking Interventions" adds a description of two-person conflict management sessions and a description of partnering, an intervention which can assist owners and contractors in avoiding unnecessary cost overruns and delays in large construction projects.

Chapter 11: "Comprehensive Interventions" adds "getting the whole system in the room," future search conferences, and cultural analysis. In addition, Chapter 11 discusses transorganizational development (TD).

Chapter 12: "Structural Interventions" provides new material on work redesign, and additional information on sociotechnical systems (STS), and self-managed work teams. Added are sections on total quality management (TQM) large-scale systems change and a discussion of the relevance of OD to reengineering.

Chapter 13: "Training Experiences" adds the concept of career anchors and includes a more extensive discussion of the relevance of T-group experiences.

Chapter 14: "Issues in Consultant-Client Relationships" adds material on entry and contracting, and more on ethics in OD.

Chapter 15: "System Ramifications" provides more on the importance of leadership and leadership style as they relate to OD, including leadership from human resources professionals. This chapter also includes further discussion of resistance to change and provides additional material on consulting skills. The dilemma presented by layoffs and other organizational crises is examined with a discussion of recent NLRB rulings relative to employee involvement programs.

Chapter 16: "Power, Politics, and Organization Development" provides a pragmatic approach to the use of power in OD.

Chapter 17: "Research on Organization Development" is an up-to-date review of the research on OD, including a "review of the reviews."

Chapter 18: "The Future and OD" extrapolates from present trends in OD and its present environment to make conjectures about the future of OD.

ACKNOWLEDGMENTS

We acknowledge our debt to the work and writings of the pioneer practitioner-scholars about whom we write in Chapter 3, "A History of Organization Development." Corrrespondence and interviews with several of these leading figures provided us with invaluable information and helped us unravel the threads of the early history of OD. In particular, we want to thank Chris Argyris, Richard Beckhard, Kenneth Benne, Robert Blake, Rensis Likert, Ronald Lippitt, Jane Mouton, Eva Schindler-Rainman, Herbert Shepard, and Robert Tannenbaum. We also wish to thank the clients and internal and external consultants with whom we have worked over the years. They have taught us much about this field.

OD is a fun, exciting, evolving discipline with the worthwhile goals of improving individual and organizational performance. It is an immensely satisfying vocation for those who learn its craft, art, and science. We hope you find valuable insights in these pages.

WENDELL FRENCH
CECIL BELL

NOTES

1. The *Wall Street Journal*, August 24, 1993, p. A1. According to a count by placement firm Challenger, Gray, and Christmas, 1993 furloughs and layoffs were averaging 50,516 monthly in the U.S., more than 4,000 a month higher than the recession year of 1991.

1

THE FIELD OF ORGANIZATION DEVELOPMENT

This book tells the broad story of organization development—its history, nature and characteristics, theory, practice methods, and values. Organization development is a planned, systematic process in which applied behavioral science principles and practices are introduced into ongoing organizations toward the goal of increasing individual and organizational effectiveness. The focus is on organizations and making them function better, that is, on *total system change*. The orientation is on action— achieving desired results as a consequence of planned activities. The target is human and social processes, the human side of organizations. The setting is real organizations in the real world. We want you, the reader, to have a complete understanding of organization development (OD): what it is, how it works, why it works, and how you can use the information in this book to improve the performance of your organization.

To begin the story, this chapter introduces the field of OD, shows some of its major features in broad outline, and presents several illustrations of OD programs. Later chapters round out the story in more complete detail.

OVERVIEW OF THE FIELD OF ORGANIZATION DEVELOPMENT

Organization development is a unique organizational improvement strategy that emerged in the late 1950s and early 1960s. Originally based on insights from group dynamics and on theory and practice related to planned change, the field has evolved into an integrated framework of theories and practices capable of solving or helping to solve most of the important problems confronting the human side of organizations.

Organization development is about people *and* organizations and people *in* organizations and how they function. OD is also about planned change, that is, getting individuals, teams, and organizations to function better. Planned change involves common sense, hard work applied diligently over time, a systematic, goal-oriented approach, and valid knowledge about organizational dynamics and how to change them. Valid knowledge derives from the behavioral sciences such as psychology, social psychology, sociology, anthropology, systems theory, organizational behavior, organization theory, and the practice of management. Putting all this together, organization development offers a prescription for improving the "fit" between the individual and the organization, between the organization and its environment, and among organizational components such as strategy, structure, and processes. The prescription is implemented through interventions and activities that address specific problematic conditions.

Leaders and OD practitioners typically conduct OD programs together. Practitioners are consultants trained in the theory and practice of organization development; they understand organizational dynamics and organizational change. These persons may be members of the organization (internal consultants) or may be from outside the organization (external consultants). Two goals of OD programs are (1) to improve the functioning of individuals, teams, and the total organization, and (2) to impart the necessary skills and knowledge that will enable organization members continuously to improve their functioning on their own.

OD programs are long-term, planned, sustained efforts. A leader confronts an undesirable situation and seeks to change it. The leader establishes contact with an OD professional, and together they explore whether organization development is relevant to the task at hand. If the answer is yes, they enlist others in the organization to help design and implement the change program. A central feature of OD is widespread participation and involvement: Get as many people as possible into the act. An overall game plan or strategy is then developed that includes a series of activities, each intended to achieve an outcome that moves the organization toward the desired goals. This is the overall OD model, but in practice OD programs are not so linear and straightforward.

Organization development deals with the gamut of "people problems" in organizations. Examples would be the following: poor morale, low productivity, poor quality, interpersonal conflict, intergroup conflict, unclear goals (either corporate strategy or unit goals), inappropriate leadership styles, poor team performance, inappropriate organization structure, poorly designed tasks, insufficient attention to environmental demands, poor customer relations, different parts of the organization working at cross-purposes, and the like. In short, where individuals, teams, and organizations are not realizing their full potential, OD can improve the situation.

A PREVIEW OF THE MAJOR THEMES OF THE BOOK

Several themes underlie the theory and practice of organization development. One theme relates to planned change, another to the distinctive nature of OD consulting. A cluster of themes describes the nature of OD as a process that focuses on organizational culture, processes, and structure utilizing a total system perspective. A final theme is "action research." We will examine these themes in turn.

Planned Change

"Change" means the new state of things is different from the old state of things. Change is omnipresent; change will be one of the few constants in the late 1990s and into the next century. This book is about planned change related to organizations and the people in them. Organization development helps leaders address and embrace change from the perspective that change is an opportunity, not a threat. Most demands for change come from outside the organization—from government agencies, competitors, new technologies, customers, market forces, and the larger society. Sometimes demands for change come from within the organization—a new chief executive, obsolete products or services, a new strategic direction, declining profitability, or an increasingly diverse work force. It is necessary to understand change and planned change to understand organization development.

Change has different facets to it. For example, change can be deliberate (planned) or accidental (unplanned). The magnitude of change can be large or small. In terms of scope, it can affect many elements of the organization or only a few elements. It can be fast (abrupt, revolutionary) or slow (evolutionary). The new state of things can have an entirely different nature from the old state of things (fundamental, quantum, or "second-order" change) or the new state of things can have the same nature with new characteristics or features (incremental, "first-order" change). Each of these facets is important because they call for different actions from leaders and OD practitioners.

Organization development is all about change. Early OD efforts primarily addressed first-order change—making moderate adjustments to the organization, its people, and its processes. Today the demands on organizations are so great that second-order change is required in many instances. Organizations are being reinvented; work tasks are being reengineered; the rules of the marketplace are being rewritten; the fundamental nature of organizations is changing. Indeed, the new state of things will be vastly different from the old state of things. OD practitioners are involved in a variety of first-order and second-order change programs as you will discover in the reading ahead.

Organization Development is a Distinctive Consulting Method

A fundamental difference between organization development and other organization improvement programs is found in the OD consultant's role and relationship to clients. OD consultants establish a collaborative relationship of relative equality with organization members as they *together* identify and take action on problems and opportunities. The role of OD consultants is typically to *structure activities to help the organization members solve their own problems and learn to do that better.* OD consultants are co-learners as well as collaborators as they help organization members find effective *ways* to work on problems. OD consultants typically do not give solutions to problems; they serve as facilitators and helpers, not expert advisors.

As mentioned, OD practitioners teach clients how to solve their own problems. The aim of leaving the organization members better able to solve their own problems is a distinctive feature of organization development. It's called "self-renewal" or "learning how to learn" or "organizational learning" in the literature, but it refers to teaching clients the key skills and knowledge required for continuous self-improvement. This method of consulting fosters increased competence, growth, learning, and empowerment throughout the client system. These distinctive goals and methods of OD consultants are very powerful for causing permanent, positive change in organizations.

Organization Development is a Process That Focuses on Organizational Culture, Processes, and Structure Utilizing a Total System Perspective

This is a cluster of themes you will find throughout the book because the essence of OD is captured in the preceding sentence. A *process* is an identifiable flow of interrelated events moving over time toward some goal or end.[1] OD is a process in this sense. Organization development is a journey, not a destination; it is an unfolding and evolving series of events, not a mechanical, step-by-step procedure. Every organization has unique problems and opportunities, which means that each OD program is itself unique. Yet all OD programs are identifiable flows of interrelated events moving over time toward the goals of organizational improvement and individual development. Thinking of OD as an unfolding process will help you understand what this field is all about.

Major events in the process are: sensing something is wrong that should be corrected, diagnosing the situation to determine what is happening, planning and taking actions to change the problematic conditions, evaluating the effects of the actions, making adjustments as necessary, and repeating the sequence. OD is thus an *iterative* process of diagnosing, taking action, diagnosing, and taking action. All organizational improvement programs are really complex processes of goals → actions → redefined goals → new actions. We will add several elements to this iterative process when we discuss action research later.

Now let's look at how organizations work. A powerful insight infusing the practice of OD is that some aspects of organizations are more important than others as sources of organizational effectiveness and ineffectiveness. Specifically, organizational culture, processes, and structures were found to be crucial leverage points for intervening in the system to cause significant improvements.

Organization culture strongly influences individual and group behavior. Culture is defined as the values, assumptions, and beliefs held in common by organization members which shape how they perceive, think, and act. Every organization has a culture. The culture must be altered if permanent change is to occur. Warner Burke considers culture change the hallmark of OD: ". . . *organization development is a process of fundamental change in an organization's culture.*"[2] We agree that norms, values, and assumptions about how the world works in the organization culture significantly determine behavior and effectiveness in organizations. By implication, OD interventions that have the power to change culture can exert enormous influence on the performance of individuals and the organization. Being able to diagnose, understand, and change organization culture is increasingly important in organization development.

Organizational processes are also key leverage points for achieving organizational improvement. Processes are *how* things get done in organizations, the *methods* for arriving at results. Important organizational processes are communication, problem solving and decision making, resource allocation, conflict resolution, allocation of rewards, human resource practices, strategic management, how authority is exercised, and self-renewal or continuous learning. *How* things are done in organizations (organizational processes) is as important as *what* is done.

The importance of processes was discovered during research on group dynamics and laboratory training. Investigators found it useful to distinguish between *task* and *process*. Task was *what* the group was working on; process was *how* the group was working on the task. Often the best way to improve a group's effectiveness was to pay attention to and improve its processes. When OD practitioners started looking at organizations, they found that processes were just as critical for organizational effectiveness as they were for group effectiveness.

Peter Vaill believes that the genius of OD is its focus on organizational processes. He views OD as "a process for improving organizational processes."[3] A central theme in organization development is to improve organizational effectiveness by improving organizational processes.

Organization structure refers to the overall design of the organization, that is, the "wiring diagram" for how the parts are connected together to produce the whole. Structure also refers to how individual work tasks are designed and how these tasks are joined and grouped. A set of OD interventions called *technostructural interventions* helps leaders examine the organization's technology and structure toward the goal of making them function better. Traditional ways of structuring work and organizations have been found wanting; there is too much waste, inefficiency, inflexibility, and high cost associated with them. In addition, some structures promote responsibility, innovation, and initiative while other structures virtually prohibit such behaviors. Getting the structure right produces immediate substantial improvements in performance. This is one of the most active areas of experimentation in the field of OD today.

Organizations are complex social systems interacting with the environment. OD efforts are directed toward improving the total organization or large parts of it. The system is the target of change, not individuals, even though individuals are the instruments of change. Shafritz and Ott describe the systems perspective as follows: "The systems school views an organization as a complex set of dynamically intertwined and interconnected elements, including its inputs, processes, outputs, feedback loops, and the environment in which it operates. A change in any element of the system inevitably causes changes in its other elements."[4] A systems perspective directs leaders and OD practitioners to be aware of interdependencies, interrelatedness, multiple causes, and multiple effects. If this makes organizational change sound complicated, it is. But the systems paradigm is a strong model for understanding complexity and taking action in complex settings.

A superordinate goal of OD programs is to optimize the system by ensuring that system components are harmonious and congruent. When organization structure, strategy, culture, and processes are not aligned, performance suffers. A systems perspective suggests that changing one element of the system, say, strategy, will require changes in other elements such as structure, processes, and culture. Different OD interventions focus on alignment of the individual and the organization, on alignment of organizational components, and on alignment of the organization with environmental demands.

Organizations are open systems, that is, systems in interaction with their environments. Many of the problems of organizations today stem from rapid changes in environmental demands, threats, and opportunities. As the environment changes, the organization must adapt; that gets harder to do as the pace of change quickens and as the number of stakeholders increases. Stakeholders are groups who are affected by the organization's activities and who want a say in what the organization does, such as labor unions, government regulators, environmentalists, and investors.

The Action Research Model

Earlier we described OD as a process of diagnosing, taking action, rediagnosing, and taking new action. This process assumes a distinct form in OD called action research. Action research is essentially a mixture of three ingredients: the highly participative nature of OD, the consultant role of collaborator and co-learner, and the iterative process of diagnosis and action. The action research model as applied in OD consists of (1) a preliminary diagnosis, (2) data gathering from the client group, (3) data feedback to the client group, (4) exploration of the data by the client group, (5) action planning by the client group, and (6) action taking by the client group—with an OD practitioner acting as facilitator throughout the process. Widespread participation by client group members ensures better information, better decision making and action taking, and increased commitment to action programs. The action research model is very powerful; superior results are produced when the ideas and energies of many people are sought. Action research yields both change and new knowledge. Change occurs based on the actions taken. New knowledge results from examining the results of the actions. The client group learns what works and what doesn't work.

This introduction to organization development is intended to give you a basic understanding of what the field is about and how it operates. The themes and characteristics in this chapter will become more familiar as we continue through the book.

The following illustrations of actual OD programs provide examples from our experience and from the work of others. Notice how the programs are initiated, how they are planned and executed, and how the central themes of OD are translated into action.

ILLUSTRATION 1: PROBLEMS IN A BUSINESS FIRM

Problems of lack of cooperation between subunits, increasing complaints from customers, sagging morale, and rapidly increasing costs induced the president of a medium-sized company to confer with an OD consultant about ways to improve the situation. The two talked at length, and it became apparent to the consultant that the executive, while having some apprehensions, was generally agreeable to the desirability of examining the dynamics of the situation, including decision-making processes and his own leadership behavior. He and the consultant agreed that certain organization development efforts might be worthwhile. It was decided that a three-day workshop away from the usual routine, with the executive and his entire work team, might be an appropriate way in which to start.

The president then sounded out several of his subordinates about the possibility of the workshop, and reactions ranged from enthusiasm to some uneasiness. It was agreed to have the consultant meet with the executive and all his immediate subordinates to explain the typical format of such a meeting and to discuss the probable content of such a workshop. At the end of this meeting, the group decided to give it a try.

A few days before the off-site session, the consultant spent an hour interviewing each member of the team. In essence he asked them, "What things are going well?" and "What things are getting in the way of this group and this organization being as successful as you would like it to be?" The purpose of these interviews was to obtain the data around which the design of the workshop was to be built.

At the beginning of the workshop, the consultant first reported back to the group the general themes in the interviews, which he had grouped under these problem headings: "The Boss," "Meetings," "Administrative Services," "Customer Relations," "Relations Between Departments," and "Long-Range Goals." The group then ranked these problem themes in terms of importance and immediacy and chose the problem areas to be worked on. With the consultant acting more as a coach than as a moderator, the group then examined the underlying dynamics of each problem area and examined optional solutions to problems. In addition to making suggestions for breaking into subgroups to tackle certain agenda items, and in addition to providing several 10-minute lectures on such topics as decision making and team effectiveness, the consultant, upon request, intervened from time to time to comment on the way in which the group was working together and to help make explicit the norms under which the group seemed to be operating.

During the three days, time was provided for such recreation activities as jogging, basketball, swimming, and billiards. On two of the three days, the group worked until 6:00 or 6:30 P.M. and then adjourned the sessions for the day to provide for a relaxed dinner and socializing. By and large, the three days, although involving intense work, were fun for the participants. Some misunderstandings and tensions were worked through in the group setting; others were worked out informally during breaks from the work agenda. It seemed to the consultant that there was a sense of enhanced camaraderie and team spirit.

The last morning was spent developing "next action steps" relative to a dozen or so items discussed under the headings listed earlier. One of the decisions was to spend half a day with the consultant three months in the future for the purpose of reviewing progress toward problem solutions.

During a subsequent meeting between the company president and the consultant, the executive reported that the morale of the group was up substantially and customer complaints and costs were beginning to go down but that "we still have a long way to go, including making our staff meetings more effective." The two then agreed to have the consultant sit in on two or three staff meetings prior to the three-month review session.

The three-month review session with the consultant revealed that significant progress had been made on some action steps but that improvement seemed to be bogged down, particularly in areas requiring delegation of certain functions by the president to his key subordinates. This matter was extensively worked on by the group, and the president began to see where and how he could "loosen the reins," thus freeing himself for more long-range planning and for more contacts with key customers.

During the following years, the top-management team institutionalized an annual three-day "problem-solving workshop" involving the consultant. In addition, all the top managers utilized the consultant's services in conducting comparable workshops with their own subordinates. Over this period, the consultant and the human resources director, whose hiring had been a direct outgrowth of one of the sessions, began to work as a consulting team to the organization, with the human resources director gradually assuming more and more of the role of a "change agent." In addition to having planning and control responsibilities in the areas of employment and compensation and in other traditional personnel functions, the new human resources director also coordinated a management development program designed to supplement the company's problem-solving workshops. For example, managers were supported in their requests to attend specialized seminars in such areas as budgeting and finance, group dynamics, and long-range planning. The human resources director thus assumed an expanded role in which he served as an internal OD consultant to the operating divisions, as a linking pin with the external (original) consultant, and as a coordinator of the traditional human resources functions.

ILLUSTRATION 2: FROM "MUDDLING THROUGH" TO MAKING MILLIONS

The president and seven senior executives of a parts manufacturing company spent a year and a half working through a strategic planning process facilitated by an OD consultant. At the end of that time they had a clear and uplifting mission, specific goals for customer relations, quality, employee relations, and profits, and a well-conceived strategy for achieving the goals and fulfilling the corporate mission. It was a long, arduous journey; intense three-day work sessions every three to four months were combined with "homework" assignments to prepare for the next work session. Tough decisions were made. New initiatives were launched. Product lines were streamlined. As the new strategy was implemented, profits, which had been minimal for years (make a million dollars this year, lose a million dollars next year), started to soar. Profitability increased substantially every year for a number of years.

The story began with a phone call to the consultant from an assistant to the president. The assistant explained that the top-management team of the company had decided that its single most important problem was lack of a clear, agreed-upon strategic plan, that the executives wanted to conduct a thorough strategic planning process, and that they needed the help of an outsider. Previous do-it-yourself strategic planning attempts had ended in frustration and stalemate. The consultant replied that outside help on strategic planning comes in two forms: from an expert on strategic planning *content*, or from an expert on *facilitating a process* where the executives themselves generated the content through a series of activities facilitated by the consultant. "I can facilitate a strategic planning process if that is the kind of help that is wanted," the consultant said.

Several phone calls later, a two-day visit was arranged. The consultant met with the president and each executive individually for lengthy interviews and exploration. At a meeting of the top-management team on the second day, the consultant reported in general terms what he had learned, stated that strategic planning was indeed appropriate, and described a process for creating a strategic plan. The process called for five three-day planning sessions stretched over about a year and a half. The activities and desired outcomes for each session were explained in detail.

A "go" decision was made. The consultant supplied reading materials on strategic management to the executives. The first session was arranged. Information on company performance was prepared for the session.

Three goals of the first session were (1) to understand the industry, the competitors, and the critical success factors for the industry; (2) to determine what the executives wanted the company to be and to do; and (3) to generate the first draft of a corporate mission statement embodying their aspirations for the company. Activities were structured to achieve the three goals. Assignments were given to individuals, subgroups, and the total group throughout the three days. It quickly became apparent that the group did not work well as a group: Several strong personalities pushed hard for their positions without compromise, considerable scapegoating and intimidating occurred, people did not listen to or accept the opinions of others, the group jumped from topic to topic without getting closure on subjects, and there were vast differences about what the company should be and do.

One half day was spent examining the industry and the competition. The following questions were explored: What are industry trends? Industry success factors? Who are the main competitors? What are their strategies? What do they do well? What do they do that you want to avoid? Next a specific environmental analysis was conducted using a SWOT analysis (company strengths/weaknesses, environmental opportunities/threats).

Discussions and activities centered on the question: What do you want the company to be and to do? The differences of opinion were great, as was the strength of conviction for opinions held by the various executives. The consultant's major tasks were to keep the group focused on the topic at hand, to highlight areas of agreement, to force in-depth exploration of areas of disagreement, and to ensure that all ideas were given a fair hearing.

The charge for the third day was to complete the first draft of a corporate mission statement that incorporated what they wanted the company to be and to do. Individuals wrote their own versions of a mission statement; subgroups used this information to construct a subgroup mission statement; next the total group discussed the subgroup reports. A second iteration ensued in which subgroups wrote revised statements, and then the total group hammered out a draft of a proposed corporate mission statement. The executives were generally pleased with the progress they had made and with the mission statement they produced. Arrangements were made for the next three layers of management to critique the mission statement prior to the next work session.

The goals of the second session, three months later, were to finalize the mission statement based on three months of reflection and on the inputs from additional managers, and to agree on corporate goals for the next two to five years. Finalizing the mission statement was difficult. This document would constitute the guiding principles for the corporation. The input from additional managers provided a healthy reality check, but old differences of opinion among the executives surfaced again and were explored until resolved. (In retrospect, the most valuable feature of the strategic planning process was to surface, confront, and resolve differences among the executives. They could not move forward as a company until their differences were resolved and all were committed to a common course of action. But the common course of action had never been achievable in the past.)

After the mission statement was finalized, goals were set for quality, customer relations, employee relations, and company profitability. The executives agreed it would be impossible to achieve gains in profits without attending to the *foundation* of profits, employees, and customers. Arrangements to report the results of the second work session to the next three levels of management were agreed upon.

The goal of the third session, four months later, was to develop the strategy or strategies to enact the corporate mission and achieve the corporate goals. The main tasks of the consultant were to cause exploration of multiple possibilities, prevent premature closure on discussion of new ideas, and to continually test for commitment to the mission and goals that had been developed in prior sessions. The executives identified five new strategic initiatives that would enable the company to achieve its goals. To ensure implementation and follow through, a "champion" was assigned responsibility for each initiative by the group.

The goal of the fourth session, three months later, was to assess progress on the five initiatives. Each champion reported on progress to date. Refinements, needed adjustments, additional clarification, and obstacles were all explored. If necessary, additional resources were allocated to the initiatives. Recommitment to the mission, goals, and strategy was obtained. The executives felt good about what they had done because significant positive results were beginning to occur.

The fifth and final session was held four months later. The goals were to assess progress on implementation, to build support mechanisms for the five initiatives, and to revisit the corporate goals for the present year. Because profitability was greater than expected, and because they had five months until the end of the fiscal year, they decided to set new, very ambitious performance goals for the current year. They subsequently achieved these goals, made a lot of money for themselves, the company, and the employees (who had a gainsharing program in place), and started a record of achievement that the company had never seen before.

Strategic planning is really about alignment—alignment with environmental demands and opportunities, and alignment and agreement among the top executives regarding what they want to do and how they intend to do it. The OD approach to strategic planning is to facilitate a process whereby the key executives align their efforts toward common goals and a common "game plan."

*fits in well w/ Balanced Scorecard

ILLUSTRATION 3: ORGANIZATIONAL IMPROVEMENT IN AN INDIAN TRIBE

A request to a graduate school of business from the tribal council and the executive director of an American Indian tribe for a management development workshop resulted in a counterproposal by a professor who had been approached for his reactions. The professor, who was also an organization development consultant, suggested, with the concurrence and support of a colleague, that the two faculty members visit the reservation, interview the key people in the tribal organization, and develop a workshop around the problems being experienced by the organization. This particular tribal organization was charged with responsibilities for the management of the natural resources of the reservation, for maintenance and development of utilities and services, for welfare and health, for law and order, for economic development, for management of tribal enterprises, and for preservation of the best of the tribal culture. The tribal organization was the governing body of the tribal members.

With the support of the chairman of the five-person tribal council, the council, and the executive director, it was agreed that a group of approximately 20 key people would be invited to the workshop as proposed by the consultants. These people included the total council, the executive director, his key subordinates, the staff of the Community Action Program, the Bureau of Indian Affairs resident forester, and an educator in charge of vocational education in the high school located on the reservation. All these people were interviewed by the consultants and were asked, in effect, What things are going right? and What things in the organization are getting in the way of accomplishing objectives? The two consultants extracted the central positive and negative themes from the interview data. These themes became the basic issues or problems around which the workshop was designed.

The first workshop, spanning an entire week, was held on the university campus and had two basic components that were intermixed throughout the week: (1) a continuation of the use of the *action research model* and (2) a lecture-exercise component. The action research model provided the basic flow of the workshop strategy as follows: data gathering (the preworkshop interviews plus additional data gathering during the workshop), data feedback, ranking of the problems, work on the problems, and action planning to solve the problems. This working of the problems that had been identified by the group served as the backdrop for the week's activities.

Several different types of interventions were initiated by the consultants during the problem-working phases of the workshop. Early in the workshop they presented the *force-field analysis* technique to the participants, who were then asked to use the diagnostic tool in analyzing several of the issues the group had identified as high-priority items. At another point, a modified *role analysis* technique was used relative to the roles of council members and executive director. With the council listening, the other participants discussed the following topic printed on a large sheet of newsprint: "If the council members were operating in an optimally effective and efficient way, what would they be doing?" Responses about which there seemed to be substantial consensus were made visible on large sheets taped on the wall. Council members then were encouraged to respond, and subsequent discussion resulted in some modifications on the sheets. The exercise was then repeated for the executive director's role. With the executive director listening, the rest of the group discussed the question: "If the executive director were operating in an optimally effective and efficient way, what would he be doing?" One of the outcomes of this exercise was a gradual, but significant, shift in delegation of day-to-day operating decisions from the council to the executive director and staff.

The workshop also included several short lectures on a number of relevant topics including leadership, group process, decision making, problem diagnosis, and communications. This component also included some instrumented exercises that permitted participants to compare different decision-making models and to evaluate their usefulness.

The humor of the members of the group appeared frequently and prompted a good deal of laughter. For example, in the review of the roles of the council members and the executive director, it was observed by one of the tribal elders that "We have too many chiefs and not enough Indians." Their humor relative to themselves and to each other usually carried messages of affection and inclusion, including messages of inclusion to the few non-Native American employees on the staff. Ethnic divisions seemed not to be important issues; but problems of role clarification, delegation, and planning were the issues of highest concern.

By the end of the workshop, the participants had worked through a dozen or so important problems or issues and had agreed on next action steps, that is, "who was going to do what when." Results of a questionnaire administered on the last day of the workshop indicated overwhelming enthusiasm for the process and what had been accomplished. The consultants also perceived what they thought was a substantially higher level of openness, trust, and support among the participants at the end of the workshop compared with what was evident during the early part of the workshop.

One of the action steps that was agreed upon was a two-day follow-up visit to the reservation by the consultants to occur in five or six months. During ensuing weeks it became apparent that a follow-up visit sooner than that would be beneficial. The implementation of some action plans had bogged down, although important progress had been made on a number of others.

During the first follow-up visit, the consultants interviewed a cross section of the workshop participants to assess the degree of progress, met with the council to assist in a further review of council activities, and assisted in correcting a misunderstanding as to who was to be on one of the task forces created at the workshop. During the second follow-up visit the time of the consultants was primarily devoted to meetings with the executive director and the council members, although some discussions with key supervisors also occurred.

Subsequently, the council and the executive director requested a second workshop, with the suggestion that this workshop be shorter and that more time be devoted to follow-up on the reservation. The workshop was held at a resort; it started on a Tuesday evening and ended Friday afternoon.

Although the same basic pattern was followed for the second workshop, including preworkshop interviews, less time was spent on lectures and instrumented exercises, and almost all the time was spent on substantive issues. Since tensions between two subunits of the organization and the need for clarification of responsibilities appeared to be the most pressing issues, a significant amount of time was spent on these matters. The first problem was addressed through a three-way intergroup exercise in which each of the major groups—the council, the tribal staff, and the Community Action Program staff—developed the following lists about the other two groups and shared them in a general session:

What we like about what the _____ group is doing.
What concerns us about the _____ group.
What we predict the _____ group will say about us.

During the sharing of the lists, discussion was limited to explanation and questions requesting clarification. This phase was followed by subgroup discussion and, finally, by total group discussion and action planning.

The problem of clarification of responsibilities was addressed by asking each participant to follow a suggested outline in writing his or her own job description, to make the descriptions visible on large newsprint, and to discuss the job descriptions with his or her particular work team, including the supervisor. Revised job descriptions were then posted in the general conference room for perusal and informal discussion during breaks in the sessions.

At the end of the workshop, the consultants, the council chairman, and the executive director agreed on the approximate date of two follow-up sessions at the tribal reservation and agreed to keep in touch by telephone.

ILLUSTRATION 4: PRODUCTIVITY IMPROVEMENTS THROUGH GROUP PROBLEM SOLVING

Production increased from about 825 logs per shift to about 1,500 logs per shift across the "quad saw" at a sawmill in the course of six months. This occurred after a series of one-hour weekly meetings lasting four months between an OD consultant and the crew. The new production level was maintained and even increased after the meetings were discontinued.

What caused the 80 percent increase in productivity?

The background to this story begins with a three-year organization development program conducted by two behavioral scientists at a large wood products company. The program consisted of a variety of activities—first-line supervisor training, survey feedback, team building with various salaried work teams, and numerous other problem-specific interventions. One consultant worked with half of the 2,000-person organization; the other consultant worked with the other half. Some consulting activities, such as supervisor training, cut across the entire organization.

The consultant conducting team-building meetings with sawmill superintendents and their salaried staff members was asked by the superintendent of one sawmill to help solve production problems with the "quad saw," one of two production lines in the mill. A quad saw is a machine in which four saws cutting simultaneously process small logs into finished-dimension lumber. The quad saw had been installed several years earlier, and the engineers had projected 1, 150 logs per shift as the expected production rate. But production had peaked at 800 to 825 logs per shift, and attempts to increase that rate had been unsuccessful. Team problem solving had worked well with the superintendent and his management team; he wanted it applied to the crew on the quad saw. A series of group problem-solving meetings was chosen as the vehicle for understanding and correcting the situation.

The first step was for the consultant to become known to the mill employees and to become familiar with the mill operations, processes, and flows. A total of about 15 persons working at ten different machine stations comprised the "quad saw system." The entire mill had about 35 employees, all under the direction of a production supervisor. The mill operated two shifts, a day shift and a swing shift.

The next step was to hold a series of weekly problem-solving meetings devoted to understanding and solving whatever problems were getting in the way of production. The meetings were attended by the quad saw crew, their supervisor, the master mechanic servicing that production line, the mechanic's supervisor, and the consultant. The meetings were held immediately after work in the sawmill conference room; they lasted about one hour; hourly employees were paid overtime for attending. The mill superintendent launched the first meeting by saying that he wanted 1,150 logs across the quad saw and was getting only 825. He further stated that he wanted the crew to figure out how to accomplish that goal. He said he would support them in their efforts to improve production. He introduced the consultant as a person who would "help them" as they worked on the problem. Then he answered a few questions and left.

The first meeting was wild and tumultuous: long-standing complaints were aired; dissatisfactions and frustrations were voiced; a general pessimism that nothing could *or would* be done was in evidence. The consultant insisted that they were the people with the knowledge and ability to improve the situation and assured them that the superintendent was sincere in asking for their help. The consultant laid out two broad questions to guide the discussions: How can we do the job better? and How can we make this a better place to work?

At later meetings, the process was more systematic. Every machine station was analyzed in detail by the operators to discover barriers and impediments to production. Every step in the operations flow was examined and studied. At this stage the predominant theme was that mechanical problems were the major source of difficulty. A long list of mechanical and maintenance "wants" was generated. The list was overwhelming for the two maintenance supervisors, so each operator was asked for his three highest-priority items. With the more manageable list, the maintenance people went to work with enthusiasm. Interaction and problem solving between maintenance and operators increased. The weekly meetings were used to report progress and check for effectiveness of repairs, adjustments, and modifications. The equipment began to run significantly better.

Next the group turned to an analysis of "human factors" such as communication, coordination, operator technique, operator training needs, and the like. Again numerous specific problems were raised and systematically addressed, and corrective actions were planned and implemented. Several persons, including the production supervisor, had to modify their behavior for overall system improvements to occur.

As changes were implemented, production began to go up, slowly at first, then more rapidly and dramatically. The superintendent's target of 1,150 was achieved and surpassed about three months after the meetings were begun. But the maintenance people kept improving the equipment, the operators kept improving their flows and technique, and the supervisor kept improving communication and coordination. Production increased to 1,550 logs and then leveled off at a steady, stable 1,500 logs per shift.

The crew members were pleased and proud of their accomplishments. The consultant became even more firmly convinced of the power of group problem solving. The superintendent was amazed at the results.

ILLUSTRATION 5: A NEW PLANT MANAGER

Several years ago a new plant manager arrived at a continuous process facility (a plant where there is a continuous shaping of raw materials into finished products, as, for example, in a steel-making plant or an oil refinery). He surveyed the scene and found the following characteristics: the plant had over 2,000 employees, there were several layers of managers arranged in functional departments (production, maintenance, technical research, purchasing and stores, engineering, and so on); the plant performed fairly well in terms of productivity and profitability. The new manager's predecessor had been an energetic and autocratic man who had made all the operational and administrative decisions at the plant. The rest of the upper and middle management were called "superintendents"—they superintended their bailiwicks, supplied information to the plant manager, and received orders from the manager about what should be done in their departments and divisions, as the plant was run on a day-to-day basis.

The new manager had a different managerial philosophy and a different leadership style: he believed in delegating as much responsibility to his subordinates as possible; he believed in allowing wide participation in the important decisions affecting the works and the work force; he believed that better information and decisions would come from involved, committed managers; he wanted to develop subordinates so that they would move to higher positions of responsibility; and, as he told the managers at one of his first meetings with them, he wanted them to "share in the work and share in the fun." The new manager knew that he needed to build strong individual managers, an effective "management team," and that he needed to change the managerial culture and climate in the plant. He knew that this change in the way things were done would require new skills and a new management climate in the plant. And that would require training; the habits of ten years could not be changed just by his issuing an order. He called in several consultants, told them his desires, and solicited their aid.

As things evolved, there turned out to be six goals of the change project: (1) to increase the abilities and skills of the individual managers; (2) to build an effective top management team; (3) to build stronger division and department teams; (4) to improve the relations between work groups, such as between production and maintenance, and thus reduce the level of energy spent in competition; (5) to change the managerial culture from one in which one person made all the decisions to one in which all managers made or participated in decisions that affected them; and (6) to improve the long-range planning and decision-making abilities of managers at all levels. These change goals and the ideas of the new plant manager were public knowledge, just as was the information about the consultants and the OD program. Team-building meetings were held with the top management group and the new plant manager. Similar meetings were held with the department managers and their supervisory subordinates. And finally, meetings were held with representatives from several "interface" groups—two or more independent groups with overlapping responsibilities or work flow duties. Also attending these meetings were the external consultants and several internal organization members who were being groomed as internal "change agents." The typical role of the consultants was to assist the groups to identify, work through, and learn from their problems.

This OD program was in operation for four years. During the first year the intervention strategy called mainly for team-building meetings with intact working groups consisting of a superior and key subordinates. These groups met to explore their culture and their methods of problem solving related to their assigned tasks within the organization. It was an important feature of the OD strategy that the first team-building meeting involved the plant manager and his key subordinates, the plant division managers. Following this successful venture, the division managers met with their subordinates in team-building sessions in an effort to improve division functioning. Significant issues surfaced during these meetings related to leadership styles, team processes and dynamics, and new ways of solving specific operational problems.

The second year's activities continued the team-building sessions and introduced a new dimension: interface meetings with groups that had problems working together. The fact that the groups had previously been successful in working on their own problems in family groups and analyzing their own dynamics seemed to facilitate the progress of the interface sessions. Greater understanding of the complexities of interdependence and the problems inherent in effective coordination of effort led to rapid and accurate diagnosis of the intergroup problems in most cases. Also during this year, task forces were formed to investigate various facets of effectively managing the plant. These task forces were typically temporary problem-solving teams with specific charges, but the charges had far-reaching implications for the plant. For example, task forces tackled industrial safety problems, labor and union relations issues, and external interface problems with the local community and region. An especially important task force outcome was the development of a new philosophy about career planning and also new career development planning and implementation procedures. These procedures provide better ways for utilizing and developing the human talent in the organization and also ensure the development of more managerial talent.

During the third year, the top management team, including the plant manager, turned their attention to developing better long-range strategic planning models. They also instituted some management development programs for the purpose of upgrading the managerial skills of the middle-level supervisors. Some intergroup sessions continued to be utilized when conditions appeared to warrant them. Occasional team-building sessions were devoted to problem solving and long-range strategic planning activities.

In the fourth year, the OD activities were moved to the shop floor. One of the consultants became a familiar and friendly face to the hourly employees in several critical areas of the plant. He observed the work and work flow and interacted with the employees to elicit their opinions about how to do the job better and how they felt about the work, the supervision, and the company. The consultant initiated meetings between supervisors and hourly employees in which they systematically evaluated various ideas that had been suggested for improving the work flow and working conditions. The consultant also acted as an "idea conduit" for suggestions that the hourly employees wanted transmitted to higher levels of management.

At the conclusion of the fourth year, the plant manager and the consultants decided to terminate the OD program. It was agreed that the goals of the program had been met. It was noted that many of the "OD activities"—problem-solving task forces, intergroup sessions, strategic planning—were now an integral part of the plant's culture and organizational processes.

ILLUSTRATION 6: LARGE-SCALE SYSTEMS CHANGE

The manufacturing company was in serious trouble: Losses were enormous, and in-company analyses showed that the competition could produce the same products at lower cost with higher quality. The survival of the organization was threatened. Significant changes needed to be made *quickly*. But how does one make changes, quickly or otherwise, in a 12,000-person organization that is divided into three major divisions, that has 12 layers in the management hierarchy, and that has a long history of authoritarian management, an inflexible bureaucracy, and managers running their units like fiefdoms? Large-scale systems change methods, developed by OD practitioners and others, helped change the culture of the company so that it became competitive and profitable again.

Realizing the need for outside help, the chief executive of the organization asked an OD consultant to develop a program that would produce rapid changes in the way the company operated. The consultant enlisted the help of a colleague who had experience with large-scale change projects, and together they developed a proposal for a program of action. The proposal was accepted, and work began.

The essence of large-scale systems change programs is to stage "events" in which large numbers of organization members simultaneously collaborate to articulate a desired future for the organization and commit to taking the necessary actions to make that desired future a reality. Follow-up events ensure the actions are being taken and desired results are forthcoming.

A design team/steering committee of 24 people from all three divisions was appointed to help the consultants diagnose the situation, plan the events, and evaluate the results. The design team interviewed the chief executive and top-management team to learn what they wanted to accomplish with the program. The executives wanted the following: to create a company that was competitive in the global marketplace, to make the company profitable again, to replace authoritarian management practices with increased employee involvement and participative management, to break down the barriers between functional units, and to increase cooperation and coordination between related units. In addition, they wanted to impart a sense of urgency about the need for rapid change and a sense of crisis about customer satisfaction and product quality. Next the design team collected additional information—from employees, managers, and major customers—to get a picture of current conditions. The interviews and surveys showed numerous problems, considerable dissatisfaction with the status quo, and also considerable doubt that the company could or would change.

With this information, the design team developed an intensive five-day seminar for middle and upper management of each of the three divisions. The seminars were specifically structured to cause increased interaction and communication among the participants, to create an awareness of the trouble the company was in, to get agreement on where the company was going and how it was going to get there, and to encourage an in-depth exploration of better ways to run the company. To cause these things to happen, the seminars contained the following elements: (1) "get a large part of the total system in the same room at the same time"; (2) conduct a business case analysis using the company as the case to be analyzed; (3) have the participants generate a "desired future" for the company and the division; and (4) take the first steps on action plans to change the company's ways of operating. It was believed that these elements would create the necessary critical mass for change to occur within each division, would demonstrate by example the value of participative management, and would immediately move the company forward.

Each seminar would begin with a three-day, off-site, highly interactive and participative program attended by the top six levels of management in each division, followed two months later by a two-day, off-site follow-up meeting. (Seminars ranged in size from 60 to 90 people; both staff and line managers attended.) The seminars were launched with one division; a week later the second division had its seminar; a week later the third division had its seminar.

The seminars themselves were designed to *get people talking to each other across hierarchical and functional boundaries* about what was going well, what needed to change if the company was to survive and prosper, and what people really wanted the company to be. A variety of small-group and large-group configurations provided the medium for

At P&B, we determined "the future" for them — certainly did not have a "large part of the total system in the same room at the same time."

discussions. Configurations included "maximum mix" groups composed of a cross section of management levels and functions, functional department groups with multiple levels of management, natural work groups of bosses and subordinates, and total group sessions where the whole group heard reports, agreed on goals, and authorized action plans.

During the first day of the seminars, the participants analyzed environmental demands and trends, became aware of the company's inadequate responses to external demands, and identified areas where the division and the company performed well or poorly. The second day was spent clarifying the "desired future" that people wanted for the division and the company. This included not only future products and services, but *how* they wanted to achieve these goals in terms of management practices, employee relations, and customer relations. These two days caused a heightened awareness of cross-functional and cross-hierarchical interdependence. People also became aware of the enormous pool of talent and goodwill contained in the division. As the three days progressed, people endorsed the desired future and new ways of operating which they had helped to create. It became clear to all that making better use of all the human resources of the company and promoting greater cooperation between functions were necessary ingredients for achieving the desired future.

The third day was spent examining the implications of the business analysis and the desired future—what it meant in terms of needed changes, needed collaboration, and needed resources. First steps were planned to correct deficiencies, remove barriers, and to move forward on opportunities. Specific plans were developed, assignments were made, and feedback and monitoring systems were established. The three-day seminars were uniformly well received.

The two-day follow-up sessions two months later continued to maximize cross-functional and cross-hierarchical interactions and communications. At each seminar people recommitted themselves to the desired future, division and company goals, and the action steps. First steps were evaluated to determine if they produced the desired effects. Follow-up action steps were developed and assigned. Enthusiasm and energy levels were higher than they had been in years.

The rousing success experienced by the first division to participate in the seminar was sufficient to "sell" the program to the other two divisions. Cross-divisional communications increased as seminar participants compared notes about "desired futures" and "first steps." Changes in interaction patterns and management practices were immediate and positive. Interunit cooperation increased significantly. Improvements in product quality and customer relations were made. The chief executive declared: "This program was exactly what the company needed at this time."

ILLUSTRATION 7: COMPETITIVE ADVANTAGE THROUGH SELF-DIRECTED TEAMS

A company engaged in the design and manufacture of high-technology specialty items appointed an eight-person task force to find ways to improve the company's performance in its highly competitive field. After numerous visits to model companies utilizing the latest techniques, such as human resource "best practices," high-technology manufacturing methods, total quality programs, and the like, the team recommended the construction of a new plant to be operated by self-directed teams (SDTs). Thus, the plant would reflect the latest technological advances and the latest organizational advances at the same time. Self-directed teams are an organizational arrangement in which all activities required for team success are performed by team members themselves without the aid of a boss or supervisor. SDTs plan their own work, set production and performance goals, acquire needed resources, hire and train team members, measure their own performance, and assume complete responsibility for a complex task.

The rationale for recommending the use of self-directed teams was simple: Properly functioning SDTs are usually 30 percent to 50 percent more productive than conventionally organized work groups. Productivity gains of this magnitude would give the company a competitive advantage in its hotly contested markets. The recommendation was accepted; the plant was built and the task of developing self-directed teams was initiated. The company enlisted the services of an OD consultant known for his work on SDTs.

The role of the consultant was that of advisor, helper, coach, teacher, and friend all rolled into one. Establishing self-directed teams is difficult because most people are steeped in the organizational paradigm that calls for "manager's work" and "workers' work." The consultant served as a helper and catalyst as they all "learned together" how to give *all* the work to the teams. Some of the critical issues the organization and consultant had to resolve follow.

First, five leadership functions that the teams had to learn to perform were identified: (1) daily operations, (2) facilities management, (3) process facilitator, (4) the human resource function, and (5) quality assurance. These functions are typically performed by supervisors, but in the new team environment they would be performed by team members. Daily operations refers to production goals and scheduling, to problem solving and troubleshooting. Facilities management refers to handling plant and equipment needs, supplies, and so forth. Process facilitator is a new function dictated by the nature of SDTs. Team members must gain the skills to *manage their own processes*—how they work together to get the job done. Good meeting-management processes, conflict resolution processes, goal-setting processes, interfacing with other groups, and the like are required for the teams to function effectively. The process facilitator's job is to monitor, teach, and enhance these processes.

The human resource leadership function refers to the fact that SDTs learn to handle all personnel functions, such as hiring, firing, training, performance appraisal, career development, and so forth. Skills and knowledge to manage the human resource function are acquired by team members over time. Quality assurance refers to all the means available to ensure the reliability and high quality of team products. When teams are fully functioning, responsibility for each of the five leadership functions is assigned to a team member. Tenure is usually for six months, at which time new members rotate into the leadership functions.

Second, moving to self-directed teams was conceptualized as an *evolutionary* process. The consultant developed a five-stage model in which the supervisor's traditional role of planning, organizing, motivating, and controlling gradually evolved into something quite different. Similarly, team members gradually learned the five leadership functions described previously. The supervisor's role evolved into that of a coach—a role that was conceptualized as a resource to several teams in the areas of long-range planning and dealing with external stakeholders, including customers. Since the new coaches assisted two or more teams, excess supervisors were offered transfers to other parts of the organization or assignments on the new self-directed teams. Pay was not reduced for those supervisors who chose the latter option, but was frozen until such time as the wages of other team members would reach that pay level. The evolution from traditional structures to self-directed teams required from six to fifteen months to complete for the different teams.

Third, a variety of training programs was initiated so the team members could learn the necessary skills for manufacturing the products, running self-directed teams, and measuring their performance. Team members were expected to learn multiple skills. A competency-based pay system was established in which members received pay increases for each new skill they learned. Planning, scheduling, quality control, procurement, personnel management, and all the other duties of team members required extensive training. This resulted in a very talented work force—a clear "win" for the individuals and the company alike.

The consultant worked with the plant manager, the teams, and the coaches. Progress was steady and apparent to all. Eighteen months after the plant opened, the entire plant was run by SDTs. There were two layers in the hierarchy, the plant manager and the self-directed teams, with the coaches typically attached to three or four teams. Morale and satisfaction were high. Quality was outstanding. "The numbers" regarding productivity, costs, quality, customer satisfaction, and the like greatly exceeded expectations. The plant manager, team members, and coaches firmly believe: "This is what the organization of the future will look like, and we have created it today!"

CONCLUDING COMMENTS

The nature of organization development and its central themes were examined to establish a foundation for understanding the field. OD is a strategy for change that intervenes in the human and social processes of organizations. The illustrations demonstrate the themes in action—the use of action research, of teams of various configurations, of a consultant-facilitator, and of interventions into the organization's culture, structure, and processes.

In later chapters we will look more closely at the techniques, at the underlying theory and assumptions of OD, and at some of the pitfalls and challenges involved in attempting to improve organizations through behavioral science methods.

NOTES

1. Wendell L. French, *Human Resources Management*, 3rd ed. (Boston: Houghton Mifflin, 1994), p. 5.
2. W. Warner Burke, *Organization Development: A Process of Learning and Changing*, 2nd ed. (Reading, MA: Addison-Wesley Publishing Company, 1994), p. 9.
3. Peter B. Vaill, "Seven Process Frontiers for Organization Development," in *The Emerging Practice of Organization Development*, Walter Sikes, Allan B. Drexler, and Jack Gant, eds. (La Jolla, CA: Copublished by NTL Institute and University Associates, 1989), p. 261.
4. Jay M. Shafritz and J. Steven Ott, *Classics of Organization Theory*, 2nd ed. (Chicago: The Dorsey Press, 1987), p. 234.

2

DEFINITIONS OF
ORGANIZATION DEVELOPMENT

The literature contains numerous definitions of organization development. We examine several here and present one of our own. A good way to gain an appreciation for what OD is all about is to see how various authors have described the field over the years. No single accepted definition of OD exists, but there is general agreement on the nature of the field and its major characteristics.

Some early definitions of organization development follow.[1]

Organization development is an effort (1) *planned*, (2) *organization-wide*, and (3) *managed* from the *top*, to (4) *increase organization effectiveness* and *health* through (5) *planned interventions* in the organization's "processes," using *behavioral-science* knowledge. (Beckhard, 1969)

Organization development (OD) is a response to change, a complex educational strategy intended to change the beliefs, attitudes, values, and structure of organizations so that they can better adapt to new technologies, markets, and challenges, and the dizzying rate of change itself. (Bennis, 1969)

OD can be defined as a planned and sustained effort to apply behavioral science for system improvement, using reflexive, self-analytic methods. (Schmuck and Miles, 1971)

Organization development is a process of planned change—change of an organization's culture from one which avoids an examination of social processes (especially decision making, planning and communication) to one which institutionalizes and legitimizes this examination. (Burke and Hornstein, 1972)

More recent definitions of organization development are these.[2]

[The aims of OD are] . . . (1) enhancing congruence between organizational structure, processes, strategy, people, and culture; (2) developing new and creative organizational solutions; and (3) developing the organization's self-renewing capacity. (Beer, 1980)

Organization development is an organizational process for understanding and improving any and all substantive processes an organization may develop for performing any task and pursuing any objectives. . . . A "process for improving processes"—that is what OD has basically sought to be for approximately 25 years. (Vaill, 1989)

Organizational development is a set of behavioral science-based theories, values, strategies, and techniques aimed at the planned change of the organizational work setting for the purpose of enhancing individual development and improving organizational performance, through the alteration of organizational members' on-the-job behaviors. (Porras and Robertson, 1992)

[OD is] . . . *a systemwide application of behavioral science knowledge to the planned development and reinforcement of organizational strategies, structures, and processes for improving an organization's effectiveness.* (Cummings and Worley, 1993)

Organization development is a planned process of change in an organization's culture through the utilization of behavioral science technologies, research, and theory. (Burke, 1994, p. 12)

As you can see, these definitions contain a great deal of overlap (that's encouraging), and several unique insights (that's enlightening). All authors agree that OD is a field of applied behavioral science related to planned change. Likewise, they agree that the target of change is the total organization or system. The goals of OD are increased organizational effectiveness and individual development.

Schmuck and Miles provide an important insight into the OD process with the words "reflexive, self-analytic methods." In OD, organization members systematically *critique* how they are doing in order to learn how to do better. Burke and Hornstein's idea of "legitimizing" an "examination of social processes" speaks to the same issue of becoming more self-analytical.

Several definitions emphasize the importance of organization *processes* (Beckhard, Burke and Hornstein, and Vaill). Vaill depicts OD as a "process for improving processes"—a keen, accurate observation. Likewise, several definitions emphasize the crucial role of organization *culture* (Burke and Hornstein and Burke). Organization culture and processes are high-priority targets in most OD programs.

Achieving *congruence* among the components of the organization such as strategy, structure, culture, and processes is emphasized by Beer and by Cummings and Worley. Cummings and Worley suggest getting the components right (planned development), and keeping them right (reinforcement). Porras and Robertson suggest that OD is a "package" of theories, values, strategies, and techniques. This package is what gives OD its distinct character compared to other improvement strategies.

Bennis calls OD both a response to change and an educational strategy intended to change beliefs, attitudes, values, and organization structure—all directed toward making the organization better able to respond to changing environmental demands. His definition is as relevant today as when it was first written. Porras and Robertson state that the aim of OD is to alter people's behaviors by changing organizational work settings. Beer's definition is the only one to mention "developing the organization's self-renewing capacity"—a central goal in all OD programs—but the desirability of creating self-renewing, "learning organizations" is found in the writings of all these authors.

These definitions collectively convey a sense of what organization development is and does. They describe in broad outline the nature and methods of OD. There is no set definition of OD, and no agreement on the boundaries of the field, that is, what practices should be included and excluded. But these are not serious constraints given the fact that the field is still evolving, and the fact that there is a central core of understanding about the field, as shown in the preceding definitions.

Now let's turn to our definition of organization development. We do not propose it as the "right" definition, but as one that includes characteristics we think are important for the present and future of the field. *Organization development is a long-term effort, led and supported by top management, to improve an organization's visioning, empowerment, learning, and problem-solving processes, through an ongoing, collaborative management of organization culture—with special emphasis on the culture of intact work teams and other team configurations—utilizing the consultant-facilitator role and the theory and technology of applied behavioral science, including action research.* This is a lengthy definition, but it includes a number of components we consider essential. We will explain this definition in some detail.

By *long-term effort* we mean that organizational change and development take time—several years in most cases. Ralph Kilmann's book, *Beyond the Quick Fix*, tells the story correctly: There is no "quick fix" when it comes to lasting organizational improvement.[3] In fact, it is more accurate to describe "improvement" as a never-ending journey of continuous change. A program or initiative moves the organization to a higher plateau, then another initiative moves it to yet a higher plateau of effectiveness.

The phrase *led and supported by top management* states a virtual imperative: Top management must lead and actively encourage the change effort. Organizational change is hard, serious business; it includes pain and setbacks as well as successes. Top management must initiate the improvement "journey" and be committed to seeing it through to completion. Most OD programs that fail do so because top management was ambivalent, lost its commitment, or became distracted with other duties.

By *visioning processes* we mean those processes through which organization members develop a viable, coherent, and shared picture of the nature of the products and services offered by the organization, how those goods will be produced and delivered to customers, and what the organization and its members can expect from each other. Visioning means creating a picture of the desired future that includes salient features of the human side of the organization and then working together to make that picture a reality.

By *empowerment processes* we mean those leadership behaviors and human resource practices that enable organization members to develop and utilize their talents as fully as possible toward the goals of individual growth and organizational success. Involving large numbers of people to help build the vision of tomorrow, develop the strategy for getting there, and making it happen is what we mean by empowerment. For empowerment to become a fact of life, it must be built into the very fabric of the organization—its strategy, structure, processes, and culture.

By *learning processes* we mean those interacting, listening, and self-examining processes that facilitate individual, team, and organizational learning. Peter Senge describes learning organizations as ". . . organizations where people continually expand their capacity to create the results they truly desire, where new and expansive patterns of thinking are nurtured, where collective aspiration is set free, and where people are continually learning how to learn together."[4] As Chris Argyris advises, people and organizations must avoid the trap of "defensive routines," those habitual reactions to situations that prevent embarrassment and threat, but that also prevent learning.[5]

Problem-solving processes refer to the ways organization members diagnose situations, solve problems, make decisions, and take actions in relation to problems, opportunities, and challenges in the organization's environment and its internal functioning. Recall that Michael Beer's definition called for "developing new and creative organizational solutions." We believe such solutions are enhanced by tapping deeply into the creativity, commitment, vitality, and common purposes of all members of the organization, in contrast to having only a select few be involved in problem solving. We further believe that having a compelling vision of a desired future that is widely shared and endorsed creates the best climate for effective problem solving by all the organization's members. Empowerment means involving people in problems and decisions and letting them be responsible for results.

By *ongoing collaborative management of the organization's culture* we mean, first, that one of the most important things to manage in organizations is the *culture*, the prevailing pattern of values, attitudes, beliefs, assumptions, expectations, activities, interactions, norms, sentiments, and artifacts.[6] And second, managing the culture should be a *collaborative* business—widespread participation in creating and managing a culture that satisfies the wants and needs of individuals at the same time that it fosters the organization's purposes is the best way to do this. Collaborative management of the culture means that everyone, not just a few, has a stake in making the organization work. Just as visioning, empowerment, learning, and problem-solving processes are opportunities for collaboration in organization development, so is managing the culture.

By including culture so prominently in our definition, we affirm our belief that culture is the bedrock of behavior in organizations. There is reciprocal influence between culture, strategy, structure, and processes; each is important and each influences the others. But culture is of primary importance. Edgar Schein clarifies the nature and power of culture in his definition: "Culture can now be defined as (a) a pattern of basic assumptions, (b) invented, discovered, or developed by a given group, (c) as it learns to cope with its problems of external adaptation and internal integration, (d) that has worked well enough to be considered valid and, therefore (e) is to be taught to new members as the (f) correct way to perceive, think, and feel in relation to those problems."[7] So culture consists of basic assumptions, values, and norms of behavior that are viewed as the correct way to perceive, think, and feel—that is why culture change is necessary for true organizational improvement.

Our definition places roughly equal weight on culture and processes, in the belief that both are central in OD programs. Processes are *how* things get done, and we highlight the importance of visioning, empowerment, learning, and problem-solving processes. Processes are relatively easy to change, so this is where OD programs often begin—stop doing things one way and start doing them a different way. But change becomes permanent when the culture changes and the new ways are accepted as the "right" ways. We believe that when the culture promotes collaboration, empowerment, and continuous learning the organization is bound to succeed.

By *intact work teams and other team configurations* we recognize the centrality of teams for accomplishing work in organizations. We think teams are the basic building blocks of organizations. When teams function well, individuals and the total organization function well. Team culture can be collaboratively managed to ensure effectiveness.

Intact work teams consisting of superior and subordinates with a specific job to perform are the most prevalent form of teams in organizations. Team building and role and goal clarification interventions are standard activities in OD programs directed toward intact work teams. But in many organizations today, intact work teams do not have a boss in the traditional sense—the teams manage themselves. These self-directed teams assume complete responsibility for planning and executing work assignments. In addition to team building and role and goal clarification, members have to be trained in additional competencies such as planning, quality control, and using management information. Over time, performance appraisals, hiring, firing, and training become tasks controlled by self-directed teams. The results are usually highly gratifying both for the team members and for the organization.

In today's organizations there is also increased use of ad hoc teams that assemble, perform a specific task, and disband when the task is completed. The current method for getting complex tasks done in organizations is to assemble a *cross-functional team* comprised of members from all the functional specialties required to get the job done, such as design, engineering, manufacturing, and procurement. The old method was to have functional specialists work on the problem in *serial* or sequential fashion. When one function was finished with its part of the project, it "threw the results over the wall" to the next functional unit in sequence. This method resulted in loss of synergy, wasted time, much rework, and considerable antagonism between the separate functional specialists.

In *Liberation Management,* Tom Peters predicts that the work of tomorrow (most of which will be "brain work") will be done by *ad hoc teams* brought together to accomplish a task, and then disbanded with the people going on to new tasks.[8] *Multifunctional projectization* and *horizontal systems* are the terms he uses to describe these teams and their work. Temporary, multifunctional, constantly shifting teams will be the dominant configuration for getting work done, according to Peters. The thesis of *Liberation Management* is that contemporary bureaucratic structures with their functional specialties and rigid hierarchies are *all wrong* for the demands of today's fast-paced marketplace. He writes,

> But I've come to realize that, in this madcap world, turned-on and theoretically empowered people . . . will never amount to a hill of beans in the vertically oriented, staff-driven, thick-headquarters corporate structures that still do most of the world's business. Empower

until you're blue in the face. Call in the best consultants and create the best strategies. It'll make no difference unless the arteries are unclogged (the "structure" part), then radically rewired (the "systems" part).[9]

The skills required to work effectively in teams will be at a premium in such a world.

The phrase *utilizing the consultant-facilitator role* conveys our belief that leaders can benefit from seeking the assistance of professional help in planning and implementing OD initiatives. In the early phases, at least, it is desirable to have the services of a third-party consultant-facilitator. The third-party role is very powerful: That person is typically seen as bringing objectivity, neutrality, and expertise to the situation. The third party also is not captive to the culture of the unit undertaking the program. This does not mean that the third party cannot be a member of the organization; rather, it means that he or she should not be a member of the particular unit that is initiating the OD effort.

Part of an effective OD effort is a growing awareness of the significance of the consultant-facilitator role and a growing capability of many organizational members to perform that role, whether on an ad hoc or a more formalized basis. Numerous members should be encouraged to increase their consultation skills and use these skills in various ways such as helping to run more effective meetings or provide counsel to peers. We are thus calling attention to the facilitator *role* in organizations as well as facilitator *persons*.

By *the theory and technology of applied behavioral science* we mean insights from the sciences dedicated to understanding people in organizations, how they function, and how they can function better. OD *applies* knowledge and theory. Therefore, in addition to the behavioral sciences such as psychology, social psychology, sociology, and so on mentioned earlier, applied disciplines such as adult education, psychotherapy, social work, economics, and political science have contributions to make to the practice of OD. Porras and Robertson state:

> Organizational development (OD) is the practical application of the science of organizations. Drawing from several disciplines for its models, strategies, and techniques, OD focuses on the planned change of human systems and contributes to organization science through the knowledge gained from its study of complex change dynamics.[10]

And finally, by *action research* we mean the participative model of collaborative and iterative diagnosis and action taking in which the leader, organization members, and OD practitioner work together to define and resolve problems and opportunities. Because of the extensive applicability of this model in OD, another definition of organization development could be *organization improvement through participant action research.*

This definition contains the elements we believe are important for OD. To summarize, here are the primary distinguishing characteristics of organization development:

1. OD focuses on culture and processes.

2. Specifically, OD encourages collaboration between organization leaders and members in managing culture and processes.

3. Teams of all kinds are particularly important for task accomplishment and are targets for OD activities.

4. OD focuses on the human and social side of the organization primarily, and in so doing also intervenes in the technological and structural sides.

5. Participation and involvement in problem solving and decision making by all levels of the organization are hallmarks of OD.

6. OD focuses on total system change and views organizations as complex social systems.

7. OD practitioners are facilitators, collaborators, and co-learners with the client system.

8. An overarching goal is to make the client system able to solve its problems on its own by teaching the skills and knowledge of continuous learning through self-analytical methods. OD views organization improvement as an ongoing process in the context of a constantly changing environment.

9. OD relies on an action research model with extensive participation by client system members.

10. OD takes a developmental view that seeks the betterment of both individuals and the organization. Attempting to create "win-win" solutions is standard practice in OD programs.

These characteristics of organization development depart substantially from traditional consultation modes. Schein identifies the three following basic models of consultation—the first two are not OD, the third model is a good description of OD.[11]

In the "purchase of expertise model" a leader or unit identifies a need for information or expertise, which the organization cannot supply, and hires a consultant to meet that need. Examples include hiring a consultant to (1) survey consumers or employees about some matter, (2) find out how other organizations organize certain units, or (3) search out such information as the marketing strategy of a competitor. The consultant then makes recommendations.

In the "doctor-patient model" a leader or group detects symptoms of ill health in a unit or more broadly in the organization, and employs a consultant to diagnose what is causing the problem or problems. The consultant, like a physician, then prescribes a course of action to remedy the ailment.

In the "process consultation model" the consultant *works with* the leader and group to diagnose strengths and weaknesses and to develop action plans. Furthermore, in this model the consultant assists the client organization to become more effective in diagnosing and solving problems.

The first two models depict traditional management consulting; the third model is more typical of OD consulting. In OD the clients are assisted in the ways they go about solving problems. The consultant suggests general processes and procedures for addressing problems of concern. The consultant helps the clients to generate valid data and learn from them. In short, the OD consultant is an expert on *process*—how to structure effective problem solving and decision making.

CONCLUDING COMMENT

These definitions clarify the distinctive features of the field of OD and suggest why it is such a powerful change strategy. The participative, collaborative, problem-focused nature of OD marshals the experience and expertise of organization members as they work on their most important problems and opportunities in ways designed to lead to successful outcomes. Where these ideas came from is presented in the next chapter on the history of OD.

NOTES

1. See Richard Beckhard, *Organization Development: Strategies and Models* (Reading, MA: Addison-Wesley Publishing Company, 1969), p. 9; Warren G. Bennis, *Organization Development: Its Nature, Origins, and Prospects* (Reading, MA: Addison-Wesley Publishing Company, 1969), p. 2; Richard Schmuck and Matthew Miles, *Organization Development in Schools* (Palo Alto, CA: National Press Books, 1971), p. 2; and Warner Burke and Harvey A. Hornstein, *The Social Technology of Organization Development* (Fairfax, VA: Learning Resources Corp., 1972), p. xi.
2. See Michael Beer, *Organization Change and Development* (Santa Monica, CA: Goodyear Publishing, 1980), p. 10; Peter B. Vaill, "Seven Process Frontiers for Organization Development," in *The Emerging Practice of Organization Development*, Walter Sikes, Allan B. Drexler, and Jack Gant, eds. (La Jolla, CA: Copublished by NTL Institute and University Associates, 1989), p. 261; Jerry I. Porras and Peter J. Robertson, "Organizational Development: Theory, Practice, and Research," in Marvin D. Dunnette and Leaetta M. Hough, eds., *Handbook of Industrial and Organizational Psychology*, 2nd ed., vol. 3 (Palo Alto, CA: Consulting Psychologists Press, 1992), p. 272; Thomas G. Cummings and Christopher G. Worley, *Organization Development and Change*, 5th ed. (St. Paul, MN: 1993), p. 2; W. Warner Burke, *Organization Development: A Process of Learning and Changing*, 2nd ed. (Reading, MA: Addison-Wesley Publishing Company, 1994), p. 12.
3. Ralph H. Kilmann, *Beyond the Quick Fix: Managing Five Tracks to Organizational Success* (San Francisco: Jossey-Bass, 1984).

4. Peter M. Senge, *The Fifth Discipline: The Art and Practice of the Learning Organization* (New York: Doubleday/Currency, 1990), p. 3.

5. Chris Argyris, *Strategy, Change, and Defensive Routines* (Boston: Pitman, 1985).

6. A. L. Kroeber and Clyde Kluckhohn, *Culture: A Critical Review of Concepts and Definitions* (New York: Vintage Books, 1952). They examined 164 definitions of culture and arrived at the following synthesis: *"Culture consists of patterns, explicit and implicit, of and for behavior acquired and transmitted by symbols, constituting the distinctive achievement of human groups, including their embodiments in artifacts; the essential core of culture consists of traditional (i.e., historically derived and selected) ideas and especially their attached values; culture systems may, on the one hand, be considered as products of action, on the other as conditioning elements of further action."* pp. 291, 357, authors' emphasis. Our definition is congruent with their synthesis. See also Ralph H. Kilmann, Mary J. Saxton, Roy Serpa, and Associates, *Gaining Control of the Corporate Culture* (San Francisco: Jossey-Bass Publishers, 1985), p. ix.

7. Edgar H. Schein, "Organizational Culture," *American Psychologist*, 45 (February 1990), p. 111.

8. Tom Peters, *Liberation Management: Necessary Disorganization for the Nanosecond Nineties* (New York: Alfred A. Knopf, 1992).

9. Ibid., p. 13.

10. Porras and Robertson, "Organizational Development: Theory, Practice, and Research," p. 720.

11. Edgar H. Schein, *Process Consultation, Vol. I: Its Role in Organization Development* (Reading, MA: Addison-Wesley Publishing Company, 1988), pp. 5–11.

3

A HISTORY OF ORGANIZATION DEVELOPMENT

The history of organization development is rich with the contributions of behavioral scientists and practitioners, many of whom are well known, and the contributions of many people in client organizations. Even if we were aware of all the significant contributors, which we are not, we could not do justice to the richness of this history in a short essay. Therefore, all we can do is write about what we believe to be the central thrusts of that history based on our research to date and hope that the many people who are not mentioned will not be offended by our incompleteness. Our focus will be largely on the early origins of OD plus some discussion of current trends and the current extent of application.

Systematic organization development activities have a recent history and, to use the analogy of a mangrove tree, have at least four important trunk stems. One trunk stem of OD consists of innovations in the application of laboratory training insights to complex organizations. A second major stem is survey research and feedback methodology. Both stems are intertwined with a third stem, the emergence of action research. Paralleling these stems, and to some extent linked, is a fourth stem—the emergence of the Tavistock sociotechnical and socioclinical approaches. The key actors in these stems interact with each other and are influenced by experiences and concepts from many fields, as we will see.

THE LABORATORY TRAINING STEM

The T-Group

One stem of OD, laboratory training, essentially unstructured small-group situations in which participants learn from their own inter-actions and the evolving dynamics of the group, began to develop in about 1946 from various experiments in the use of discussion groups to achieve changes in behavior in back-home situations. In particular, an Inter-Group Relations workshop held at the State Teachers College in New Britain, Connecticut, in the summer of 1946 was important in the emergence of laboratory training. This workshop was sponsored by the Connecticut Interracial Commission and the Research Center for Group Dynamics, then at MIT.

The Research Center for Group Dynamics (RCGD) had been founded in 1945 under the direction of Kurt Lewin, a prolific theorist, researcher, and practitioner in interpersonal, group, intergroup, and community relationships.[1] Lewin had been recruited to MIT largely through the efforts of Douglas McGregor of the Sloan School of Management who had convinced MIT President Carl Compton of the wisdom of establishing a center for group dynamics. Lewin's original staff included Marian Radke, Leon Festinger, Ronald Lippitt, and Dorwin Cartwright.[2] Lewin's field theory and his conceptualizing about group dynamics, change processes, and action research were of pro-found influence on the people who were associated with the various stems of OD.

What was later to be called the "T-group" began to emerge through a series of events at the New Britain workshop of 1946. The staff consisted of Kurt Lewin, Kenneth Benne, Leland Bradford, and Ronald Lippitt. The latter three, along with other responsibilities, served as leaders of "learning groups." Each group, in addition to group members and a leader, had an observer who made notes about interactions among members. At the end of each day, the observers met with the staff and reported what they had seen. At the second or third evening session, three women members of the workshop asked if they could sit in on the reporting session, and were encouraged to do so. One woman disagreed with the observer as to the meaning of her behavior during the day's sessions, and a lively discussion ensued. The three women then asked to return to the next reporting session, and, because of the liveliness and the richness of the discussions, Lewin and the staff enthusiastically agreed. By the next evening, about half of the 50-60 members of the workshop were attending the feedback session. These sessions soon be-came the most significant learning experiences of the conference.[3]

From this experience emerged the National Training Laboratory in Group Development, which was organized by Benne, Bradford, and Lippitt (Lewin died in early 1947) and which held a three-week session during the summer of 1947 at the Gould Academy in Bethel, Maine.[4] Participants met with a trainer and an observer in Basic Skill Training Groups (later called T-groups) for a major part of each day. The 1947 laboratory was sponsored by the Research Center for Group Dynamics (MIT), the National Education Association (NEA), Teachers College of Columbia University, University of California at Los Angeles (UCLA), Springfield College, and Cornell University. The work of that summer was to evolve into the National Training Laboratory, later called NTL Institute for Applied Behavioral Science, and into contemporary T-group training. Out of the Bethel experiences and NTL grew a significant number of laboratory training centers sponsored by universities. One of the first was the Western Training Laboratory, headed by Paul Sheats and sponsored by UCLA. The Western Training Laboratory offered its first program in 1952.

In addition to Lewin and his work, influences on Bradford, Lippitt, and Benne relative to the invention of the T-group and the subsequent emergence of OD included extensive experience with role playing and Moreno's psychodrama.[5] Further, Bradford and Benne had been influenced by John Dewey's philosophy of education, including concepts about learning and change and about the transactional nature of humans and their environment.[6] Benne, in collaboration with R. Bruce Raup and others, had built on Dewey's philosophy and focused on the processes by which policy agreements are reached between people who differ.[7] In addition, Benne had been influenced by the works of Mary Follett, an early management theorist, including her ideas about integrative solutions to problems in organizations.[8]

As a footnote to the emergence of the T-group, the widespread use of flip-chart paper as a convenient way to record, retrieve, and display data in OD activities and in training sessions was invented by Ronald Lippitt and Lee Bradford during the 1946 New Britain sessions. As Lippitt reports,

> The blackboards were very inadequate, and we needed to preserve a lot of the material we produced. So I went down to the local newspaper and got a donation of the end of press runs. The paper was still on the rollers. We had a "cutting bee" of Lee, Ken, myself and several others to roll the sheets out and cut them into standard sizes that we could put up in quantity with masking tape on the blackboards and walls of the classrooms. We took the practice back to MIT and I had the shop make some boards with clamps across the top. We hung them in our offices and the seminar room, and Lee did the same thing at the NEA in Washington. . . . The next summer at Bethel we had a large supply

of cut newsprint and used some of the boards on easels, as well as using the walls.[9]

Bradford also reports that he and Ronald Lippitt used "strips of butcher paper" in their early work with organizations. [10]

In a sense, the invention of the T-group grew out of an awareness that had been growing for a decade or more of the importance of helping groups and group leaders focus on group and leadership *processes*. This growing awareness was particularly evident in adult education and group therapy.[11]

Over the next decade, as trainers began to work with social systems of more permanency and complexity than T-groups, they began to experience considerable frustration in the transfer of laboratory behavioral skills and insights of individuals into the solution of problems in organizations. Personal skills learned in the "stranger" T-groups setting were very difficult to transfer to complex organizations. However, the training of "teams" from the same organization had emerged early at Bethel and undoubtedly was a link to the total organizational focus of Douglas McGregor, Herbert Shepard, Robert Blake, and Jane Mouton and subsequently the focus of Richard Beckhard, Chris Argyris, Jack Gibb, Warren Bennis, Eva Schindler-Rainman, and others.[12] All had been T-group trainers in NTL programs.

Robert Tannenbaum

Within our present awareness, some of the earliest sessions of what would now be called "team building" were conducted by Robert Tannenbaum in 1952 and 1953 at the U. S. Naval Ordnance Test Station at China Lake, California.[13] According to Tannenbaum, the term "vertically structured groups" was used, with groups dealing with "personal topics (such as departmental sociometrics, interpersonal relationships, communication, and self-analysis), and with organizational topics (such as deadlines, duties and responsibilities, policies and procedures, and— quite extensively—with interorganizational-group relations)."[14] These sessions, which stimulated a 1954 *Personnel* article by Tannenbaum, Kallejian, and Weschler, were conducted "with all managers of a given organizational unit present."[15] The more personally oriented dynamics of such sessions were described in a 1955 *Harvard Business Review* article by the same authors.[16]

Tannenbaum, along with Art Shedlin, also was the leader of what appears to be the first nondegree training program in OD, the Learning Community in Organizational Development at UCLA. This annual program was first offered as a full-time, ten-week, residential program, January–March 1967.[17]

Tannenbaum, who held a Ph.D. in Industrial Relations from the School of Business at the University of Chicago, had early been influenced by such authors as Mary Parker Follett in management theory, V. V. Anderson's *Psychiatry in Industry,* Roethlisberger and Dickson's *Management and the Worker,* and Burleigh Gardner's *Human Relations in Industry.* He was on the planning committee for the Western Training Laboratory (WTL) and a staff member for the first session (1952). During that first session he co-trained with a psychiatric social worker who had attended a Bethel program, and in subsequent sessions, in his words, "co-trained with a psychiatrist, an educator, a clinical psychologist . . . and I learned much from them."[18]

Chris Argyris

Chris Argyris, then a faculty member at Yale University (later at Harvard), in 1957 was one of the first to conduct team building sessions with a CEO and the top executive team. Two of Argyris's early clients were IBM and Exxon. His early research and interventions with a top executive group are reported in his 1962 book *Interpersonal Competence and Organizational Effectiveness.*[19]

In 1950, Argyris, while working on a Ph.D. at Cornell University, had visited Bethel as a member of NTL's research staff in order to study T-groups. In his words, "I became fascinated with what I saw, and wanted to become a trainer. Several years later . . . I was invited to become a staff member . . ."[20]

Argyris was later to make extensive contributions to theory and research on laboratory training, OD, and organizational learning. One of his several books on OD, *Intervention Theory and Method,*[21] stands as a classic in the field.

According to Argyris, three people had the greatest impact on his early career:

> Number one was Kurt Lewin[22]. . . . I was at Clark, finishing my undergraduate degree. I would go over (to MIT) and sit in on his seminars[23]. . . . But his writings . . . had the greatest impact.[24] Next came Roger Barker, and his studies on psychological ecology and behavioral settings. I worked with Roger for several years. His greatest impact was not only on helping me to understand how to study behavioral settings more rigorously, but his whole approach to knowledge, which was to explore, to enquire, and to experiment. Finally, there was Bill Whyte at Cornell University, with whom I received my Ph.D. (in organizational behavior). Bill was not only a very thoughtful and encouraging advisor, but he was very smart and learned about field work. He had a sensitivity for what it meant to be an ethnographer that helped me to learn a lot about what to do in the field.[25]

Argyris interacted with many of the early leaders in the T-group and OD fields. For example, in referring to Douglas McGregor, he states, "I had many wonderful discussions with him in the advanced president's programs at Bethel and in Florida." In referring to Bradford, with whom he worked numerous times from 1950 on, he states that "he was, without any doubt, the person who helped make NTL come alive."[26]

Douglas McGregor

Douglas McGregor, as a professor-consultant, working with Union Carbide, beginning about 1957, was also one of the first behavioral scientists to begin to solve the transfer problem and to talk systematically about and to help implement the application of T-group skills to complex organizations.[27] John Paul Jones, who had come up through industrial relations at Union Carbide, in collaboration with McGregor and with the support of a corporate executive vice president and director, Birny Mason, Jr. (later president of the corporation), established a small internal consulting group that in large part used behavioral science knowledge in assisting line managers and their subordinates to learn how to be more effective in groups. McGregor's ideas were a dominant force in this consulting group; other behavioral scientists who had had an influence on Jones's thinking were Rensis Likert and Mason Haire. Jones's organization was later called an "organization development group."[28]

Among the many influences on Douglas McGregor, of course, was Kurt Lewin, a colleague at MIT whom McGregor had help recruit. It is also clear that he was influenced by Leland Bradford, Edwin Boring, Irving Knickerbocker, Jay Forrester, and Gordon Allport.[29] McGregor also must have been influenced by Carl Rogers, the leading theorist and practitioner in client-centered therapy, because McGregor assigned Rogers' writings to his classes at MIT.[30] McGregor's classic work, *The Human Side of Enterprise*, which has had a great impact on managers since its publication in 1960, cites an extensive list of psychologists, sociologists, and management theorists, including Peter Drucker.[31] (See the discussion of Richard Beckhard, which refers to the influence of McGregor's consulting work at General Mills on *The Human Side of Enterprise*.)

Herbert Shepard

During the same year, 1957, Herbert Shepard, through introductions by Douglas McGregor, joined the employee relations department of Esso Standard Oil (now Exxon) as a research associate. Shepard was to have a major impact on the emergence of OD. While we will focus mainly on Shepard's work at Esso, it should also be noted that Shepard was later involved in community development activities and, in 1960, at the Case Institute of Technology, founded the first doctoral program devoted to training OD specialists.

Before joining Esso, Shepard had completed his doctorate at MIT and had stayed for a time as a faculty member in the Industrial Relations Section. Among influences on Shepard were Roethlisberger and Dickson's *Management and the Worker* (1939) and a biography of Clarence Hicks. (As a consultant to Standard Oil, Hicks had helped to develop participative approaches to personnel management and labor relations.) Shepard was also influenced by Farrell Toombs, who had been a counselor at the Hawthorne plant and had trained under Carl Rogers. In addition, Shepard had been heavily influenced by the writings of Kurt Lewin. NTL influence was also an important part of Shepard's background; he attended an NTL lab in 1950 and subsequently was a staff member in many of its programs.[32]

In 1958 and 1959 Shepard launched three experiments in organization development at major Esso refineries: Bayonne, New Jersey; Baton Rouge, Louisiana; and Bayway, Texas. At Bayonne an interview survey and diagnosis were made and discussed with top management, followed by a series of three-day laboratories for all members of management.[33] Paul Buchanan, who had worked earlier at the Naval Ordnance Test Station and more recently had been using a somewhat similar approach in Republic Aviation, collaborated with Shepard at Bayonne and subsequently joined the Esso staff.

Herbert Shepard and Robert Blake

At Baton Rouge, Robert Blake joined Shepard, and the two initiated a series of two-week laboratories attended by all members of "middle" management. At first, an effort was made to combine the case method with the laboratory method, but the designs soon emphasized T-groups, organizational exercises, and lectures. One innovation in this training program was an emphasis on intergroup as well as interpersonal relations. Although working on interpersonal problems affecting work performance was clearly an organizational effort, between-group problem solving had even greater organization development implications in that a broader and more complex segment of the organization was involved.

At Baton Rouge, efforts to involve top management failed, and as a result follow-up resources for implementing organization development were not made available. By the time the Bayway program started, two fundamental OD lessons had been learned: the requirement for active involvement in and leadership of the program by top management and the need for on-the-job application.

At Bayway, there were two significant innovations. First,

Shepard, Blake, and Murray Horwitz utilized the instrumented laboratory, which Blake and Jane Mouton had been developing in social psychology classes at the University of Texas and which they later developed into the Managerial Grid approach to organization development.[34] (An essential dimension of the instrumented lab is the use of feedback based on scales and measurements of group and individual behavior during sessions.)[35] Second, at Bayway more resources were devoted to team development, consultation, intergroup conflict resolution, and so forth than were devoted to laboratory training of "cousins," that is, organization members from different departments. As Robert Blake stated, "It was learning to *reject* T-group stranger-type labs that permitted OD to come into focus," and it was intergroup projects, in particular, that "triggered real OD."[36]

Robert Blake and Jane Mouton

As in the case of Shepard and others, influences on Robert Blake up to that point were important in the emergence of OD. While at Berea College majoring in psychology and philosophy (later an M.A., University of Virginia, and a Ph. D., University of Texas), Blake had been strongly influenced by the works of Korzybski and the general semanticists and found that "seeing discrete things as representative of a continuous series was much more stimulating and rewarding than just seeing two things as 'opposites.'" This thinking contributed in later years to Blake's conceptualization of the Managerial Grid with Jane Mouton and to their intergroup research on win-lose dynamics. This intergroup research and the subsequent design of their intergroup conflict management workshops were also heavily influenced by Muzafer Sherif's fundamental research on intergroup dynamics.[37] Jane Mouton's influence on Blake's thinking and on the development of the Grid stemmed partly, in her words, "from my undergraduate work (at Texas) in pure mathematics and physics which emphasized the significance of measurement, experimental design, and a scientific approach to phenomena."[38] (Mouton later attained an M.A. from the University of Virginia and a Ph.D. from the University of Texas.)

During World War II, Blake served in the Psychological Research Unit of the Army Air Force where he interacted with a large number of behavioral scientists, including sociologists. This contributed to his interest in "looking at the system rather than the individuals within the system on an isolated one-by-one basis."[39] (This is probably one of many links between systems concepts or systems theory and OD.)

Another major influence on Blake had been the work of John Bowlby, a medical member of the Tavistock Clinic in London, who was working in family group therapy. Blake, after completing his Ph.D. work in clinical psychology, went to England for 16 months in 1948 and 1949 to study, observe, and do research at Tavistock. As Blake states it,

Bowlby had the clear notion that treating mental illness of an individual out of context was an. . .ineffective way of aiding a person. . . . As a result, John was unprepared to see patients, particularly children, in isolation from their family settings. He would see the intact family: mother, father, siblings. . . . I am sure you can see from what I have said that if you substitute the word organization for family and substitute the concept of development for therapy, the natural next step in my mind was organization development.[40]

Among others at Tavistock who influenced Blake were Wilfred Bion, Henry Ezriel, Eric Trist, and Elliott Jaques.

After returning from Tavistock and taking an appointment at Harvard, Blake joined the staff for the summer NTL programs at Bethel. His first assignment was co-responsibility for a T-group with John R. P. French. Blake was a member of the Bethel staff from 1951 to 1957 and continued after that with NTL labs for managers at Harriman House, Harriman, New York. Among other influences on Blake were Jacob Moreno's action orientation to training through the use of psychodrama and sociodrama and E. C. Tolman's notions of purposive behavior in humans.[41]

Richard Beckhard

Richard Beckhard, another major figure in the emergence and extension of the OD field, came from a career in the theater. In his words,

I came out of a whole different world—the theater—and went to NTL in 1950 as a result of some discussions with Lee Bradford and Ron Lippitt. At that time they were interested in improving the effectiveness of the communications in large meetings and I became involved as head of the general sessions program. But I also got hooked on the whole movement. I made a career change and set up the meetings organization, "Conference Counselors." My first major contact was the staging of the 1950 White House conference on children and youth. . . . I was brought in to stage the large general sessions with six thousand people. . . . I had been doing a lot of large convention participative discussion type things and had written on the subject. . . . At the same time I joined the NTL summer staff. . . . My mentors in the field were Lee Bradford, in the early days, and Ron Lippitt and later, Ren Likert, and very particularly, Doug McGregor, who became both mentor, friend, father figure. . . and in the later years, brother. Doug had left MIT and was at Antioch as president. . . . Doug and I began appearing on similar programs. One day coming back on the train from Cincinnati to Boston, Doug asked if I was interested in joining MIT. . . .

In the period 1958-63, I had worked with him (McGregor) on two or three projects. He brought me to Union Carbide, where I replaced him in working with John Paul Jones, and later, George Murray and the group. We (also) worked together at . . . Pennsylvania Bell and . . . at General Mills.[42]

Beckhard worked with McGregor at General Mills in 1959 or 1960, where McGregor was working with Dewey Balsch, vice president of personnel and industrial relations, in an attempt to facilitate "a total organizational culture change program which today might be called quality of work life or OD." Beckhard goes on to say, "The issues that were being worked were relationships between workers and supervision; roles of supervision and management at various levels; participative management for real. . . . This experience was one of the influences on Doug's original paper, 'The Human Side of Enterprise'. . . and from which the book emerged a year or so later."[43]

Beckhard developed one of the first major nondegree training programs in OD, NTL's Program for Specialists in Organizational Training and Development (PSOTD). The first program was an intensive four-week session held in the summer of 1967 at Bethel, Maine, the same year that UCLA launched its Learning Community in OD. Core staff members the first year in the NTL program were Beckhard as dean, Warner Burke, and Fritz Steele. Additional resource persons the first year were Herbert Shepard, Sheldon Davis, and Chris Argyris. In addition, along with McGregor, Rensis Likert, Chris Argyris, Robert Blake, Lee Bradford, and Jack Gibb, Beckhard was a founder of NTL's Management Work Conferences that are essentially laboratory training experiences for middle managers. As an extension of this program, Beckhard was also active in the development and conducting of NTL's senior executive conferences and presidents' labs.[44]

Eva Schindler-Rainman

Probably one of the first persons to be an NTL staff member doing OD work and who was almost exclusively trained in the social work field was Eva Schindler-Rainman. Schindler-Rainman was awarded both a masters and doctorate in social work from the University of Southern California with specialties in group work, organizational behavior, and community organization. While employed as director of personnel and training for the Los Angeles Girl Scouts Council, in the early 1950's she attended one of the first events of the Western Training Laboratory. Her T-group trainers there were Gordon Hearn and Marguerite Vanderworker.

Around 1959, Schindler-Rainman was on the staff of an NTL-sponsored Community Development Laboratory at UCLA's Arrowhead Conference Center where she was a T-group co-trainer with Leland Bradford. Others on the staff were Warren Schmidt, Kenneth Benne, and Max Birnbaum.

Some of Schindler-Rainman's recollections about transferring her social work, community development experiences, and T-group training to the emerging field of OD are as follows:

> . . . I would say that I began consciously doing OD work when I was the Director of Training and Personnel for the Girl Scouts . . . I did OD-type work with school districts, organizing a coordinating council that made it possible to bring in-service classes from UCLA to teachers from all of those districts . . .[45]

Schindler-Rainman goes on to describe her work with the Health Department in Los Angeles, and the Education Extension department at UCLA where she was at one time assistant director. Along with Charles Ferguson, she later became one of the associate directors of the Department of Conferences at UCLA, headed by Warren Schmidt. She also worked with Robert Tannenbaum, Irv Weschler, Joan Lasko, and Jerry Reisel. In addition, she worked with Richard Beckhard who was doing a series of interventions with the California Cancer Society.

Schindler-Rainman's formal link to NTL came with a staff assignment at Bethel around 1966. Ronald Lippitt was the dean. Other staff members included Dorothy Mial, Cyril Mill, and Matthew Miles. Some of the other women with whom Schindler-Rainman worked, in addition to Dorothy Mial, were Edith Seashore, Miriam Ritvo, and Peggy Lippitt. Referring to the women in the field, Schindler-Rainman recounts, "Edie [Edith Seashore] was the person doing more OD interventions than anybody else as far as I know."[46]

Schindler-Rainman works with a wide range of clients, both in the United States and internationally. A few of her well-known publications are *The Creative Volunteer Community: A Collection of Writings*,[47] *Building the Collaborative Community*,[48] *The Volunteer Community*,[49] and *Team Training for Community Change*.[50] (The latter three were co-authored with Ronald Lippitt.) Schindler-Rainman's extensive professional training, her collaboration with a number of key men and women in the early days of NTL and the OD movement, and her early and extensive contribution to the community development movement, clearly identify her as one of the pioneers in the laboratory training stem of OD.

The Term *Organization Development*

It is not entirely clear who coined the term *organization development*, but it is likely that the term emerged more or less simultaneously in two or three places through the conceptualization of Robert Blake, Herbert Shepard, Jane Mouton, Douglas McGregor, and Richard Beckhard.[51] The phrase *development group* had earlier been used by Blake and Mouton in connection with human relations training at the University of Texas and appeared in their 1956 document that was distributed for use in the Baton Rouge experiment.[52] (The same phrase appeared in a Mouton and Blake article first published in the journal *Group Psychotherapy* in 1957.)[53] The Baton Rouge T-groups run by Shepard and Blake were called *development groups*,[54] and this program of T-groups was called "organization development" to distinguish it from the complementary management development programs already underway.[55]

Referring to his consulting with McGregor at General Mills, Beckhard gives this account of the term emerging there:

> At that time we wanted to put a label on the program at General Mills. . . . We clearly didn't want to call it management development because it was total organization-wide, nor was it human relations training although there was a component of that in it. We didn't want to call it organization improvement because that's a static term, so we labeled the program "Organization Development," meaning system-wide change effort.[56]

Thus, the term emerged as a way of distinguishing a different mode of working with organizations and as a way of highlighting its developmental, systemwide, dynamic thrust.

The Role of Human Resources Executives

It is of considerable significance that the emergence of organization development efforts in three of the first corporations to be extensively involved, Union Carbide, Esso, and General Mills, included human resources people seeing themselves in new roles. At Union Carbide, John Paul Jones, in industrial relations, now saw himself in the role of a behavioral science consultant to other managers.[57] At Esso, the headquarters human relations research division began to view itself as an internal consulting group offering services to field managers rather than as a research group developing reports for top management.[58] At General Mills, the vice president of personnel and industrial relations, Dewey Balsch, saw his role as including leadership in conceptualizing and coordinating changes in the culture of the total organization.[59] Thus, in the history of OD we see both external consultants and internal staff departments departing from their traditional roles and collaborating in a new approach to organization improvement.

THE SURVEY RESEARCH AND FEEDBACK STEM

Survey research and feedback,[60] a specialized form of action research (see Chapter 7) constitutes the second major stem in the history of organization development. The history of this stem, in particular, revolves around the techniques and approach developed by staff members at the

Survey Research Center of the University of Michigan over a period of years.

Rensis Likert

The SRC was founded in 1946 after Rensis Likert, director of the Division of Program Surveys of the Federal Bureau of Agricultural Economics, and other key members of the division, moved to Michigan. Likert held a Ph.D. in psychology from Columbia, and his dissertation, *A Technique for the Measurement of Attitudes*, was the classic study in which the widely used five-point Likert scale was developed. After a period of university teaching, Likert had been employed by the Life Insurance Agency Management Association where he conducted research on leadership, motivation, morale, and productivity. He had then moved to the U.S. Department of Agriculture, where his Division of Program Surveys furthered a more scientific approach to survey research in its work with various federal departments, including the Office of War Information.[61] After helping to develop and direct the Survey Research Center, following World War II, in 1948 Likert then became the director of a new Institute for Social Research, which included both the SRC and the Research Center for Group Dynamics, the latter moving to Michigan from MIT after Lewin's death.

Floyd Mann, Rensis Likert, and Others

Part of the emergence of survey research and feedback was based on refinements made by SRC staff members in survey methodology. Another part was the evolution of the feedback methodology. As related by Rensis Likert,

> In 1947, I was able to interest the Detroit Edison Company in a company-wide study of employee perceptions, behavior, reactions and attitudes which was conducted in 1948. Floyd Mann, who had joined the SRC staff in 1947, was the study director on the project. I provided general direction. Three persons from D.E.: Blair Swartz, Sylvanus Leahy and Robert Schwab with Mann and me worked on the problem of how the company could best use the data from the survey to bring improvement in management and performance. This led to the development and use of the survey-feedback method. Floyd particularly played a key role in this development. He found that when the survey data were reported to a manager (or supervisor) and he or she failed to discuss the results with subordinates and failed to plan with them what the manager and others should do to bring improvement, little change occurred. On the other hand, when the manager discussed the results with subordinates and planned with them what to do to bring improvement, substantial favorable changes occurred.[62]

Another aspect of the Detroit Edison study was the process of feeding back data from an attitude survey to the participating departments in what Mann calls an "interlocking chain of conferences."[63] Additional insights are provided by Baumgartel, who participated in the project and who drew the following conclusions from the Detroit Edison study:

> The results of this experimental study lend support to the idea that an intensive, group discussion procedure for utilizing the results of an employee questionnaire survey can be an effective tool for introducing positive change in a business organization. It may be that the effectiveness of this method, in comparison to traditional training courses, is that it deals with the system of human relationships as a whole (superior and subordinate can change together) and it deals with each manager, supervisor, and employee in the context of his own job, his own problems, and his own work relationships.[64]

Links between the Laboratory Training Stem and the Survey Feedback Stem

Links between people who were later to be key figures in the laboratory training stem of OD and people who were to be key figures in the survey feedback stem occurred as early as 1940 and continued over the years. These links were undoubtedly of significance in the evolution of both stems. Of particular interest are the links between Likert and Lewin and between Likert and key figures in the laboratory training stem of OD. As Likert states it, "I met Lewin at the APA annual meeting at State College, Pa., I believe in 1940. When he came to Washington during the War, I saw him several times and got to know him and his family quite well."[65] In 1944 Likert arranged a dinner at which Douglas McGregor and Kurt Lewin explored the feasibility of a group dynamics center at MIT.[66]

Likert further refers to McGregor: "I met McGregor during the war and came to know him very well after Lewin had set up the RCGD at MIT. After the War, Doug became very interested in the research on leadership and organizations that we were doing in the Institute for Social Research. He visited us frequently and I saw him often at Antioch and at MIT after he returned." Likert goes on to refer to the first NTL lab for managers that was held at Arden House in 1956: "Douglas McGregor and I helped Lee Bradford launch it. . . . Staff members in the 1956 lab were: Beckhard, Benne, Bradford, Gordon Lippitt, Malott, Shepard and I. Argyris, Blake and McGregor joined the staff for the 1957 Arden House lab."[67]

Argyris refers to Likert:

> Rensis Likert was also a leader in the field when I was a graduate student, and I had the highest respect for him and his commitment to trying to connect theory with practice. Indeed, I've always been a bit sad to see how many of his colleagues, who saw themselves as more re-

searchers, at times would downplay Rensis' commitment to practice. They saw him as being too . . . committed to the world of practice. I never felt that. I felt that it was the combination of practice and theory that made him an important member of our community. I would put Lewin first on that dimension, and Ren Likert and Doug McGregor next, each in his own way making important contributions.[68]

Links between group dynamics and survey feedback people were extensive, of course, after the RCGD moved to Michigan with the encouragement of Rensis Likert and members of the SRC. Among the top people in the RCGD who moved to Michigan were Leon Festinger, Dorwin Cartwright, Ronald Lippitt, and John R. P. French, Jr. Cartwright, who was selected by the group to be the director of the RCGD, was particularly knowledgeable about survey research, since he had been on the staff of the Division of Program Surveys with Rensis Likert and others during World War II.[69]

THE ACTION RESEARCH STEM

In earlier chapters we briefly described action research as a collaborative, client-consultant inquiry consisting of preliminary diagnosis, data gathering from the client group, data feedback to the client group, data exploration and action planning by the client group, and action. As we will describe in Chapter 7, there are at least four versions of action research, one of which, participant action research, is used with the most frequency in OD. The laboratory training stem in the history of OD has a heavy component of action research; the survey feedback stem is the history of a specialized form of action research; and Tavistock projects have had a strong action research thrust, as we will discuss shortly.

Because we will treat the history of action research in some detail later we will mention only a few aspects here. For example, William F. Whyte and Edith L. Hamilton were using action research in their work with Chicago's Tremont Hotel in 1945 and 1946; John Collier, commissioner of Indian Affairs, was describing action research in a publication in 1945; Kurt Lewin and his students conducted numerous action research projects in the mid-1940s and early 1950s. The work of these and other scholars and practitioners in the invention and utilization of action research was basic in the evolution of OD.

THE SOCIOTECHNICAL AND SOCIOCLINICAL STEM

A fourth stem in the history of OD is the evolution of socioclinical and sociotechnical approaches to helping groups and organizations. Parallel to the work of the RCGD, the SRC, and NTL was the work of the Tavistock

Clinic in England. The clinic had been founded in 1920 as an outpatient facility to provide psychotherapy based on psychoanalytic theory and insights from the treatment of battle neurosis in World War I. A group focus emerged early in the work of Tavistock in the context of family therapy in which the child and the parent received treatment simultaneously.[70] The action research mode also emerged at Tavistock in attempts to give practical help to families, organizations, and communities.

W. R. Bion, John Rickman, and Others

The staff of the Tavistock Clinic was extensively influenced by such innovations as World War II applications of social psychology to psychiatry, the work of W. R. Bion and John Rickman and others in group therapy, Lewin's notions about the "social field" in which a problem was occurring, and Lewin's theory and experience with action research. Bion, Rickman, and others had been involved with the six-week "Northfield Experiment" at a military hospital near Birmingham during World War II. In this experiment each soldier was required to join a group that both performed some task such as handicraft or map reading and discussed feelings, interpersonal relations, and administrative and managerial problems as well. Insights from this experiment were to carry over into Bion's theory of group behavior.[71]

Eric Trist

It is of significance that Tavistock's sociotechnical approach to restructuring work grew out of Eric Trist's visit to a coal mine and his insights as to the relevance of Lewin's work on group dynamics and Bion's work on leaderless groups to mining problems.[72] Trist was also influenced by the systems concepts of Von Bertalanffy and Andras Angyal.[73] Trist's subsequent experiments in work redesign and the use of semiautonomous work teams in coal mining were the forerunners of other work redesign experiments in various industries in Europe, India, Australia, and the United States. Thus, there is a clear historical link between the group dynamics field and sociotechnical approaches to assisting organizations.

Tavistock–U.S. Links

Tavistock leaders, including Trist and Bion, had frequent contact with Kurt Lewin, Rensis Likert, Chris Argyris, and others in the United States. One product of this collaboration was the decision to publish the journal *Human Relations* as a joint publication between Tavistock and MIT's Research Center for Group Dynamics.[74] Some Americans prominent in the emergence and evolution of the OD field, for example, Robert

Blake, as we noted earlier, and Warren Bennis,[75] studied at Tavistock. Chris Argyris held several seminars with Tavistock leaders in 1954.[76]

The sociotechnical approach focused on the nonexecutive ranks of organizations and especially the redesign of work. The focus on teams and the use of action research and participation was consistent with OD approaches. Some contemporary quality of work life (QWL) and some total quality management (TQM) programs are amalgamations of OD, sociotechnical, and other approaches.

THE CHANGING CONTEXT

While it is important to understand how OD emerged, it is also important to understand the changing milieu in which contemporary OD activities are occurring. That context has changed dramatically throughout the 1980s and 1990s. As authors are prone to say, the environment has become increasingly "turbulent." In the United States, the plethora of technological innovations, company mergers, acquisitions, leveraged buyouts, bankruptcies, success stories, downsizings, and changes in laws has intensified. At the same time, while the frequency of startups has slowed somewhat, thousands of small companies are born each year. Globalization of companies is commonplace. Worldwide, many previously centralized and autocratic societies are moving in the direction of creating democratic institutions and privatizing business and industry. All of these changes create opportunities for OD applications, but also stretch the capabilities of leaders and OD practitioners to the utmost.

It is in this context that what might be called *second-generation OD* is evolving. There is still a major reliance on the first-generation techniques of OD that are highly relevant to adaptive, incremental change such as action research, a focus on teams, team building, the use of facilitators, process consultation, survey feedback, intergroup problem solving, sociotechnical systems approaches to job design, and participative management. Indeed, there is growing application and theory building and/or research relative to all of these OD basics. But the field is growing beyond these first-generation approaches in the sense that many applications of OD are now more complicated and more multifaceted.

SECOND-GENERATION OD

Considerable attention to theory and practice is now being given to emerging concepts, interventions, and areas of application, which might be called second-generation OD. Each, to some extent, overlaps with some or all of the others. Second-generation OD, in particular, has a focus on second-order change, that is, on organizational transformation.

Interest in Organizational Transformation

More and more, practitioners and scholars are talking and writing about "organizational transformation." Amir Levy and Uri Merry give one of the most complete explorations of this topic in their book by the title *Organizational Transformation*. They define the term as follows: "Second-order change (organization transformation) is a multi-dimensional, multi-level, qualitative, discontinuous, radical organizational change involving a paradigmatic shift."[77]

Increasingly, OD professionals are making a distinction between the more modest, or evolutionary, efforts toward organization improvement and those that are massive and, in a sense, revolutionary. For example, Nadler and Tushman refer to "transitions" on the one hand, and "frame bending" on the other.[78] Goodstein and Burke contrast "fine tuning" with "fundamental, large-scale change in the organization's strategy and culture."[79] Barczak, Smith, and Wilemon differentiate "adaptive, incremental change" from "large-scale change."[80] Beckhard and Pritchard contrast "incremental" change strategies and "fundamental" change strategies.[81] Organizational transformation is seen as requiring more demands on top leadership, more visioning, more experimenting, more time, and the simultaneous management of many additional variables.

Interest in Organizational Culture

Efforts to define, measure, and change organizational culture have become more sophisticated. Schein in particular has written extensively about culture,[82] and has devised interventions to help leaders and employees identify those cultural assumptions that will assist the organization in attaining its goals and those that hinder goal attainment. This is done through a joint exploration to identify sequentially the organization's *artifacts*, such as office layout and status symbols; the *values* underlying these artifacts; and the *assumptions* behind those values.[83] Others have helped organizations focus on culture through the use of questionnaires that are aimed at identifying actual and desired norms. Agreements are then made as to new norms and how to monitor and reinforce the changes.[84] (For more detail, see Chapter 11.)

Interest in the Learning Organization

Largely stimulated by the works of Argyris,[85] Argyris and Schon,[86] and Senge, there has been considerable interest in the conditions under which individuals, teams, and organizations learn. Argyris, for example, has focused on the defensive routines of organizational members, or "master programs in their heads that tell them how to deal with embarrassment and threat." Basically, according to Argyris, individuals tend to follow these rules:

1. Bypass embarrassment and threat whenever possible.
2. Act as though you are not bypassing them.
3. Don't discuss steps 1 and 2 while they are happening.
4. Don't discuss the undiscussability of the undiscussable.[87]

Workshops with top-management teams are designed to tackle simultaneously major tasks such as strategy formulation plus learning how to recognize defensive routines toward improvements in communications and the quality of team decision making.[88]

Senge writes extensively about the importance of systems thinking ("the fifth discipline") relative to organizations, and about the learning disabilities that plague organizations. One learning disability, for example, is a focus on one's own job exclusively with little sense of responsibility for the collective product. Another is to do a lot of blaming of the "enemy out there" for things that are wrong, whether it's another department in the same organization or a competitor overseas.[89] Senge is noted for his workshops in which games and exercises are used to create an awareness of these disabilities and to develop different ways of thinking about complex problems.[90]

Intensified Interest in Teams

A focus on intact work teams and other team configurations has been a central aspect of OD since the emergence of the field, but recent years have seen a widening and deepening interest in teams, especially what are called high-performance teams, cross-functional teams, and self-managed teams. Interest has intensified particularly in self-managed or self-directed teams. An extension of the semiautonomous team concept from the sociotechnical systems stem of OD, interest in self-managed or seemingly self-managed teams has accelerated due to converging pressures on organizations to improve quality, to become more flexible, to reduce layers of management, and to enhance employee morale.[91]

Laboratory training methods have been found to be highly useful in training team members in effective membership and leadership behaviors, and in training supervisors and managers in the arts of delegation and empowerment. Furthermore, many organizations have used team-building approaches to assist self-managed teams and cross-functional teams in getting started. In addition, as self-managed teams have assumed many functions previously performed by management, supervisors and middle managers have utilized team-building approaches within their own ranks to help reconceptualize their own roles. Furthermore, since some supervisors and managers are likely to be displaced in the process of "delayering," in many instances top management has used OD professionals to look at various options to minimize the distress of those affected by job changes, demotions, or layoffs.

Total Quality Management (TQM)

Interest in and efforts toward total quality management (TQM) are worldwide and growing rapidly. Ciampa, who acknowledges the pioneering contributions of Joseph Juran, W. Edwards Deming, and Armand Feigenbaum to the development of TQM[92], provides a clear statement regarding the relationship between TQM and OD. First, his definition: "Total Quality is typically a companywide effort seeking to install and make permanent a climate where employees continuously improve their ability to provide on demand products and services that customers will find of particular value."[93] He then goes on to say that one element that separates successful TQ efforts from less successful ones is

> . . . a particular set of values about the individual and the individual's role in the organization. TQ efforts in these companies encourage true employee involvement, demand teamwork, seek to push decision-making power to lower levels in the company, and reduce barriers between people. . . . These values are at the core of Organization Development (OD), as well."[94]

OD values and approaches have been key aspects of many successful TQM processes. Burke comments on the role of OD in TQM as follows: "Moreover, the quality movement, to be successful, is highly dependent on effective process—and process is the OD practitioner's most important product."[95]

Interest in Visioning

Interventions designed to help organizational members look to the future—visioning—are not new to OD, but renewed interest in the use of interventions to look at trends projected into the future and their organizational implications has developed. Marvin Weisbord, for example, has built on the work and experience of Ronald Lippitt and Edward Lindaman,[96] Ronald Fox, Ronald Lippitt, and Eva Schindler-Rainman,[97] and Eric Trist and Fred Emery [98] to develop "future search conferences." In a two- or three-day conference, participants are asked to "(a) build a data base, (b) look at it together, (c) interpret what they find, and (d) draw conclusions for action."[99] This last part of the conference asks participants to develop next action steps and a structure for carrying them out, including task forces and specific assignments.[100]

Senge believes that "the origin of the vision is much less important than the process whereby it comes to be shared." He strongly urges that "shared visions" be based on encouraging organizational members to develop and share their own personal visions, and that a vision is not truly shared "until it connects with the personal visions of people throughout the organization."[101] This obviously requires OD-like processes to implement.

Rediscovering Large Meetings and Getting the "Whole System" in the Room

As described earlier, one of the contributing factors in the emergence of the OD movement was the experience of people like Leland Bradford, Ronald Lippitt, and Richard Beckhard in improving the effectiveness of large meetings. Early on, Beckhard wrote an article entitled "The Confrontation Meeting" which was really about getting the total management group of an organization together in a one-day session to diagnose the state of the system and to make plans for quickly improving conditions.[102] In recent years, Marvin Weisbord and others have written about the importance of OD consultants "getting the whole system in the room." For example, with reference to future search conferences, he advises that such conferences involve all of top management and "people from as many functions and levels as feasible." Again, the final products are action plans and specific assignments to carry the process forward.[103]

Other Directions and Areas of Interest

There are other visible areas of interest and attention in second-generation OD. Assistance in developing diversity awareness workshops and in "managing" and "valuing" diversity have been much in evidence in recent years. Expanded interest in sociotechnical systems design, interrelated with interest in self-managed teams and in total quality management, has been apparent. OD applications to quality of work life (QWL) programs has continued but is less evident because of the heightened attention to TQM. Partially as a result of a focus on teams and teamwork, a great deal of attention has been directed toward developing congruent reward systems, including productivity gainsharing plans and skills-based pay plans. Research and conceptualizing about action research, process consultation, and third-party roles have continued and perhaps increased. There is renewed interest in the concept of community relative to organizational transformation and the creation of high-performance organizations. Considerable work has been done with "appreciative inquiry" workshops.[104] Interest in physical settings is by no means dormant.

All of these directions are fruitful areas for OD theory and practice. With the diffusion of OD techniques to so many areas it becomes difficult to identify what is and what is not OD. Thus, it has become increasingly important to examine the processes underlying various improvement efforts—not because there is anything inherently sacred about OD, but because the fundamental building blocks of OD are vital ingredients to participant satisfaction and development and to organizational effectiveness and survival.

EXTENT OF APPLICATION

Applications emerging from one or more of the stems described previously are evident in contemporary organization development efforts occurring in many countries, including England, Japan, Norway, Italy, Belgium, Switzerland, Canada, Sweden, Germany, Finland, Australia, New Zealand, the Philippines, Mexico, France, Venezuela, and the Netherlands, as well as in the United States. Among the large number of organizations in America that have at one time or another embarked on organization development efforts are Union Carbide and Exxon (the first two companies), Connecticut General Insurance Company, Hewlett-Packard, Tektronix, Graphic Controls, Equitable Life Assurance Company, Digital Equipment Corporation, Procter & Gamble, Microelectronics and Computer Technology Corporation (MCC), Mountain Bell Telephone, Searle Laboratories, the Boeing Company, Bankers Trust, Ford Motor Company, Heinz Foods, Polaroid, Sun Oil, and TRW Inc.

Applications have varied, with the total organization involved in many instances, but with only some divisions or plants in others. Further, some efforts have moved ahead rapidly, only to flounder at a later time. In many situations, OD approaches have become an ongoing way of managing with little program visibility and under different terminology. Thus, it is difficult to report with any precision the extent of application.

Applications at TRW Space & Electronics Group (S&EG) were of major significance in the emergence and history of OD. Among the key figures in the beginnings of OD there in the early 1960s (then called TRW Systems Group) were Jim Dunlap, director of industrial relations; Shel Davis, who was later promoted to that position; Ruben Mettler, president; and Herb Shepard. T-group labs conducted by internal trainers, NTL, and UCLA staff members were also important in providing impetus to the effort in its early phases. Early applications of OD at TRW Systems included team building, intergroup team building, interface laboratories between departments and between company and customers, laboratory training, career assessment workshops, and organization redesign and structuring for improved productivity and quality of working life.[105]

After successful applications in the 1960s, OD activities tended to decline during the 1970s and 1980s. However, according to Michael Thiel, director of leadership and organization effectiveness at S&EG, "radical structural change within the defense industry has forced TRW (and other defense contractors) to critically examine and shift basic operating paradigms."[106] Thiel goes on to say:

> This has led to the rebirth of "OD-like" activities as part of cultural change and organization transformation efforts. Since 1989, S&EG has been actively pursuing the creation/implementation of a total quality culture, incorporating continuous process improvement, employee empowerment, performance management, and the use of concurrent engineering/integrated product development with cross-functional teams. OD methodologies such as organizational diagnosis, values clarification, offsite meetings, sensing, etc. have been used where appropriate in these activities. Other tools include team facilitation, team-based experimental education and survey/feedback systems.
>
> Most of these "organization effectiveness" interventions are spearheaded by the Human Resources organization, either HR generalists, or specialists from my office. In addition, there are a number of line/technical managers involved in various facets (specifically team facilitation/process improvement, and self-managed work teams).[107]

Business and industrial organizations are by no means the only kinds of institutions involved. There are applications, for example, in public school systems; colleges; medical schools; social welfare agencies; police departments; professional associations; governmental units at the local, county, state, and national levels; the White House;[108] various health care delivery systems; churches; American Indian tribes; and the U.S. military.

OD activities in the U.S. military have waxed and waned, partly depending upon top command interest and support. Reduced support for the program in the Army appears to be partly due to lack of systematic measurement of the results. At one time, the Army ran an Organizational Effectiveness Center and School at Fort Ord, California and graduated some 1,702 officers as internal consultants. The Center started in 1975 with a complement of 19 officers, six enlisted personnel, and 21 civilians; ten years later the complement had been reduced to three officers and one civilian who were reassigned to the Soldier Support Center to teach basic human resource skills.[109] The Navy, on the other hand, conducted a year-long study of all aspects of its OE program and concluded that the program had "definite value but would be best utilized with a major change in its structure."[110]

Some community development strategies have a number of elements in common with organization development, such as the use of action research, the use of a change agent, and an emphasis on facilitating decision-making and problem-solving processes.[111] Undoubtedly, some of the commonality stems from OD practitioners working in the community development field. For example, in 1961 Herbert Shepard conducted community development laboratories at China Lake, California, sponsored by the Naval Ordnance Test Station. These one-week labs involved military persons and civilians and people of all ages and socioeconomic levels. Outcomes included the resolution of some community and intercommunity issues.[112]

In addition to emphasizing the diversity of types of systems using OD consultants, we want to emphasize that intraorganization development efforts have not focused on just top-management teams, although the importance of top-management involvement will be discussed in later chapters. The wide range of occupational roles that have been involved in OD is almost limitless and has included production workers,[113] managers, soldiers, military officers, miners, scientists and engineers, ministers, psychologists, geologists, lawyers, accountants, nurses, physicians, teachers, computer specialists, foresters, technicians, secretaries, clerical employees, board members, and flight crews.

Symptomatic of the widespread application of organization development concepts is the emergence and growth of the OD Network, which began in 1964 and in late 1993 had a membership of about 2,450 and 27 regional networks. Most members either have major roles in the OD efforts of organizations or are scholar-practitioners in the OD field. While most OD Network members reside in the United States, in 1993 there were about 200 international members, the majority from Canada. 24 countries were represented in addition to the United States.

The OD Network began with discussions at the Case Institute of Technology between Herbert Shepard, Sheldon Davis of TRW Systems, and Floyd Mann of the University of Michigan,[114] and through the initiative of Leland Bradford and Jerry Harvey of NTL and a number of industrial people who had attended labs at Bethel. Among the industrial founders of the organization, originally called the Industrial Trainers Network, were Sheldon Davis of TRW Systems, George Murray of Union Carbide, John Vail of Dow Chemical, and Carl Albers of the Hotel Corporation of America. Other early members were from Procter & Gamble, Weyerhaeuser, Bankers Trust, West Virginia Pulp and Paper Company, the U.S. State Department, the U.S. National Security Agency, Pillsbury, Eli Lilly, Polaroid, Esso, Parker Pen, American Airlines, Goodrich-Gulf Chemicals, RCA, Sandia, National Association of Manufacturers, General Foods, Armour & Company, Heublein, and Du

Pont. Jerry Harvey was the first secretary/coordinator of the emerging organization, and Warner Burke assumed that role in 1967 shortly after joining NTL on a full-time basis. There were fewer than 50 members at that time; when Warner Burke stepped aside as executive director in 1975, there were approximately 1,400 members.[115] That same year the OD Network became independent of NTL.

An OD Division of the American Society for Training and Development was established in 1968 and had 6,233 members by the spring of 1993. It is also significant that the Academy of Management, whose members are mostly professors in management and related areas, established a Division of Organization Development within its structure in 1971. This unit, renamed The Division of Organization Development and Change, had approximately 1,500 members by 1993. The Society of Industrial-Organizational Psychology of the American Psychological Association has held workshops on organization development at the annual APA conventions; several annual conventions going back at least to 1965 have included papers or symposia on organization development or related topics.[116] In 1974 the *Annual Review of Psychology* for the first time devoted a chapter entirely to a review of research on organization development.[117] Chapters on OD have appeared at other times, for example, 1977,[118] 1982, 1987,[119] and 1991.[120] The 1982 chapter was written by authors from the Netherlands and France, indicative of OD's international applications.[121]

The first doctoral program devoted to training OD specialists was founded by Herbert Shepard in 1960 at the Case Institute of Technology. Originally called The Organizational Behavior Group, this program is now part of the Department of Organizational Behavior, School of Management, Case Western Reserve University. Masters degree programs in organization development or masters programs with concentrations in OD have been offered in recent years by several universities, including New York University, Brigham Young, Pepperdine, Loyola, Bowling Green, New Hampshire, Central Washington University, Columbia, and Case Western Reserve and Sheffield Polytechnic in England. The American University and NTL Institute jointly offer a masters degree program in Human Resource Development. The John F. Kennedy University and NTL cosponsor a masters program which has organization development and change as a major component. Many other major universities, if not most, now have graduate courses directly bearing on organization development, including UCLA, Stanford, Harvard, University of Washington, University of Southern California, Hawaii, Oklahoma, Colorado, Indiana, and Purdue, and in England, such courses are found at the University of Manchester Institute of Science and Technology and the University of Bath.[122]

This rapid growth in OD interest and attention has been given impetus by NTL's Program for Specialists in Organization Development (originally called PSOTD), discussed earlier in this chapter. PSOD started as an intensive, four-week session held in the summer at Bethel and was partly an outgrowth of an Organization Intern Program that had included some OD training. PSOD subsequently became a one-week program for managers/practitioners with several years of professional experience, and also became a capstone course for participants in an OD certificate program. Other NTL programs include Consultation Skills; Process Consultation; Developing High-Performing, Culturally Diverse Organizations; Team Building; TQM Implementation; and Tavistock Workshop. Other professional programs in OD have been or are now being offered in the United States, Canada, the United Kingdom, Australia, New Zealand, and elsewhere under the sponsorship of universities, foundations, professional associations, and other institutions.

SUMMARY

Organization development has emerged largely from applied behavioral sciences and has four major stems: the invention of the T-group and innovations in the application of laboratory training insights to complex organizations, the invention of survey feedback technology, the emergence of action research, and the evolution of the Tavistock sociotechnical and socioclinical approaches.

Key figures in this early history interacted with each other and across these stems and were influenced by concepts and experiences from a wide variety of disciplines and settings. These disciplines included social psychology, clinical psychology, family group therapy, ethnography, military psychology and psychiatry, the theater, general semantics, social work, systems theory, mathematics and physics, philosophy, psychodrama, client-centered therapy, survey methodology, experimental and action research, human resources management, organizational behavior, general management theory, and large conference management.

The context for the application of OD approaches has changed to an increasingly more turbulent environment. While there is still a major reliance on OD basics, considerable attention is being given to new concepts, interventions, and areas of application. Second-generation OD includes interest in organizational transformation, organizational culture, the learning organization, teams and their various configurations, total quality management, visioning, and "getting the whole system in the room."

The history of OD is emergent in that a rapidly increasing number of behavioral scientists and practitioners are building on the research and insights of the past as well as rediscovering the utility of some of the earlier insights. These efforts, often under different terminology, are now expanding and include a wide range of organizations, types of institutions, occupational categories, and geographical locations around the world.

In the chapters that follow, the assumptions, theory, and techniques of organization development, as well as problems with implementation of OD processes, will be examined in considerable depth. We will also speculate on the future viability of OD or OD-like processes.

NOTES

1. The phrase *group dynamics* was coined by Kurt Lewin in 1939. See Warrent Bennis, address to the Academy of Management, San Diego, California, August 3, 1981.
2. This and the next paragraph are based on Kenneth D. Benne, Leland P. Bradford, Jack R. Gibb, and Ronald O. Lippitt, eds., *The Laboratory Method for Changing and Learning: Theory and Application* (Palo Alto, CA: Science and Behavior Books, 1975), pp. 1–6; and Alfred J. Marrow, *The Practical Theorist: The Life and Work of Kurt Lewin* (New York: Basic Books, 1969), pp. 210–214. For additional history, see Leland P. Bradford, "Biography of an Institution," *Journal of Applied Behavioral Science*, 3 (April–June 1967), pp. 127–143; and Alvin Zander, "The Study of Group Behavior During Four Decades," *The Journal of Applied Behavioral Science*, 15 (July–September 1979), pp. 272–282. We are indebted to Ronald Lippitt for his correspondence, which helped to clarify this and the following paragraph.
3. Jerrold I. Hirsch, *The History of the National Training Laboratories 1947–1986* (New York: Peter Lang publishing, 1987), pp. 17–18; and address by Ronald Lippitt, Academy of Management annual conference, Chicago, Illinois, August 1986. For more on Bradford, see David L. Bradford, "A Biography of Leland P. Bradford," *Journal of Applied Behavioral Science*, 26, no. 1 (1990), viii.
4. See also Nancie Coan, "A History of NTL Institute in Bethel," *NTL Institute News & Views* (February 1991), pp. 11–15.
5. Peter B. Smith, ed., *Small Groups and Personal Change* (London: Methuen & Co. 1980), pp. 8–9.
6. Robert Chin and Kenneth D. Benne, "General Strategies for Effecting Changes in Human Systems," in Warren G. Bennis, Kenneth D. Benne, and Robert Chin, eds., *The Planning of Change*, 2nd ed. (New York: Holt, Rinehardt and Winston, 1969), pp. 100–102.
7. Correspondence with Kenneth Benne. Raup was Benne's Ph.D. major professor at Columbia. Benne states that he was also influenced by Edward Lindeman. For more on Benne, see Paul Nash, "Biography of Kenneth D. Benne," *Journal of Applied Behavioral Science*, 28 (June 1992), p. 167.
8. Chin and Benne, op cit., p. 102.
9. Correspondence with Ronald Lippitt.
10. Conversation with Lee Bradford, conference on current theory and practice in organization development, San Francisco, March 16, 1978.
11. See, for example, S. R. Slavson, *An Introduction to Group Therapy* (New York: The Commonwealth Fund, 1943); and S. R. Slavson, *Creative Group Education* (New York: Association press, 1937), especially Chapter 1.
12. Based largely on correspondence with Ronald Lippitt. According to Lippitt, as early as 1945 Bradford and Lippitt were conducting "three-level training" at Freedman's Hospital in Washington, D.C., in an effort "to induce interdependent changes in all parts of the same system." Lippitt also reports that Leland Bradford very early was acting on a basic concept of "multiple entry," that is, simultaneously training and working with several groups in the organization.

13. Correspondence with Robert Tannenbaum.

14. Tannenbaum correspondence; memorandum of May 12, 1952, U. S. Naval Ordnance Test Station from E. R. Toporeck to "Office, Division and Branch Heads, Test Department," and "Minutes, Test Department Management Seminar, 5 March 1953."

15. Robert Tannenbaum, Verne Kallejian, and Irving R. Weschler, "Training Managers for Leadership," *Personnel,* 30 (January 1954), p. 3.

16. Verne J. Kallejian, Irving R. Weschler, and Robert Tannenbaum, "Managers in Transition," *Harvard Business Review,* 33 (July–August 1955), pp. 55–64.

17. Tannenbaum correspondence.

18. Ibid.

19. Correspondence with Chris Argyris; and Chris Argyris, *Interpersonal Competence and Organizational Effectiveness* (Homewood, IL: Richard D. Irwin, 1962).

20. Argyris correspondence.

21. Chris Argyris, *Intervention Theory and Method* (Reading, MA: Addison-Wesley, 1970).

22. Argyris correspondence.

23. Donald D. Bowen, "Competence and Justice: A Conversation with Chris Argyris," p. 4.2 of a manuscript accepted for publication in the 1988 *OD Annual.*

24. Argyris correspondence.

25. Ibid. Argyris's Ph.D. in organizational behavior may have been the first ever awarded.

26. Argyris correspondence.

27. See Richard Beckhard, W. Warner Burke, and Fred I. Steele, "The Program for Specialists in Organization Training and Development," p. ii, mimeographed paper (NTL Institute for Applied Behavioral Science, December 1967); and John Paul Jones, "What's Wrong with Work?" in *What's Wrong with Work?* (New York: National Association of Manufacturers, 1967), p. 8. According to correspondence with Rensis Likert, the link between McGregor and John Paul Jones occurred in the summer of 1957. Discussion took place between the two when Jones attended one of the annual two-week seminars at Aspen, Colorado, organized by Hollis Peter of the Foundation for Research on Human Behavior and conducted by Douglas McGregor, Mason Haire, and Rensis Likert.

28. Gilbert Burck, "Union Carbide's Patient Schemers, " *Fortune,* 72 (December 1965), pp. 147–149. For McGregor's account, see "Team Building at Union Carbide," in Douglas McGregor, *The Professional Manager* (New York: McGraw-Hill, 1967), pp. 106–110.

29. See the Editor's Preface to Douglas McGregor, *The Professional Manager* (New York: McGraw-Hill, 1967), p. viii.

30. Conversation with George Strauss, Western Division of the Academy of Management conference, San Diego, California, March, 1985. For a brief overview of Rogers's life and career, see "Carl Rogers (1902–1987)," *American Psychologist,* 43 (February 1988), pp. 127–128. Carl Rogers was also on the staff of several NTL president's labs in the early days. Seminar with Carl Rogers, Western Division of the Academy of Management conference, San Diego, California, March, 1985.

31. Douglas McGregor, *The Human Side of Enterprise* (New York: McGraw-Hill, 1960). For more on McGregor, see Marvin R. Weisbord, *Productive Workplaces* (San Fransisco: Jossey-Bass Publishers, 1987), pp. 106–122.

32. This paragraph is based on interviews with Herbert Shepard, August 3, 1981. For a brief discussion of the career of Clarence Hicks, see Wendell French, *The Personnel Management Process,* 6th ed. (Boston: Houghton Mifflin, 1987), Chap. 2.

33. Much of the historical account in this paragraph and the following three paragraphs is based on correspondence and interviews with Herbert Shepard, with some information added from correspondence with Robert Blake.

34. Correspondence with Robert Blake and Herbert Shepard. For further reference to Murray Horowitz and Paul Buchanan, as well as to comments about the innovative contributions of Michael Blansfield, see Herbert A. Shepard, "Explorations in Observant Participation," in Bradford, Gibb, and Benne, eds., *T-Group Theory,* pp. 382–383. See also Marshall Sashkin, "Interview with Robert R. Blake and Jane Srygley Mouton," *Group and Organization Studies,* 3 (December 1978), pp. 401–407.

35. See Robert Blake and Jane Srygley Mouton, "The Instrumented Training Laboratory," in Irving R. Weschler and Edgar M. Schein, eds., *Selected Readings Series Five: Issues in Training* (Washington, DC: National Training Laboratories, 1962), pp. 61– 85. In this chapter, Blake and Mouton credit Muzafer and Carolyn Sherif with important contributions to early intergroup experiments. Reference is also made to the contributions of Frank Cassens of Humble Oil and Refinery in the early phases of the Esso program. For a brief description of the development of the two-dimensional Managerial Grid, see Robert Blake and Jane Srygley Mouton, *Diary of an OD Man* (Houston: Gulf 1976), pp. 332–336. For more on Sherif, see O. J. Harvey, "Muzafer Sherif (1906–1988)," *American Psychologist*, 44 (October 1989), pp. 1325–1326.

36. Based on correspondence with Robert Blake. See also Robert R. Blake and Jane Srygley Mouton, "Why the OD Movement Is 'Stuck' and How to Break It Loose," *Training and Development Journal*, 33 (September 1979), pp. 12–20.

37. Blake correspondence.

38. Mouton correspondence.

39. Blake correspondence.

40. Ibid. For more on Bowlby, see Mary D. Salter Ainsworth, "John Bowlby (1907–1993)," *American Psychologist*, 47 (May 1992), p. 668.

41. Blake correspondence.

42. Correspondence with Richard Beckhard.

43. Ibid.

44. Based on Beckhard correspondence and other sources.

45. The previous three paragraphs and the following three are based on correspondence with Eva Schindler-Rainman. For additional material, see Anthony J. Reilly, "Interview" (with Eva Schindler-Rainman and Ron Lippitt) *Group & Organization Studies*, 2 (September 1977), pp. 265–281.

46. For more on Edith Seashore, see Charleen Alderfer, "A Biography of Edith Whitfield Seashore," *Journal of Applied Behavioral Science*, 28 (March 1992), pp. 7–8.

47. Eva Schindler-Rainman, *The Creative Volunteer Community: A Collection of Writings by Eva Schindler-Rainman, D.S.W.* (Vancouver, BC: Vancouver Volunteer Centre, 1987).

48. Eva Schindler-Rainman and Ronald Lippitt, *Building the Collaborative Community: Mobilizing Citizens for Action* (Riverside, CA: University of California Extension, 1980.) (Third printing available through ENERGIZE, 5450 Wissahickon Avenue, Philadelphia, PA, 19144.)

49. Eva Schindler-Rainman and Ronald Lippitt, *The Volunteer Community: Creative Use of Human Resources*, 2nd ed. (San Diego: University Associates, 1975.) (Available through ENERGIZE.)

50. Eva Schindler-Rainman and Ronald Lippitt, *Team Training for Community Change: Concepts, Goals, Strategies and Skills* (Bethesda, MD: Development Publications, 1972). (Third printing, 1993, available through Dr. Eva Schindler-Rainman, 4267 San Rafael Avenue, Los Angeles, CA 90042.)

51. Interpretations of Blake correspondence, Shepard interview, Beckhard correspondence, and Larry Porter, "OD: Some Questions Some Answers—An Interview with Beckhard and Shepard," *OD Practitioner*, 6 (Autumn 1974), p. 1.

52. Blake correspondence.

53. Jane Srygley Mouton and Robert R. Blake, "University Training in Human Relations Skills," *Selected Readings Series Three: Forces in Learning* (Washington DC: National Training Laboratories, 1961), pp. 88–96, reprinted from *Group Psychotherapy*, 10 (1957), pp. 342–345.

54. Shepard and Blake correspondence.

55. Interview with Herbert Shepard, San Diego, California, August 3, 1981.

56. Beckhard correspondence.

57. Burck, "Union Carbide's Patient Schemers," p. 149.

58. Harry D. Kolb, "Introduction" to *An Action Research Program for Organization Improvement* (Ann Arbor, MI: Foundation for Research on Human Behavior, 1960), p. i. The phrase *organization development* is used several times in this monograph based on a 1959 meeting about the Esso programs and written by Kolb, Shepard, Blake, and others.
59. Based on Beckhard correspondence.
60. This history is based largely on correspondence with Rensis Likert and partially on "The Career of Rensis Likert," *ISR Newsletter,* (Winter 1971); and *A Quarter Century of Social Research,* Institute for Social Research, 1971. See also Charles Cannell and Robert Kahn, "Some Factors in the Origins and Development of The Institute for Social Research, The University of Michigan," *American Psychologist,* 39 (November 1984), pp. 1256–1266.
61. "Rensis Likert," *ISR newsletter,* p. 6.
62. Likert correspondence. Floyd Mann later became the first director of the Center for Research on the Utilization of Scientific Knowledge (CRUSK) when the center was established by ISR in 1964. See also Floyd C. Mann, "Studying and Creating Change," in Bennis, Benne, and Chin, eds. *Planning of Change,* pp. 605–613.
63. Mann, "Studying and Creating Change," p. 609.
64. Howard Baumgartel, "Using Employee Questionnaire Results for Improving Organizations: The Survey (Feedback) Experiment," *Kansas Business Review,* 12 (December 1959), pp. 2–6.
65. Likert correspondence.
66. Marrow, *The Practical Theorist,* p. 164. This book about the life and work of Kurt Lewin is rich with events that are important to the history of OD.
67. Likert correspondence.
68. Argyris correspondence.
69. Likert correspondence.
70. H.V. Dicks, *Fifty Years of the Tavistock Clinic* (London: Routledge & Kegan Paul, 1970), pp. 1, 32.
71. Based on Ibid., 5, 7, 133, 140; and Robert DeBoard, *The Psychoanalysis of Organizations* (London: Tavistock 1978), pp. 35–43.
72. Eric Trist and Marshall Sashkin, "Interview," *Group & Organization Studies,* 5 (June 1980), pp. 150–151.
73. Ibid., p. 155. See also William A. Pasmore and Guruder S. Khalsa, "The Contributions of Eric Trist to the Social Engagement of Social Science," *Academy of Management Review,* 18 (July 1993), pp. 546–569.
74. This and the previous three paragraphs are based largely on Ibid., pp. 144–151. The brief statement about action research is also partly based on Alfred J. Marrow, "Risks and Uncertainties in Action Research," *Journal of Social Issues* 20, no. 3 (1964), p. 17.
75. Bennis address, Academy of Management, August 3, 1981.
76. Argyris correspondence.
77. Amir Levy and Uni Merry, *Organizational Transformation* (New York: Praeger Publishers, 1986), p. 5.
78. David A. Nadler and Michael L. Tushman, "Organizational Frame Bending: Principles for Managing Reorientation," *The Academy of Management EXECUTIVE,* 3 (August 1989), pp. 194–204.
79. Leonard D. Goodstein and W. Warner Burke, "Creating Successful Organization Change," *Organizational Dynamics,* 19 (Spring 1991), pp. 5–17.
80. Gloria Barczak, Charles Smith, and David Wilemon, "Managing Large-Scale Organizational Change," *Organizational Dynamics* (Autumn 1987), pp. 23–35.
81. Richard Beckhard and Wendy Pritchard, *Changing the Essence* (San Fransisco: Jossey-Bass Publishers, 1992), p. 3; and Richard Beckhard, "Choosing and Leading a Fundamental Change," *Academy of Management ODC Newsletter* (Summer 1993), pp. 6–8.

82. Edgar H. Schein, *Organizational Culture and Leadership* (San Francisco: Jossey-Bass Publishers, 1985).

83. Edgar H. Schein, "Organization Development and the Study of Organizational Culture," *Academy of Management OD Newsletter* (Summer 1990), pp. 3–5.

84. Ralph H. Kilmann, "Five Steps for Closing Culture-Gaps," pp. 351–369, and Robert F. Allen, "Four Phases for Bringing About Cultural Change," pp. 332–350 in Ralph H. Kilmann, Mary J. Saxton, and Roy Serpa, eds. *Gaining Control of the Corporate Culture* (San Francisco: Jossey-Bass Publishers, 1985). See also William G. Ouchi and Raymond L. Price, "Hierarchies, Clans, and Theory Z: A New Perspective on Organization Development," *Organizational Dynamics,* 21 (Spring 1993), pp. 62–70.

85. Chris Argyris, *Overcoming Organizational Defensive Routines* (Boston: Allyn and Bacon, 1990).

86. Chris Argyris and Donald Schon, *Organizational Learning* (Reading, MA: Addison-Wesley, 1976).

87. Chris Argyris, "Strategy Implementation and Experience in Learning, " *Organizational Dynamics,* 18 (Autumn 1989), pp. 8, 9.

88. Ibid., pp. 5–15; and Chris Argyris, "Teaching Smart People How to Learn," *Harvard Business Review,* 69 (May–June 1991), pp. 99–109.

89. Peter M. Senge, *The Fifth Discipline: The Art and Practice of the Learning Organization* (New York: Doubleday/Currency, 1990), pp. 12, 18, 19, 44.

90. John A. Byrne, "Management's New Gurus," *Business Week,* August 31, 1992, pp. 44–52.

91. For more on teams, see Jon R. Katzenbach and Douglas K. Smith, *The Wisdom of Teams* (Boston: Harvard Business School Press, 1993); Richard S. Wellins, William C. Byham, and Jeanne M. Wilson, *Empowered Teams* (San Francisco: Jossey-Bass Publishers, 1991); David Barry, "Managing the Bossless Team: Lessons in Distributed Leadership," *Organizational Dynamics,* 20 (Summer 1991), pp. 31–46; Eric Sundstrom, Kenneth P. De Meuse, and David Futrell, "Work Teams: Applications and Effectiveness," *American Psychologist,* 45 (February 1990), pp. 120–133; Glenn M. Parker, *Team Players and Teamwork* (San Fransisco: Jossey-Bass Publishers, 1990); and Larry Hirschhorn, *Managing in the New Team Environment* (Reading, MA: Addison-Wesley Publishing Company, 1991).

92. Dan Ciampa, *Total Quality* (Reading, MA: Addison-Wesley Publishing Company, 1992), p. xxi. See also Marshall Sashkin and Kenneth J. Kiser, *Total Quality Management* (Seabrook, MD: Ducochon Press, 1991).

93. Ciampa, *Total Quality,* p. xxii.

94. Ibid., p. xxiv.

95. W. Warner Burke, *Organization Development: A Process of Learning and Changing* (Reading, MA: Addison-Wesley Publishing Company, 1994), p. 199.

96. Edward Lindaman and Ronald Lippitt, *Choosing the Future You Prefer* (Washington, DC: Development Publications, 1979).

97. Ronald Fox, Ronald Lippitt, and Eva Schindler-Rainman, *The Humanized Future: Some New Images* (LaJolla, CA: University Associates, 1973).

98. Merrelyn Emery, *Searching: For New Directions, in New Ways for New Times* (Canberra: Centre for Continuing Education, Australian National University, 1982).

99. Marvin R. Weisbord, "Future Search: Toward Strategic Integration," in Walter Sikes, Allan Drexler, and Jack Gant, eds., *The Emerging Practice of Organization Development* (Alexandria, VA: NTL Institute for Applied Behavioral Science, and San Diego, CA: University Associates, 1989), p. 171; and Marvin R. Weisbord, "Future Search: Innovative Business Conference," *Planning Review,* 12 (July 1984), pp. 16–20.

100. Marvin R. Weisbord, *Productive Workplaces* (San Francisco: Jossey-Bass Publishers, 1987), pp. 289–292.

101. Senge, *The Fifth Discipline,* p. 214.

102. Richard Beckhard, "The Confrontation Meeting," *Harvard Business Review,* 45 (March–April 1967), pp. 149–155. See also W. Warner Burke and Richard Beckhard, *Conference Planning,* 2nd ed. (San Diego: University Associates, 1970).

103. Marvin R. Weisbord, "Toward Third-Wave Managing and Consulting," *Organizational Dynamics*, 15 (Winter 1987), pp. 19–20.
104. See Frank J. Barrett and David L. Cooperrider, "Generative Metaphor Intervention: A New Approach for Working with Systems Divided by Conflict and Caught in Defensive Perception," *The Journal of Applied Behavioral Science*, 26, no. 2 (1990), 219–239.
105. Interview with Sam Shirley, February 4, 1982; correspondence with Sheldon A. Davis; Sheldon A. Davis, "An Organic Problem-Solving Method of Organizational Change," *Journal of Applied Behavioral Science*, 3 (November 1, 1967), pp. 3–21; and the case study of the TRW Systems Group in Gene Dalton, Paul Lawrence, and Larry Greiner, *Organizational Change and Development* (Homewood, IL: Irwin-Dorsey, 1970), pp. 4–153.
106. Correspondence with Michael Thiel, June 1993.
107. Ibid.
108. *The Wall Street Journal*, March 5, 1993, p. B7A.
109. Mel R. Spehn, "Reflections on the Organizational Effectiveness Center and School," mimeographed paper, compiled in the summer/fall of 1985, Fort Ord, California, p. 3.
110. Ibid., p. 11.
111. See Eva Schindler-Rainman, "Community Development Through Laboratory Methods," in Benne, Bradford, Gibb, eds; and Lippitt, *Laboratory Method of Changing and Learning*, pp. 445–463. See also John W. Selsky, "Lessons in Community Development," *Journal of Applied Behavioral Science*, 27 (March 1991), pp. 91–115.
112. Shepard correspondence. Starting in 1967, Herbert Shepard was involved in the applications of OD to community problems in Middletown, Connecticut.
113. See Scott Myers, "Overcoming Union Opposition to Job Enrichment," *Harvard Business Review*, 49 (May–June 1971), pp. 37–49; and Robert Blake, Herbert Shepard, and Jane Mouton, *Managing Intergroup Conflict in Industry* (Houston: Gulf, 1964), pp. 122–138.
114. Shepard correspondence.
115. Correspondence with W. Warner Burke and memoranda and attendance lists pertaining to 1967–1969 Network meetings furnished by Burke.
116. For example, the following topics were included in the program of the 1965 convention: "Strategies for Organization Improvement: Research and Consultation," "Managerial Grid Organization Development," and "The Impact of Laboratory Training in Research and Development Environment," *American Psychologist*, 20 (July 1965), pp. 549, 562, 565.
117. Frank Friedlander and L. Dave Brown, "Organization Development," *Annual Review of Psychology*, 25 (1974), pp. 313–341.
118. Clay Alderfer, "Organization Development," *Annual Review of Psychology*, 28 (1977), pp. 197–223.
119. Michael Beer and Anna Elise Walton, "Organizational Change and Development," *Annual Review of Psychology*, 38 (1987), pp. 339–367.
120. Jerry I. Porras and Robert C. Silvers, "Organization Development and Transformation," *Annual Review of Psychology*, 42 (1991), pp. 51–78.
121. Claude Faucheux, Gilles Amada, and André Laurent, "Organizational Development and Change," *Annual Review of Psychology*, 33 (1982), pp. 343–370.
122. D. D. Warrick, ed., *OD Newsletter*, OD Division, Academy of Management (Spring 1979), p. 7.

4

VALUES, ASSUMPTIONS, AND BELIEFS IN OD

A set of values, assumptions, and beliefs constitutes an integral part of organization development, shaping the goals and methods of the field and distinguishing OD from other improvement strategies. Most of these beliefs were formulated early in the development of the field, and they continue to evolve as the field itself evolves. A *belief* is a proposition about how the world works that the individual accepts as true; it is a cognitive fact for the person. *Values* are also beliefs, and are defined as: "Beliefs about what is a desirable or a 'good' (e.g., free speech) and what is an undesirable or a 'bad' (e.g., dishonesty)."[1] *Assumptions* are beliefs that are regarded as so valuable and obviously correct that they are taken for granted and rarely examined or questioned. Thus, values, assumptions, and beliefs are all cognitive facts or propositions, with values being beliefs about good and bad, and assumptions being strongly held, relatively unexamined beliefs accepted as the truth. Values, assumptions, and beliefs provide structure and stability for people as they attempt to understand the world around them.

OD values and assumptions developed from research and theory by behavioral scientists and from the experiences and observations of practicing managers. OD values tend to be humanistic, optimistic, and democratic. Humanistic values proclaim the importance of the individual. Respect the whole person, treat people with respect and dignity, assume that everyone has intrinsic worth, view all people as having the potential for growth and development—these beliefs flow from humanistic values. Optimistic values posit that people are basically good, that progress is possible and desirable in human affairs, and that rationality, reason, and goodwill are the tools for making progress. Democratic values assert the sanctity of the individual, the right of people to be free from arbitrary misuse of power, fair and equitable treatment for all, and justice through the rule of law and due process. Evidence for the validity of these values and their supporting assumptions came from many sources—the Hawthorne studies, the human relations movement, the laboratory training movement, the clash between fascism and democracy in World War II, increasing awareness of the dysfunctions of bureaucracies, research on the effects of different leadership styles, greater understanding of individual motivation and group dynamics, and the like.

Values and assumptions do not spring full grown from individuals or societies; they are formed from the collective beliefs of an era—the *zeitgist,* or spirit of the time. Major ingredients of the *zeitgist* that influenced OD values and assumptions are presented here in a brief chronology. As these ingredients accumulated, they were fashioned into a coherent value foundation for the theory and practice of organization development.

CHRONOLOGY OF EVENTS IN MANAGEMENT AND ORGANIZATION THOUGHT

- 1911 Frederick Winslow Taylor's *The Principles of Scientific Management* launched the scientific management movement with its emphasis on time and motion studies and breaking jobs into small, repetitive tasks in an attempt to find "the one best way" to do each job. Expert engineers and supervisors designed each task and ensured it was done correctly. Piece-rate pay systems were designed to increase motivation and to prevent "soldiering," or slacking off. Simple, repetitive tasks minimized the skills required to do the job. Taylor's methods quickly swept the country and the world as the way to organize work.[2]

- 1922 The great German sociologist Max Weber introduced the concept of "bureaucracy" as the best, most efficient way to organize people. A strong hierarchy of authority, extensive division of labor, Impersonal rules, and rigid procedures would create a well-oiled human machine called the organization.[3]

- Scientific management as the way to organize work and bureaucracy as the way to organize people were the prevailing paradigms for organizations in the early 1900s. These approaches possessed many desirable features, but also contained serious flaws that led to unintended consequences. In a sense, much of the research, theory, and practice since the late 1920s has focused on the shortcomings of these two paradigms and how to overcome the limitations.

- 1926 Mary Parker Follett, a management theorist and astute observer of labor-management relations, wrote an article on "The Giving of Orders" advocating participative leadership and joint problem solving by labor and management. Much of her career was devoted to finding ways to reduce adversarial relationships between workers and management. Her papers were collected and published as a book in 1941.[4]

- 1927 to 1932 The famous Hawthorne studies were conducted at the Hawthorne plant of Western Electric Company. Reports on these studies by Mayo in 1933 and 1945, by Roethlisberger and Dickson in 1939, and by Homans in 1950 profoundly and irreversibly affected people's beliefs about organizational behavior. The research demonstrated the *primacy* of social factors on productivity and morale. People came to work as whole people; their feelings and attitudes about the work, the work environment, and the supervisor determined their performance. Their simple, repetitive jobs left them feeling alienated and dispirited. Group norms had more powerful effects on productivity than economic incentives. People were not cogs; organizations were not machines.[5]

- 1938 *The Functions of the Executive* by Chester I. Barnard presented insights from his experience as president of the New Jersey Bell Telephone Company. Barnard viewed organizations as social systems that must be effective (achieve goals) and efficient (satisfy the needs of employees). His acceptance theory of authority proposed that authority derives from the willingness of subordinates to comply with directions rather than from position power.[6]

- 1939 Research by Lewin, Lippitt, and White demonstrated the superiority of democratic leadership compared to authoritarian leadership and laissez-faire leadership in terms of the effects on group climate and group performance. Democratic leadership seemed to bring out the best in the groups; authoritarian leadership caused dependency, apathy, aggressiveness, and poor performance.[7]

- 1940s Group dynamics—the scientific study of groups using experimental research methods—was launched by Kurt Lewin and his students.[8] Some early experiments were conducted in the late 1930s.

- 1940s to 1960s The Hawthorne studies spawned the human relations movement that was in full flower from the 1930s to the 1960s. The human relations movement advocated participative management, greater attention to workers' social needs, training in interpersonal skills for supervisors, and a general "humanizing" of the workplace.

- 1946 and 1947 These years witnessed the beginnings of the laboratory training movement, a direct precursor of OD. Improved interpersonal relations, increased self-understanding, and awareness of group dynamics were lessons learned in laboratory training. Humanistic and democratic values suffused the movement.[9]

- 1948 Ken Benne and Paul Sheats, pioneers in laboratory training, proposed that the leadership functions of a group should be shared between the leader and group members and showed how that could be done.[10]

- 1948 Lester Coch and John R. P. French's article, "Overcoming Resistance to Change," reported that resistance to change could be minimized by communicating the need for change and allowing the people affected by the change to participate in planning it.[11]

- 1950 Ludwig von Bertalanffy introduced general systems theory concepts and showed their application to physics and biology. His article on general systems theory followed in 1956.[12]

- 1951 Carl Rogers's *Client-Centered Therapy* demonstrated the efficacy of nondirective psychotherapy, which holds that individuals have within themselves the capacity to assume responsibility for their behavior and mental health when provided with a supportive, caring social climate. Rogers's focus on effective interpersonal communications was applicable to superior-subordinate relations.[13]

- 1951 Eric Trist and Ken Bamforth of the Tavistock Clinic published the results of their work in British coal mines. This article introduced the concept of organizations as sociotechnical systems, which postulates that organizations are comprised of a social system and a technological system and that changes in one system will produce changes in the other system.[14]

- 1954 *Motivation and Personality* by Abraham Maslow presented a new view of human motivation. Maslow suggested that human motivation is arranged in a hierarchy of needs from lower-level needs such as physiological and survival needs to higher-level needs such as esteem and self-actualization. The theory postulated that when lower-level needs are satisfied, higher-level needs become dominant.[15]

- 1957 Chris Argyris's *Personality and Organization* was the first of several books in which he stated that there is an inherent conflict between the needs of organizations and the needs of mature, healthy adults.[16]

- 1960 Douglas McGregor wrote *The Human Side of Enterprise* in which he described his famous Theory X and Theory Y assumptions. Those who subscribe to Theory X assume that people are lazy, lack ambition, dislike responsibility, are self-centered, indifferent to the organization's needs, resist change, and need to be led. Those who subscribe to Theory Y assume that people have the potential to develop, to assume responsibility, and to pursue organizational goals if given the chance and the social environment to do so. The task of management is to change organizational structures, management practices, and human resource practices to allow individual potential to be released. In addition to presenting Theory X and Y, this book popularized Maslow's motivation theory, and introduced the concepts of need hierarchy and self-actualization to practicing managers.[17]

- 1961 Burns and Stalker described two very different forms of organization structure—mechanistic and organic. In an environment of slow change, a mechanistic organization structure may be appropriate; in an environment of high change, an organic organization form is preferred. Organic structures encourage decentralized decision making and authority, open communications, and greater individual autonomy.[18]

- 1961 Rensis Likert's *New Patterns of Management* presented data and theory showing the overwhelming superiority of a democratic leadership style in which the leader is group oriented, goal oriented, and shares decision making with the work group. This leadership style was compared to an authoritarian, one-on-one leadership style.[19]

- 1966 *The Social Psychology of Organizations* by Daniel Katz and Robert L.

Kahn presented the first comprehensive exposition of organizations as open systems.[20]

- 1969 The Addison-Wesley Publishing Company "OD Six-Pack," a set of six little books on OD by prominent practitioners, summarized the state of organization development a decade or so after its inception. These six books presented the theory, practice, and values of the field.[21]

Most of the significant influences from research, theory, and observations utilized by OD practitioners are captured in this chronology. To summarize the intellectual climate of this period, the initial enthusiasm for scientific management, bureaucracy, and authoritarian leadership gave way to increasing doubts about these organizational practices as theory and research pointed up their limitations, dysfunctions, and negative consequences. Out of this *zeitgist*, organization development practitioners formulated a set of values and assumptions regarding people, groups, and organizations that was, as we have said, humanistic, optimistic, and democratic.

EARLY STATEMENTS OF OD VALUES AND ASSUMPTIONS

Values have always been an integral part of the OD package. We will examine three early statements regarding OD values that had a significant impact on the field. The Bennis and Beckhard quotations come from their books in the Addison-Wesley Six-Pack. Tannenbaum and Davis presented their ideas in an article appearing in *Industrial Management Review*.

Writing in 1969, Warren Bennis proposed that OD practitioners (change agents) share a set of *normative goals* based on their humanistic/democratic philosophy. He listed these normative goals as follows:

1. Improvement in interpersonal competence.
2. A shift in values so that human factors and feelings come to be considered legitimate.
3. Development of increased understanding between and within working groups in order to reduce tensions.
4. Development of more effective "team management," that is, the capacity for functional groups to work more competently.
5. Development of better methods of conflict resolution. Rather than the usual bureaucratic methods which rely mainly on suppression, compromise, and unprincipled power, more rational and open methods of conflict resolution are sought.
6. Development of organic rather than mechanical systems. This is a strong reaction against the idea of organizations as mechanisms which managers "work on," like pushing buttons.[22]

Bennis clarified some of the salient differences between mechanical systems and organic systems. For example, mechanical systems rely on "authority-obedience relationships" while organic systems rely on "mutual confidence and trust." Mechanical systems insist on "strict division of labor and hierarchical supervision" while organic systems foster "multigroup membership and responsibility." Mechanical systems encourage "centralized decision making" while organic systems encourage "wide sharing of responsibility and control."[23]

Another major player in the field was Richard Beckhard. In his 1969 book he described "several assumptions about the nature and functioning of organizations" held by OD practitioners. Here is his list.

1. The basic building blocks of an organization are groups (teams). Therefore, the basic units of change are groups, not individuals.

2. An always relevant change goal is the reduction of inappropriate competition between parts of the organization and the development of a more collaborative condition.

3. Decision making in a healthy organization is located where the information sources are, rather than in a particular role or level of hierarchy.

4. Organizations, subunits of organizations, and individuals continuously manage their affairs against goals. Controls are interim measurements, not the basis of managerial strategy.

5. One goal of a healthy organization is to develop generally open communication, mutual trust, and confidence between and across levels.

6. "People support what they help create." People affected by a change must be allowed active participation and a sense of ownership in the planning and conduct of the change.[24]

Robert Tannenbaum, professor at UCLA, and Sheldon Davis, director of organization development at TRW Systems, presented their view of OD values in a 1969 article. They asserted that an important shift in values was occurring and that this shift signaled a more appropriate and accurate view of people in organizations. They listed these *values in transition* as follows:

Away from a view of people as essentially bad toward a view of people as basically good.

Away from avoidance of negative evaluation of individuals toward confirming them as human beings.

Away from a view of individuals as fixed, toward seeing them as being in process.

Away from resisting and fearing individual differences toward accepting and utilizing them.

Away from utilizing an individual primarily with reference to his or her job description toward viewing an individual as a whole person.

Away from walling off the expression of feelings toward making possible both appropriate expression and effective use.

Away from maskmanship and game playing toward authentic behavior.

Away from use of status for maintaining power and personal prestige toward use of status for organizationally relevant purposes.

Away from distrusting people toward trusting them.

Away from avoiding facing others with relevant data toward making appropriate confrontation.

Away from avoidance of risk taking toward willingness to risk.

Away from a view of process work as being unproductive effort toward seeing it as essential to effective task accomplishment.

Away from a primary emphasis on competition toward a much greater emphasis on collaboration.[25]

These values and assumptions may not seem profound today, but in the 1950s and 1960s they represented a radical departure from the accepted beliefs and assumptions at the time. Beliefs such as trust and respect for the individual, the legitimacy of feelings, open communication, decentralized decision making, participation and contribution by all organization members, collaboration and cooperation, appropriate uses of power, authentic interpersonal relations, and so forth were seldom espoused and rarely implemented in the vast majority of organizations at that time. We think most organization development practitioners held these humanistic and democratic values with their implications for different and "better" ways to run organizations and deal with people. The democratic values prompted a critique of authoritarian, autocratic, and arbitrary management practices as well as the dysfunctions of bureaucracies. The humanistic values prompted a search for better ways to run organizations and develop the people in them.

IMPLICATIONS OF OD VALUES AND ASSUMPTIONS

Let's examine specific assumptions and their implications for organization leaders and members. We answer the question: What are some of the implications of OD assumptions and values for dealing with individuals, groups, and organizations?

Implications for Dealing with Individuals.   Two basic assumptions about individuals in organizations pervade organization development. The first assumption is that most individuals have drives toward personal growth and development if provided an environment that is both supportive and challenging. Most people want to develop their potential. The second assumption is that most people desire to make, and are capable of making, a higher level of contribution to the attainment of organization goals than most organizational environments permit. A tremendous amount of constructive energy can be tapped if organizations realize and act on these assumptions. The people doing the work are generally experts on how to do it—and how to do it better. The implications of these two assumptions are straightforward: Ask, listen, support, challenge, encourage risk taking, permit failure, remove obstacles and barriers, give autonomy, give responsibility, set high standards, and reward success.

Implications for Dealing with Groups.   Several assumptions relate to the importance of work teams and the collaborative management of team culture. First, one of the most psychologically relevant reference groups for most people is the work group, including peers and boss. What occurs in the work group, at both the formal and informal levels, greatly influences feelings of satisfaction and competence. Second, most people wish to be accepted and to interact cooperatively with at least one small reference group, and usually with more than one group, such as a work group, the family, a church or club group, and so on. Third, most people are capable of making greater contributions to a group's effectiveness and development. Implications of these assumptions are several. *Let teams flourish* because they are often the best way to get work done and, in addition, are the best way to satisfy social and emotional needs at work. Also, *leaders should invest* in groups: Invest the time required for group development, invest training time and money to increase group members' skills, invest energy and intelligence in creating a positive climate. It is especially important that leaders *adopt a team leadership style*, not a one-on-one leadership style. To do this, leaders need to give important work to teams, not individuals.

Another assumption is that the formal leader cannot perform all the leadership and maintenance functions required for a group to optimize its effectiveness. Hence, group members should assist the leader in performing the multiple roles required for group effectiveness. One implication is to have group members receive training in group effectiveness skills such as group problem solving and decision making, conflict management, facilitation, and interpersonal communication. And since suppressed feelings and attitudes adversely affect problem solving, personal growth, and job satisfaction, group members should be encouraged to learn to deal effectively with positive and negative feelings. This too is a trainable skill. Dealing appropriately with feelings and attitudes increases the level of interpersonal trust, support, and cooperation within the group.

Finally, it is assumed that many attitudinal and motivational problems in organizations require interactive and transactional solutions. Such problems have the greatest chance of constructive solution if all parties in the system alter their mutual relationships. The question becomes not how A can get B to perform better, but *how A and B can work together to modify their interactions toward the goal of B becoming more effective and A and B becoming more mutually effective.* Frequently the challenge is broader, including *how persons C, D, and E can support and assist in these changes.* By implication, this requires a shift in perspective from viewing problems as "within the problem person" to viewing problems and solutions as transactional and as embedded in a system.

Implications for Designing and Running Organizations.   It is becoming increasingly clear that traditional hierarchical forms of organization—fairly steep pyramid, emphasis on top-down directives, grouping by specialized function, adherence to the chain of command, formalized cross-functional communication, and so on—are obsolete in terms of meeting the demands of the marketplace. The clear implication is that experimenting with new organization structures and new forms of authority is imperative. In addition, there is growing awareness that "win-lose" organizational situations, in which one side wins and the other side loses, are dysfunctional over the long run and need to be replaced by "win-win" situations. Creating cooperative organizational dynamics rather than competitive ones is a primary task of the organization's leaders.

A key assumption in organization development is that the needs and aspirations of human beings are the reasons for organized effort in society. This suggests it is good to have a developmental outlook and seek opportunities in which people can experience personal and professional growth. This orientation creates a self-fulfilling prophecy. The belief that people are important tends to result in their being important. The belief that people can grow and develop in terms of personal and organizational competency tends to produce that result. By implication, an optimistic, developmental set of assumptions about people is likely to reap rewards beneficial to both the organization and its members.

Finally, it is possible to create organizations that on the one hand are humane, developmental, and empowering, and on the other hand are high performing in terms of productivity, quality of output, and profitability. Evidence for this assumption comes from numerous examples where "putting people first" paid off handsomely in profits and performance. The implication is that people are an organization's most important resource; they are the source of productivity and profits and should be treated with care.

In this section we have shown that values and assumptions have direct implications in how to organize work and people, and how to realize the best from human potential. Much of the practice of OD is concerned with designing organizational practices to incorporate the implications of these assumptions and values.

A VALUES STUDY

We close this chapter by reviewing the results of a values survey recently given to OD practitioners by Robert Hurley, Allan Church, Warner Burke, and Donald Van Eynde.[26] The authors randomly selected 1,000 OD practitioners from the rosters of the OD Network and the OD Division of the American Society of Training and Development, sent them a brief survey, and received 289 responses in return. The survey addressed three broad areas: (1) What attracted you to OD? (2) Which values do you believe are associated with OD work today? (3) Which values do you think *should* be associated with OD work today?

In answer to the first question, the five most frequent response categories in order of frequency were: A desire to . . . (1) create change, (2) positively impact people and organizations, (3) enhance the effectiveness and profitability of organizations, (4) learn and grow, and (5) exercise power and influence.[27]

To answer the two value questions, respondents rated 31 value statements on a five-point scale from 1 ("of little importance") to 5 ("extremely important"), and the rankings were averaged. For the question asking which values respondents believe are associated with OD work today, the top five values considered most important were (1) increasing effectiveness and efficiency, (2) creating openness in communication, (3) empowering employees to act, (4) enhancing productivity, and (5) promoting organizational participation. For the question concerning which values respondents think *should* be associated with OD work today, the top five values considered most important were (1) empowering employees to act, (2) creating openness in communication, (3) facilitating ownership of process and outcome, (4) promoting a culture of collaboration, and (5) promoting inquiry and continuous learning.[28]

These results appear congruent with the discussion in this chapter. The hoped-for values all relate to humanistic and democratic concerns; the existing values relate to both organizational effectiveness and to humanistic and democratic concerns.

Values are never static; they change over time. The rapid technological, societal, and organizational changes taking place virtually assure that tomorrow will bring new definitions of what is "true" and new beliefs about what is "good," as behavioral scientists and managers continue to develop better understanding of authority structures, organizing structures, and ways to optimize human potential.

CONCLUDING COMMENT

The field of organization development rests on a foundation of values and assumptions about people and organizations. These beliefs help to define what OD is and guide its implementation. This discussion was intended to provide you with an appreciation of OD values and explain where they came from. These OD values were considered revolutionary in the 1950s but are widely accepted today.

NOTES

1. David Krech, Richard S. Crutchfield, and Egerton Ballachey, *Individual in Society* (New York: McGraw-Hill, 1962), p. 102.
2. Frederick W. Taylor, *The Principles of Scientific Management* (New York: Harper, 1911).
3. Max Weber, "The Essentials of Bureaucratic Organization: An Ideal-Type Construction." Reprinted in H. H. Gerth and C. W. Mills, (trans. and eds.), *Max Weber: Essays in Sociology* (New York: Oxford University Press, 1946).
4. Mary Parker Follett, "The Giving of Orders," in H. C. Metcalf, ed., *Scientific Foundations of Business Administration* (Baltimore, MD: Williams and Wilkins Company, 1926). See also H. C. Metcalf, ed., *Dynamic Administration: The Collected Papers of Mary Parker Follett* (New York: Harper, 1941).
5. Elton Mayo, *The Human Problems of an Industrial Civilization* (Cambridge, MA: Harvard University, Graduate School of Business, Division of Research, 1933); Elton Mayo, *The Social Problems of an Industrial Civilization* (Cambridge, MA: Harvard University Press, 1945); F. W. Roethlisberger and W. J. Dickson, *Management and the Worker* (Cambridge, MA: Harvard University Press, 1939); George C. Homans, *The Human Group* (New York: Harcourt, Brace & World, Inc., 1950).
6. Chester I. Barnard, *The Functions of the Executive* (Cambridge, MA: Harvard University Press, 1938).
7. K. Lewin, R. Lippitt, and R. White, "Patterns of Aggressive Behavior in Experimentally Created Social Climates," *Journal of Social Psychology*, 10 (1939), pp. 271–299.
8. See D. Cartwright and A. Zander, *Group Dynamics: Research and Theory* (New York: Harper and Row, 1953).
9. See Edgar Schein and Warren G. Bennis, *Personal and Organizational Change Through Group Methods* (New York: John Wiley & Sons, 1965).
10. K. D. Benne and P. Sheats, "Functional Roles of Group Members," *Journal of Social Issues*, 4, no. 2 (1948), 41–49.
11. Lester Coch and John R. P. French, Jr., "Overcoming Resistance to Change," *Human Relations*, 1 (1948), pp. 512–532.
12. Ludwig von Bertalanffy, "The Theory of Open Systems in Physics and Biology," *Science*, 3 (1950), pp. 23–29. Ludwig von Bertalanffy, "General System Theory" *General Systems: Yearbook of the Society for General Systems Theory*, 1 (1956), pp. 1–10.
13. Carl R. Rogers, *Client-Centered Therapy* (Boston, MA: Houghton-Mifflin, 1951).
14. E. L. Trist and K. W. Bamforth, "Some Social and Psychological Consequences of the Long-Wall Method of Coal-Getting," *Human Relations*, 4 (1951), pp. 3–38.
15. Abraham Maslow, *Motivation and Personality* (New York: Harper, 1954).
16. Chris Argyris, *Personality and Organization* (New York: Harper, 1957). Chris Argyris, *Interpersonal Competence and Organizational Effectiveness* (Homewood, IL: Irwin-Dorsey, 1962).
17. Douglas McGregor, *The Human side of Enterprise* (New York: McGraw-Hill, 1960).
18. T. Burns and G. M. Stalker, *The Management of Innovation* (London: Tavistock, 1961).
19. Rensis Likert, *New Patterns of Management* (New York: McGraw-Hill, 1961); Rensis Likert, *The Human Organization* (New York: McGraw-Hill, 1967).
20. Daniel Katz and Robert L. Kahn, *The Social Psychology of Organizations* (New York: John Wiley & Sons, 1966).

21. The Six-Pack consisted of the following books: Richard Beckhard, *Organization Development: Strategies and Models*; Warren Bennis, *Organization Development: Its Nature, Origins, and Prospects*; Paul Lawrence and Jay Lorsch, *Developing Organizations: Diagnosis and Action*; Edgar Schein, *Process Consultation: Its Role in Organization Development*; Richard Walton, *Interpersonal Peacemaking: Confrontations and Third-Party Consultation*; Robert Blake and Jane Srygley Mouton, *Building a Dynamic Corporation Through Grid Organization Development*. All were published in 1969 by Addison-Wesley Publishing Company.

22. Bennis, *Organization Development: Its Nature, Origins, and Prospects*, p. 15.

23. Ibid., p. 15.

24. Beckhard, *Organization Development: Strategies and Models*, pp. 26–27.

25. Robert Tannenbaum and Sheldon A. Davis, "Values, Man, and Organizations," *Industrial Management Review*, 10 (Winter 1969), pp. 67–83.

26. Robert F. Hurley, Allan H. Church, W. Warner Burke, and Donald F. Van Eynde, "Tension, Change and Values in OD," *OD Practitioner*, 24 (September 1992), pp. 1–5.

27. Ibid., p. 3.

28. Ibid., p. 4.

5

FOUNDATIONS OF ORGANIZATION DEVELOPMENT

This chapter describes the foundations that underlie organization development theory and practice, art and science. These foundations form the knowledge base upon which OD is constructed. This knowledge base is used by leaders and OD practitioners to plan and implement effective change programs. In this discussion you will learn *what* OD practitioners think and *how* they think as they engage in the inherently complicated task of improving organizational functioning.

The knowledge base of OD is extensive and is constantly being upgraded. In this chapter we describe what we think are the most important underpinnings for the field. We will examine the following concepts:

Models and theories of planned change
Systems theory
Participation and empowerment
Teams and teamwork
Parallel learning structures
A normative-reeducative strategy of changing
Applied behavioral science
Action research

MODELS AND THEORIES OF PLANNED CHANGE

Organization development is planned change in an organizational context. The development of models of planned change facilitated the development of OD. Models and theories depict, in words or pictures, the important features of some phenomenon, describe those features as variables, and specify the relationships between the variables. Planned change theories are rather rudimentary as far as explaining relationships between variables, but pretty good in terms of identifying the important variables involved in change. Several recent theories show great promise for increasing our understanding of what happens and how it happens in planned change situations. Our purpose here is to provide a framework for thinking about planned change by exploring several models from the literature.

Kurt Lewin introduced two ideas about change that have been very influential since the 1940s.[1] The first idea states that what is occurring at any point in time is a *resultant* in a field of opposing forces. The status quo—whatever is happening right now—is the result of forces pushing in opposing directions. For example, the production level of a manufacturing plant can be thought of as a resultant *equilibrium point* in a field of forces, with some forces pushing toward higher levels of production and some forces pushing toward lower levels of production. The production level tends to remain fairly constant because the field of forces remains fairly constant. Likewise, the level of morale in that plant can be thought of as a resultant equilibrium point. Although morale may get a little better or a little worse on occasion, it generally hovers around some *equilibrium point* that is the resultant in a field of forces, some forces pushing toward higher morale, and some pushing toward lower morale. With a technique called the force-field analysis, one can identify the major forces that make up the field of forces and then develop action plans for moving the equilibrium point in one direction or the other. This concept that the status quo is the result of a field of forces is a powerful one for thinking about the dynamics of change situations.

Lewin's second idea was a model of the change process itself. He suggested that change is a three-stage process: *unfreezing* the old behavior (or situation), *moving* to a new level of behavior, and *refreezing* the behavior at the new level. Change entails moving from one equilibrium point to another equilibrium point. Take the example of a man who is a cigarette smoker who wants to quit. The three-stage model says he must first unfreeze the old behavior of smoking, that is, believe that cigarette smoking is bad for him, and that he should stop smoking. Next he must move, that is, change his behavior from being a smoker to being a nonsmoker. Finally, the nonsmoking behavior must become permanent so that not smoking becomes the new equilibrium point. To do this a new field of forces must be established to support the new behavior.

Table 5-1   A Three-Stage Model of the Change Process

Stage 1.	*Unfreezing:* Creating motivation and readiness to change through a. Disconfirmation or lack of confirmation b. Creation of guilt or anxiety c. Provision of psychological safety
Stage 2.	*Changing through Cognitive Restructuring:* Helping the client to see things, judge things, feel things, and react to things differently based on a new point of view obtained through a. Identifying with a new role model, mentor, etc. b. Scanning the environment for new relevant information
Stage 3.	*Refreezing:* Helping the client to integrate the new point of veiw into a. The total personality and self-concept b. Significant relationships

Source: Edgar H. Schein, *Process Consulation,* Vol. II (Table 6-1), p. 93. © 1987 by Addison-Wesley Publishing Company, Inc. Reprinted by permission of the publisher.

Lewin's three-stage model is a powerful cognitive tool for understanding change situations. Edgar Schein took this excellent idea and improved it by specifying the psychological mechanisms involved in each stage as shown in Table 5-1.[2]

In stage 1, *unfreezing,* disconfirmation creates pain and discomfort, which cause guilt and anxiety, which motivate the person to change. But unless the person feels comfortable with dropping the old behaviors and acquiring new ones, change will not occur. That is, the person must experience a sense of psychological safety in order to replace the old behaviors with new behaviors.

In stage 2, *moving,* the person undergoes cognitive restructuring. The person needs information and evidence to show that the change is desirable and possible. This is gained by modeling the behavior of an exemplar or by gathering relevant information from the environment.

The primary task in stage 3, *refreezing,* is to integrate the new behaviors into the person's personality and attitudes. That is, stabilizing the changes requires testing to see if they fit—fit with the individual, and fit with the individual's social surroundings. The phrase *significant relationships* refers to important people in the person's social environment—do these significant others accept and approve of the changes? We believe Lewin's model and Schein's extension of the model provide excellent ways to think about change and the planning of change.

Another modification of Lewin's model was proposed by Ronald Lippitt, Jeanne Watson, and Bruce Westley, who expanded the three-stage model into a seven-stage model representing the consulting process. Their seven stages are as follows:

Phase 1. The development of a need for change. This phase corresponds to Lewin's *unfreezing* phase.

Phase 2. The establishment of a change relationship. In this phase a client system in need of help and a change agent from outside the system establish a working relationship with each other.

Phase 3. The clarification or diagnosis of the client system's problem.

Phase 4. The examination of alternative routes and goals; establishing goals and intentions of action.

Phase 5. The transformation of intentions into actual change efforts. Phases 3, 4, and 5 correspond to Lewin's *moving* phase.

Phase 6. The generalization and stabilization of change. This corresponds to Lewin's *refreezing* phase.

Phase 7. Achieving a terminal relationship, that is, terminating the client-consultant relationship.[3]

The seven-stage model by Lippitt, Watson, and Westley lays out the logical steps involved in OD consulting; most practitioners know this model. Similar models have been developed by Kolb and Frohman and by Burke.[4] These "road maps" are useful for thinking about change.

A comprehensive change model by Ralph Kilmann specifies the critical leverage points to manipulate for change to occur. We will briefly describe the "total system change" model presented in his book, *Managing Beyond the Quick Fix.*[5] There are five sequential stages in this model: (1) initiating the program; (2) diagnosing the problems; (3) scheduling the "tracks"; (4) implementing the "tracks"; and (5) evaluating the results. Change programs take from one to five years to complete.

Initiating the program entails securing commitment and support from top management. Diagnosing the problems entails conducting a thorough analysis of the problems and opportunities facing the organization. These problems and opportunities will be the targets of later interventions. Scheduling and implementing the "tracks" entail intervening in five critical leverage points (called "tracks") found in all organizations, that, when functioning properly, cause the organization to be successful. Kilmann's five tracks are: (1) the culture track; (2) the management skills track; (3) the team-building track; (4) the strategy-structure track; and (5) the reward system track. Interventions include training programs, problem-solving sessions, critique of current practices and procedures, and so forth. Kilmann describes the five tracks:

> What does each track do for the organization? The culture track enhances trust, communication, information sharing, and willingness to change among members—the conditions that must exist before any other improvement effort can succeed. The management-skills track provides all management personnel with new ways of coping with complex problems and hidden assumptions. The team-building track infuses the new culture and updated management skills into each work unit—thereby instilling cooperation organization-wide so that complex problems can be addressed with all the expertise and infor-

mation available. The strategy-structure track develops either a completely new or a revised strategic plan for the firm and then aligns divisions, departments, work groups, jobs, and all resources with the new strategic direction. The reward-system track establishes a performance-based reward system that sustains all improvements by officially sanctioning the new culture, the use of updated management skills, and cooperative team efforts within and among all work groups.[6]

The tracks are implemented in a phased sequence, beginning with the culture track, then moving to the management skills track, then moving to the team-building track, and so forth. Kilmann has tested his model at AT&T, Eastman Kodak, Ford, General Electric, General Foods, TRW, Westinghouse, and Xerox with good results. We like this model because of its comprehensive nature, its identification of the five tracks as critical leverage points, and its holistic view of organization change and development.

Another useful model is "stream analysis" developed by Jerry Porras.[7] Stream analysis is a system for graphically displaying the problems of an organization, examining the interconnections between the problems, identifying core problems (those with many interconnections), and graphically tracking the corrective actions taken to solve the problems. Stream analysis is complicated and somewhat difficult to use, but as a model for thinking about change and a method for managing change, it is quite valuable.

Porras categorized the important features of the *organizational work setting* (the environment in which people work), into four *classes of variables* labeled "organizing arrangements," "social factors," "technology," and "physical setting." "Organizing arrangements" include such things as goals, strategies, structure, administrative policies and procedures, administrative systems, reward systems, and ownership. "Social factors" include culture, management style, interaction processes, informal patterns and networks, and individual attributes. "Technology" includes tools, equipment, and machinery, information technology, job design, work flow design, technical expertise, technical procedures, and technical systems. "Physical setting" includes space configuration, physical ambiance, interior design, and architectural design.[8] These four classes of variables constitute the four "streams" of stream analysis.

Next a thorough diagnosis of the organization's problems and barriers to effectiveness is performed, via brainstorming sessions, interviews, questionnaires, and other methods. A task force of representatives from all parts of the organization reviews the problems and barriers, discusses them until there is agreement on what they mean, and categorizes each problem into one of the "streams." Four columns are drawn on paper; the column headings are labeled "organizing arrangements," "social factors," "technology," and "physical setting." Porras writes:

> As the problems are categorized, they are placed on Stream Charts in their appropriate columns. After all identified problems have been classified, an analysis of the entire set usually reveals much overlap among the various problem statements. What is usually required then is a grouping of problems and a condensation of the larger set of problems into a much smaller collection of relatively unique issues.[9]

Next the interconnections between the problems are noted; problems that have many interconnections are identified as core problems. Action plans are developed to correct the core problems. The action plans and their results are tracked on stream charts.

The action plans are OD interventions directed toward solving the core problems. The OD program systematically addresses and resolves the issues identified, and by so doing corrects dysfunctional aspects of the four classes of variables that make up the organizational work setting. OD programs modify organizing arrangements, social factors, technology, and physical settings, which in turn causes changes in individuals' on-the-job behaviors. *Thus, in stream analysis, OD programs change the work setting, which leads to changes in behavior, which leads to organizational improvement.* Porras and Robertson say: "Since the work setting is the environment in which people work, and since the environment plays a key role in determining the behavior of people, these factors define the characteristics that, if changed, will induce change in on-the-job behaviors of individual employees."[10] We believe stream analysis is a valuable model for understanding planned change processes.

The final model to be examined is the Burke-Litwin model of individual and organizational performance, developed by Warner Burke and George Litwin.[11] This model identifies the variables involved in creating first-order and second-order change, which the authors call "transactional change" and "transformational change," respectively. Recall that first-order change is evolutionary, adaptive change in which features of the organization are changed, but its fundamental nature remains the same. Second-order change is revolutionary, fundamental change in which the nature of the organization is altered in significant ways. To understand the model it is necessary to distinguish between organizational climate and culture, and between transactional and transformational change.

Organizational climate is people's collective assessment of an organization in terms of whether it is a good or bad place to work, whether it is friendly, warm, cold, hard-working, easy-going, and so forth. These perceptions are based on managerial practices and organizational systems and procedures; they are relatively malleable and they will change with changes in the organizational processes on which they are based. Litwin demonstrated that different climates could be induced in laboratory "organizations" by manipulating managerial goals and practices. Furthermore, these different climates produced significantly different kinds of behavior from organization members. Organization culture is also a collective assessment of the organization, but culture is based on deeper, relatively enduring, often unconscious, values, norms, and assumptions.

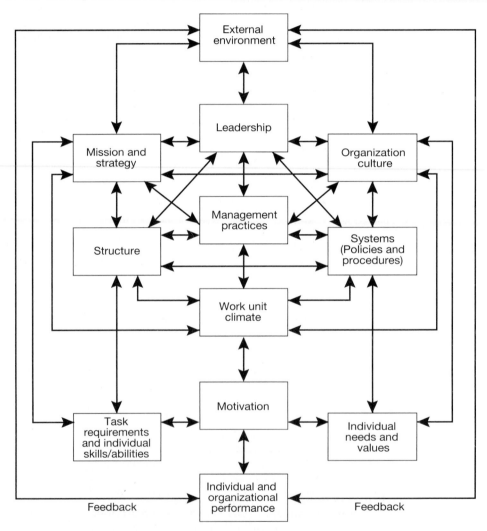

Figure 5-1   The Burke-Litwin Model of Organizational Performance and Change

Source: W. Warner Burke, *Organization Development, Second Edition* (Figure 7.1), p. 128, © 1994 by Addison-Wesley Publishing Company, Inc. Reprinted by permission of the publisher.

The transactional/transformational concepts come from leadership research where it was observed that some leaders are capable of obtaining extraordinary performance from followers while other leaders are not.[12] Transformational leaders are "leaders who inspire followers to transcend their own self-interest for the good of the organization and who are capable of having a profound and extraordinary effect on their followers." Transactional leaders are "leaders who guide or motivate their followers in the direction of established goals by clarifying role and task requirements."[13] Transactional leadership implies a fair exchange between leader and follower that leads to "normal" performance; transformational leadership implies inspiration that leads to new heights of performance. Transactional implies first-order change; transformational implies second-order change. The Burke-Litwin model is shown in Figure 5-1.

This model looks quite complicated, but it becomes more understandable when we see it disaggregated in Figure 5-2 and Figure 5-3.

Burke and Litwin propose that interventions directed toward leadership, mission and strategy, and organization culture produce *transformational change* or fundamental change in the organization's culture. (This is shown in Figure 5-2.) On the other hand, interventions directed toward management practices, structure, and systems produce *transactional change* or change in organizational climate. (This is shown in Figure 5-3.) Burke says:

> Thus there are two distinct sets of organizational dynamics. One set primarily is associated with the transactional level of human behav-

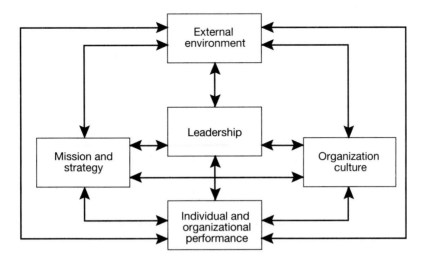

Figure 5-2 The Transformational Factors

Source: W. Warner Burke, *Organization Deveolopment, Second Edition* (Figure 7.2), p. 130, © 1994 by Addison-Wesley Publishing Company, Inc. Reprinted by permission of the publisher.

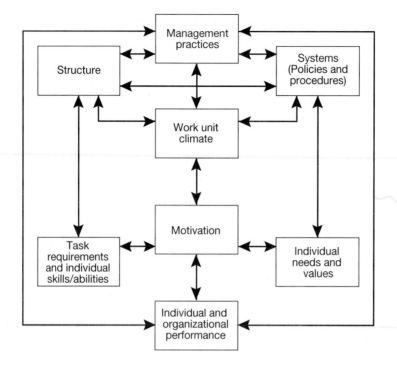

Figure 5-3 The Transactional Factors

Source: W. Warner Burke, *Organization Development, Second Edition*, (Figure 7.3), p. 131, © 1994 by Addison-Wesley Publishing Company, Inc. Reprinted by permission of the publisher.

ior or the everyday interactions and exchanges that create the climate. The second set of dynamics is concerned with processes of human transformation; that is, sudden "leaps" in behavior; these transformational processes are required for genuine change in the culture of an organization.[14]

The top half of Figure 5-1 displays the variables related to transformational change. These variables carry more weight, in that they change the culture in fundamental ways. The bottom half of Figure 5-1 shows the variables related to transactional change; these variables cause change in organization climate. These variables are less powerful for effecting organizational change.

We consider the Burke-Litwin model to be a significant advance in thinking about planned change. The OD practitioner sizes up the change situation, determines what kind of change is required (transactional or transformational), and then targets interventions toward those elements of the organization that produce the desired change. Research by Burke and his students suggests that the model performs as intended.[15] Such confirmation is heartening to see.

In summary, models and theories of planned change provide

an important foundation for organization development. The models reviewed here contribute to that foundation.

SYSTEMS THEORY

A second foundation of organization development is systems theory, which views organizations as open systems in active exchange with their surrounding environments. The aim of this section is to explain systems theory, describe the characteristics of systems, and show how systems theory enhances the practice of OD.

Ludwig von Bertalanffy first articulated the principles of general systems theory in 1950, and Katz and Kahn were the first to apply open systems theory to organizations in a comprehensive way in 1966.[16] Systems theory is one of the most powerful conceptual tools available for understanding the dynamics of organizations and organizational change. Fagen defines *system* as "a set of objects together with relationships between the objects and between their attributes."[17] Von Bertalanffy refers to a system as a set of "elements standing in interaction."[18] Kast and Rosenzweig define *system* as "an organized, unitary whole composed of two or more interdependent parts, components, or subsystems, and delineated by identifiable boundaries from its environmental suprasystem."[19] Hanna says: "A *system* is an arrangement of interrelated parts. The words *arrangement* and *interrelated* describe interdependent elements forming an entity that is the system. Thus, when taking a systems approach, one begins by identifying the individual parts and then seeks to understand the nature of their collective interaction."[20] To summarize, *system* denotes interdependency, interconnectedness, and interrelatedness of a set of elements that constitute an identifiable whole or gestalt.

The nature, dynamics, and characteristics of open systems are well known. Organizations are open systems. Therefore, studying open systems leads to a good understanding of organizations. The characteristics of open systems are examined here in a discussion based on expositions by Katz and Kahn and Hanna.[21]

All open systems are *input-throughput-output* mechanisms. Systems take in *inputs* from the environment in the form of energy, information, money, people, raw materials, and so on. They do something to the inputs via *throughput, conversion, or transformation* processes that change the inputs; and they export products to the environment in the form of *outputs*. Each of these three system processes must work well if the system is to be effective and survive. Figure 5-4 shows a system in diagrammatic form.

Every system has a *boundary* that separates it from its *environment*. The boundary delineates the system; what is inside the boundary

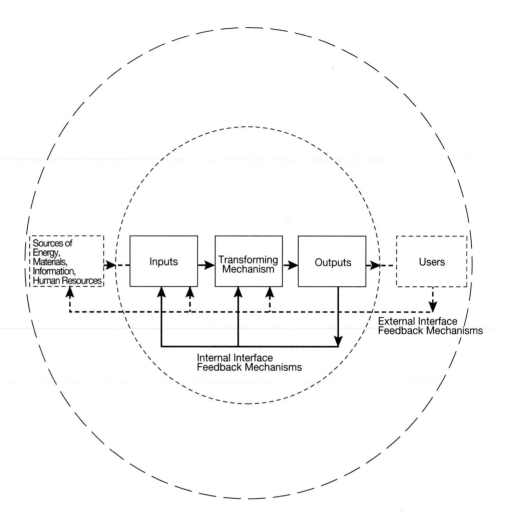

Figure 5-4   A System in Interaction With Its Environment

is the system and what is outside the boundary is the environment. A good rule of thumb for drawing the boundary is that more energy exchange occurs *within* the boundary than *across* the boundary. Boundaries of open systems are *permeable*, in that they permit exchange of information, resources, and energy between system and environment. The *environment* is everything outside the system.

Open systems have *purposes and goals*, the reasons for their existence. It is important to note that these purposes must align with purposes or needs in the environment; for example, the organization's purposes will be reflected in its outputs, and if the outputs are not wanted by the environment, the organization will cease to exist.

The law of entropy states that all systems "run down" and disintegrate unless they reverse the entropic process by importing more energy than they use. Organizations achieve *negative entropy* when they are able to exchange their outputs for enough inputs to keep the system from running down. *Information* is important to systems in several different ways. *Feedback* is information from the environment about system performance. Systems require two kinds of feedback, negative and positive. Hanna writes: "Negative feedback measures whether or not the output is on course with the purpose and goals. It is also known as *deviation-correcting* feedback. . . . Positive feedback measures whether or not the purpose and goals are aligned with environmental needs. It is sometimes called deviation-amplifying feedback."[22] For example, if a rocket ship traveling to the moon strays off its trajectory, it receives information to that effect in the form of negative feedback, and makes a course correction. If the mission (target) changes, however, that information is called positive feedback, and the system adjusts to a new goal, say, "return to earth." Here is another example of negative and positive feedback. Say your company makes buggy whips, and the production plan calls for 100 buggy whips per month. Negative feedback tells you if you are on track regarding your scheduled production output. Positive feedback comes from the environment; it will signal whether or not the environment needs and/or wants buggy whips. Hanna states: "The usefulness of the two concepts is that they demonstrate that it is not enough to merely measure our outputs versus the intended targets. Survival of the system is equally influenced by whether or not the targets themselves are appropriate."[23]

Systems are bombarded by all kinds of information, some information is useful, and most information is not useful. So systems "code" useful information and incorporate it, while screening out other information. For example, organizations in the fast-food industry pay a lot of attention to information about their industry—information about nutrition, eating fads, competitors, and the like. By the same token, they usually ignore information about other industries such as electronics, mining, aerospace, and so on.

Another characteristic of open systems is *steady state* or *dynamic homeostasis*. Systems achieve a steady state or equilibrium point and seek to maintain this equilibrium against disruptive forces, either internal or external. As Katz and Kahn say: *"The basic principle is the preservation of the character of the system."*[24] Also, systems tend to get more elaborated, differentiated, specialized, and complex over time; this is called *differentiation*. And, with increased differentiation, there is a need for increased *integration and coordination*. Another characteristic of systems is *equifinality*, the principle that there are multiple ways to arrive at a particular outcome or state—in systems there are multiple paths to goals. There can be *subsystems* within larger systems. And systems can be arranged into a *hierarchy of systems* moving from less important to more important.

These characteristics of open systems explain many phenomena we observe in organizations. Why do organizations resist change? Because of a desire to preserve the character of the system via steady state and dynamic homeostasis. Why does Plan A fail, and fail again, then succeed? Equifinality. Why do organizations become increasingly bureaucratic and complex? Differentiation, with its attendant integration and coordination. Why do businesses go bankrupt? Because they are unable to create negative entropy. Why did the American automobile industry fail to react to the Japanese challenge of small cars? Because the companies lacked appropriate coding processes and adequate positive feedback mechanisms.

Viewing organizations as input-throughput-output systems is very useful. All organizations import energy, materials, information, and the like as *inputs* that provide fuel for the system. These inputs are *transformed* and infused with value in the *throughput* process. Goods and services are exported to the environment as *outputs* to be exchanged for money, raw materials, and labor that become new inputs.

Two major variations of open systems theory—sociotechnical systems theory (STS) and open systems planning (OSP)—play an especially important role in organization development. We will discuss these briefly.

Sociotechnical systems theory was developed by Eric Trist, Fred Emery, and others at the Tavistock Institute in the 1950s. The thesis of STS is that all organizations are comprised of two interdependent systems, a social system and a technical system, and that changes in one system produce effects in the other system. To achieve high productivity and employee satisfaction, organizations must be structured to optimize both systems. STS is the principal conceptual foundation for efforts in work redesign and organization restructuring, two very active segments of OD today.

A number of design principles have been developed to implement sociotechnical systems theory. Principles such as optimization of the social and technical systems, the formation of autonomous work groups, training group members in multiple skills, giving information and feedback to the people doing the work, and identifying the core tasks to be accomplished are some of the STS principles used to structure organizations and tasks for maximum effectiveness and efficiency. High-performance organizations almost always utilize principles from sociotechnical systems theory, especially autonomous work groups (self-regulated teams or self-directed teams), multiskilled teams, controlling variance at the source, and information to the point of action, that is, to the workers doing the job. Excellent reviews of STS theory, principles, and practice can be found in works by Passmore, Pava, Cummings, Hanna, and Bushe and Shani.[25]

Another important application of systems theory to organization development is open systems planning. Hanna writes:

In the late 1960s a small team of consultants led by James Clark, Charles Krone, G. K. Jayaram, and Will McWhinney developed a technology for addressing the interface between organization and the environment. Their technology became known as Open Systems Planning (OSP). It was the first attempt to help organizations methodically analyze the environmental demands and expectations placed on them and plan to successfully meet these demands and expectations.[26]

Open systems planning entails scanning the environment to determine the demands and expectations of external organizations and stakeholders; developing scenarios of possible futures of the organization, both realistic (likely to happen if the organization continues on its current course) and ideal (what the organization would like to see happen); and developing action plans to ensure that a desirable future occurs. Most OD practitioners engaged in redesign projects use a combination of sociotechnical systems theory and open systems planning. For example, this combination is often used in designing high-performance organizations.

Open systems thinking is a requirement for creating learning organizations, according to Peter Senge. Learning organizations are able to cope effectively with rapidly changing environmental demands. Senge believes five disciplines must be mastered in order to create a learning organization: personal mastery, mental models, building shared vision, team learning, and systems thinking. Of all these disciplines, the fifth discipline, systems thinking, is the most important. He says of systems thinking:

> It is the discipline that integrates the disciplines, fusing them into a coherent body of theory and practice. It keeps them from being separate gimmicks or the latest organization change fads. Without a systemic orientation, there is no motivation to look at how the disciplines interrelate. By enhancing each of the other disciplines, it continually reminds us that the whole can exceed the sum of its parts.[27]

Systems theory pervades all of the theory and practice of organization development, from diagnosis to intervention to evaluation. Some consequences of viewing organizations from this perspective are the following. First, issues, events, forces, and incidents are not viewed as isolated phenomena, but are seen in relation to other issues, events, and forces. Second, a systems approach encourages analysis of events in terms of multiple causation rather than single causation. Most phenomena have multiple causes. Third, one cannot change one part of a system without influencing other parts in some ways. OD practitioners expect multiple effects, not single effects, from their activities. Fourth, according to field theory (Kurt Lewin), the forces in the field at the time of the event are the relevant forces for analysis. This idea moves the practitioner away from an analysis of historical events and dictates an examination of the contemporary events and forces—to a more existential vantage point. And fifth, if one wants to change a system, one changes the system, not just its component parts. Systems theory and systems thinking are invaluable in OD.

PARTICIPATION AND EMPOWERMENT

One of the most important foundations of organization development is its use of a participation/empowerment model. Participation in OD programs is not restricted to elites or the top people; it is extended broadly throughout the organization. Increased participation and empowerment have always been central goals and prominent values of the field. These pillars of OD practice are validated by both research and practice.

Research on group dynamics began in the 1940s and achieved exponential growth in the 1950s and 1960s.[28] This research demonstrated that increased involvement and participation were desired by most people, had the ability to energize greater performance, produced better solutions to problems, and greatly enhanced acceptance of decisions. It was found that such group dynamics worked to overcome resistance to change, increased commitment to the organization, reduced stress levels, and generally made people feel better about themselves and their worlds.[29] Participation is a powerful elixir—it is good for people, and it dramatically improves individual and organizational performance.

To empower is to give someone power. This is done by giving individuals the authority to participate, to make decisions, to contribute their ideas, to exert influence, and to be responsible. That is why participation is such an effective form of empowerment. Participation enhances empowerment, and empowerment in turn enhances performance and individual well-being.

OD interventions are deliberately designed to increase involvement and participation by organization leaders and members. For example, autonomous work groups, quality circles, team building, survey feedback, quality of work life programs, future search conferences, and the culture audit are all predicated on the belief that increased participation will lead to better solutions to problems and opportunities. Rules of thumb like "Involve all those who are part of the problem or part of the solution," and "Have decisions made by those who are closest to the problem," push decision making lower in the organization, treat those closest to the problem as the relevant experts, and give more power to more people. OD interventions are basically methods for increasing participation. The entire field of OD is about empowerment.

Let us look briefly at additional sources of information about empowerment. A good manual for implementing empowerment strategies is James Belasco's *Teaching the Elephant to Dance: The Manager's Guide to Empowering Change.*[30] Belasco presents numerous examples in which leaders reap extraordinary gains by empowering their employees. Belasco uses a simple four-step model to describe the empowerment process: "preparation," "create tomorrow," "vision," and "change." He believes (1) that only massive changes will suffice to keep organizations viable in the future, (2) that people will not naturally embrace the needed changes, and (3) that empowerment is the key to getting people to want to participate in change. One of the most important ingredients of empowerment is vision—a coherent, credible picture of the desired future. Developing a clear vision, devising a strategy to achieve the vision, and unleashing the intelligence and energy of the work force to accomplish the vision are what empowerment is all about, according to Belasco. This valuable book is filled with interesting stories of successes and failures by managers using empowerment strategies to foster change.

The Leadership Challenge by Kouzes and Posner is another excellent manual on empowerment.[31] For many years, Kouzes and Posner conducted leadership seminars in which, among other things, they asked participants to describe a "personal best" leadership situation from their own experience. Analysis of hundreds of these "personal best" leadership stories led to the identification of five leadership practices and ten behavioral commitments exhibited by successful, empowering leaders. The five practices, each with two behavioral commitments, are the following:

Challenging the Process
  Search for Opportunities
  Experiment and Take Risk
Inspiring a Shared Vision
  Envision the Future
  Enlist Others
Enabling Others to Act
  Foster Collaboration
  Strengthen Others
Modeling the Way
  Set the Example
  Plan Small Wins
Encouraging the Heart
  Recognize Individual Contributions
  Celebrate Accomplishments[32]

We have used this book and the "personal best" exercise, and find this to be an excellent way to start people thinking about empowerment in practical, specific, behavioral terms.

Donald Petersen was president of Ford Motor Company from 1980 to 1985 and CEO and chairman of the board from 1985 to his retirement in 1990. In his book, *A Better Idea*, written with John Hillkirk, he describes the turnaround of that 370,000-person company from one that was losing money and market share to one that produced high-quality products, made big profits, and created the Ford Taurus, one of the best-selling cars in American history. The primary vehicle for the turnaround was employee involvement, participation, and empowerment. In the early 1980s, Ford launched programs in EI (employee involvement), participative management training for supervisors, employee involvement teams, and total quality management. The net effect was a significant change in the company's culture from being a top-down, autocratic, functionally oriented company to one that gave responsibility and power to cross-functional teams at all levels of the organization. Ford became a different company, and a much more successful company, by empowering its employees.[33]

Tom Peters is one of the strongest advocates for participation and empowerment on the American scene, and it is instructive to follow the development of his thinking on this topic. In the book, *In Search of Excellence*, written with Robert Waterman, one of the eight attributes they say characterizes excellent, innovative companies is "productivity through people."[34] Excellent companies value their employees and consider them their most important single asset; excellent companies have people-oriented cultures. In the book, *A Passion for Excellence: The Leadership Difference*, written with Nancy Austin, the theme is empowering people through visionary leadership.[35] Peters and Austin say that excellent companies pay attention to four things: customers, innovation, people, and leadership. The challenge for leaders is to empower employees so that they create great customer relations and continuous innovation.

In *Thriving on Chaos*, by Tom Peters, the same themes appear: (1) creating total customer responsiveness, (2) pursuing fast-paced innovation, (3) achieving flexibility by empowering people, (4) learning to love change—a new view of leadership at all levels, and (5) building organizational systems that support, not inhibit, the first four themes.[36] These conditions can only be met through having "turned on," empowered employees, and the role of the leader is to empower others. Peters offers the following "prescriptions" for "achieving flexibility by empowering people": involve everyone in everything; use self-managing teams; listen/celebrate/recognize; spend time lavishly on recruiting; train and retrain; provide incentive pay for everyone; provide an employment guarantee; simplify/reduce structure; reconceive the middle manager's role; and eliminate bureaucratic rules and humiliating conditions.[37] This advice is powerful, practical, and cogent.

In his latest book, *Liberation Management*, Peters continues to advocate the importance of empowered people, customer satisfaction, innovation, and visionary leadership.[38] But he introduces an important new insight; he takes aim at the inappropriateness of today's organization structures. Large bureaucratic organizations with their bloated corporate headquarters staffs, rigid hierarchies, and smothering rules and procedures stifle even empowered people led by enlightened leaders; this renders the organization unable to compete in the "nanosecond nineties." Today's jobs are best accomplished through empowered people working in highly autonomous project teams, he says, and organizations must be *redesigned* to allow that to happen. Tom Peters's insights on empowerment are quite valuable for OD practitioners.

Participation/empowerment works. That is why it is part of the foundation of organization development.

TEAMS AND TEAMWORK

A fundamental belief in organization development is that work teams are the building blocks of organizations. A second fundamental belief is that teams must manage their culture, processes, systems, and relationships if they are to be effective. Theory, research, and practice attest to the central role teams play in organizational success. Teams and teamwork are part of the foundation of organization development.

The previous discussion focused on empowerment and concluded that the act of empowering individuals greatly increased their performance and satisfaction. The message of this section is to put those empowered individuals into *teams*, and the effects on performance and satisfaction will be extraordinary.

Teams and teamwork are the "hottest" thing happening in organizations today—gurus extol the virtues of teams; the noun *team* has become a verb, *teaming*; and team-related acronyms abound—SDTs (self-directed teams), QCs (quality circles), HPOs (high-performance organizations), HPWSs (high-performance work systems), STS (sociotechnical systems), to name just a few. Teams at Motorola produced its best-selling cellular phones; Team Taurus developed Ford's best-selling automobile; Team Saturn produced the Saturn automobile; teams at 3M generate the hundreds of innovations that keep 3M ahead of its competition; cross-functional "design-build" teams are developing the Boeing 777. Teams and teamwork are "in." The evidence is abundantly clear: Effective teams produce results far in excess of the performance of unrelated individuals.

Teams are important for a number of reasons. First, much individual behavior is rooted in the sociocultural norms and values of the work team. If the team, as a team, changes those norms and values, the effects on individual behavior are immediate and lasting. Second, many tasks are so complex they cannot be performed by individuals; people must work together to accomplish them. Third, teams create synergy, that is, the sum of the efforts of members of a team is far greater than the sum of the individual efforts of people working alone. Synergy is a principal reason teams are so important. Fourth, teams satisfy people's needs for social interaction, status, recognition, and respect—teams nurture human nature. In this section, we examine the potential of teams and teamwork, and explore ways to realize that potential.

A number of OD interventions are specifically designed to improve team performance. Examples are team building, intergroup team building, process consultation, quality circles, parallel learning structures, sociotechnical systems programs, Grid OD, and techniques such as role analysis technique, role negotiation technique, and responsibility charting. These interventions apply to formal work teams as well as startup teams, cross-functional teams, temporary teams, and the like. Team-building activities are now a way of life for many organizations. Teams periodically hold team-building meetings, people are trained in group dynamics and group problem-solving skills, and individuals are trained as group leaders and group facilitators. Organizations using autonomous work groups or self-directed teams devote considerable time and effort to ensure that team members possess the skills to be effective in groups. The net effect is that teams perform at increasingly higher and higher levels, that synergy is achieved, and that teamwork becomes more satisfying for team members.

Investigators are discovering why some teams are successful while others are not. Larson and LaFasto studied a number of high-performance teams, including collegiate football national champions, heart transplant surgical teams, the crew of the USS *Kitty Hawk,* and others, to determine the characteristics that make them successful. They found eight characteristics that are always present: (1) a clear, elevating goal; (2) a results-driven structure; (3) competent team members; (4) unified commitment; (5) a collaborative climate; (6) standards of excellence; (7) external support and recognition; and (8) principled leadership.[39] All these characteristics are required for superior team performance; when any one feature is lost, team performance declines. High-performance teams regulate the behavior of team members, help each other, find innovative ways around barriers, and set ever-higher goals. Larson and LaFasto also discovered that the most frequent cause of team failure was letting personal or political agendas take precedence over the clear and elevating team goal.

Another excellent source of information about teams is *The Wisdom of Teams: Creating the High-Performance Organization,* by Jon Katzenbach and Douglas Smith.[40] They, too, studied a number of teams in a wide variety of settings. For them, a group of individuals becomes a team when, and only when, they commit to achieving high-performance goals. Without demanding performance goals, groups never jell into teams. Therefore, they write, "Organizational leaders can foster team performance best by building a strong performance ethic, rather than by establishing a team-promoting environment alone."[41] A key characteristic of high-performance teams is *discipline*. "Groups become teams through *disciplined action*. They *shape* a common purpose, *agree* on performance goals, *define* a common working approach, *develop* high levels of complementary skills, and *hold* themselves mutually accountable for results. And, as with any effective discipline, they never stop doing any of these things."[42] It's hard work for groups to become teams, but this is what is required to create high-performance organizations.

Katzenbach and Smith believe teams will become even more important in the future. They write: "In fact, most models of the 'organization of the future' that we have heard about—'networked,' 'clustered,' 'nonhierarchical,' 'horizontal,' and so forth—are premised on *teams surpassing individuals as the primary performance unit in the company*."[43] This book gives examples of high-performing teams, teaches the basics of team development, and offers how-to advice for turning groups into teams.

Tom Peters asserts in *Liberation Management* that cross-functional, autonomous, empowered teams are what the best organizations are using right now to outdistance the competition.[44] Examples from EDS (Electronic Data Systems), Union Pacific Railroad, Asea Brown Boveri, Titeflex, and countless other organizations are used to demonstrate the ability of small project teams to produce high quality, superior customer service, flexible response, and continuous learning. High responsibility, clear objectives, and high accountability drive these project teams to outperform traditional organization structures on every measurable dimension. Projects are the work of the future; projects will be performed by teams. Interestingly, normal hierarchical considerations become obsolete for these project teams—you could be the boss of one team, and report to one of your subordinates on another team.

Sources for learning about team effectiveness are plentiful. Michael Doyle and David Straus's *How to Make Meetings Work*, contains valuable instruction about the roles of leaders, facilitators, and recorders of groups.[45] Advice on team building, facilitation, and team effectiveness is found in William G. Dyer's *Team Building* and Larry Hirschhorn's *Managing in the New Team Environment*.[46] Edgar Schein's *Process Consultation* books show how to manage group processes for greater effectiveness.[47] Many large organizations provide team-effectiveness training for their members through courses in team problem-solving skills, leading team problem-solving meetings, facilitator skills, and meeting-management skills offered to employees at all levels. Many managers routinely enlist the services of facilitators to help them run meetings. As teams become more important to organizations, resources are being made available to upgrade team skills.

An emerging development is the application of technology to improve team performance. *Groupware* is the generic term used to describe electronic and nonelectronic tools designed to help teams, especially business teams, function better. To our knowledge, the book, *Leading Business Teams*, by Johansen, Sibbet, Benson, Martin, Mittman, and Saffo is the first complete exposition on this subject.[48] These authors describe the gamut of possible tools available today—telephones, computers, electronic mail, voice mail, audio teleconferencing, video teleconferencing, copyboards, local-area networks (LANs), and the like—and show how they can be used separately or in combination to help teams get the job done. Regarding the origin of the term *groupware,* the authors write:

> Peter and Trudy Johnson-Lenz, who work over an electronic information network called EIES (New Jersey Institute of Technology) are credited with first using the term *groupware*. Cal Pava of Harvard is another early user of the word. There were probably other early users of the term, and, as is usual in such cases, it is very difficult to determine who really coined it. The first time we saw the term *groupware* in the mass-market press was in the *Fortune* article called "Software Catches the Team Spirit" (June 1987). Since then the term has come into much wider use, and many network-based products carry the label.[49]

The authors also explain how to design a team room—a room filled with tools, gadgets, and furniture to help teams be more effective. A key goal is to help teams make better decisions; therefore, a variety of decision-support tools, including computer workstations, are available to team members. Experimentation with groupware is certain to increase in the future. (We were relieved to discover that flip charts and magic markers were included in the team room.)

Teams have always been an important foundation of OD, but there is a growing awareness of the unique ability of teams to create synergy, respond quickly and flexibly to problems, innovate and find new ways to get the job done, and satisfy social needs in the workplace.

PARALLEL LEARNING STRUCTURES

Parallel learning structures, specially created organizational structures developed to plan and guide change programs, constitute another important foundation of organization development. Dale Zand introduced this concept under the label *collateral organization* in 1974, and defined it as: "a supplemental organization coexisting with the usual, formal organization."[50] The purpose of the collateral organization is to deal with "ill-structured" problems that the formal organization is unable to resolve.

Considerable experimentation with collateral organizations occurred in the 1970s and 1980s.

Gervase Bushe and Abraham (Rami) Shani summarized and extended the work on this concept in their comprehensive treatment titled, *Parallel Learning Structures.*[51] We will use the terms *parallel learning structures* and *parallel structures* to refer to this structural intervention. Parallel learning structures are a mechanism to facilitate innovation in large bureaucratic organizations where the forces of inertia, hierarchical communication patterns, and standard ways of addressing problems inhibit learning, innovation, and change. In essence, parallel structures are a vehicle for *learning* how to change the system, and then *leading* the change process.

Bushe and Shani describe the idea as follows: "We offer the term 'parallel learning structure' as a generic label to cover interventions where: (a) a 'structure' (that is, a specific division and coordination of labor) is created that (b) operates 'parallel' (that is, tandem or side-by-side) with the formal hierarchy and structure and (c) has the purpose of increasing an organization's 'learning' (that is, the creation and/or implementation of new thoughts and behaviors by employees)."[52] In its most basic form, a parallel learning structure consists of a steering committee and a number of working groups that study what changes are needed, make recommendations for improvement, and monitor the change efforts. Additional refinements include having a steering committee plus idea groups, action groups, work groups, or implementation groups, with the groups serving specific functions as designated by the steering committee. The parallel structure should be a microcosm of the larger organization, that is, it should have representatives from all parts of the organization. One or more top executives should be members of the steering committee to give the parallel structure authority, legitimacy, and clout.

The charge to members of the parallel learning structure is to think and behave in ways that are different from the normal roles and rules of the organization. Bushe and Shani say:

> The key thing about parallel structures is that they create a bounded space and time for thinking, talking, deciding, and acting differently than normally takes place at work. If you don't implement different norms and procedures, you don't have a parallel structure. The most important and difficult task for the people creating the parallel learning structure is to create a different culture within it. It isn't the supplemental structure that's important. What's important is that people act in a way that promotes learning and adaptation.[53]

Parallel structures help people break free of the normal constraints imposed by the organization, engage in genuine inquiry and experimentation, and initiate needed changes.

We believe parallel learning structures are a foundation of OD because they are prevalent in so many different OD programs. The quality of work life programs of the 1970s and 1980s used parallel structures composed of union leaders, managers, and employees. Most sociotechnical systems redesign efforts and open systems planning programs use parallel structures. Parallel structures are often used to coordinate self-directed teams in high-performance organizations. A steering committee and working groups were used to coordinate the employee involvement teams at Ford Motor Company. Parallel learning structures are often the best way to initiate change in large bureaucratic organizations, especially when the change involves a fundamental shift in the organization's methods of work and/or culture. Bushe and Shani recount a number of examples from a variety of settings where this intervention was used to great advantage. Parallel learning structures are a powerful tool for creating organizational change.

A NORMATIVE-REEDUCATIVE STRATEGY OF CHANGING

At the beginning of this chapter, we spoke of the importance of models and theories of planned change. Here we address another foundation of OD in terms of the *strategy* of change that underlies most organization development activities.

Organization development involves change, and it rests on a particular strategy of changing that has implications for practitioners and organization members alike. Chin and Benne describe three types of strategies for changing.[54] First there are the empirical-rational strategies, based on the assumptions that people are rational, will follow their rational self-interest, and will change if and when they come to realize the change is advantageous to them. The second group of strategies is the normative-reeducative strategies, based on the assumptions that norms form the basis for behavior, and change comes through a reeducation process in which old norms are discarded and supplanted by new ones. The third set of strategies is the power-coercive strategies, based on the assumption that change is compliance of those with less power to the desires of those with more power. Evaluated against these three change strategies, OD clearly falls within the normative-reeducative category, although often OD represents a combination of the normative-reeducative and the empirical-rational strategies. The nature of the normative-reeducative strategy is indicated by Chin and Benne:

> A second group of strategies we call normative-reeducative. These strategies build upon assumptions about human motivation different from those underlying the first. The rationality and intelligence of men are not denied. Patterns of action and practice are supported by sociocultural norms and by commitments on the part of the individu-

als to these norms. Sociocultural norms are supported by the attitude and value systems of individuals—normative outlooks which undergird their commitments. Change in a pattern of practice or action, according to this view, will occur only as the persons involved are brought to change their normative orientations to old patterns and develop commitments to new ones. And changes in normative orientations involve changes in attitudes, values, skills, and significant relationships, not just changes in knowledge, information, or intellectual rationales for action and practice.[55]

An illustration may clarify these three strategies of changing. Suppose that the Salk polio vaccine has just been invented, tested, and cleared for public use, and that you are in charge of disseminating it to the public. The procedures you use would depend upon the strategy of changing you believed in. If you espoused the empirical-rational strategy, then you would assume that all rational, self-interested people (and that is just about everyone) would use the vaccine if only they had information and knowledge about its availability and its efficacy. Your program, therefore, would be to disseminate the knowledge and information, and as a consequence, everyone would take the vaccine, since it would be in his or her best interests.

On the other hand, if you believed in a normative-reeducative strategy of changing, you would do additional things. While you do not disbelieve or disregard people's intelligence, rationality, and self-interest, you also believe that many behaviors are rooted in sociocultural norms, values, and beliefs that must be changed if people are to accept and use the vaccine. Some of these beliefs might be that "all new drugs are dangerous until they have been on the market for ten years"; "My neighbor, Mrs. Jones, isn't going to use the vaccine, and neither am I since she's always right about these things"; "Well, no one in my family has ever had polio, so I'm not afraid of getting it and don't need to be vaccinated." Holding a normative-reeducative strategy of changing, you would assume that norms and values had to be changed, in addition to making the information available to the public. You would mount both an education campaign about the new drug and a reeducation campaign to change people's norms and values.

If you believed in a power-coercive strategy of changing, your task would be straightforward: You would pass a law stating that all persons must get vaccinated, and you would ensure and enforce compliance to the law. If you had the power to pass the law, and power to enforce the law, the people would take the vaccine.

The point here is that there are different strategies for effecting change, and OD is based primarily on a normative-reeducative strategy and secondarily on a rational-empirical strategy. Chin and Benne suggest that a normative-reeducative strategy has the following implications for the practice of OD. The client system members define what changes and improvements they want to make, rather than the OD practitioner; the practitioner intervenes in a collaborative way with the clients, and together they define problems and seek solutions. Anything hindering effective problem solving is brought to light and publicly examined; that is, doubts, anxieties, and negative feelings are surfaced for "working through." Behavioral science knowledge is used as a resource for both clients and practitioner, and solutions to problems are not a priori assigned to greater technical information or knowledge but may reside in values, attitudes, relationships, and customary ways of doing things.[56] The norms to be changed and the form of reeducation are decided by the client system members. These implications give clients considerable choice and control over the situation; they impel a collaborative effort rather than a "doing something to" effort, and they give more options and alternatives to both the clients and the practitioner.

Our definition of organization development refers to improving and managing the organization's culture—a clear reference to sociocultural norms and to the normative nature of organizational change. Since norms are socially accepted beliefs about appropriate and inappropriate behaviors held by groups, norms can best be changed by focusing on the group, not the individual. Burke writes:

> If one attempts to change an attitude or the behavior of an individual without attempting to change the same attitude or behavior in the group to which the individual belongs, then the individual will be a deviate and either will come under pressure from the group to get back into line or will be rejected entirely. Thus, the major leverage point for change is at the group level; for example, by modifying a group norm or standards.[57]

The discovery of the importance of norms for determining individual behavior led to the normative-reeducative strategy of changing becoming a foundation of OD.

APPLIED BEHAVIORAL SCIENCE

This foundation of OD relates to the primary knowledge base of the field, behavioral science knowledge. OD programs apply scientific and practice principles from the behavioral sciences to intervene in the human and social processes of organizations. Although human behavior in organizations is far from being an exact science, there are lawful patterns of events that produce effectiveness and ineffectiveness, and OD practitioners know about these patterns because of research and theory. The aim of this discussion is to look briefly at how behavioral science knowledge becomes *applied* behavioral science knowledge because OD is the *application* of behavioral science knowledge, practices, and skills in ongoing systems in collaboration with system members.

A conventional distinction is usually made between (1) "pure" or basic science, the object of which is knowledge for its own sake, and (2) "technology," applied science, or practice, the object of which is knowledge to solve practical, pressing problems.[58] Greenwood discusses the activities of the practitioner as follows: "The problem that confronts a practitioner is customarily a state of disequilibrium that requires rectification. The practitioner examines the problem situation, on the basis of which he or she prescribes a solution that, hopefully, reestablishes the equilibrium, thereby solving the problem. This process is customarily referred to as diagnosis and treatment."[59] Both diagnosis and treatment consist of observing a situation, and on the basis of selected variables, placing it in a classification scheme or typology. The diagnostic typology allows the practitioner to know what category of situation he or she has examined; the treatment typology allows the practitioner to know what remedial efforts to apply to correct the problem. On this point, Greenwood states:

> The diagnostic and treatment typologies are employed together. Each type description of the diagnostic typology contains implications for a certain type of treatment. The practitioner uses treatment as the empirical test of his diagnosis, success corroborating the diagnosis, failure negating it and thus requiring rediagnosis. The principles of diagnosis and of treatment constitute the principles of practice, i.e., with their elaborations and implications constitute practice theory.[60]

It is from this "practice theory" that the OD practitioner works: first diagnosing the situation, then selecting and implementing treatments based on the diagnosis, and finally evaluating the effects of the treatments.

Organization development is both a result of applied behavioral science and a form of applied behavioral science; perhaps more accurately, it is a program of applying behavioral science to organizations. Figure 5-5 shows some of the inputs to applied behavioral science. The two bottom inputs, behavioral science research and behavioral science theory, are intended to represent contributions from pure or basic science; the two top inputs, practice research and practice theory, are intended to represent contributions from applied science.

Some examples of contributions from these four sources that are relevant for organization development are the following:

Contributions from behavioral science theory are these:

The importance of social norms in determining perceptions, motivations, and behaviors (Sherif)

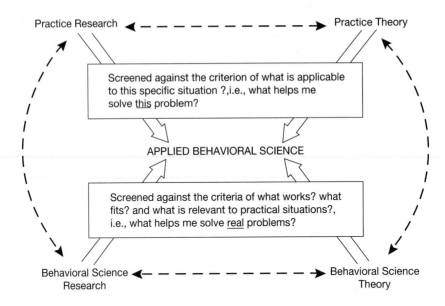

Figure 5-5 Composition of Applied Behavioral Science

The role of an exchange theory of behavior that postulates that people tend to exchange approximately equivalent units to maintain a balance between what is given and received (Gouldner, Homans)

The importance of the existing total field of forces in determining and predicting behavior (Lewin)

The relevance of role theory in accounting for stability and change in behavior (G. H. Mead)

The possibilities inherent in views of motivation different from those provided by older theories (McGregor, Herzberg, Maslow)

The importance of individual goal setting for increasing productivity and improving performance (Locke)

The place of social cognitive theory, general theories of learning, effects of reward and punishment, attitude change theories, and so on in understanding organizational behavior (Bandura, Skinner, McGuire)[61]

Contributions from behavioral science research are these:

Studies on the causes, conditions and consequences of induced competition on behavior within and between groups (Sherif and Blake and Mouton)

Results on the effects of cooperative and competitive group goal structures on behavior within groups (Deutsch)

Studies on the effects of organizational and managerial climate on leadership style (Fleishman)

Studies on the variables relevant for organizational health (Likert)

Studies showing the importance of the social system in relation to the technical system (Trist and Bamforth)

Studies on different communication networks (Leavitt), causes and consequences of conformity (Asch), group problem solving (Kelley and Thibaut), and group dynamics (Cartwright and Zander)[62]

Contributions from practice theory are these:

Implications from the theory and practice of the laboratory training method (Bradford, Benne, and Gibb)

Implications from theories of group development (Bion and Bennis and Shepard)

New dimensions in the helping relationship and specifically the client-consultant relationship (Rogers)

Codification of the practice of management (Drucker)

New ideas about the education process (Dewey)

The concept of "management by objectives" (Drucker, McGregor)

Implications of social learning theory and behavior modeling for supervisor training (Goldstein and Sorcher)

Explorations in intervention theory and method (Argyris)

Developments in consultation typologies and theory (Blake and Mouton)

Implications and applications from theories of *planned change* (Lippitt, Watson, and Westley; Bennis, Benne, and Chin)[63]

Contributions from practice research are these:

Studies showing that feeding back survey research data can bring about organization change (Mann, Likert, Baumgartel)

Results indicating the importance of the informal work group on individual and group performance (Roethlisberger and Dickson)

Results showing the efficacy of grid organization development in large organizations (Blake, Mouton, Barnes, and Greiner)

Results documenting improved organizational performance and improved organization climate stemming from a long-term OD effort in a manufacturing firm (Marrow, Bowers, and Seashore)

Results showing the ability of behavior modeling training to improve supervisory human relations skills (Latham and Saari) and organizational effectiveness (Porras)

Results from the action research studies in Chapter 7 showing how to change organizational practices[64]

These contributions are not meant to be exhaustive, but only to show some of the sources and kinds of information/knowledge that OD practitioners, as applied behavioral scientists, bring to the organizational setting. In fact, most of the citations listed throughout this book represent contributions to the behavioral science theory and research, or practice theory and research underlying OD.

ACTION RESEARCH

A basic model underlying most organization development activities is the action research model—a data-based, problem-solving method that replicates the steps involved in the scientific method of inquiry. Three processes are involved in action research: data collection, feedback of the data to the client system members, and action planning based on the data.[65] Action research is especially well suited for planned change programs and has been a foundation of OD from the very beginning.

Action research is a method for *learning* and *doing*—learning about the dynamics of organizational change, and doing or implementing change efforts. Kurt Lewin, who developed the concept of action research, had this to say about it:

> The research needed for social practice can best be characterized as research for social management or social engineering. It is a type of action-research, a comparative search on the conditions and effects of various forms of social action, and research leading to social action. . . .
>
> This by no means implies that the research needed is in any respect less scientific or "lower" than what would be required for pure science in the field of social events. I am inclined to hold the opposite to be true.[66]

Chapter 7 describes action research in detail, so we defer discussion of it until then. For now, we simply note that the many similarities between organization development and action research make this one of the most important foundations of OD.

CONCLUDING COMMENTS

These foundations of organization development form the theoretical and practice underpinnings of the field. Taken separately, each is a powerful conceptual tool for thinking about and implementing change. Taken collectively, they constitute the beginning of a theory of organization development and change that has enormous potential for improving organizational performance and individual development. These foundations are solid, valid, and of great value to OD theorists and practitioners. They are also of great value to organization leaders and members who stand to benefit from the change programs erected on this collective foundation.

NOTES

1. See Kurt Lewin, *Field Theory in Social Science* (New York: Harper, 1951).
2. Edgar Schein, *Process Consultation: Lessons for Managers and Consultants*, vol. 2 (Reading, MA: Addison-Wesley Publishing Company, 1987). This discussion is based on pp. 92–114. Table 5-1 is taken from p. 93.

3. R. Lippitt, J. Watson, and B. Westley, *Dynamics of Planned Change* (New York: Harcourt and Brace, 1958).

4. See, for example, D. Kolb and A. Frohman, "An Organization Development Approach to Consulting," *Sloan Management Review*, 12, no. 1 (1970), 51–65. Also, W. Warner Burke, *Organization Development: A Process of Learning and Changing* (Reading, MA: Addison-Wesley Publishing Company, 1994).

5. R. H. Kilmann, *Managing Beyond the Quick Fix* (San Francisco: Jossey-Bass, 1989). See also R. H. Kilmann, "A Completely Integrated Program for Creating and Maintaining Organizational Success," *Organizational Dynamics* (Summer 1989), pp. 5–19.

6. Kilmann, "A Completely Integrated Program," pp. 13–14. These stages and tracks are reminiscent of Grid OD; see R. R. Blake and J. S. Mouton, *Building a Dynamic Corporation Through Grid Organization Development* (Reading, MA: Addison-Wesley Publishing Company, 1969).

7. Jerry I. Porras, *Stream Analysis: A Powerful Way to Diagnose and Manage Organizational Change* (Reading, MA: Addison-Wesley Publishing Company, 1987).

8. This discussion comes from Jerry I. Porras and Peter J. Robertson, "Organizational Development: Theory, Practice, and Research," in Marvin D. Dunnette and Leaetta M. Hough, eds., *Handbook of Industrial and Organizational Psychology*, 2nd ed., vol. 3 (Palo Alto, CA: Consulting Psychologists Press, 1992), pp. 719–822. The work-setting elements are listed on p. 729.

9. Porras, *Stream Analysis*, p. 23.

10. Porras and Robertson, "Organizational Development," p. 728.

11. See Warner Burke, *Organization Development*, Chap. 7.

12. The leadership research can be found in James M. Burns, *Leadership* (New York: Harper & Row, 1978); B. M. Bass, *Leadership and Performance Beyond Expectations* (New York: The Free Press, 1985); and N. M. Tichy and M. A. Devanna, *The Transformational Leader* (New York: Wiley and Sons, 1986).

13. These definitions are from Stephen P. Robbins, *Organizational Behavior*, 4th ed. (Englewood Cliffs, N.J.: Prentice Hall, 1989), p. 329.

14. W. Warner Burke, *Organization Development*, pp. 126–127.

15. See, for example, W. W. Burke and P. Jackson, "Making the Smith Kline Beecham Merger Work," in *Human Resource Management*, 30 (1991), pp. 69–87. See also W. M. Bernstein and W. W. Burke, "Modeling Organizational Meaning Systems," in R. W. Woodman and W. A. Pasmore, eds., *Research in Organizational Change and Development* (Greenwich, CT: JAI Press, 1989), pp. 117–159.

16. Ludwig von Bertalanffy, "The Theory of Open Systems in Physics and Biology," *Science*, 111 (1950), pp. 23–28. D. Katz and R. L. Kahn, *The Social Psychology of Organizations* (New York: Wiley, 1966). A second edition appeared in 1978.

17. See A. D. Hall and R. E. Fagen, "Definition of a System," *General Systems*, Yearbook of the Society for the Advancement of General Systems Theory, 1956, 1, pp. 18–28.

18. L. von Bertalanffy, "General System Theory," *General Systems*, Yearbook of the Society for the Advancement of General Systems Theory, 1956, 1, pp. 1–10.

19. Fremont E. Kast and James E. Rosenzweig, *Organization and Management: A Systems Approach*, 4th ed. (New York: McGraw-Hill, 1985), p. 15.

20. David P. Hanna, *Designing Organizations for High Performance* (Reading, MA: Addison-Wesley Publishing Company, 1988), p. 8.

21. This discussion follows the descriptions of Katz and Kahn, *The Social Psychology of Organizations* 2nd ed., pp. 18–34; and Hanna, *Designing Organizations for High Performance*, pp. 1–31.

22. Hanna, pp. 14–15.

23. Ibid., p. 16.

24. Katz and Kahn, p. 27.

25. See W. A. Pasmore, *Designing Effective Organizations: The Sociotechnical Systems Perspective* (New York: Wiley, 1988); C. Pava, "Redesigning Sociotechnical Systems Design: Concepts and Methods for the 1990s," *Journal of Applied Behavioral Science*, 22

(1986), 201–221; T. G. Cummings, "Future Directions of Sociotechnical Systems Theory and Research," *Journal of Applied Behavioral Science*, 22 (1986), 355–360; D. P. Hanna, *Designing Organizations for High Performance*; and G. R. Bushe and A. B. Shani, *Parallel Learning Structures* (Reading, MA: Addison-Wesley Publishing Company, 1991).

26. Hanna, *Designing Organizations for High Performance*, p. 97.
27. Peter M. Senge, *The Fifth Discipline: The Art and Practice of the Learning Organization* (New York: Doubleday/Currency, 1990), p. 12.
28. See Dorwin Cartwright, "Achieving Change in People: Some Applications of Group Dynamics Theory," *Human Relations*, 4, no. 4 (1951), 381–392.
29. J. E. McGrath, *Groups: Interaction and Performance* (Englewood Cliffs, NJ: Prentice Hall, 1984).
30. James A. Belasco, *Teaching the Elephant to Dance: The Manager's Guide to Empowering Change* (New York: Plume Publishing, 1990)
31. James M. Kouzes and Barry Z. Posner, *The Leadership Challenge* (San Francisco: Jossey-Bass Publishers, 1990).
32. Ibid., p. 14.
33. Donald E. Petersen and John Hillkirk, *A Better Idea: Redefining the Way Americans Work* (Boston: Houghton Mifflin Company, 1991).
34. Thomas J. Peters and Robert H. Waterman, Jr., *In Search of Excellence* (New York: Harper & Row, Publishers, 1982).
35. Tom Peters and Nancy Austin, *A Passion for Excellence* (New York: Warner Books, Inc., 1985).
36. Tom Peters, *Thriving on Chaos* (New York: Alfred A. Knopf, 1988).
37. Ibid., pp. 281–386. The full list of "Prescriptions for a World Turned Upside Down" is reproduced inside the front and back covers.
38. Tom Peters, *Liberation Management* (New York: Alfred A. Knopf, 1992).
39. Carl E. Larson and Frank M. J. LaFasto, *TeamWork* (Newbury Park, CA: Sage Publications, Inc., 1989).
40. Jon R. Katzenbach and Douglas K. Smith, *The Wisdom of Teams: Creating the High Performance Organization* (Boston: Harvard Business School Press, 1993).
41. Ibid., p. 13.
42. Ibid., pp. 14–15.
43. Ibid., p. 19.
44. Tom Peters, *Liberation Management*.
45. Michael Doyle and David Straus, *How to Make Meetings Work* (New York: Playboy Press, 1976).
46. See William G. Dyer, *Team Building: Issues and Alternatives*, 2nd ed. (Reading, MA: Addison-Wesley Publishing Company, 1987); and Larry Hirschhorn, *Managing in the New Team Environment: Skills, Tools, and Methods* (Reading, MA: Addison-Wesley Publishing Company, 1991).
47. See Edgar H. Schein, *Process Consultation: Its Role in Organization Development*, vol. 1, 2nd ed. (Reading, MA: Addison-Wesley Publishing Company, 1988); and Edgar H. Schein, *Process Consultation: Lessons for Managers and Consultants*, vol. 2 (Reading, MA: Addison-Wesley Publishing Company, 1987).
48. Robert Johansen, David Sibbet, Suzyn Benson, Alexia Martin, Robert Mittman, and Paul Saffo, *Leading Business Teams* (Reading, MA: Addison-Wesley Publishing Company, 1991).
49. Ibid., p. 10.
50. Dale Zand, "Collateral Organization: A New Change Strategy," *Journal of Applied Behavioral Science*, 10 (1974), pp. 63–89. This quotation is from p. 64.
51. Bushe and Shani, *Parallel Learning Structures*.
52. Ibid., p. 9.
53. Ibid., p. 10.
54. Robert Chin and Kenneth D. Benne, "General Strategies for Effecting Changes in

Human Systems," in W. G. Bennis, K. D. Benne, R. Chin, and K. E. Corey, eds.,*The Planning of Change*, 3rd ed. (New York: Holt, Rinehart, and Winston, 1976), pp. 22–45.

55. Ibid., p. 23.

56. Based on a discussion in Chin and Benne, "General Strategies," pp. 32–33.

57. Warner Burke, *Organization Development*, p. 151.

58. Robert K. Merton and Daniel Lerner, "Social Scientists and Research Policy," in W. G. Bennis, K. D. Benne, and R. Chin, eds., *The Planning of Change* (New York: Holt, Rinehart, and Winston, 1961), pp. 53–69.

59. Ernest Greenwood, "The Practice of Science and the Science of Practice," in Bennis, Benne, and Chin, eds., *The Planning of Change*, 1961, p. 78.

60. Ibid., p. 79.

61. These citations, listed in order of mention in the text, are: (1) M. Sherif, *The Psychology of Social Norms* (New York: Harper & Bros., 1936). (2) A. W. Gouldner, "The Norm of Reciprocity: A Preliminary Statement," *American Sociological Review*, April 1960, 25, pp. 161–178. (3) C. G. Homans, *The Human Group* (New York: Harcourt, Brace & World, 1950). (4) K. Lewin, *Field Theory in Social Science* (New York: Harper & Bros., 1951). (5) G. H. Mead, *Mind, Self, and Society* (Chicago: University of Chicago Press, 1934). (6) D. M. McGregor, *The Human Side of Enterprise* (New York: McGraw-Hill, 1960). (7) F. B. Herzberg, B. Mausner, and B. Snyderman, *The Motivation to Work* (New York: John Wiley, 1959). (8) A. Maslow, *Motivation and Personality* (New York: Harper & Row, 1964). (9) E. A. Locke, "Toward a Theory of Task Motivation and Incentives," *Organizational Behavior and Human Performance*, 3 (1968), pp. 157–189. (10) A. Bandura, *Social Foundations of Thought and Action: A Social Cognitive Theory* (Englewood Cliffs, NJ: Prentice Hall, 1986). (11) B. F. Skinner, *About Behaviorism* (New York: Alfred A. Knopf, 1974). (12) W. J. McGuire, "The Nature of Attitudes and Attitude Change," in G. Lindzey and E. Aronson, eds., *Handbook of Social Psychology*, 2nd ed., vol. 3 (Reading, MA: Addison-Wesley Publishing Company, 1969), pp. 136–314.

62. These citations, listed in order of mention in the text, are: (1) M. Sherif, O. J. Harvey, B. J. White, W. R. Hood, and C. Sherif, *Intergroup Conflict and Cooperation: The Robbers Cave Experiment* (Norman, OK: University Book Exchange, 1961). (2) R. R. Blake, "Conformity, Resistance, and Conversion," in I. A. Berg and B. M. Bass, eds., *Conformity and Deviation* (New York: Harper & Row, 1961), pp. 1–37. (3) M. Deutsch, "A Theory of Cooperation and Competition," *Human Relations*, 2, no. 2 (1949), 129–152. (4) E. A. Fleishman, "Leadership Climate, Human Relations Training and Supervisory Behavior," *Personnel Psychology*, 6 (Summer 1953), pp. 205–222. (5) R. Likert, *New Patterns of Management* (New York: McGraw-Hill, 1961). (6) E. L. Trist and K. W. Bamforth, "Some Social and Psychological Consequences of the Longwall Method of Coal-Getting," *Human Relations*, 4, no. 1 (1951), 1–38. (7) H. J. Leavitt, "Some Consequences of Certain Communication Patterns on Group Performance," *Journal of Abnormal and Social Psychology*, 46 (January 1951), pp. 38–50. (8) S. Asch, "Studies of Independence and Conformity: A Minority of One Against a Unanimous Majority," *Psychological Monographs*, 7, no. 9 (1956). (9) H. H. Kelley and J. W. Thibaut, "Group Problem Solving," in G. Lindzey and E. Aronson, eds., *Handbook of Social Psychology*, 2nd ed., vol. 4 (Reading, MA: Addison-Wesley Publishing Company, 1969), pp. 1–101. (10) D. Cartwright and A. Zander, *Group Dynamics*, 2nd ed. (New York: Harper & Row, 1960).

63. These citations, listed in order of mention in the text, are: (1) L. P. Bradford, J. R. Gibb, and K. D. Benne, eds., *T-Group Theory and Laboratory Method* (New York: John Wiley, 1964). (2) W. R. Bion, *Experiences in Groups* (New York: Basic Books, 1961). (3) W. G. Bennis and H. A. Shepard, "A Theory of Group Development," *Human Relations*, 9, no. 4 (1956), 415–438. (4) C. R. Rogers, *Client-Centered Therapy* (Boston: Houghton Mifflin, 1951). (5) P. F. Drucker, *The Practice of Management* (New York: Harper & Row, 1954). (6) J. Dewey, *How We Think*, (rev. ed.) (New York: Heath, 1933). (7) P. F. Drucker, *The Practice of Management* (New York: Harper & Row, 1954). (8) D. M. McGregor, *The*

Human Side of Enterprise (New York: McGraw-Hill, 1960). (9) A. P. Goldstein and M. Sorcher, *Changing Supervisor Behavior* (New York: Pergamon Press, 1974). (10) C. Argyris, *Intervention Theory and Method: A Behavioral Science View* (Reading, MA: Addison-Wesley Publishing Company, 1970). (11) R. R. Blake and J. S. Mouton, *Consultation* (Reading, MA: Addison-Wesley Publishing Company, 1976). (12) R. Lippitt, J. Watson, and B. Westley, *The Dynamics of Planned Change* (New York: Harcourt, Brace & World, 1958). (13) W. G. Bennis, K. D. Benne, and R. Chin, eds., *The Planning of Change* (New York: Holt, Rinehart and Winston, 1961).

64. These citations, listed in order of mention in the text, are: (1) F. C. Mann, "Studying and Creating Change," in W. G. Bennis, K. D. Benne, and R. Chin, eds., *The Planning of Change* (New York: Holt, Rinehart and Winston, 1961), pp. 605–613. (2) R. Likert, *New Patterns of Management* (New York: McGraw-Hill, 1961). (3) H. Baumgartel, "Using Employee Questionnaire Results for Improving Organizations: The Survey 'Feedback' Experiment," *Kansas Business Review*, 12 (December 1959), pp. 2–6. (4) F. J. Roethlisberger and W. J. Dickson, *Management and the Worker* (Cambridge, MA: Harvard University Press, 1939). (5) R. R. Blake, J. S. Mouton, L. B. Barnes, and L. E. Greiner, "Breakthrough in Organization Development," *Harvard Business Review*, 42 (November-December 1964), pp. 133–155. (6) A. J. Marrow, D. G. Bowers, and S. E. Seashore, *Management by Participation* (New York: Harper & Row, 1967). (7) G. P. Latham and L. M. Saari, "The Application of Social Learning Theory to Training Supervisors Through Behavior Modeling," *Journal of Applied Psychology*, 64 (1979), pp. 239–246. (8) J. I. Porras, K. Hargis, K. J. Patterson, D. G. Maxfield, N. Roberts, and R. J. Bies, "Modeling-Based Organizational Development: A Longitudinal Assessment," *The Journal of Applied Behavioral Science*, 18, no. 4 (1982), 433–446.

65. Richard Beckhard, *Organization Development: Strategies and Models*, (Reading, MA: Addison-Wesley Publishing Company, 1969), p. 28.

66. Kurt Lewin, "Frontiers in Group Dynamics," *Human Relations*, 1, no. 2 (1947), 150–151.

6

MANAGING THE OD PROCESS

In this chapter we examine what leaders, organization members, and OD practitioners do as they implement and manage organization development programs. By now you know that *diagnosis* forms a foundation for *intervening*, and that intervening involves *implementing various change-inducing action programs*. Thinking about how to manage this process is the focus of the present discussion. First we take an in-depth look at diagnosis from several different perspectives or approaches. This is followed by an examination of the considerations that go into selecting and implementing interventions. Finally, guidelines for the overall management of OD programs are presented and explained.

DIAGNOSIS

There are three basic components of all OD programs: *diagnosis, action,* and *program management*. The diagnostic component represents a continuous collection of data about the total system or its subunits, and about system processes, culture, and other targets of interest. The action component consists of all the activities and interventions designed to improve the organization's functioning. The program management component encompasses all activities designed to ensure the success of the program, such as developing the overall OD strategy, monitoring events along the way, and dealing with the complexities and surprises inherent

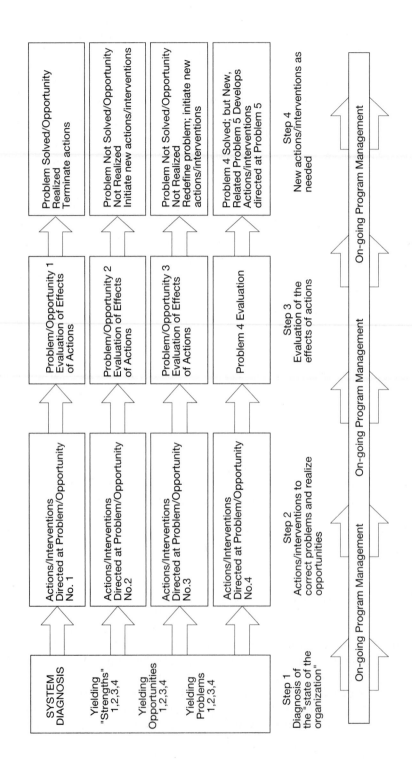

Figure 6-1 Components of the OD Process: Diagnosis, Action, Program Management

in all programs. (In fact, all three of these components are interventions into the organization in that all have impacts on organization members. They are separated here for analysis purposes.) Figure 6-1 shows what we mean when we describe the OD process in terms of diagnosis, action, and program management components.

The first step is to diagnose the state of the system regarding the client's focus of interest—whether the total system or some part of the whole. What are its strengths? What are its problem areas? What are the unrealized opportunities that are being pursued? Is there a discrepancy between the vision of the desired future and the current situation? From the diagnosis comes identification of strengths, opportunities, and problem areas. Action plans are developed in step 2 to correct problems, seize opportunities, and to maintain areas of strength. These action plans are OD interventions specifically tailored to address issues at the individual, group, intergroup, or organizational levels, as well as address issues related to selected processes, such as communication or decision making. Step 3 consists of fact-finding concerning the results of the actions taken. Did the actions have the desired effects? Is the problem solved or the opportunity achieved? If the answer is yes, organization members move on to new and different problems and opportunities; if the answer is no, the members initiate new action plans and interventions to resolve the issue (step 4). Often when problems remain unsolved after an initial attack on them, steps 3 and 4 entail redefining and reconceptualizing the problem areas. Steps 5, 6, 7, and so on may be required for some problems and opportunities, but further steps are just iterations of the basic sequence of diagnosis-action-evaluation-action. Again, this process looks logical and linear in Figure 6-1, but in practice it is more complicated.

During the entire sequence, attention is also directed to managing the OD process itself. Energy and effort are expended to ensure that the program is supported by the organization members, that the program is relevant to the organization's priority concerns, and that the program is making discernible progress. Managing the OD program is a constant concern and a continuous activity.

Diagnosing the System, Its Subunits, and Processes

Organization development is at heart an action program based on valid information about the status quo, current problems and opportunities, and effects of actions as they relate to goal achievement. An OD program thus starts with diagnosis and continuously employs data collecting and data analyzing throughout. The requirement for diagnostic activities—activities designed to provide an accurate account of things as they really are—stems from two needs: the first is to know the state of

Table 6-1 Diagnosing Organizational Subsystems

DIAGNOSTIC FOCUS OR TARGET	EXPLANATION AND IDENTIFYING EXAMPLES	TYPICAL INFORMATION SOUGHT	COMMON METHODS OF DIAGNOSIS
The total organization (having a common "charter" or mission and a common power structure)	The total system is the entity assessed and analyzed. The diagnosis might also include, if relevant, extrasystem (environmental) organizations, groups, or forces, such as customers, suppliers, and governmental regulations. Examples are a manufacturing firm, a hospital, a school system, a department store chain, or a church denomination.	What are the norms ("cultural oughts") of the organization? What is the organization's culture? What are the attitudes, opinions, and feelings of system members toward various "cognitive objects" such as compensation, organization goals, supervision, and top management? What is the organization climate—open vs. closed, authoritarian vs. democratic, repressive vs. developmental, trusting vs. suspicious, cooperative vs. competitive? How well do key organizational processes, such as decision making and goal setting, function? What kind and how effective are the organization's "sensing mechanisms" to monitor internal and external demands? Are organization goals understood and accepted?	Questionnaire surveys are most popular with a large organization. Interviews, both group and individual, are useful for getting detailed information, especially if based on effective sampling techniques. A panel of representative members who are surveyed or interviewed periodically is useful to chart changes over time. Examination of organizational "potsherds"—rules, regulations, policies, symbols of office and/or status, etc., yields insight into the organization's culture. Diagnostic meetings held at various levels within the organization yield a great amount of information in a short time period.
Large subsystems that are by nature complex and heterogeneous	This target group stems from making different "slices" of the organization, such as by hierarchical *level*, *function*, and geographical *location*. Two criteria help to identify this set of subsystems: first they are viewed as a subsystem by themselves or others; and second, they are heterogeneous in makeup, that is, the members have some differences in common, but many differences from each other, too. Examples would be the middle-management group, consisting of managers from	All of the above, plus: How does this subsystem view the whole and vice versa? How do the members of this subsystem get along together? What are the unique demands of this subsystem? Are organization structures and processes related to the unique demands? Are there "high" and "low" subunits within the subsystem in terms of performance? How do the major problems confronting this subsystem and its subunits? Are the subsystem's goals compatible	If the subsystems are large or widely dispersed, questionnaire and survey techniques are recommended. Interviews and observations may be used to provide additional supporting or hypothesis-testing information. Organization records, reports, and information are good sources of information about performance and problems.

Subsystem	Description	Diagnostic Questions	Methods
(continued)	diverse functional groups; the personnel department members of an organization that has widely dispersed operations with a personnel group at each location; everyone in 1 plant in a company that has 10 plants; a division made up several different businesses.	with organization goals? Does the heterogeneity of role demands and functional identity get in the way of effective subsystem performance?	Typical methods include the following: individual interviews followed by a group meeting to review the interview data; questionnaires; observation of staff meetings and other day-to-day operations; and a formal group meeting for self-diagnosis.
Small subsystems that are simple and relatively homogeneous	These are typically formal work groups or teams that have frequent face-to-face interaction. They may be permanent groups, temporary task forces, or newly constituted groups (e.g., the group charged with the "start-up" of a new operation, or the group formed by an acquisition or merger). Examples are the top-management team, any manager and his or her key subordinates, committees of a permanent or temporary nature, task force teams, the work force in an office, the teachers in a single school, etc.	The questions on culture, climate, attitudes, and feelings are relevant here, plus: What are the major problems of the team? How can team effectiveness be improved? What do people do that gets in the way of others? Are member/leader relations those that are desired? Do individuals know how their jobs relate to group and organizational goals? Are the group's working processes, i.e., the way they get things done as a group, effective? Is good use made of group and individual resources?	Questionnaires or interviews are frequently used. Descriptive adjective questionnaires can be used to obtain a quick reading on the culture, "tone," and health of the organization. Diagnostic group meetings can be useful. Organizational records can be examined.
Small, total organizations that are relatively simple and homogeneous	An example would be a local professional organization or small company. Typical problems as seen by officers might be declining membership, low attendance, difficulty in manning special task forces, or poor quality and declining profits.	How do the officers and the members see the organization and its goals? What do they like and dislike about it? What do they want it to be like? What is the competition like? What significant external forces are impacting on the organization?	
Interface or intergroup subsystems	These consist of subsets of the total system that contain members of two subsystems, such as a matrix organizational structure requiring an individual or a group to have two reporting lines. But more often this	How does each subsystem see the other? What problems do the two groups have in working together? In what ways do the subsystems get in each other's way? How can they collaborate to improve the perform-	Confrontation meetings between both groups are often the method for data gathering and planning corrective actions. Organization mirroring meetings are used when three or more groups are involved. Inter-

Table 6-1 *(cont.)*

	target consists of members of one subsystem having common problems and responsibilities with members of another subsystem. We mean to include subsystems with common problems and responsibilities such as production and maintenance overlaps, marketing and production overlaps.	ance of both groups? Are goals, subgoals, areas of authority and responsibility clear? What is the nature of the climate between the groups? What do the members want it to be?	views of each subsystem followed by a "sharing the data" meeting or observation of interactions can be used.
Dyads and/or triads	Superior/subordinate pairs, interdependent peers, linking pins—i.e., persons who have multiple group memberships—all these are subsystems worthy of analysis.	What is the quality of the relationship? Do the parties have the necessary skills for task accomplishment? Are they collaborative or competitive? Are they effective as a subsystem? Does the addition of a third party facilitate or inhibit their progress? Are they supportive of each other?	Separate interviews followed by a meeting of the parties to view any discrepancies in the interview data are often used. Checking their perceptions of each other through confrontation situations may be useful. Observation is an important way to assess the dynamic quality of the interaction.
Individuals	Any individual within the organization, such as president, division heads, key occupants of positions in a work flow process, e.g., quality control, R&D. In school systems, this would be students, teachers, or administrators.	Do people perform according to the organization's expectations? How do they view their place and performance? Do certain kinds of problems typically arise? Do people meet standards and norms of the organization? Do they need particular knowledge, skills, or ability? What career development opportunites do they have/want/need? What pain are they experiencing?	Interviews, information derived from diagnostic work team meetings, or problems identified by the human resources department are sources of information. Self-assessment growing out of team or subsystem intervention is another source.
Roles	A role is a set of behaviors enacted by a person as a result of occupying a certain position within the organization. All persons in the organization have roles requiring certain	Should the role behaviors be added to, subtracted from, or changed? Is the role defined adequately? What is the "fit" between the person and role? Should the role performer be given	Usually information comes from observations, interviews, role analysis technique, a team approach to "management by objectives." Career planning activities yield this information

behaviors, such as secretaries, production supervisors, accountants, scientists, custodians.	special skills and knowledge? Is this the right person for this role?	as an output.
Between-organization systems constituting a suprasystem—this is the arena of transorganizational OD. An example might be the system of law and order in a region, including local, county, state, federal police or investigative and enforcement agencies, courts, prisons, parole agencies, prosecuting officers and grand juries. Most such suprasystems are so complex that change efforts tend to focus on a pair or a trio of subparts.	How do the key people in one segment of the suprasystem view the whole and the subparts? Are there frictions or incongruities between subparts? Are there high-performing and low-performing subunits? Why?	Organizational mirroring, or developing lists of how each group sees each other, is a common method of joint diagnosis. Questionnaires and interviews are useful in extensive long-term interventions.

things or "what is"; the second is to know the effects or consequences of actions.

The importance of diagnostic activities is emphasized by Beckhard as follows:

> The development of a strategy for systematic improvement of an organization demands an examination of the present state of things. Such an analysis usually looks at two broad areas. One is a diagnosis of the various subsystems that make up the total organization. These subsystems may be natural "teams" such as top management, the production department, or a research group; or they may be levels such as top management, middle management, or the work force.
>
> The second area of diagnosis is the organization processes that are occurring. These include decision-making processes, communications patterns and styles, relationships between interfacing groups, the management of conflict, the setting of goals, and planning methods.[1]

Table 6-1 shows how one would proceed to diagnose a system and its subsystems (the whole and its subunits). For each of the major targets or subsystems in an organization, the typical information desired and common methods of obtaining the information are given. The OD practitioner may be interested in all these target groups or in only one or two of them; he or she may work with one subsystem during one phase of the program and other subsystems during subsequent phases. Frequently, the improvement strategy (the overall OD intervention strategy) calls for concentrating on different organizational targets in a planned sequence. For example, the program may start at an important subsystem, move to another subsystem, and then extend to the total organization; or the initial focus could be on the total organization and then move to selected subsystems.

An alternative way to conceptualize the diagnostic component emphasizes the organization's principal processes rather than its primary target groups. Such a scheme is presented in Table 6-2 showing the principal organization processes, the typical desired information concerning the processes, and the common methods of obtaining the information.

In practice the OD consultant works from both tables simultaneously. Although interested in some specific target group from Table 6-1 and the information about that group, the consultant is also interested in the processes found in that group and would rely on Table 6-2. Organizational processes are the *what* and the *how* of the organization, that is, What is going on? and How is it being accomplished? To know about the organization's processes is to know about the organization in its dynamic and complex reality. Organization development practitioners typically pay special attention to the processes listed in Table 6-2 because of their centrality for effective organization functioning, because of their ubiquitous nature in organizations, and because significant organizational problems often stem from them. Careful examination of the two tables will give a good sense of the inner workings of an OD program and its thrusts, emphases, and mechanics.

These tables are intended as tools for diagnosing organizations, their processes, and their subunits. For example, say the vice president of a large heterogeneous division composed of several different businesses with multiple manufacturing and marketing organizations is worried about decreasing profitability. The questions the vice president needs answers to are those listed for the total organization and large subsystems from Table 6-1, as well as questions about organizational processes such as goal setting, decision making, technology, and strategic management from Table 6-2. This knowledge would likely be gained in the diagnostic phase of an OD effort sponsored by the vice president.

Continual diagnosis is thus a necessary ingredient of any planned change effort. Such diverse activities as getting rich, managing your time, and losing weight, for example, all begin with an audit of "what is"—the status quo—and then require continual monitoring of the changing status quo over time. From a comparison of "what is" with "what should be" comes a discovery of the gap between actual and desired conditions. Action plans are then developed to close the gap between the actual and the desired conditions; and the effects (consequences) of these action plans are continuously monitored to measure progress or movement toward the goal.[2] Diagnostic activities are therefore basic to all goal-seeking behaviors.

Organization development, with its emphasis on moving the organization from "what is" to "what should be," requires continuous generation of system data. In this regard, Argyris states that the consultant ("interventionist" in his terms) has three "primary intervention tasks": to help the client system generate valid data; to enable the client system to have free, informed choice; and to help the client system generate internal commitment to the choices made.[3] Argyris says: "One condition that seems so basic as to be defined axiomatic is the generation of *valid information*. Without valid information it would be difficult for the client to learn and for the interventionist to help. . . . Valid information is that which describes the factors, plus their interrelationships, that create the problem for the client system."[4]

Granted that diagnosis is a sine qua non of effective organization development, two issues remain. First, is the diagnosis systematically planned and structured in advance so that it follows an extensive category system and structured question format, or is the diagnosis more emergent—following the data wherever they may lead? Second, what diagnostic categories are to be used? Practice varies widely on these two dimensions. We tend to be about in the middle of the "structured in ad-

Table 6-2 Diagnosing Organizational Processes

ORGANIZATIONAL PROCESS	IDENTIFYING REMARKS AND EXPLANATION	TYPICAL INFORMATION SOUGHT	COMMON METHODS OF DIAGNOSIS
Communications patterns, styles and flows	Who talks to whom, for how long, about what? Who initiates the interaction? Is it two-way or one-way? Is it top-down; down-up; lateral?	Is communication directed upward, downward, or both? Are communications filtered? Why? In what way? Do communications patterns "fit" the nature of the jobs to be accomplished? What is the "climate" of communications? What is the place of written communications vs. oral?	Observations, especially in meetings; questionnaires for large-sized samples; interviews and discussions with group members—all these methods may be used to collect the desired information. Analysis of videotaped sessions by all concerned is especially useful.
Goal setting	Setting task objectives and determining criteria to measure accomplishment of the objectives takes place at all organizational levels.	Do they set goals? How is this done? Who participates in goal setting? Do they possess the necessary skills for effective goal setting? Are they able to set long-range and short-range objectives?	Questionnaires, interviews, and observation all afford ways of assessing goal-setting ability of individuals and groups within the organization.
Decision making, problem solving, and action planning	Evaluating alternatives and choosing a plan of action are integral and central functions for most organization members. This includes getting the necessary information, establishing priorities, evaluating alternatives, and choosing one alternative over all others.	Who makes decisions? Are they effective? Are all available sources utilized? Are additional decision-making skills needed? Are additional problem-solving skills needed? Are organization members satisfied with the problem-solving and decision-making processes?	Observation of problem-solving meetings at various organizational levels is particularly valuable in diagnosing this process. Analysis of videotaped sessions by all concerned is especially useful.
Conflict resolution and management	Conflict—interpersonal, intrapersonal, and intergroup—frequently exists in organizations. Does the organization have effective ways of dealing with conflict?	Where does conflict exist? Who are the involved parties? How is it being managed? What are the system norms for dealing with conflict? Does the reward system promote conflict?	Interviews, third-party observations, and observation meetings are common methods for diagnosing these processes.
Managing interface relations	Interfaces represent these situations wherein two or more groups (subsystems) face common problems or overlapping responsibility. This is most often seen when members of two separate groups are interdependently related in achieving an objective but have separate accountability.	What is the nature of the relations between two groups? Are goals clear? Is responsibility clear? What major problems do the two groups face? What structural conditions promote/inhibit effective interface management?	Interviews, third-party observations, and observation of group meetings are common methods for diagnosing these processes

Table 6-2 *(cont.)*

Superior-subordinate relations	Formal hierarchical relations in organizations dictate that some people lead and others follow: these situations are often a source of many organizational problems.	What are the extant leadership styles? What problems arise between superiors and subordinates?	Questionnaires can show overall leadership climate and norms. Interviews and questionnaires reveal the desired leadership behaviors.
Technological and engineering systems	All organizations rely on multiple technologies—for production and operations, for information processing, for planning, for marketing, etc., to produce goods and services.	Are the technologies adequate for satisfactory performance? What is the state of the art and how does this organization's technology compare with that? Should any changes in technology be planned and implemented?	Generally this is not an area of expertise of the OD consultant. He or she must then seek help from "experts" either inside the organization or outside. Interviews and group discussions focused on technology are among the best ways to determine the adequacy of technological systems. Sometimes outside experts conduct an audit and make recommendations; sometimes inside experts do so.
Strategic management and long-range planning Vision/Mission formulation	Monitoring the environment, adding and deleting "products," predicting future events, and making decisions that affect the long-term viability of the organization must occur for the organization to remain competitive and effective. Vision and mission establish the framework for strategy.	Who is responsible for "looking ahead" and for making long-range decisions? Do they have adequate tools and support? Have recent long-range decisions been effective? What is the nature of current and future environmental demands? What are the unique strengths and competencies of the organization? What are the threats to the organization? Is mission clear? Widely shared?	Interviews of key policy-makers, group discussions, and examination of historical records give insights to this dimension.
Organizational learning	Learning from past successes and failures, from present "blind spots" and from all organizational members is essential to remain competitive, vital, and to develop new paradigms.	What are our strengths, problem areas? What observations, ideas, suggestions are available from all organizational members? Does our present behavior square with what we espouse? What are the "learning disabilities" (Senge) of this organization? Are the present paradigms changing? What will the new paradigms be like? Are we recording our learnings, our philosophy, our progress?	Interviews, questionnaires, group methods of diagnosis; examination of assumptions and culture (Schein[b]); games and exercises to create awareness of organizational learning disabilities; examination of defensive routines (Argyris,[c] Senge[c]); visioning, including environment analysis.

[a] Peter M. Senge, *The Fifth Discipline: The Art and Practice of the Learning Organization* (New York: Doubleday/Currency, 1990), pp. 12, 18–19, 44.
[b] Edgar Schein, "Organization Development and the Study of the Organizational Culture," *Academy of Management Newsletter* (Summer 1990). pp. 3–5.
[c] Chris Argyris, "Teaching Smart People How to Learn," *Harvard Business Review*, 69 (May–June 1991), pp. 99–109.
[d] Peter M. Senge, *The Fifth Discipline*, pp. 237–238.

vance—emergent" continuum. We have some structured questions but follow up on leads as they develop in the course of the diagnosis. We also tend to use the diagnostic categories of Tables 6-1 and 6-2 because we focus on system and subsystem cultures and processes.

Furthermore, in an OD program, not only are the *results* of diagnostic activities important but *how the information is collected* and *what is done with the information* are also significant aspects of the process. There is active collaboration between the OD practitioner and the organization members about such issues as what target groups are to be diagnosed, how the diagnosis is best accomplished, what processes and dynamics should be analyzed, what is to be done with the information, how the data will be worked with, and how the information will be used to aid action planning. Usually information is collected through a variety of methods—interviews, observations, questionnaires, and organization records. Information is generally considered to be the property of those persons who generated it; the data serve as the foundation for planning actions. This is basically an action research model. Therefore, the diagnostic component and the action component are intimately related in organization development.

The Six-Box Model

Another diagnostic tool is Marvin Weisbord's six-box model, a diagnostic framework published in 1976, and still widely used by OD practitioners.[5] This model tells practitioners where to look and what to look for in diagnosing organizational problems. As shown in Figure 6-2, Weisbord identifies six critical areas—purposes, structure, rewards, helpful mechanisms, relationships, and leadership—where things must go right if the organization is to be successful. Practitioners use this model as a cognitive map, systematically examining the processes and activities of each box, looking for signs of trouble. Assume there are problems with a major product produced by the organization. These problems will have their causes in dysfunctional processes located in one or more of the six boxes. The problems could be caused by ill-advised structures, poor leadership, unclear purposes or purposes at variance with the product, lack of helpful mechanisms, and so on. The six-box model is a simple but powerful diagnostic tool.

According to Weisbord, the consultant must attend to both the *formal* and *informal* aspects of each box. The formal system represents the official ways things are supposed to happen; the informal system represents the ways things really happen. For example, the formal reporting of relationships and organization of tasks and people prescribed in the structure box may not reflect the real structural arrangements found in the informal system. The practitioner needs answers to two questions: First, are the arrangements and processes called for by the *formal* system

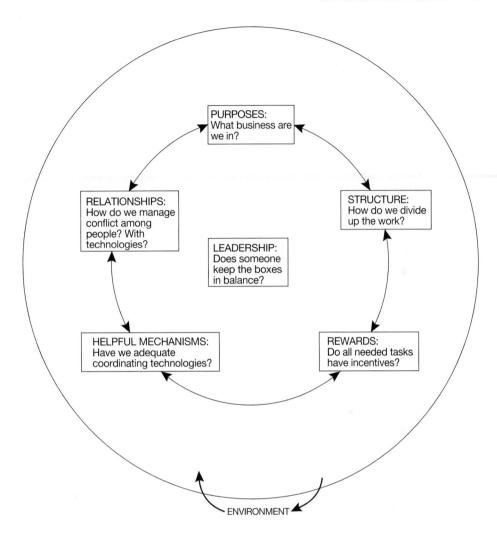

Figure 6–2. The Six-Box Organizational Model

Source: Marvin R. Weisbord, "Organizational Diagnosis: Six Places to Look With or Without a Theory," *Group and Organizational Studies*, 1 (1976), pp. 430–447. Reprinted by permission.

correct for each box? Second, are the arrangements and processes developed by the *informal* system *correct* for each box? It is common to find that formal arrangements are inappropriate, but the informal system works around that by developing methods to correct the deficiency. By the same token, it is common to find that the formal system is correctly designed, but the informal system is not following those correct procedures and consequently performance suffers. The formal/informal distinction, that is, what's supposed to happen versus what is really happening, is a powerful element of OD practice theory and one of the secrets to understanding organizational dynamics. Weisbord recommends a thorough diagnosis, looking at multiple boxes, before choosing interventions.

"Third-Wave Consulting"

About ten years after the six-box model appeared, Weisbord wrote an article titled, "Toward Third-Wave Managing and Consulting," in which he reconsiders the issues of diagnosis and intervention.[6] "Third wave" refers to the assertion by futurist Alvin Toffler that the world has progressed through the agricultural revolution (the first wave) and the industrial revolution (the second wave), and is poised on the brink of an information and technological revolution (the third wave), in which the hallmark will be rampant change in virtually all institutions of society. Weisbord believes this requires new paradigms for managing and consulting. As far as diagnosis and intervention are concerned, Weisbord no longer likes a problem-centered, "sickness" model of organizational diagnosis where the diagnosis leads to a list of problems, and interventions are designed to cure the problems. Instead, he prefers to focus on "wellness," to help people achieve the desired futures chosen by them, and to create workplaces that have meaning and community. Operationally, this means moving from a view of the consultant as an expert on diagnosis and intervention, to a view of the consultant as a stage manager of *events to help people do what they are trying to do.*

Weisbord identifies four "useful practices" for the third-wave consultant: (1) assess the potential for action (look for conditions where there are committed leadership, good business opportunities, and energized people); (2) get the "whole system" in the room; (3) focus on the future; and (4) structure tasks that people can do for themselves. This optimistic, goal-oriented view for helping people in organizations is a valuable perspective on diagnosis. More information on this approach can be found in Chapter 11 and in Weisbord's *Productive Workplaces.*[7]

THE ACTION COMPONENT: OD INTERVENTIONS

Organization development is a process for improving organizational performance by causing changes in the organization's culture and processes. Improving processes and culture is done through OD interventions, which are *sets of structured activities* in which selected organizational units (target groups or individuals) engage with a task or sequence of tasks where the task goals are related to organizational improvement. Interventions are actions taken to produce desired changes.

Typically, one of four conditions gives rise to the need for OD interventions. First, there is a problem; something is "broken." Corrective actions—interventions—are implemented to "fix" the problem. Second, there is an unrealized opportunity; something we want is beyond our reach. Enabling actions—interventions—are developed to seize the opportunity. Third, features of the organization are out of alignment; parts of the organization are working at cross-purposes. Alignment activities—interventions—are developed to get things back "in sync." Fourth, the vision that guides the organization changes; yesterday's vision is no longer good enough. Actions to build the necessary structures, processes, and culture to support the new vision—interventions—are developed to make the new vision a reality. In summary, interventions are planned sets of actions to change those situations the organization members want to change.

The range of OD interventions is quite extensive. Interventions have been developed to solve most problems related to the human side of organizations. For example, interventions focus on the target groups of Table 6-1 and the organizational processes of Table 6-2. Thus, when problems are discovered in organizational systems, subsystems, or processes, intervention activities can be initiated to remedy the problems. An inventory of OD interventions is given in Chapters 9 through 13.

The Nature of OD Interventions

To intervene in the client system is to interpose or interject activities into the normal activities of the organization in such a way that the intervention activities are done *in addition to* the normal activities or are done *instead of* the normal activities. An example of an "in addition to" intervention would be for a staff group to include a "process critique" at the end of each staff meeting. This simply means that a few minutes are set aside to look at "how we worked"—the process—during the meeting. Critiquing "how we worked" can enable the group to correct any deficient processes and become more effective in its deliberations. An example of an "instead of" intervention would be getting a key service department of an organization to hold an "organization mirroring" workshop with its user-clients to determine how the clients view the services provided and how they want the services changed or improved. In this case, instead of the normal activities of begging, cajoling, or coercing the user-clients to utilize the staff services, a problem-solving workshop called the organization mirror is convened in which the clients give feedback to the service group regarding services and a two-way dialogue is established between service providers and service users. Such a meeting would probably not be a normal activity in the organization.

A well-designed OD program unfolds according to a strategy or game plan, called the *overall OD strategy*. This strategy may be planned in advance or may emerge over time as events dictate. The strategy is based on answers to such questions as the following: What are the overall change/improvement goals of the program? What parts of the organization are most ready and receptive to the OD program? What are the key leverage points (individuals and groups) in the organization? What are the most pressing problems of the client organization? What resources are available for the program in terms of client time and energy and internal and external facilitators? Answers to these questions lead the practitioner to develop a game plan for where to intervene in the system, what to do, the sequencing of interventions, and so forth.

It can be seen that planning actions, executing actions, and evaluating the consequences of actions are an integral and essential part of organization development. This emphasis on action planning and action taking is a powerful feature of OD and, in some respects, is a distinguishing one. In many traditional educational and training activities, learning and action taking are separated in that the knowledge and skills are "learned" in one setting, say, in a classroom, and are then taken back to the organization with the learner being admonished to practice what he or she has learned, that is, to take actions. This artificial separation is minimized in most OD interventions in several ways. First, in many intervention activities there are two goals: a learning or educational goal and an accomplishing-a-task goal. Second, OD problem-solving interventions tend to focus on real organization problems that are central to the needs of the organization rather than on hypothetical, abstract problems that may or may not fit the members' needs. Third, OD interventions utilize several learning models, not just one. Let us examine these three points in more detail.

The dual aspect of OD interventions can be clarified with an illustration. Let us say that the top executives of an organization spend three days together in a workshop in which they do the following things: (1) explore the need for and desirability of a long-range strategic plan for the organization; (2) learn how to formulate such a strategy by analyzing other strategies, determining what the strategic variables are, being shown a sequence of steps for preparing a comprehensive plan, and so forth; and (3) actually make a three-year strategic plan for the organization.[8] This intervention combines the dual features of learning and action: the executives engaged in activities in which they learned about strategic planning, and they then generated a strategy. In some OD interventions, the "learning aspect" predominates, and in others, the "action aspect" predominates; but both aspects are present in most interventions.

Organization development interventions tend to focus on real problems rather than on abstract problems. The problems facing organization members are real, not hypothetical; the problems members get rewarded for solving are real, not hypothetical; and the problems central to the needs of organization members are real, not hypothetical.

Developing the skills and knowledge to solve real problems as they arise in their "natural state" means that the educational problem of "transfer of learning" from one situation to another is minimized (although the problem of generalization, that is, knowing the appropriate times and places to apply this particular set of skills and knowledge, is still present.)

An additional feature of working on real problems in OD interventions is that the real set of individuals involved in the problem is the group the problem solvers work with. For example, in a human relations class, if a manager were having trouble understanding and working with minority subordinates, he or she would perhaps "role play" the situation with the instructor or fellow students. In OD, the manager would probably interact with the minority employees with whom he or she was having difficulties—but would do so in carefully structured activities that have a high probability of resulting in learning for both parties and a high probability of being a "success experience" for both parties.

Organization development programs rely on several learning models. For example if "learning how to" do something precedes "doing" it, then we have a somewhat traditional approach to learning that most people are familiar with. If the "doing" precedes the "learning how to," then we have a "deficiency" model of learning in which the learning comes primarily from critiquing the actions after the fact to see how they could have been done differently and, presumably, better. Both models are viable learning modes, and both are used extensively in organization development.

Action programs in OD are closely linked with explicit goals and objectives. Careful attention is given to the problem of translating goals into observable, explicit, and measurable actions or behaviors, and equal care is given to the related problem of ensuring that actions are relevant to and instrumental for goal attainment. Such questions as the following thus become an integral part of organizational life: How does this action relate to the goal we have established? What are the action implications of that goal for me, my subordinates, my group? When we say we want to achieve a certain goal, what do we really mean by that, in measurable terms? Given several alternative forms of action, which one seems most appropriate to achieve the goal we have set?

Diagnosis, action taking, and goal setting are inextricably related in an OD program. Diagnostic activities are precursors to action programs; that is, fact-finding is done to provide a foundation for action. Actions are continuously evaluated for their contribution to goal accomplishment. Goals are continuously evaluated in terms of their appropriateness—whether or not they are attainable and whether or not they can be translated into action programs. Organization development is a continuous process of the cycling of setting goals and objectives, collecting data about the status quo, planning and taking actions based on hypotheses and on the data, and evaluating the effects of action through additional data collection.

Analyzing Discrepancies

A useful model for thinking about diagnosis and intervention could be termed *discrepancy analysis*—examination of the discrepancies or gaps between what is happening and what should be happening, and discrepancies between where one is and where one wants to be. Discrepancies, therefore, define both problems and goals. Discrepancies require *study* (diagnosis and planning) and *action* if the gaps are to be eliminated. We believe that a good part of OD is problem solving, hence, discrepancy analysis. Action research describes an iterative problem-solving process that is essentially discrepancy analysis and linking that to action taking. Any manager's primary task is essentially discrepancy analysis—the study of problems and opportunities (goals) or the study of the discrepancies between where one is and where one wants to be. Organization development provides technologies for studying and closing gaps.

This simple but powerful analytical model is presented clearly and effectively by Charles Kepner and Benjamin Tregoe in *The Rational Manager* and *The New Rational Manager*.[9] Their ideas have been translated into training seminars to improve problem-solving and decision-making skills. Kepner and Tregoe state, "The problem analyzer has an expected standard of performance, a 'should' against which to compare actual performance. . . . A problem is a deviation from a standard of performance."[10] According to these authors, a problem is a gap; problem solving is discovering the *cause* of the gap; decision making is discovering a *solution*—a set of actions—to close the gap.

In *The New Science of Management Decision*, Herbert Simon proposed a discrepancy model of problem analysis.[11] He stated that a problem is a deviation from an expected standard and a cause of a problem is a *change* of some sort. Simon's conclusions were derived from his studies of human cognitive processes and computer science. His model is one of analyzing gaps. Kepner and Tregoe call Simon's book "the best statement of problem-solving theory to be found in the literature on the subject."[12]

Goals also represent gaps—gaps between where we are and where we want to be. Goal setting is the process of defining or imposing a gap; goal accomplishment is made possible by taking actions to close the gap.

Organization development is more than just problem solving and goal seeking. But a large part of any OD program is devoted to these two critical activities. The discrepancy analysis approach is a fruitful way to conceptualize problems and goals.

THE PROGRAM MANAGEMENT COMPONENT

Just as OD practitioners apply behavioral science principles and practices to improve organizational functioning and individual development, they apply these same principles and practices as they plan, implement, and manage OD programs. They attend equally to task and process, consider system ramifications of the program, involve organization members in planning and execution, use an action research model, create feedback loops to ensure relevance and timeliness, and so forth. Managing the OD program effectively means the difference between success and failure. The aim of this section is to provide guidelines to help ensure success in managing OD programs. Specifically, we examine the phases involved in OD programs, a change management model, and a procedure for creating parallel learning structures.

Phases of OD Programs

OD programs follow a logical progression of events—a series of phases that unfolds over time. An important part of managing an OD program well is to execute each phase well. Warner Burke describes the following phases of OD programs:

1. Entry
2. Contracting
3. Diagnosis
4. Feedback
5. Planning change
6. Intervention
7. Evaluation[13]

Entry represents the initial contact between consultant and client, exploration of the situation that stimulated the client to seek a consultant, and exploration aimed at determining whether the problem or opportunity, the client, and the consultant constitute a good match. *Contracting* involves establishing mutual expectations, reaching agreement on expenditures of time, money, resources, and energy, and generally clarifying what each party expects to get from the other and give to the other. (We say more about entry and contracting in Chapter 14.) *Diagnosis* is the fact-finding phase in which a picture of the situation is gained through interviews, observations, questionnaires, examination of organization documents and information, and the like. Burke observes that there are two steps within the diagnostic phase—gathering information and analyzing it. *Feedback* represents the return of the analyzed information to the client system; exploration of the information by the clients for understanding, clarification, and accuracy; and the beginning of ownership of the data by the clients as their data, their picture of the situation, and their problems and opportunities. *Planning change* involves the clients deciding what action steps to take based on the information they have just learned. Alternative possibilities are explored and critiqued; plans for action are selected and developed. *Intervention* implements sets of actions designed to correct the problems or seize the opportunities. *Evaluation* represents assessing the effects of the program: Was it successful? What changes occurred? What were the causal mechanisms? Are we satisfied with the results?

These phases are straightforward and logical in description, but in practice they often overlap a great deal and look more like an evolving process than a linear progression. But the most important point is that each phase builds the foundation for subsequent phases; therefore, each phase must be executed with care and precision. For example, if expectations are not clear in the contracting phase, this mismatch will surface later in unmet expectations and dissatisfaction. Or, if the analysis of the data during the diagnosis phase is incorrect, interventions may not be relevant or appropriate. These phases of OD programs serve as an overall road map for practitioners.

A Model for Managing Change

Another way to think about managing OD programs is to ask the question: What are the key ingredients involved in successful change efforts? Cummings and Worley identify five sets of activities required for effective change management: (1) motivating change, (2) creating a vision, (3) developing political support, (4) managing the transition, and (5) sustaining momentum.[14] These are shown in Figure 6-3.

Getting people to want to change, to believe change is necessary, and to commit to abandoning the status quo for an uncertain future is the first step. Cummings and Worley suggest three methods for *creating readiness to change*: sensitize people about the pressures for change, that is, why change must occur; show discrepancies between the current (undesirable) state of affairs and the future (more desirable) state of affairs; and communicate positive, realistic expectations for the advantages of the change. Concerning readiness, one of the greatest motivators for change is *pain*—things aren't working, profits and market share are dropping, survival is in doubt—these conditions increase readiness for change. The next set of activities, *overcoming resistance to change*, is achieved through three methods: dealing empathetically with feelings of loss and anxiety, providing extensive communication about the change effort and how it is proceeding, and encouraging participation and involvement by organization members in planning and executing the change. As the authors write: "One of the oldest and most effective strategies for overcoming resistance is to involve organizational members directly in planning and implementing change."[15]

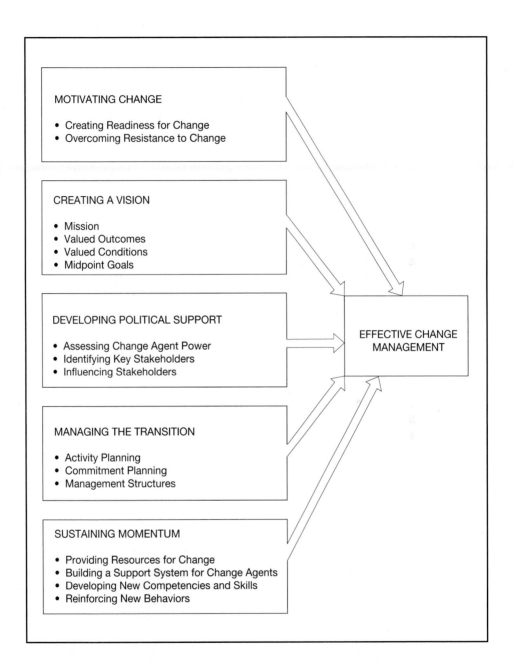

Figure 6–3 Activities Contributing to Effective Change Management

Source: Reprinted by permission from p. 145 of *Organization Development and Change*, 5th ed., by T. G. Cummings and C. G. Worley; Copyright © 1993 by West Publishing Company. All rights reserved.

Creating a *vision* provides a picture of the future and shows how individuals and groups will fit into that future. Visions reduce uncertainty, serve as goals to energize behavior, show that the future will be beneficial, and demonstrate that the future is attainable. The mission, values, and conditions provide tangible goals to which organization members can direct their energies. *Developing political support* is a critical factor in successful change efforts. Powerful individuals and groups must be convinced that the change is *good for them* or at least will not significantly harm them, or else they will resist and even sabotage the effort. Cummings and Worley suggest that the practitioner should assess his or her own power in the situation, identify the key players whose support is required for success, and persuade those key players that the change will have positive benefits for them.

Activities related to *managing the transition* are extremely important. Richard Beckhard and Reuben Harris addressed this topic in their book, *Organizational Transitions: Managing Complex Change.*[16] Beckhard and Harris proposed that change efforts move through three states: the current state, the transition state, and the desired future state in that order, and they suggest three sets of activities for managing the transition state. "Activity planning" involves specifying the sequence of activities, events, and milestones that must occur during the transition. This serves as a road map for the organization members and as a checklist for measuring progress. "Commitment planning" involves getting the support and commitment from those key players in the organization whose leadership, resources, and energy are needed to make the transition succeed. "Management structures" involve setting up parallel learning structures to initiate, lead, monitor, and facilitate the change. Finally, the Cummings and Worley model lists several methods for *sustaining momentum* in order to complete and stabilize the change. We think this model is valuable for managing OD programs.

Creating Parallel Learning Structures

Earlier we discussed the important role of parallel learning structures as devices for introducing and managing change in large bureaucratic organizations. Change programs in large-scale systems almost always utilize parallel structures. Bushe and Shani developed what they call the *generic parallel learning structure intervention process*, which is shown in Figure 6-4.[17]

Phases 1 and 2 focus on establishing the need for change, building readiness and commitment, and creating an infrastructure that has sufficient political support and executive leadership to sustain the change program. The steering committee includes members from a cross section of the organization; it is headed by one or more top executives. Phase 3 communicates openly what is happening and why. Phase 4 solic-

Phase 1:	Initial Definition of Purpose and Scope
Phase 2:	Formation of a Steering Committee
	2.1 Re-examining the need for change
	2.2 Creating a vision statement
	2.3 Defining boundaries, strategies, expectations, and rewards
Phase 3:	Communicating to Organization Members
Phase 4:	Formation and Development of Study Groups
	4.1 Selecting and developing internal facilitators
	4.2 Selecting study group members
	4.3 Study group development
	4.4 Establishing working procedures and norms
Phase 5:	The Inquiry Process
Phase 6:	Identifying Potential Changes
Phase 7:	Experimental Implementation of Proposed Changes
Phase 8:	System-wide Diffusion and Evaluation

Figure 6-4   The Generic Parallel Learning Structure Intervention Process

Source: Gervase R. Bushe and A. B. Shani, *Parallel Learning Structures* (Table 7.1), p. 125. © 1991 by Addison-Wesley Publishing Company, Inc. Reprinted by permission of the publisher.

its widespread participation and involvement from organization members; this increases involvement and ownership of the change and increases the number of good ideas available. Phases 5, 6, and 7 represent extensive study, data collection, targeting of high-priority problems, and experimentation to find solutions to problems. Solutions (changes) that work are then diffused throughout the organization. This model is presented here to show the flow of events and the things to consider when managing large-scale OD programs.

Summary of Program Management Issues

These ideas about managing OD programs describe some of the important factors OD practitioners take into account as they plan and implement change efforts. Program management is complex, dynamic, difficult, and great fun. The challenges are many, but the sense of accomplishment is great for practitioners, leaders, and organization members alike as successes build upon successes and the organization realizes its goals.

We close this section with a comment by Warner Burke, who writes:

> The toughest job is to *manage* the change process. In writing about this management process, I can be logical, rational, and perhaps convey that dealing with organizational change is indeed subject to management. In reality, however, managing change is sloppy—people never do exactly as we plan. And it follows Murphy's Law—if anything can go wrong, it will. Moreover, organizational politics is always present and change, after all, affects us all emotionally.[18]

CONCLUDING COMMENTS

Three components—diagnosis, intervention, and program management—critical to all organization development programs have been explored in this chapter. Each is important in its own right; all are vital to success. The more people learn about these three components, the more effective they will become in their organizational improvement efforts. Organization development is a complex blend of art, science, and craft that is gained through the study and mastery of these three components.

NOTES

1. Richard Beckhard, *Organization Development: Strategies and Models* (Reading, MA: Addison-Wesley Publishing Company, 1969), p. 26.
2. This "actual condition" versus "ideal condition" discrepancy model is an integral feature of Kurt Lewin's force-field analysis, and appears, in fact, to be basic to all human goal-seeking and problem-solving activities. See K. Lewin, *Field Theory in Social Science* (New York: Harper & Row, 1951). See also George A. Miller, Eugene Galanter, and Karl H. Pribram, *Plans and the Structure of Behavior* (New York: Holt, Rinehart and Winston, 1960).
3. Chris Argyris, *Intervention Theory and Method: A Behavioral Science View* (Reading, MA: Addison-Wesley Publishing Company, 1970).
4. Ibid., pp. 16–17.
5. Marvin R. Weisbord, "Organizational Diagnosis: Six Places to Look for Trouble With or Without a Theory," *Group & Organization Studies* (December 1976), pp. 430–447.
6. Marvin R. Weisbord, "Toward Third-Wave Managing and Consulting," *Organizational Dynamics* (1987), pp. 5–24. See also Alvin Toffler, *The Third Wave* (New York: Bantam Books, 1980).
7. Marvin R. Weisbord, *Productive Workplaces* (San Francisco: Jossey-Bass Publishers, 1987).
8. Actually, in a real strategic planning session, steps 1 and 2 might take place during the first session, with that session concluding with homework assignments to the team in order that the necessary information for the strategic plan could be generated. Then, in a second session, step 3 would be finalized.
9. Charles H. Kepner and Benjamin B. Tregoe, *The Rational Manager* (New York: McGraw-Hill, 1965). A revised edition appeared in 1981 titled *The New Rational Manager*. These books are highly recommended for OD practitioners.
10. Kepner and Tregoe, *The Rational Manager*, p. 44.
11. Herbert A. Simon, *The New Science of Management Decision* (New York: Harper & Row, 1960).
12. Kepner and Tregoe, *The Rational Manager*, p. 252.
13. W. W. Burke, *Organization Development: A Process of Learning and Changing* (Reading, MA: Addison-Wesley Publishing Company, 1994), see Chapter 4.
14. T. G. Cummings and C. G. Worley, *Organization Development and Change* (Minneapolis, MN: West Publishing Company, 1993), see Chapter 8.
15. Ibid., p. 148.
16. R. Beckhard and R. T. Harris, *Organizational Transitions: Managing Complex Change*, 2nd ed. (Reading, MA: Addison-Wesley Publishing Company, 1987).
17. G. R. Bushe and A. B. Shani, *Parallel Learning Structures* (Reading, MA: Addison-Wesley Publishing Company, 1991), see Chapter 7. This figure is from p. 125.
18. Burke, *Organization Development*, pp. 146–147.

7

ACTION RESEARCH AND ORGANIZATION DEVELOPMENT

Action research is research on action with the goals of making that action more effective while simultaneously building a body of scientific knowledge. Action refers to programs and interventions designed to solve problems and improve conditions. Kurt Lewin, the consummate applied social scientist, proposed action research as a new methodology in behavioral science because of his interest in eradicating the problems of society. Lewin believed that *research on action programs*, especially social change programs, was imperative if progress was to be made in solving social problems. Action research, he thought, would address several needs simultaneously: the pressing need for greater knowledge about the causes and dynamics of social ills; the need to understand the laws of social change; the need for greater collaboration and joint inquiry between scientists and practitioners; the need for "richer" data about real-world problems; the need to discover workable, practical solutions to problems; and the need to discover general laws explaining complex social phenomena.[1]

Action research is one of the cornerstones of organization development, underlying both the theory and practice of the field. We first examine action research from two perspectives, as a process and as a problem-solving approach. Next the history and varieties of action research are explored. Finally, examples of action research in OD are given.

ACTION RESEARCH: A PROCESS AND AN APPROACH

Action research may be described as a process, that is, as an ongoing series of events and actions. Used in this way, it is defined as follows: Action research is the process of systematically collecting research data about an ongoing system relative to some objective, goal, or need of that system; feeding these data back into the system; taking actions by altering selected variables within the system based both on the data and on hypotheses; and evaluating the results of actions by collecting more data. This definition characterizes action research in terms of the activities comprising the process. First, a static picture is taken of an organization. On the basis of "what exists," hunches and hypotheses suggest actions; these actions typically entail manipulating variables in the system that are under the control of the action researcher (this often means doing something differently from the way it has always been done). Later a second static picture is taken of the system to examine the effects of the action taken. These steps are very similar to the steps OD practitioners use when they execute OD programs.

Several authors have noted the importance of viewing action research as a process. In a study of the Tremont Hotel in Chicago, William F. Whyte and Edith L. Hamilton described their work as follows:

> What was the project? It was an action-research program for management. We developed a process for applying human relations research findings to the changing of organization behavior. The word *process* is important, for this was not a one-shot affair. The project involved a continuous gathering and analysis of human relations research data and the feeding of the findings into the organization in such a way as to change behavior.[2]

This study by Whyte and Hamilton is a cogent example of the relation of action research to OD. Although the study itself was conducted in 1945 and 1946—before the term *organization development* was introduced—it would be considered an OD program today, even though it was based solely on an action research model.

French shows how action research can be used as a generic process in organization development (see Figure 7-1). The process is iterative and cyclical.[3] He clarifies the model as follows:

> The key aspects of the model are *diagnosis, data gathering, feedback to the client group, data discussion and work by the client group, action planning, and action.* The sequence tends to be cyclical, with the focus on new or advanced problems as the client group learns to work more effectively together.[4]

Action research is a process in two different ways. It is a sequence

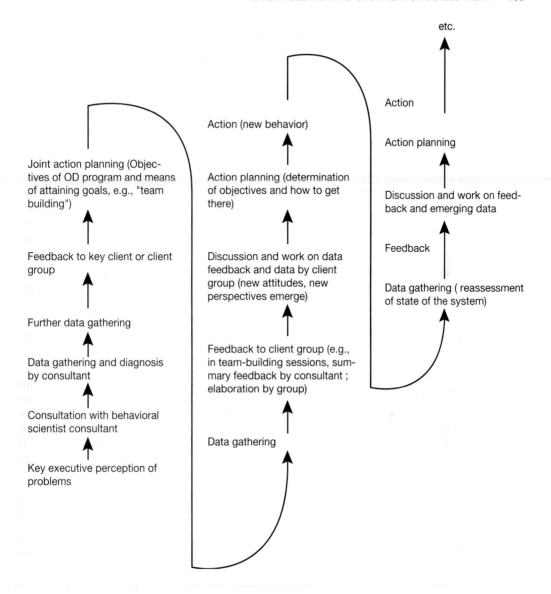

Figure 7-1   An Action Research Model for Organization Development

Source: Copyright 1969 by the Regents of the University of California. Reprinted from *California Management Review*, Vol. XII, No. 2, p. 26, Figure 1. By permission of the Regents.

of events and activities within each iteration (data collection, feedback and working with the data, and taking action based on the data); and it is a cycle of iterations of these activities, sometimes treating the same problem through several cycles and sometimes moving to different problems in each cycle.

Action research may also be described as an approach to problem solving, thus suggesting its usefulness as a model, guide, or paradigm. Used in this way, *action research* may be defined as follows: action research is the application of the scientific method of fact-finding and experimentation to practical problems requiring action solutions and involving the collaboration and cooperation of scientists, practitioners, and laypersons. The desired outcomes of the action research approach are solutions to the immediate problems and a contribution to scientific knowledge and theory. Viewing action research from this perspective points up additional features that are important.

Action research was the conceptual model for an early organization improvement program in a group of oil refineries. Herbert Shepard, one of the behavioral scientists involved in that program, defines the nature of action research as follows:

> The action-research model is a normative model for learning, or a model for planned change. Its main features are these. In front of intelligent human action there should be an objective, be it ever so fuzzy or distorted. And in advance of human action there should be planning, although knowledge of paths to the objective is always inadequate. Action itself should be taken a step at a time, and after each step it is well to do some fact-finding. The fact-finding may disclose whether the objective is realistic, whether it is nearer or more distant than before, whether it needs alteration. Through fact-finding, the present situation can be assessed, and this information, together with information about the objective, can be used in planning the second step. Movement toward an objective consists of a series of such cycles of planning-acting-fact-finding-planning.[5]

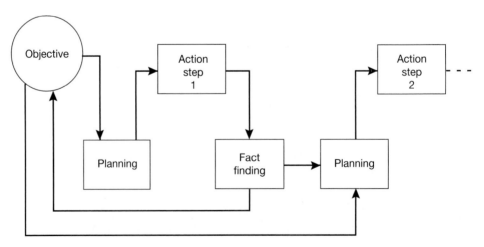

Figure 7-2 Action Research Model

Source: Herbert A. Shepard, "An Action Research Model" in *An Action Research Program for Organization Improvement*, Ann Arbor, MI: Foundation for Research on Human Behavior, 1960. Used with permission.

Shepard's concept of the action research model is shown in Figure 7-2.[6]

Shepard highlights the relations among goals (objectives), planning, and action in his diagram—a point we think is a very important feature of action research. And both he and French emphasize that action research is research inextricably linked to action; it is research with a purpose, that is, to guide present and future action.

In an action research approach, the role of the consultant/ change agent takes on a special form, as shown by Shepard:

> The role is to help the manager plan his actions and design his fact-finding procedures in such a way that he can learn from them, to serve such ends as becoming a more skillful manager, setting more realistic objectives, discovering better ways of organizing. In this sense, the staff concerned with follow-up are research consultants. Their task is to help managers formulate management problems as experiments.[7]

By viewing action research as an approach to problem solving we have noted the following features: the normative nature of this model, the importance and centrality of goals and objectives, and the different role requirements of the consultant/change agent vis-à-vis the clients. Three additional features deserve discussion: first, the elements of the action research model that link it to the scientific method of inquiry, second, the collaborative relation among scientists, practitioners, and laypersons that often is a component of action research, and third, the increased richness of the knowledge that can be derived from action research programs.

The paradigm for problematical inquiry that serves both as the model for the scientific method and as the model for action research was introduced by the philosopher John Dewey in his book *How We Think*.[8] He identified the following five phases of reflective thinking: suggestion, intellectualization, hypothesizing, reasoning, and testing the hypothesis by action. This approach to problem solving is translated into the scientific method as follows. First, the scientist is confronted with a *problem, obstacle, or new idea* that he or she wants to understand (Dewey's suggestion phase). The scientist identifies the problem, intellectualizes about it (what we usually call "thinking"), and arrives at the point where an *hypothesis* about the problem can be formulated. (An *hypothesis* is a conjectural statement positing the relations between two or more phenomena, usually referred to as a "cause" and an "effect.") The next step, a critical one, consists of the scientist *reasoning or deducing the consequences of the hypothesis*. The final step consists of *observing, testing, or experimenting* to see if the relation between the two phenomena expressed in the hypothesis is verified or disconfirmed.[9]

These steps for the scientific method are identical with the steps outlined by Corey for action research:

The significant elements of a design for action research are

1. The identification of a problem area about which an individual or a group is sufficiently concerned to want to take some action.

2. The selection of a specific problem and the formulation of a hypothesis or prediction that implies a goal and a procedure for reaching it. This specific goal must be viewed in relation to the total situation.

3. The careful recording of actions taken and the accumulation of evidence to determine the degree to which the goal has been achieved.

4. The inference from this evidence of generalizations regarding the relation between the actions and the desired goal.

5. The continuous retesting of these generalizations in action situations.

If the problem under attack is one of concern to many people, or if it is likely that the experiment will affect many people, the action research should involve these people. It then becomes *cooperative* action research.[10]

An example applying action research to a typical organizational problem might be helpful. Suppose that the problem is unproductive staff meetings—they are poorly attended, members express low commitment and involvement in them, and they are generally agreed to be unproductive. Suppose also that you are the manager in charge of both the meetings and the staff and that you desire to make the meetings a vital, productive instrument for your organization. Following the action research model, the first step is to gather data about the status quo. Assume that this has been done and that the data suggest the meetings are generally disliked and regarded as unproductive. The next step is to search for causes of the problem and to generate one or more hypotheses from which you deduce the consequences that will allow the hypotheses to be tested. Say you come up with the following four hypotheses. Note the very important feature that an action research hypothesis consists of two aspects: a goal and an action or procedure for achieving that goal.

1. Staff meetings will be more productive if I solicit and use agenda topics from the staff rather than have the agenda made up just by me.

2. Staff meetings will be more productive if I rotate the chair of the meeting among the staff rather than my always being chairperson.

3. Staff meetings will be more productive if we hold them once a week instead of twice a week.

4. I have always run the staff meetings in a brisk "all-business no-nonsense" fashion; perhaps if I encourage more discussion and am more open about how I am reacting to what is being said, then staff meetings will be more productive.

Each of these action research hypotheses has a goal, or objective (better staff meeting productivity), and each has an action, or procedure, for achieving the goal. Additional work would be done to clarify and specify the goal and the actions in more detail, and then the hypotheses would be systematically tested (implemented) one at a time and evaluated for their effects through data collection.

Another distinguishing feature of action research is collaboration between individuals inside the system—clients—and individuals outside the system—change agents or researchers. Almost all authors stress the collaborative nature of action research, with some seeing it as the primary reason for the model's efficacy.[11] It is a widely held belief that people support what they have helped to create. Such a belief is highly congruent with the collaborative aspect of the action research model and impels practitioners and researchers alike to cooperate extensively with client system members. Such a point of view implies that the client system members and the researcher should *jointly* define the problems they want to address, define the methods used for data collection, identify the hypotheses relevant to the situations, and evaluate the consequences of actions taken. This collaborative ingredient of action research is particularly important in organization development.

As scientists and laypersons work together to understand and change a problematic condition, that joint inquiry process typically yields rich data and insights about the phenomenon of interest. The problem is a real one, not hypothetical; the actors know more about the situation than the outsiders do; and the actors have a vested interest in getting to the true facts since they will benefit from the solution. As Shani and Bushe observe: "It is the development of high-quality relations between action researchers and organizational members that creates access to important information that otherwise might not be available to outsiders. . . ."[12] As Deutsch observes, this was an appealing characteristic of action research for Kurt Lewin:

> In addition to the value that action research might have for social agencies, Lewin felt that linking research to social action might give the social scientist access to basic social processes which he would otherwise be unable to study. Furthermore, Lewin's orientation to dynamics in individual and group psychology led him to the conclusion that change studies are necessary to reveal underlying processes. Since the social scientist is rarely in the position to create social change on his own initiative, he has much to gain through cooperation with social agencies that attempt to produce social and community change.[13]

Because the data available in action research are so rich, this adds to the value of action research as a problem-solving approach.

HISTORY AND VARIETIES OF ACTION RESEARCH

John Dewey translated the scientific method of problem solving into terms understandable by practitioners and laypersons, and these seminal ideas were incorporated into action research several years later. The origin of action research can be traced to two independent sources. One source, John Collier, was a man of practical affairs; the other, Kurt Lewin, was a man of science. John Collier was commissioner of Indian Affairs from 1933 to 1945, a role in which he had to diagnose problems and recommend remedial programs for the improvement of race relations. Collier found that effecting changes in ethnic relations was an extremely difficult process and required *joint effort* on the part of the scientist (researcher), the administrator (practitioner), and the layperson (client).

> Principle seven I would call the first and the last: that research and then more research is essential to the program, that in the ethnic field research can be made a tool of action essential to all the other tools, indeed, that it ought to be the master tool. But we had in mind a particular kind of research, or, if you will, particular conditions. We had in mind research impelled from central areas of needed action. And since action is by nature not only specialized but also integrative to more than the specialities, our needed research must be of the integrative sort. Again, since the findings of the research must be carried into effect by the administrator and the layman, and must be criticized by them through their experience, the administrator and the layman must themselves participate creatively in the research, impelled as it is from their own area of need.[14]

Collier called this form of research *action research.* Taking effective actions requires research directed to important practical problems, and the solutions must be relevant and feasible. To be able to implement a good action plan also requires cooperation of the client. Action research seemed to afford a means to mesh these diverse elements.

The other major source for theory and practice of action research, Kurt Lewin, a social psychologist, was profoundly interested in applying social science knowledge to help solve social problems. In the mid-1940s and early 1950s, Lewin and his students conducted action research projects in many different behavioral domains: Lewin applied action research principles to inter-group relations and to changing eating habits; Lippitt and Lippitt and Radke applied the tool to an extensive community relations project; Bavelas conducted an action research project on leadership training; Coch and French applied the model to studying resistance to change in an industrial plant.[15] As Lewin succinctly stated the issue, "No action without research, and no research without action."

Lewin's work with social agency practitioners engaged in eradicating prejudice led him to conclude that research to help the practitioner was imperative. His answer to the need was action research. Only by conducting research could action people generate standards by which to measure progress. Speaking to this problem he said,

> In a field that lacks objective standards of achievement, no learning can take place. If we cannot judge whether an action has led forward or backward, if we have no criteria for evaluating the relation between effort and achievement, there is nothing to prevent us from making the wrong conclusions and to encourage the wrong work habits. Realistic fact-finding and evaluation is a prerequisite for any learning. Social research should be one of the top priorities for the practical job of improving inter-group relations.[16]

For the Lewin group, action research represented a linking of experimentation and application, and at the same time, people of science and people of action.

Other noteworthy action research projects may be found in the literature.[17] Whyte and Hamilton studied the effects of human relations practices in a large hotel; Elliott Jaques used the action research model to change the culture of a factory in England; Cyril Sofer applied the methods in three diverse organizations undergoing change for which he was a researcher-consultant; Floyd Mann and Seashore and Bowers applied the methods to industrial plants undergoing changes in leadership; Shepard, Katzell, and others, working at a large refinery, used action research to effect a planned change program; Morse and Reimer's field experiment investigating leadership styles and participation in an insurance company is an example of action research; and Miles, Hornstein, Callahan, Calder, and Schiavo used action research to investigate the processes of self-renewal in a school system. Abraham Shani, writing in 1981, found over 100 published reports of action research projects and over 100 theoretical statements about this methodology. Shani found that many of these action research efforts were linked to OD programs.[18]

The payoff from a good action research project is high: practical problems get solved, a contribution is made to theory and to practice in behavioral science, and greater understanding grows among scientist, practitioner, and layperson. Some varieties of action research emphasize one kind of payoff over others, as we see in the next section on different kinds of action research.

Action research projects may be directed toward diverse goals, thereby giving rise to several variations of the model. Lewin, for example, suggested two broad categories of action research: the investigation of general laws and the diagnosis of a specific situation.[19] The study of general laws leads to contributions to theory and practice, and to generalizations about natural phenomena; the diagnosis of a specific situation leads to solving immediate, practical problems.

Raymond Katzell, in the refinery action research project, suggested three types of situations in which the research consultant staff were providing data feedback to managers: the first situation was described as "adventitious," that is, the research group happened to have already collected data that turned out to be quite useful to someone at a later time; the second situation represented data collection on a refinerywide basis of a preplanned, systematic nature, that is, a periodic pulse taking of the organization; the third situation was to work intensively with a small "demonstration" group, continuously collecting data on all sorts of topics and feeding them back to the group as they were needed.[20] The second situation is often found in programs involving surveys taken, say, annually. In this situation it is possible to measure changes in various parts of the organization over time. The third situation is also found in organization development programs where a team of consultants has time and energy to spend on researching the consequences of behaviors within a small group with whom they are working intensively.

Chein, Cook, and Harding enumerate four varieties of action research—diagnostic, participant, empirical, and experimental.[21] In *diagnostic action research,* the scientist enters a problem situation, diagnoses it, and makes recommendations for remedial treatment to the client. The recommendations are intuitively derived, not pretested, and usually come from the scientist's experience or knowledge. Often the recommendations are not put into effect by the client group. This gave rise to a second kind of action research, *participant action research,* in which the people who are to take action are involved in the entire research and action process from the beginning. This involvement both facilitates a carrying out of the actions once decided upon and keeps the recommended actions feasible and workable.

Empirical action research is that in which the actor keeps a systematic, extensive record of what he or she did and what effects it had. This is similar to the practitioner's keeping a day-to-day diary. Limitations of this method are the difficulties found in any clinical data collecting: the actor may have too few experiences to draw from; he or she may encounter situations too divergent from one another to compare them; the situation may be unique and may not permit generalizations; the actor may lack objectivity in evaluating his or her own performance; and there are difficulties inherent in being both researcher and change agent simultaneously.

A fourth variety of action research, the *experimental,* is controlled research on the relative effectiveness of various action techniques. There is almost always more than one possible way of trying to accomplish something. The problem is to find which is the best. This is research *on* action in the strictest sense of both words.[22]

These authors indicate that experimental action research may make the greatest contribution to the advancement of scientific knowledge, but at the same time it is the most difficult to accomplish. The experimental nature of the research permits definitive testing of hypotheses and that is good. Controlling conditions to the extent that the hypothesis is tested in exactly the same way over several situations is difficult to do, however, when clients want immediate answers to pressing problems. In situations like these, the research aspects of the project often become subordinated to the problem-solving/remedial treatment requirements of the situation.

Organization development practitioners typically utilize participant action research and, occasionally, experimental action research. The participant model is highly congruent with current OD practices, and the experimental model, while being congruent, is simply harder to implement. In this regard, we maintain that the practice of organization development itself is in a sense a result of the experimental action research model, in that certain kinds of interventions (actions and hypotheses) were found to be effective by practitioners for achieving organization improvement and they were kept in the repertoire, while other interventions were found to be ineffective and were dropped from use.

Argyris promotes action research under the label of "action science" and he believes action science (action research) is more appropriate and effective for the study of social change and social action than is "normal science."[23] He criticizes traditional scientific methods for focusing on trivial problems, distorting human subjects and researchers alike, generating unreliable data, and being generally unable to answer questions about everyday life. According to Argyris, Lewin's action research was characterized by six features: ". . . (1) it was problem-driven, (2) it was client-centered, (3) it challenged the status quo and was simultaneously concerned with (4) producing empirically disconfirmable propositions that (5) could be systematically interrelated into a theory designed to be (6) usable in everyday life. . . ."[24] All six characteristics should be present in action research programs but often are not. Specifically, researchers become overly client-centered and focus only on action, not research; they do not define problems from the perspective of the client; they do not study the processes of their own interventions; they neglect to test hypotheses; and they continue to work within the paradigm of "normal science." Given these shortcomings, there should be a return to pure action research. And the use of action science will prove to be a better method for studying complex social situations, Argyris believes. Action science is similar to participant action research as identified by Chein, Cook, and Harding, according to a recent article by Argyris and Schon.[25]

Another variation of action research is "appreciative inquiry." David Cooperrider and Suresh Srivastva criticize current action research as too problem-centered and action-oriented, and not sufficiently concerned with creating theory.[26] They propose *appreciative inquiry* to augment contemporary action research and introduce their article with these words:

> The position that is developed can be summarized as follows: For action-research to reach its potential as a vehicle for social innovation it needs to begin advancing theoretical knowledge of consequence; that good theory may be one of the best means human beings have for affecting change in a postindustrial world; that the discipline's steadfast commitment to a problem-solving view of the world acts as a primary constraint on its imagination and contribution to knowledge; that appreciative inquiry represents a viable complement to conventional forms of action-research; and finally, that through our assumptions and choice of method we largely create the world we later discover.[27]

In essence, appreciative inquiry contends that the fact of organizations is not a problem to be solved, but "a miracle to be embraced." They write:

> Here we will move to the heart of the chapter and argue that the generative incapacity of contemporary action-research derives from the discipline's unquestioned commitment to a secularized problem-oriented view of the world and thus to the subsequent loss of our capacity as researchers and participants to marvel, and in marvelling to embrace, the miracle and mystery of social organization.[28]

And they add:

> In distinction to conventional action-research, the knowledge-interest of appreciative inquiry lies not so much in problem solving as in social innovation. Appreciative inquiry refers to a research perspective that is uniquely intended for discovering, understanding, and fostering innovations in social-organizational arrangements and processes. Its purpose is to contribute to the generative-theoretical aims of social science and to use such knowledge to promote egalitarian dialogue leading to social-system effectiveness and integrity. . . . Thus, appreciative inquiry refers to both a search for knowledge and a theory of intentional collective action which are designed to help evolve the normative vision and will of a group, organization, or society as a whole.[29]

Appreciative inquiry advocates four principles for research on organizations. Such research should begin with appreciation, should be applicable, should be provocative, and should be collaborative. Cooperrider and Srivastva have provided an intriguing new look at action research that is worthy of study.

Several other varieties of action research exist. The concept of grounded theory in sociological research appears to be similar to action research, as does Edgar Schein's clinical inquiry.[30] Shani and Pasmore, and Shani and Bushe present good recent reviews of action research.[31]

The final variant of action research to be discussed comes from the quality movement. The action research model is very similar to the Shewhart cycle of plan, do, check, act—a virtual mantra in total quality management (TQM) programs. Walter A. Shewhart was the "father" of statistical process control and TQM. Shewhart introduced the cycle in his four lectures on statistics at the Graduate School of the U.S. Department of Agriculture in March 1938.[32] Shewhart had been invited to present the lectures by W. Edwards Deming who was in charge of courses in advanced mathematics and statistics.[33] To improve quality, Shewhart advised, you should: *plan* a test or change intended to improve something; *do* a small-scale test; *check* the effects of the test; and *act* on the new learning. Then plan new tests based on the knowledge gained and repeat the cycle again and again. This was the road to continuous quality improvement, he asserted. W. Edwards Deming introduced the Shewhart cycle to Japanese executives and engineers in the summer of 1950 when he launched the quality revolution in Japan. (The Japanese call it the Deming cycle due to their respect for Dr. Deming.) The plan, do, check, act cycle is a key ingredient in quality control. It looks a lot like action research.

EXAMPLES OF ACTION RESEARCH IN ORGANIZATION DEVELOPMENT

The OD process is basically an action research program in an organization designed to improve the functioning of that organization. Effective improvement programs almost always require a data base, that is, they rely on systematically obtained empirical facts for planning action, taking action, and evaluating action. Action research supplies an approach and a process for generating and utilizing information about the system itself that will provide a base for the action program.

The collaborative inquiry feature of action research suggests to practitioners and laypersons alike the desirability for jointly determining central needs, critical problems, and hypotheses and actions. The potential experimental nature of actions inherent in action research provides a different perspective for managers as they try to solve problems, that is, viewing problems in cause-effect terms and viewing solutions to problems as only one action hypothesis from a range of several. The systematic collection of data about variables related to the organization's culture and testing the effects of managerial actions on these variables offers a new tool for understanding organizational dynamics. All these features fit with a program to improve the organization.

Several examples will show how action research is used in organization development. Gavin conducted a comprehensive survey feedback program in a mining company of approximately 400 employees in the southwestern United States.[34] In several respects the OD program was a success—it was well received by the hourly employees and many key managers; it led to the solution of many immediate problems; and it led to numerous long-term organizational changes that increased the effectiveness of the mine. And in several respects it was a failure—increasing lack of trust of the consultants by some managers led to increasingly strained relations between higher management and the consultant team which led to the premature termination of the program. But Gavin and his doctoral students had conceptualized the project from the beginning as an action research project, not just an OD effort using survey feedback methodology. Therefore, they simultaneously studied the effects of the OD program, their own intervention's processes and dynamics, and the changing client-consultant relations over time. The result was a rich case study yielding vital new information about both research and practice.

Shani and Eberhardt conducted an action research project at a medical rehabilitation hospital designed to improve the effectiveness of health care teams.[35] Patient care was provided by clinical teams comprised of professionals from many different medical specialties. Some teams were more effective than others. What caused the differences? How could less effective teams be made more effective? As one can imagine, the causes, correlates, and conditions of health care team effectiveness are complex and multifaceted. The expertise and cooperation of organization members were needed to discover the causal mechanisms and to plan and implement changes. The authors established a "parallel organization" consisting of a steering committee to guide the project and a study group to do the work. Shani and Eberhardt define a parallel organization as ". . . an institutionalized supplemental organizational form coexisting alongside the formal,"[36] and argue that such vehicles are particularly valuable for conducting action research programs. The parallel organization defined the data needs, conducted several iterations of data collection and making sense of the information, formulated hypotheses to be tested, and suggested alternatives for future steps to the hospital management. A major conclusion was that the action research approach yields better, richer information than the usual methods of social science research.

Another example of action research is provided by Santalainen and Hunt, who used the occurrence of a massive OD program in a Finnish banking group to gain new knowledge about how the change program was utilized differentially by high- and low-performing banks.[37] A comprehensive, multidimensional, OD change program was implemented in the 80 largest banks of the 270-bank system. The program was called *results management* (ReMa) and focused on teaching the top teams of the banks better strategic planning and operational planning methods, better ways to define desired results, consensus decision making, and better ways to meet the needs and values of employees. Although all banks received the same training, wide latitude was permitted in how each bank implemented the program. What makes this action research is the fact that research was conducted on the OD program itself and at the same time knowledge was gained on organizational dynamics in general, specifically, high and low performance.

The 18 highest-performing and 18 lowest-performing banks out of the total of 80 were examined to see how they had utilized and implemented the learning from the OD program. At the end of three years the high-performing banks had made more strategic changes and fewer operational changes; the low-performing banks had made more operational changes, and fewer strategic changes. At the end of six years, the high-performing banks had made more "deep-seated" (fundamental and significant) changes than the low-performing banks. The payoff from this action research was high—knowledge about the results management intervention, and knowledge about the ingredients of high and low performance. This was an excellent blend of action and research.

In *Productive Workplaces* Marvin Weisbord takes the reader through a number of action research projects, explains and critiques them, and shows how his thinking about such projects evolved. Over time he became disenchanted with the terms *diagnosis* and *action*, and started using *snapshooting* and *moviemaking* to refer to those activities instead. He stopped focusing on problems and sickness, and began focusing on wellness, potential, and desired futures. He came to realize that the most successful action research projects were not expert-centered (what the consultant wanted to do), but stakeholder-centered (what the organizational members wanted to do).[38] Readers interested in a fresh approach to action research can benefit from this book.

Most sociotechnical systems theory change projects are conceptualized as action research—research precedes action, and research follows action as OD practitioners and organizational members collaborate to discover what should be done and how. The same is true for open systems planning efforts and parallel learning structure interventions. Action research is a big part of contemporary organization development.

The natures of organization development and action research are very similar. They are both variants of applied behavioral science; they are both action oriented; they are both data based; they both call for close collaboration between insider and outsider; and they are both problem-solving social interventions. This is why we believe a sound organization development program rests on an action research model.

CONCLUDING COMMENTS

Two philosophical and pragmatic values underlie action research. The first value is that action plans and programs designed to solve real problems should be based on valid public data generated collaboratively by clients and consultants. This belief calls for actions to be based on diagnostic research—an *action-should-follow-research* mode of thinking. Or, to state it another way, diagnose the problem situation and base action plans on that diagnosis. The second value is that action in the real world should be accompanied by research on that action so that we can build up a cumulative body of knowledge and theory of the effects of various actions directed to solving real-world problems—a *research-should-follow-action* mode of thinking. Only if we systematically evaluate (do research on) actions can we know what the real effects of these actions are. And only if we systematically and cumulatively build a body of knowledge can we build better social science theories.

Thus actions to solve real-world problems offer a unique opportunity for both the scientist-researcher and the administrator-layperson if the problems are approached from the standpoint of the action research model: the administrator's problems will be solved and the scientist's quest for theory and empirical validation of theory will be furthered. The applied behavioral science discipline of organization development is a fertile ground for action research projects.[39]

NOTES

1. Kurt Lewin, "Frontiers in Group Dynamics," *Human Relations*, 1, no. 2 (1947), 143–153.
2. William F. Whyte and Edith L. Hamilton, *Action Research for Management* (Homewood, IL: Irwin-Dorsey, 1964), pp. 1–2.
3. Wendell French, "Organization Development Objectives, Assumptions, and Strategies," *California Management Review,* 12 (Winter 1969), pp. 23–34.
4. Ibid., p. 26.
5. Herbert A. Shepard, "An Action Research Model," in *An Action Research Program for Organization Improvement* (Ann Arbor: The Foundation for Research on Human Behavior, University of Michigan, 1960), pp. 33–34.
6. Figure 7–2 is from Herbert A. Shepard, "An Action Research Model," in *An Action Research Program for Organization Improvement* (Ann Arbor: The Foundation for Research on Human Behavior, 1960), p. 33, and is used with permission.
7. Ibid., p. 34.
8. John Dewey, *How We Think,* rev. ed. (New York: Heath, 1933).
9. Based on a discussion in Fred N. Kerlinger, *Foundations of Behavioral Research,* 2nd ed. (New York: Holt, Rinehart and Winston, 1973), pp. 11–15.
10. Corey, *Action Research to Improve School Practices* (New York: Bureau of Publications, Teachers College, Columbia University, 1953), pp. 40–41.
11. In this regard, the work of Collier (cited later in this chapter), Corey, and Lippitt (cited later) indicates a heavy emphasis on the importance of collaboration between all the individuals affected by a change project of this nature. And in an article on

action research and OD, client-consultant collaboration is cited as one of the basic processes of the action research model. Mark A. Frohman, Marshall Sashkin, and Michael J. Kavanagh, "Action-Research as Applied to Organization Development," *Organization and Administrative Sciences*, 7, nos. 1 and 2 (Spring-Summer 1976), pp. 129–161.

12. Abraham B. Shani and Gervase R. Bushe, "Visionary Action Research: A Consultation Process Perspective," *Consultation*, 6, no. 1, (Spring 1987) 8.

13. Deutsch, "Field Theory in Social Psychology," in *The Handbook of Social Psychology*, Gardner Lindzey and Elliott Aronson, eds., Vol. 1, pp. 465–466.

14 John Collier, "United States Indian Administration as a Laboratory of Ethnic Relations," *Social Research*, 12 (May 1945), pp. 275–276.

15. The relevant sources for Lewin's work are as follows: Kurt Lewin, "Action Research and Minority Problems," *Journal of Social Issues*, 2, no. 4 (1946), 34–46; *Resolving Social Conflicts* (New York: Harper & Bros., 1948); in addition, Ronald Lippitt, *Training in Community Relations* (New York: Harper & Row, 1951); Ronald Lippitt and Marion Radke, "New Trends in the Investigation of Prejudice," *Annals of the American Academy of Political and Social Science*, 244 (March 1946), pp. 167–176; and Lester Coch and J.R.P. French, Jr., "Overcoming Resistance to Change," *Human Relations*, 1 (1948), pp. 512–532.

16. Lewin, "Action Research and Minority Problems," p. 35.

17. Whyte and Hamilton, *Action Research for Management*; Elliott Jaques, *The Changing Culture of a Factory* (New York: Dryden Press, 1952); Cyril Sofer, *The Organization from Within* (Chicago: Quadrangle Books, 1962); Floyd Mann, "Studying and Creating Change: A Means to Understanding Social Organization," in C. M. Arensberg et al., eds., *Research in Industrial Human Relations* (New York: Harper & Row, 1957); and S. E. Seashore and D. G. Bowers, *Changing the Structure and Functioning of an Organization*, Monograph No. 33 (Ann Arbor: Survey Research Center, University of Michigan, 1963). Herbert A. Shepard and Raymond A. Katzell are two of the writers for the book *An Action Research Program for Organization Improvement*. Also see Nancy Morse and E. Reimer, "The Experimental Change of a Major Organizational Variable," *Journal of Abnormal and Social Psychology*, 52 (January 1956), pp. 120–129; and Matthew Miles, Harvey Hornstein, Daniel Callahan, Paula Calder, and R. Steven Schiavo, "The Consequences of Survey Feedback: Theory and Evaluation," in Warren Bennis, Kenneth Benne, and Robert Chin, eds., *The Planning of Change*, 2nd ed. (New York: Holt, Rinehart and Winston, 1969), pp. 457–468.

18. A. B. Shani, *Understanding the Process of Action Research in Organizations: A Theoretical Perspective*. Unpublished doctoral dissertation, Case Western Reserve University, Cleveland, Ohio, 1981.

19. Lewin, "Action Research and Minority Problems," pp. 34–46.

20. Raymond Katzell, "Action Research Activities at One Refinery," in *An Action Research Program for Organization Improvement*, pp. 37–47.

21. Isadore Chein, Stuart Cook, and John Harding, "The Field of Action Research," *American Psychologist*, 3 (February 1948), pp. 43–50.

22. Ibid., p. 48.

23. C. Argyris, R. Putnam, and D. M. Smith, *Action Science* (San Francisco: Jossey-Bass, 1985). C. Argyris, *Inner Contradictions of Rigorous Research* (New York: Academic Press, 1980). C. Argyris and D. A. Schon, *Theory in Practice* (San Francisco: Jossey-Bass, 1974).

24. Chris Argyris, "Action Science and Intervention," *The Journal of Applied Behavioral Science*, 19, no. 2 (1983), 115–140. This quotation is from p. 115.

25. Chris Argyris and Donald A. Schon, "Participatory Action Research and Action Science Compared, "*American Behavioral Scientist*, 9, no. 5 (May/June 1989), 612–623.

26. David Cooperrider and Suresh Srivastva, "Appreciative Inquiry in Organizational Life," in R. W. Woodman and W. A. Pasmore, eds., *Research in Organizational Change and Development*, vol. 1 (Greenwich, CT: JAI Press, 1987), pp. 129–169.

27. Ibid., p. 129.

28. Ibid., p. 131.

29. Ibid., p. 159.

30. Edgar H. Schein, *The Clinical Perspective in Field Work* (Newbury Park, CA: Sage Publishing Company, 1987).

31. See A. B. Shani and W. A. Pasmore, "Organization Inquiry: Towards a New Paradigm of the Action Research Process," in *Contemporary Organization Development*, D. D. Warrick, ed. (Glenview, IL: Scott, Foresman, 1985). See also A. B. Shani and G. R. Bushe, "Visionary Action Research: A Consultation Process Perspective," *Consultation*, 6 (1987), pp. 3–19.

32. W. Edwards Deming, *Out of the Crisis* (Cambridge, MA: MIT Center for Advanced Engineering Study, 1986), p. 88. This is Deming's major work, a very important book.

33. Lloyd Dobyns and Clare Crawford-Mason, *Quality or Else* (Boston: Houghton Mifflin Company, 1991), p. 57. This is an excellent overview of the quality movement.

34. James F. Gavin, "Survey Feedback: The Perspectives of Science and Practice," *Group and Organization Studies*, 9, no. 1 (March 1984), 29–70.

35. Abraham B. Shani and Bruce J. Eberhardt, "Parallel Organization in a Health Care Institution," *Group and Organization Studies*, 12, no. 2 (June 1987), 147–173.

36. Ibid., p. 150.

37. Timo J. Santalainen and J. G. Hunt, "Change Differences from an Action Research, Results-Oriented OD Program in High- and Low-Performing Finnish Banks," *Group & Organization Studies*, 13, no. 4 (December 1988), 413–440.

38. Marvin R. Weisbord, *Productive Workplaces* (San Francisco: Jossey-Bass Publishers, 1987), pp. 196–252.

39. See Frohman, Sashkin, and Kavanagh, "Action-Research as Applied to Organization Development," pp. 129–161. Also Michael Peters and Viviane Robinson, "The Origins and Status of Action Research," *The Journal of Applied Behavioral Science*, 20, no. 2 (1984), 113–124.

8

OD INTERVENTIONS—
AN OVERVIEW

Work gets done in organization development by organization leaders and members systematically addressing problems and opportunities, usually guided by an OD practitioner. Over the years, practitioners have created an array of interventions to help organization members address specific problems effectively and efficiently. Interventions such as team building, survey feedback, role analysis, and intergroup conflict resolution were developed during the early years of organization development. Interventions such as quality of work life (QWL), work redesign using sociotechnical systems theory (STS), collateral organization (also known as parallel learning structures), and strategic planning methods were developed as the field continued to evolve. Today there are interventions aimed at the development of self-directed teams, high-performance work systems, and self-designing organizations, as well as large-scale systems change models to help organizations cope and survive. OD interventions thus address a host of specific problems and opportunities. But OD is much more than just reaching into the "kit bag" and executing an intervention. OD is a strategy for change that encompasses theory, practice methods, and values. Interventions are just one component of the OD formula.

    Practice methods have evolved and improved over the years as well. By practice methods we mean *how* practitioners ply their craft to cause organizational change. Principles, rules of thumb, and practical knowledge have accumulated so that a practice theory exists to tell practitioners what to do and how to do it to effect change in human systems. For example, people often resist change and there is a tendency to lapse back into old habits after change has occurred. Practice theory tells how to deal with these situations. The secrets to success in OD programs lie in the practice theory. Advances in behavioral science theory, practice theory, and the range and scope of interventions have significantly increased the power of OD as a strategy for change.

In this and the next several chapters we discuss OD interventions and describe the most important ones. The term *OD interventions* refers to the planned activities clients and consultants participate in during the course of an organization development program. These activities are designed to improve the organization's functioning by helping organization members better manage their team and organization cultures and processes. Knowing the OD interventions and the rationale for their use shows you how change takes place in OD programs because interventions are the vehicles for causing change. In this overview chapter we clarify what interventions are, examine some rules of thumb for implementing interventions, and then explore different ways to classify interventions.

OD interventions are *sets of structured activities* in which selected organizational units (target groups or individuals) engage in a task or a sequence of tasks where the task goals are related directly or indirectly to organizational improvement. Interventions constitute the action thrust of organization development. The OD practitioner is a professional versed in the theory and practice of OD. The practitioner brings four sets of attributes to the organizational setting: a set of values; a set of assumptions about people, organizations, and interpersonal relationships; a set of goals and objectives for the practitioner and the organization and its members; and a set of structured activities that are the *means* for achieving the values, assumptions, and goals. These activities are what we mean by the word *interventions*.

THINKING ABOUT OD INTERVENTIONS

We said OD is more than reaching into the "kit bag" and pulling out an intervention or two. Let's explore some of the factors leaders and practitioners consider as they plan and implement OD.

First, behind every program is an overall game plan or intervention strategy. This plan integrates the problem or opportunity to be addressed, the goals and desired outcomes of the program, and the sequencing and timing of the various interventions used to accomplish the goals. Intervention strategies are based on a combination of diagnosis and the goals set by the client system. Say the clients want to redesign the way work is done at a production facility, changing from an assembly-line arrangement of individualized simple tasks to complex tasks performed by self-managed teams. Diagnosis is required to determine if the work itself is amenable to such a system, to test the willingness of the employees to undertake such a change, to calculate the time and effort required to make the change, and to assess the probable benefits to be achieved. Sociotechnical systems theory would likely be the guiding model for the program, which would entail dozens of significant changes and dozens of different interventions—training, education, parallel structures, employee involvement, modifications of reward systems and management philosophy, and so forth. A series of activities designed to move the system in step-wise fashion from the current state to a new state would be laid out against a time line of several years duration. This overall strategy would be the road map for the change program. The key questions to be asked and answered are: What are we trying to accomplish? What activities/interventions will help us get there? What is the proper timing and sequencing of the interventions? What have we learned from the diagnosis about readiness to change, barriers and obstacles, key stakeholders, and sources of energy and leadership?

Second, some advice for structuring interventions has come from practice theory and experience. There are "better" and "worse" ways to structure activities to promote learning and change. The following points help practitioners structure activities in "better" ways:

1. Structure the activity so that the relevant people are there. The relevant people are those affected by the problem or the opportunity. For example, if the goal is improved team effectiveness, have the whole team engage in the activities. If the goal is improved relations between two separate work groups, have both work groups present. If the goal is to build linkages with some special group, say, the industrial relations people, have them there and have the linking people from the home group there. This preplanning of the group composition is a necessary feature of properly structuring the activity.

2. Structure the activity so that it is (a) problem oriented or opportunity oriented and (b) oriented to the problems and opportunities generated by the clients themselves. Solving problems and capitalizing on opportunities are involving, interesting, and enjoyable tasks for most people, whether it is due to a desire for competence or mastery (as suggested by White),[1] or a desire to achieve (as suggested by McClelland),[2] or whatever. This is especially true when the issues to be worked on have been defined by the client. There is built-in support and involvement, and there is a real payoff when clients are solving issues that they have stated have highest priority.

3. Structure the activity so that the goal is clear and the way to reach the goal is clear. Few things demotivate an individual as much as not knowing what he or she is working toward and not knowing how what the individual is doing contributes to goal attainment. Both these points are part of structuring the activity properly. (Parenthetically, the goals will be important goals for the individuals if point 2 is followed.)

4. Structure the activity so that there is a high probability of successful goal attainment. Implicit in this point is the warning that expectations of practitioners and clients should be realistic. But more than that, manageable, attainable objectives once achieved produce feelings of success, competence, and potency for the people involved. This, in turn, raises aspiration levels and feelings of self- and group-worth. The task can still be hard, complicated, taxing—but it should be attainable. And if there is failure to accomplish the goal, the reasons for this should be examined so they can be avoided in the future.

5. Structure the activity so that it contains both experience-based learning and conceptual/cognitive/theoretical-based learning. New learnings gained through experience are made a permanent part of the individual's repertoire when they are augmented with conceptual material that puts the experience into a broader framework of theory and behavior. Relating the experience to conceptual models, theories, and other experiences and beliefs helps the learning to become integrated for the individual.

6. Structure the climate of the activity so that individuals are "freed up" rather than anxious or defensive. Setting the climate of interventions so that people expect "to learn together" and "to look at practices in an experimenting way so that we can select better procedures" is what we mean by climate setting.

7. Structure the activity so that the participants learn both how to solve a particular problem and "learn how to learn" at the same time. This may mean scheduling in time for reflecting on the activity and teasing out learnings that occurred; it may mean devoting as much as half the activity to one focus and half to the other.

8. Structure the activity so that individuals can learn about both *task* and *process*. The task is what the group is working on, that is, the stated agenda items. The term *process*, as used here, refers to *how* the group is working and *what else is going on* as the task is being worked on. This includes the group's processes and dynamics, individual styles of interacting and behaving, and so on. Learning to be skillful in both of these areas is a powerful tool. Activities structured to focus on both aspects result in learnings on both aspects.

9. Structure the activity so that individuals are engaged as whole persons, not segmented persons. This means that role demands, thoughts, beliefs, feelings, and strivings should all be called into play, not just one or two of these. Integrating disparate parts of individuals in an organizational world where differentiation in terms of roles, feelings, and thoughts is common probably enhances the individual's ability to cope and grow.

These points come from practice theory. Implementing these points causes interventions to be more effective.

A third set of considerations concerns choosing and sequencing the intervention activities. Michael Beer suggests the following guidelines or decision rules to help in this regard:

> These decision rules can help a change agent focus on the relevant issues in making decisions about how to integrate a variety of interventions. They are rules for managing the implementation process.

1. *Maximize diagnostic data.* In general, interventions that will provide data needed to make subsequent intervention decisions should come first. This is particularly true when change agents do not know much about the situation. Violation of this rule can lead to choosing inappropriate interventions.

2. *Maximize effectiveness.* Interventions should be sequenced so that early interventions enhance the effectiveness of subsequent interventions. For example, interventions that develop readiness, motivation, knowledge, or skills required by other interventions should come first. Violation of this rule (leapfrogging) can result in interventions that do not achieve their objectives, regression, and the need to start a new sequence of interventions.

3. *Maximize efficiency.* Interventions should be sequenced to conserve organizational resources such as time, energy, and money. Violation of this rule will result in overlapping interventions or in interventions that are not needed by certain people or parts of the organization.

4. *Maximize speed.* Interventions should be sequenced to maximize the speed with which ultimate organizational improvement is attained. Violation of this rule occurs when progress is slower than is necessary to conform to all the other rules.

5. *Maximize relevance.* Interventions that management sees as most relevant to immediate problems should come first. In general, this means interventions that will have an impact on the organization's performance or task come before interventions that will have an impact on individuals or culture. Violation of this rule will result in loss of motivation to continue with organization development.

6. *Minimize psychological and organizational strain.* A sequence of interventions should be chosen that is least likely to create dysfunctional effects such as anxiety, insecurity, distrust, dashed expectations, psychological damage to people, and unanticipated and unwanted effects on organizational performance. Violating this rule will lower people's sense of competence and confidence and their commitment to organizational improvement.[3]

Good advice. Paying attention to these guidelines helps ensure success. Disregard of these rules has caused many an OD program to flounder.

Fourth, different interventions have different dynamics; they do different things because they are based on different causal mechanisms. It's important to know the underlying causal mechanisms of interventions to ensure the intervention fits the desired outcomes. Robert Blake and Jane Mouton identified the following types of interventions based on the underlying causal mechanisms involved:

1. *Discrepancy intervention,* which calls attention to a contradiction in action or attitudes that then leads to exploration.

2. *Theory intervention*, where behavioral science knowledge and theory are used to explain present behavior and assumptions underlying the behavior.

3. *Procedural intervention*, which represents a critiquing of how something is being done to determine whether the best methods are being used.

4. *Relationship intervention*, which focuses attention on interpersonal relationships (particularly those where there are strong negative feelings) and surfaces the issues for exploration and possible resolution.

5. *Experimentation intervention*, in which two different action plans are tested for their consequences before a final decision on one is made.

6. *Dilemma intervention*, in which an imposed or emergent dilemma is used to force close examination of the possible choices involved and the assumptions underlying them.

7. *Perspective intervention*, which draws attention away from immediate actions and demands and allows a look at historical background, context, and future objectives in order to assess whether or not the actions are "still on target."

8. *Organization structure intervention*, which calls for examination and evaluation of structural causes for organizational ineffectiveness.

9. *Cultural intervention*, which examines traditions, precedents, and practices—the fabric of the organization's culture—in a direct, focused approach.[4]

These different kinds of interventions suggest a range of different ways the OD practitioner can intervene in the client system. They also suggest the underlying dynamics of interventions.

Blake and Mouton have continued to examine and refine the nature of interventions and have proposed a theory and typology for the entire consultation field.[5] The typology, called the Consulcube™, is a 100-cell cube depicting virtually all consultation situations. The cube is built on three dimensions. The first dimension is what the consultant *does*, that is, what kind of intervention the consultant uses. There are five basic types of interventions—*acceptable* (the consultant gives the client a sense of worth, value, acceptance, and support); *catalytic* (the consultant helps the client generate data and information in order to restructure the client's perceptions); *confrontation* (the consultant points out value discrepancies in the client's beliefs and actions); *prescription* (the consultant tells the client what to do to solve the problem); and *theories and principles* (the consultant teaches the client relevant behavioral science theory so that the client can learn to diagnose and solve his or her own problems).

The second dimension is the *focal issues* causing the client's problems. Four focal issue categories are identified: power-authority, morale/cohesion, norms/standards of conduct, and goals/objectives.

The third dimension of the cube is the units of change that are the target of the consultation. Five units are proposed: individual, group, intergroup, organization, and larger social systems such as a community or even a society.

Five kinds of interventions, four different focal issues, and five different units of change are thus seen to encompass the range of consultation possibilities. Blake and Mouton's Consulcube represents a major contribution in the development of a theory of consultation and intervention. It clarifies the role of organization development and the different interventions that make up the OD technology.

As we said, interventions *do* different things; they *cause different things to happen.* One intervention's major result may be that it increases interaction and communication between parties. Another intervention's major result may be that it increases feedback, or increases accountability. These *differential* results are often exactly what is needed to produce change in the particular situation. For example, a situation requiring increased accountability will benefit more from an intervention that directly increases accountability than an intervention that increases interaction and communication. The following list shows some of the results to be expected from different OD interventions.

1. *Feedback.* This refers to learning new data about oneself, others, group processes, or organizational dynamics—data that one did not previously take active account of. Feedback refers to activities and processes that reflect or mirror an objective picture of the real world. Awareness of this new information may lead to change if the feedback is not too threatening. Feedback is prominent in such interventions as process consultation, organization mirroring, sensitivity training, coaching and counseling, and survey feedback.

2. *Awareness of Changing Sociocultural Norms or Dysfunctional Present Norms.* Often people modify their behavior, attitudes, values, and so on when they become aware of changes in the norms that are helping to determine their behavior. Thus, awareness of new norms has change potential because the individual will adjust his or her behavior to bring it in line with the new norms. The awareness that "this is a new ball game" or that "we're now playing with a new set of rules" is here hypothesized to be a cause of changes in individual behavior. Also, awareness of dysfunctional present norms can serve as an incentive to change. When people sense a discrepancy between the outcomes their present norms are causing and the desired outcomes they want, this can lead to change. This causal mechanism is probably operating in team building and intergroup team-building activities, culture analysis, Grid OD, and sociotechnical systems programs.

3. *Increased Interaction and Communication.* Increasing interaction and communication between individuals and groups may in and of itself effect changes in attitudes and behavior. Homans, for example, suggests that increased interaction leads to increased positive sentiments.[6] Individuals and groups in isolation tend to develop "tunnel vision" or "autism," according to Murphy.[7] Increasing communication counteracts this tendency. Increased communication allows one to check one's perceptions to see if they are socially validated and shared. This mechanism underlies almost all OD interventions. The rule of thumb is: Get people talking and interacting in new, constructive ways and good things will result.

4. *Confrontation.* This term refers to surfacing and addressing differences in beliefs, feelings, attitudes, values, or norms to remove obstacles to effec-

tive interaction. Confrontation is a process that actively seeks to discern real differences that are "getting in the way," surface those issues, and work on the issues in a constructive way. Many obstacles to growth and learning exist; they continue to exist when they are not actively looked at and examined. Confrontation underlies most conflict resolution interventions such as intergroup team building, third-party peacemaking, and role negotiation.

5. *Education.* This refers to activities designed to upgrade (a) knowledge and concepts, (b) outmoded beliefs and attitudes, and (c) skills. In organization development the education may be directed toward increasing these three components in several content areas: task achievement, human and social relationships and behavior, organizational dynamics and processes, and processes of managing and directing change. Education has long been an accepted change technique. Education is the primary causal mechanism in behavior modeling, force-field analysis, and life- and career-planning.

6. *Participation.* This refers to activities which increase the number of people who are allowed to be involved in problem solving, goal setting, and the generation of new ideas. Participation has been shown to increase the quality and acceptance of decisions, to increase job satisfaction, and to promote employee well-being. Participation is a principal underlying mechanism of quality circles, collateral organizations, quality of work life (QWL) programs, team building, survey feedback, and Beckhard's Confrontation Meeting. It is likely that participation plays a role in most OD interventions.

7. *Increased Accountability.* This refers to activities that clarify who is responsible for what and that monitor performance related to those responsibilities. Both of these features must be present for accountability to enhance performance. OD interventions that increase accountability are the role analysis technique, responsibility charting, Gestalt OD, life- and career-planning, quality circles, MBO, self-managed teams, and partnering.

8. *Increased Energy and Optimism.* This refers to activities that energize and motivate people through visions of new possibilities or new desired futures. The future must be desirable, worthwhile, and attainable. Increased energy and optimism are often direct results of interventions such as appreciative inquiry, visioning, "getting the whole system in the room," quality of work life programs, future search conferences, total quality programs, self-managed teams, and so forth.

These are some areas to consider when planning OD programs, choosing OD interventions, and implementing and managing OD interventions. One learns this practice theory through experience, reading, workshops, mentors, and reflecting on successes and failures.

CLASSIFYING OD INTERVENTIONS

The inventory of OD interventions is quite extensive. We will explore several classification schemes here to help you understand how various interventions "clump" together in terms of (1) the objectives of the interventions, and (2) the targets of the interventions. Familiarity with how interventions relate to one another is useful for planning the overall OD strategy.

OD programs are designed to achieve specific goals, and often several interventions are combined into a "package" to accomplish the goals. As we see it, the following are the major "families" or types of OD interventions.

1. *Diagnostic Activities.* Fact-finding activities designed to ascertain the state of the system, the status of a problem, the "way things are." Available methods range from projective devices such as "build a collage that represents for you your place in this organization" to the more traditional data collection methods of interviews, questionnaires, surveys, and meetings.

2. *Team-Building Activities.* Activities designed to enhance the effective operation of system teams. They may relate to task issues, such as the way things are done, the needed skills to accomplish tasks, the resource allocations necessary for task accomplishments; or they may relate to the nature and quality of the relationships between the team members or between members and the leader. Again, a wide range of activities is possible. In addition, consideration is given to the different kinds of teams that may exist in the organization, such as formal work teams, temporary task force teams, newly constituted teams, and cross-functional teams.

3. *Intergroup Activities.* Activities designed to improve effectiveness of interdependent groups. They focus on joint activities and the output of the groups considered as a single system rather than as two subsystems. When two groups are involved, the activities are generally designated intergroup or interface activities; when more than two groups are involved, the activities are often called *organizational mirroring.*

4. *Survey Feedback Activities.* Related to and similar to the diagnostic activities mentioned in that they are a large component of those activities. However, they are important enough in their own right to be considered separately. These activities center on actively working the data produced by a survey and designing action plans based on the survey data.

5. *Education and Training Activities.* Activities designed to improve skills, abilities, and knowledge of individuals. There are several activities available and several approaches possible. For example, the individual can be educated in isolation from his or her own work group (say, in a T-group comprised of strangers), or one can be educated in relation to the work group (say, when a work team learns how better to manage interpersonal conflict). The activities may be directed toward technical skills required for effective task performance or may be directed toward improving interpersonal competence. The activities may be directed toward leadership issues, responsibilities and functions of group members, decision making, problem solving, goal setting and planning, and so forth.

6. *Technostructural or Structural Activities.* Activities designed to improve the effectiveness of the technical or structural inputs and constraints affecting individuals or groups. The activities may take the form of (a) experi-

menting with new organization structures and evaluating their effectiveness in terms of specific goals or (b) devising new ways to bring technical resources to bear on problems. In Chapter 12 we discuss these activities and label them "structural interventions," defined as "the broad class of interventions or change efforts aimed at improving organization effectiveness through changes in the task, structural, and technological subsystems." Included in these activities are certain forms of job enrichment, management by objectives, sociotechnical systems, collateral organizations, and physical settings interventions.

7. *Process Consultation Activities.* Activities on the part of the consultant that "help the client to perceive, understand, and act upon process events which occur in the client's environment."[8] These activities perhaps more accurately describe an approach, a consulting mode in which the client is given insight into the human processes in organizations and taught skills in diagnosing and managing them. Primary emphasis is on processes such as communications, leader and member roles in groups, problem solving and decision making, group norms and group growth, leadership and authority, and intergroup cooperation and competition.

8. *Grid Organization Development Activities.* Activities invented and franchised by Robert Blake and Jane Mouton, which constitute a six-phase change model involving the total organization.[9] Internal resources are developed to conduct most of the programs, which may take from three to five years to complete. The model starts with upgrading individual managers' skills and leadership abilities, moves to team improvement activities, then to intergroup relations activities. Later phases include corporate planning for improvement, developing implementation tactics, and concluding with an evaluation phase assessing change in the organization culture and looking toward future directions.

9. *Third-Party Peacemaking Activities.* Activities conducted by a skilled consultant (the third party), which are designed to "help two members of an organization manage their interpersonal conflict."[10] They are based on confrontation tactics and an understanding of the processes involved in conflict and conflict resolution.

10. *Coaching and Counseling Activities.* Activities that entail the consultant or other organization members working with individuals to help them (a) define learning goals, (b) learn how others see their behavior, and (c) learn new modes of behavior to see if these help them to achieve their goals better. A central feature of this activity is the nonevaluative feedback given by others to an individual. A second feature is the joint exploration of alternative behaviors.

11. *Life- and Career-Planning Activities.* Activities that enable individuals to focus on their life and career objectives and how they might go about achieving them. Structured activities lead to production of life and career inventories, discussions of goals and objectives, and assessment of capabilities, needed additional training, and areas of strength and deficiency.

12. *Planning and Goal-Setting Activities.* Activities that include theory and experience in planning and goal setting, utilizing problem-solving models, planning paradigms, ideal organization versus real organization "discrepancy" models, and the like. The goal of all of them is to improve these skills at the levels of the individual, group, and total organization.

TARGET GROUP	TYPES OF INTERVENTIONS
Interventions designed to improve the effectiveness of INDIVIDUALS	Life- and career-planning activities Coaching and counseling T-group (sensitivity training) Education and training to increase skills, knowledge in the areas of technical task needs, relationship skills, process skills, decision making, problem solving, planning, goal-setting skills Grid OD phase 1 Work redesign Gestalt OD Behavior modeling
Interventions designed to improve the effectiveness of DYADS/TRIADS	Process consultation Third-party peacemaking Role negotiation technique Gestalt OD
Interventions designed to improve the effectiveness of TEAMS and GROUPS	Team building — Task directed — Process directed Gestalt OD Grid OD phase 2 Interdependency exercise Appreciative inquiry Responsibility charting Process consultation Role negotiation Role analysis technique "Startup" team-building activities Education in decision making, problem solving, planning, goal setting in group settings Team MBO Appreciations and concerns exercise Sociotechnical systems (STS) Visioning Quality of work life (QWL) programs Quality circles Force-field analysis Self-managed teams
Interventions designed to improve the effectiveness of INTERGROUP RELATIONS	Intergroup activities — Process directed — Task directed Organizational mirroring Partnering Process consultation Third-party peacemaking at group level Grid OD phase 3 Survey feedback
Interventions designed to improve the effectiveness of the TOTAL ORGANIZATION	Sociotechnical systems (STS) Parallel learning structures MBO (participation forms) Cultural analysis Confrontation meetings Visioning Strategic planning/strategic management activities Grid OD phases 4, 5, 6 Interdependency exercise Survey feedback Appreciative inquiry Future search conferences Quality of work life (QWL) programs Total quality management (TQM) Physical settings Large-scale systems change

Figure 8-1 Typology of OD Interventions Based on Target Groups

13. *Strategic Management Activities.* Activities that help key policy-makers reflect systematically on their organization's basic mission and goals and environmental demands, threats, and opportunities and engage in long-range action planning of both a reactive and proactive nature. These activities direct attention in two important directions: outside the organization to a consideration of the environment, and away from the present to the future.

14. *Organizational Transformation Activities.* Activities that involve large-scale system changes; activities designed to cause a fundamental change in the nature of the organization. Almost everything about the organization is changed—management philosophy, reward systems, the design of work, the structure of the organization, organization mission, values, and culture. Total quality programs are transformational; so are programs to create high-performance organizations or high-performance work systems. Sociotechnical systems theory and open systems planning provide the basis for such activities.

Each of these families of interventions has many activities and exercises included in it. They involve both conceptual material and actual experience with the phenomenon being studied. Some of the families are directed toward specific targets, problems, or processes. For example, the team-building activities are specific to intact work teams, while the life-planning activities are directed to individuals, although this latter activity takes place in group settings. Some interventions are *problem* specific: examples of this are the third-party peacemaking activities and the goal-setting activities. Some activities are *process* specific, that is, specific to selected processes: an example of this is the intergroup activities in which the processes involved in managing interfaces are explored.

Another way to classify OD interventions is by the primary target of the intervention, for example, individuals, dyads and triads, teams and groups, intergroup relations, and the total organization. Fig. 8-1 shows this classification scheme. Some interventions have multiple targets and multiple uses, and thus appear in several places in the figure.

These classification schemes are intended to help you understand the range and uses of OD interventions. For those interested in exploring typologies further, Porras and Robertson offer a comprehensive discussion.[11]

CONCLUDING COMMENT

This overview of OD interventions—the action component of organization development—presented some of the thinking that goes into planning and implementing OD interventions. Leaders and practitioners are encouraged to learn the full range of interventions so that change efforts will be relevant, timely, properly structured, and ultimately successful.

NOTES

1. R. W. White, "Motivation Reconsidered: The Concept of Competence," *Psychological Review*, 66 (1959), pp. 297–334.
2. D. C. McClelland, J. W. Atkinson, R. A. Clark, and E. L. Lowell, *The Achievement Motive* (New York: Appleton-Century-Crofts, 1953).
3. From Michael Beer, *Organization Change and Development* (Glenview, IL: Scott, Foresman and Company, 1980). Copyright © 1980 by Scott, Foresman and Company. Reprinted by permission.
4. Robert R. Blake and Jane S. Mouton, *The Managerial Grid* (Houston: Gulf, 1964), pp. 281–283. There is also *The Managerial Grid III* (1985) and *The Managerial Grid IV* (1990).
5. Robert R. Blake and Jane S. Mouton, *Consultation* (Reading, MA: Addison-Wesley, 1976). See also *Consultation*, 2nd ed. (1983).
6. George C. Homans, *The Human Group* (New York: Harcourt, Brace & Co., 1950).
7. Gardner Murphy, "The Freeing of Intelligence," *Psychological Bulletin*, 42, (1945), pp. 1–19.
8. E. H. Schein, *Process Consultation Vol. I* (Reading, MA: Addison-Wesley Publishing Company, 1988).
9. Robert R. Blake and Jane S. Mouton, *Building a Dynamic Corporation Through Grid Organization Development* (Reading, MA: Addison-Wesley Publishing Company, 1969). This book is a treatise showing how grid organization development programs operate. See also the excellent update on Grid OD: Robert R. Blake, Jane Srygley Mouton, and Anne Adams McCanse, *Change by Design* (Reading, MA: Addison-Wesley Publishing Company, 1989).
10. R. E. Walton, *Interpersonal Peacemaking: Confrontation and Third-Party Consultation* (Reading, MA: Addison-Wesley Publishing Company, 1969), p. 1. This entire book is devoted to a discussion of this specialized intervention technique. See also R. E. Walton, *Managing Conflict*, 2nd ed. (Reading, MA: Addison-Wesley, 1987).
11. Jerry I. Porras and Peter J. Robertson, "Organizational Development: Theory, Practice, and Research," in Marvin D. Dunnette and Leaetta M. Hough, eds., *Handbook of Industrial and Organizational Psychology*, 2nd ed., vol. 3. (Palo Alto, CA: Consulting Psychologists Press, 1992), pp. 719–822.

9

TEAM INTERVENTIONS

In Chapters 9 through 12 we will examine in detail many of the interventions that are used in contemporary OD efforts. These interventions are techniques and methods designed to change the culture of the organization, move it from "where it is" to where organizational members want it to be, and generally enable them to improve their practices so that they may better accomplish individual, team, and organizational goals. The broad nature of these interventions and a preliminary look at the different types of methods have already been presented. In this chapter we present descriptions, goals, and mechanics of the various technical tools of OD practitioners that are directed toward improving the performance of ongoing work teams—from office or plant floor to board rooms—as well as temporary team configurations.

TEAMS AND WORK GROUPS:
STRATEGIC UNITS OF ORGANIZATION

Collaborative management of the work team culture is a fundamental emphasis of organization development programs. This reflects the reality that much of the organization's work is accomplished directly or indirectly through teams and the assumption that work team culture exerts a significant influence on individual behavior. In large part, the techniques and the theory for understanding and improving team processes come from the laboratory training movement coupled with research in the area of group dynamics. An appreciation of the importance of the work team as a determinant of individual behavior and sentiments has come from cultural anthropology, sociology, organization theory, and social psychology.

Although we will use the terms somewhat synonymously, it is important to make a distinction between *groups* and *teams*. "A *work group* is a number of persons, usually reporting to a common superior and having some face-to-face interaction, who have some degree of interdependence in carrying out tasks for the purpose of achieving organizational goals."[1] A *team* is a form of group, but has some characteristics in greater degree than ordinary groups, including a higher commitment to common goals and a higher degree of interdependency and interaction. Jon Katzenbach and Douglas Smith define *team* as follows: "A team is a small number of people with complementary skills who are committed to a common purpose, set of performance goals, and approach for which they hold themselves mutually accountable."[2] This distinction is particularly relevant in conceptualizing the kinds of teams desired in organization development efforts, in the creation of self-managed teams, and in the development of high-performance teams.

Among the early writers who directed attention to the importance of team functioning were Rensis Likert and Douglas McGregor. Likert, for example, suggested that organizations are best conceptualized by systems of interlocking groups connected by *linking pins*—individuals who occupy membership in two groups by being a boss in one group and a subordinate in another.[3] It is through these interlocking groups that the work of the organization gets done. The key reality seems to be that individuals in organizations function not so much as *individuals* alone but as *members* of groups or teams. For an individual to function effectively, frequently a prerequisite is that the team must function effectively.

Both Likert and McGregor identified some of the characteristics of well-functioning, effective groups (teams). McGregor's list of characteristics is as follows:

> The atmosphere tends to be relaxed, comfortable, and informal
>
> The group's task is well understood and accepted by the members
>
> The members listen well to each other; there is a lot of task-relevant discussion in which most members participate
>
> People express both their feelings and ideas
>
> Conflict and disagreement are present but are centered around ideas and methods, not personalities and people
>
> The group is self-conscious about its own operation
>
> Decisions are usually based on consensus, not majority vote
>
> When actions are decided upon, clear assignments are made and accepted by the members[4]

According to McGregor, when these conditions are met, it is likely that the team is successfully accomplishing its mission and simultaneously satisfying the personal and interpersonal needs of its members.

Later writers and researchers have built on the work of McGregor, Likert, and others to specify the dimensions of team effectiveness. In Chapter 5 we listed eight characteristics that Carl Larson and Frank LaFasto have found in all high-performance teams.[5] Glenn Parker has also looked at the characteristics of effective teams and has developed a similar list. Here is his list (our explanations are in parentheses):

Characteristics of an Effective Team

Clear purpose (defined and accepted vision, mission, goal or task, and an action plan)

Informality (informal, comfortable, and relaxed)

Participation (much discussion and everyone encouraged to participate)

Listening (members use effective listening techniques such as questioning, paraphrasing, and summarizing)

Civilized disagreement (team is comfortable with disagreement; does not avoid, smooth over, or suppress conflict)

Consensus decision making (substantial agreement through thorough discussion, avoidance of voting)

Open communications (feelings are legitimate, few hidden agendas)

Clear roles and work assignments (clear expectations and work evenly divided)

Shared leadership (while there is a formal leader, everyone shares in effective leadership behaviors)

External relations (the team pays attention to developing outside relationships, resources, credibility)

Style diversity (team has broad spectrum of group process and task skills)

Self-assessment (the team periodically stops to examine how well it is functioning)[6]

High-performance teams have the same characteristics but to a higher degree. Katzenbach and Smith say that strong personal commitment to each other—commitment to the others' growth and success—distinguishes high-performance teams from effective teams.

> Energized by this extra sense of commitment, high-performance teams typically reflect strong extensions of the basic characteristics of teams: deeper sense of purpose, more ambitious performance goals, more complete approaches, fuller mutual accountability, interchangeable as well as complementary skills.[7]

Team interventions in OD tend to be congruent with the characteristics identified in the preceding lists and are designed to bring about these conditions. Parenthetically, when groups are asked to describe what their groups would be like if they were operating at a highly effective level, they generate lists similar to the preceding lists.

Again, teams and work groups are considered to be the fundamental units of organizations and also key leverage points for improving the functioning of the organization. The following are among the interventions that have been developed to help teams become more effective while simultaneously addressing organizational problems and challenges.

BROAD TEAM-BUILDING INTERVENTIONS

Probably the most important single group of interventions in OD are team-building activities, the goals of which are the improvement and increased effectiveness of various teams within the organization. Some interventions focus on the intact work team composed of a boss and subordinates, which we are calling the formal group. Other interventions focus on special

Figure 9–1   Varieties of Team-Building Interventions

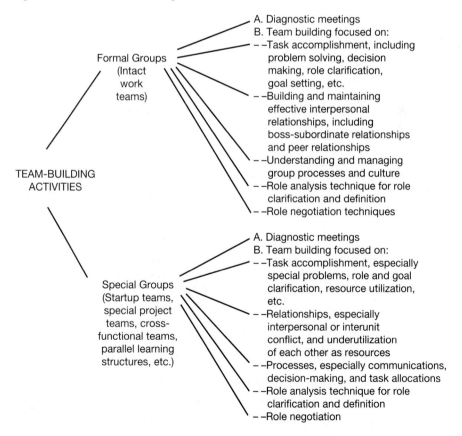

teams such as startup teams, newly constituted teams due to mergers, organization structure changes, or plant startups; task forces; cross-functional project teams; and committees.

Team-building interventions are typically directed toward four major substantive areas: diagnosis, task accomplishments, team relationships, and team and organization processes. These separate thrusts are diagrammed in Figure 9-1. In the following pages we describe major approaches to team building, such as the formal work group diagnostic meeting, formal work group team-building meeting, process consultation, and Gestalt OD, as well as a number of techniques and exercises used within team-building sessions to address specific issues.

Let us examine several of these interventions as they might be conducted with a formal group. The major actors are a consultant, who is not a member of the group (the *third party*), the group leader, and the group members.

THE FORMAL GROUP DIAGNOSTIC MEETING

The purpose of the formal group diagnostic meeting is to conduct a general critique of the performance of the group, that is, to take stock of "where we are going" and "how we are doing," and to surface and identify problems so that they may be worked on. Typically the leader and the consultant discuss the idea first, and if it appears that a genuine need for a diagnostic meeting exists, the idea is put to the group for their reactions. The leader may structure his or her testing for the group's reaction in the form of the following questions: What are our strengths? What problems do we have that we should work on? How are we doing in regard to our assigned tasks? How are our relationships with each other? What opportunities should we be taking advantage of?

If it is decided to conduct the formal group diagnostic meeting, after some thinking about their own performance, the group assembles for a half-day or a day meeting. There are several ways of getting the diagnostic data out, that is, to make the information public:

A total-group discussion involving everyone making individual contributions to the total assemblage.

Subgrouping, which involves breaking down into smaller groups where a more intensive discussion takes place, then the subgroups reporting back to the total group. (This is particularly effective because people have more "air time" and there is a higher degree of safety in the anonymity of a subgroup report.)

Pairing of two individuals who interview each other or who simply discuss their ideas with each other, each pair then reporting back to the total group.

When the data are shared throughout the group, the next steps consist of discussing the issues, grouping the issues in terms of themes (say, planning problems, interface problems, goal ambiguity problems), and getting a preliminary look at the next action steps. The next action steps may call for a team-building meeting, may assign different persons to task groups to work on the problems, or may include a number of other strategies that involve moving from the diagnostic data to corrective action taking. It should be noted however that the primary focus of the group diagnostic meeting is to surface issues and problems that should be worked on and to decide *how* to take action steps. Taking action is generally a postmeeting activity or an activity for subsequent team meetings.

The formal group diagnostic meeting permits a group to critique itself and to identify its strengths and problem areas, and it allows everyone to participate in generating the necessary data. The data then form the basis for planning future actions. Such a meeting requires only a minimal expenditure of time. Semiannual diagnostic meetings afford an excellent method for staying on top of problems. A key secret to the success of a short diagnostic meeting is the realization by all participants that the meeting is for the purpose of identifying problems, not solving problems.

Diagnostic meetings for newly constituted groups, say, task forces or new teams resulting from mergers or acquisitions, are similar in form and function to the group diagnostic meeting. These meetings may have to be held more frequently to stay ahead of the problems. Furthermore, linking diagnostic meetings with problem-solving sessions or team-building sessions may be indicated for newly constituted teams.

THE FORMAL GROUP TEAM-BUILDING MEETING

The formal group team-building meeting has the goal of improving the team's effectiveness through better management of task demands, relationship demands, and group processes. It is an inward look by the team at its own performance, behavior, and culture for the purposes of dropping out dysfunctional behaviors and strengthening functional ones. The group critiques its performance, analyzes its way of doing things, and attempts to develop strategies to improve its operation. Sometimes the purpose of the meeting is a special agenda item, such as developing the group's performance goals for the coming year. Often the purpose of the meeting is for the more general charge expressed in the questions: How can we build ourselves into a better functioning team? and How can we do the job better?

The team-building session is usually initiated by the manager in consultation with the third party. The idea is then tested for reactions with the group. (Conversely, the group may initiate the idea and take it to the boss if they sense pressing problems that need examination and solution.) A good length of time for the meeting is anywhere from one to three days. The session should be held away from the work place.

The usual practice for these sessions is to have the consultant interview each of the group members and the leader prior to the meeting, asking them what the strengths of the group are, what their problems are, how they think the group functions, and what obstacles are getting in the way of the group performing better. These interview data are categorized into themes by the consultant, who presents the themes to the group at the beginning of the meeting. The group examines and discusses the issues, ranks them in terms of their importance, examines the underlying dynamics of the problems, begins to work on solutions to the problems, and establishes some action steps to bring about the changes deemed desirable. It is imperative to have follow-up meetings to determine whether the action steps that were outlined were taken and to determine whether or not they had the desired effects. This is the flow of events for the team-building meeting. But let us look closer at the components.

The meeting may be called for a special purpose, such as a new member coming into the group, an organization structure change, or planning for the next year; or it may primarily be devoted to maintaining and managing the group's culture and processes. If it is a special-purpose meeting, time should still be allocated to an examination and critique of the group's dynamics.

As mentioned previously, it is often desirable for the consultant to interview the entire group, using an open-ended approach, such as "What things do you see getting in the way of this group being a better one?" This procedure introduces the consultant to the group members and allows the consultant to assess commitment to the team-building session. The consultant decides in advance and informs the interviewees whether or not the information each gives will be considered public or confidential. There seem to be advantages and disadvantages to either approach. For example, if the information in the interviews is confidential, the interviewees may be more candid and open than they will be if they know the information is public. On the other hand, treating the information as public data helps to set a climate of openness, trust, and constructive problem solving. If the information is considered confidential, the consultant is careful to report the findings in a general way that does not reveal the sources of information. Other ways the agenda items for the meeting are developed are through such devices as the formal group diagnostic meeting or through a survey.

The consultant presents the interview results in terms of themes. When everyone has understood the themes, these are ranked by the group in terms of their importance, and the most important ones form the agenda for the meeting. In the course of the meeting, much interpersonal and group process information will be generated, and that may be examined too. The group thus works on two sets of items: the agenda items and the items that emerge from the interactions of the participants.

As important problems are discussed, alternatives for action are developed. Generally, the team-building meeting involves deciding on action steps for remedying problems and setting target dates for "*who* will do *what when.*"

Significant variations of the team-building session entail devoting time to problem-solving methods, planning and goal-setting methods, conflict resolution techniques, and the like. These special activities are usually initiated in response to the needs demonstrated or stated by the group. The consultant often makes conceptual inputs (mini-lectures) or structures the situation so that a particular problem or process is focused on and highlighted. A wide variety of exercises may be interspersed into the three-day meeting, depending upon the problems identified and the group phenomena that emerge.

Figure 9-1 suggests that team-building sessions may be directed toward problem solving for task accomplishment, examining and improving interpersonal relationships, or managing the group's culture and processes. It may be that one of these issues is the principal reason for holding the team-building meeting. For example, suppose that the meeting is designed as a team problem-solving session to examine the impact on the team of a new function or task being added to the group's work requirements. Even in this case a portion of the session will probably be reserved for reflecting on *how* the team is solving its problems, that is, critiquing the group's processes. In this way the team becomes more effective at both the task level and the process level.

Richard Beckhard lists, in order of importance, the four major reasons or purposes involved in having teams meet other than for the sharing of information: (1) to set goals and/or priorities . . . (2) to analyze or allocate the way work is performed . . . (3) to examine the way a group is working, its processes (such as norms, decision making, communications) . . . and (4) to examine relationships among the people doing the work.[8] He notes that often all four items will be covered in a single team-building session, but it is imperative that the *primary* goal be clear and accepted by all. It is especially important that the leader and the consultant agree on the primary goal. Often the consultant will have a priority list of items that are inverse to those just given—from relationships among people as most important, to the way the group works together as next most important, to the work itself next, and to goals and priorities as least important. Lack of agreement on the primary goal can lead to wasted energy and a generally unproductive and frustrating team-building session. We agree with Beckhard when he states that the consultant should help to implement the group leader's goals for the session, not the consultant's goals.

Bell and Rosenzweig relied heavily upon team-building workshops in an OD program in a municipal government organization and came to the following assessment:

> Our experience leads us to the tentative conclusion that some relatively simple notions underlie success, namely:
>
> 1. Get the *right people* together for
> 2. A *large block of uninterrupted time*
> 3. To work on *high-priority problems or opportunities* that
> 4. *They have identified* and that are worked on
> 5. In *ways that are structured* to enhance the likelihood of
> 6. *Realistic solutions and action plans* that are
> 7. *Implemented* enthusiastically and
> 8. *Followed up* to assess actual versus expected results.[9]

These authors comment on the overall nature of team-building sessions as follows:

> We have come to believe strongly that initial improvement efforts should be task oriented rather than focused on interpersonal relations. It is usually safer, less resisted, and more appropriate in terms of the problems and opportunities identified by the client. We have tended not to focus on team building per se; rather, we find that it occurs as a natural by-product of learning to solve problems in a group setting. However, we don't avoid interpersonal or team ineffectiveness issues if they are getting in the way of effective and efficient problem solving.[10]

When a team engages in problem-solving activities directed toward task accomplishment, the team members *build something together.* It appears that the act of building something together also builds a sense of camaraderie, cohesion, and *esprit de corps.* The major ingredients involved in a team's building something together are probably the eight steps identified by Bell and Rosenzweig.

In our own consulting we have increasingly come to designate these sessions as "team-building problem-solving workshops"—a clear signal to us and the client that *both* building a more effective team and solving priority problems constitute the business at hand. We consider team-building problem-solving interventions to be a cornerstone of OD technology.

An example of a team-building program might be helpful. The top management team of a quasi-governmental agency decided collectively that they "needed help to become more goal-directed and effective." They interviewed several consultants and selected one who the executive director (the boss) and the team felt was most appropriate for them, their organization, and their problems. At a meeting the consultant explained the team-building problem-solving process, how it would be conducted, and what could be expected of the consultant and the team. Questions were answered; mutual expectations were established.

The consultant then interviewed all team members in confidential interviews to gain an understanding of the strengths and weaknesses of the team and the organization. When the interviews were completed, the consultant met with the executive director to give him an overview of the interview results. While maintaining confidentiality, the consultant described the issues uncovered in the interviews and solicited the executive director's reaction which was that the diagnosis agreed with his own perceptions. Let us explain why we include this step since not all OD practitioners give a preliminary overview to the team leader. We include this step for several reasons: so the leader will not be surprised (and possibly defensive) at the first team-building meeting; so that the leader is forewarned if he or she is viewed as a "problem"; so that we can gauge the leader's willingness to address the problems identified; and so that the leader can be coached to respond constructively to the array of problems. The leader is not allowed to censor problems or to delete problems from the agenda. This step is a useful one, in our view, in that it helps to build a foundation of trust and openness between the key client and the consultant. (The team had been informed that this step would occur.)

The next event was the first meeting, an all-day, off-site workshop. The executive director opened the meeting with remarks that established a constructive, optimistic climate. Next the consultant presented the strengths and problem areas found in the interviews and asked the team to prioritize the problem areas in terms of importance and urgency. The rest of that day was spent exploring the three highest priority problems and developing action steps to correct the problems. Four subsequent all-day meetings were held at intervals of three or four weeks until the original problem agenda was worked through. This schedule allowed enough time between meetings to implement action steps, while at the same time keeping the level of momentum and energy high. At the fifth meeting the team decided to hold quarterly team-building meetings to monitor progress and to address and solve new problems. Three quarterly meetings were held with the consultant present and later meetings were held without him. This is a typical team-building intervention sequence of activities and events.

An excellent statement of the team-building process is found in William Dyer's *Team Building: Issues and Alternatives*. He describes team building as a data gathering, diagnostic, action planning, and action taking process conducted by intact work teams. He says of the process,

> One underlying assumption regarding teams in organizations is that resources are available in the individuals in the work unit. They have

the capability to address and deal with the above questions, [issues of declining performance] and the problems behind the questions, if given the time, encouragement, and freedom needed to work honestly toward solutions. Team development in its best sense is creating the opportunity for people to come together to share their concerns, their ideas, and their experiences, and to begin to work together to solve their mutual problems and achieve common goals.[11]

The basic building blocks of organizations are teams, and one of the basic building blocks of organization development is team building.

PROCESS CONSULTATION INTERVENTIONS

The process consultation model is similar to team-building interventions except that in process consultation greater emphasis is placed on diagnosing and understanding process events. Furthermore, there is greater emphasis on the consultant being more nondirective and questioning as he or she gets the groups to solve their own problems.

Process consultation (PC) represents an approach or a method for intervening in an ongoing system. The crux of this approach is that a skilled third party (consultant) works with individuals and groups to help them learn about human and social processes and learn to solve problems that stem from process events. This approach has been around a long time; many practitioners operate from this stance. Edgar Schein pulled together the disparate practices and principles of process consultation in a comprehensive and coherent exposition.[12] Schein also describes the role of PC in organization development.

Process consultation consists of many different interventions; it is not any single thing the consultant does. The paramount goal of PC is stated by Schein as follows:

> The job of the process consultant is to help the organization solve its own problems by making it aware of organizational processes, the consequences of these processes, and the mechanisms by which they can be changed. The process consultant helps the organization to learn from self-diagnosis and self-intervention. The ultimate concern of the process consultant is the organization's capacity to do for itself what he has done for it. Where the standard consultant is more concerned about passing on his knowledge, the process consultant is concerned about passing on his skills and values.[13]

Some particularly important organizational processes are communications, the roles and functions of group members, group problem solving and decision making, group norms and group growth, leadership and authority, and intergroup cooperation and competition.[14] The

PC consultant works with the organization, typically in work teams, and helps them to develop the skills necessary to diagnose and solve the process problems that arise.

Schein describes the kinds of interventions he believes the process consultant should make:

1. Agenda-setting interventions, consisting of:
   —Questions which direct attention to interpersonal issues.
   —Process-analysis periods.
   —Agenda review and testing procedures.
   —Meetings devoted to interpersonal process.
   —Conceptual inputs on interpersonal-process topics.
2. Feedback of observations or other data, consisting of:
   —Feedback to groups during process analysis or regular work time.
   —Feedback to individuals after meetings or after data-gathering.
3. Coaching or counseling of individuals [see discussion following].
4. Structural suggestions:
   —Pertaining to group membership.
   —Pertaining to communication or interaction patterns.
   —Pertaining to allocation of work, assignment of responsibility, and lines of authority.[15]

In Schein's view, the process consultant would most often make interventions in that same order: agenda setting, feedback of observations or other data, counseling and coaching, and, least likely, structural suggestions. Specific recommendations for the solution of substantive problems are not listed because to Schein such interventions violate the underlying values of the PC model in that the consultant is acting as an expert rather than as a resource.[16]

In *coaching and counseling interventions*, which may be considered either as a part of PC or as a set of interventions in their own right, the consultant is placed in the role of responding to such questions from groups or individuals as "What do you think I should do in this instance to improve my performance?" "Now that I can see some areas for improvement, how do I go about changing my behavior?"

Schein sees the consultant's role in coaching and counseling situations to be the following: "The consultant's role then becomes one of adding alternatives to those already brought up by the client, and helping the client to analyze the costs and benefits of the various alternatives which have been mentioned."[17] Thus the consultant, when counseling either individuals or groups, continues to maintain the posture that real improvements and changes in behavior should be those decided upon by the client. The consultant serves to reflect or mirror accurate feedback, to listen to alternatives and suggest new ones (often through questions designed to expand the client's horizons), and to assist the client in evaluating alternatives for feasibility, relevance, and appropriateness.

The basic congruence between theories of counseling and the theory of process consultation is pointed out by Schein: "In both cases it is essential to help the client improve his ability to observe and process data about himself, to help him accept and learn from feedback and to help him become an active participant with the counselor/consultant in identifying and solving his own problems."[18]

A GESTALT APPROACH TO TEAM BUILDING

A form of team building that focuses more on the individual than the group is the Gestalt approach to OD. The major advocate of this orientation is Stanley M. Herman, a management and OD consultant. The approach rests on a form of psychotherapy developed by Frederick S. "Fritz" Perls called Gestalt therapy.[19] Gestalt therapy is based on the belief that persons function as whole, total organisms. And each person possesses positive and negative characteristics that must be "owned up to" and permitted expression. People get into trouble when they get fragmented, when they do not accept their total selves, and when they are trying to live up to the demands ("shoulds") of others rather than being themselves. Robert Harman lists the goals of Gestalt therapy as awareness, integration, maturation, authenticity, self-regulation, and behavior change.[20] Basically, one must come to terms with oneself, must accept responsibility for one's actions, must experience and live in the "here and now," and must stop blocking off awareness, authenticity, and the like by dysfunctional behaviors.

Stanley Herman applies a Gestalt orientation to organization development, especially in working with leader-subordinate relations and team building. The primary thrust is to make the *individual* stronger, more authentic, and more in touch with the individual's own feelings; building a better team may result, but it is not the primary desired outcome. As Herman says,

> My objective here is not to provide instruction on making the organization culture safer, more pleasant or easier for the individual, but rather to help the individual recognize, develop and experience his own potency and ability to cope with his organization world, whatever its present condition. Further, I would like to encourage him to discover for himself his own unique wants of that environment and his capacity to influence and shape it in ways that get him more of what he wants.[21]

To do this people must be able to express their feelings fully, both positive and negative. They must "get in touch" with "where they are" on issues, relations with others, and relations with selves. They must learn to "stay with" transactions with others and work them through to resolution rather than suppressing negative feelings or cutting off the transactions prematurely. They must learn to accept the polarities within themselves—weakness-strength, autocratic-democratic urges, and so forth.

The Gestalt OD practitioner fosters the expression of positive and negative feelings, encourages people to stay with transactions, structures exercises that cause individuals to become more aware of what they want from others, and pushes toward greater authenticity for everyone. The Gestalt OD practitioner often works within a group setting, but the focus is usually on individuals.

Use of the Gestalt orientation to OD is not widespread. An interesting book by Herman and Korenich gives a theoretical framework, examples, and exercises for Gestalt OD, and this intervention may become more popular in organization development.[22]

We are somewhat ambivalent about the Gestalt orientation to OD. On the one hand, better individual functioning is a laudable goal and deserves support. On the other hand, this is an intervention of considerable "depth" and one that people might not choose to expose themselves to—they may believe they are being coerced into a therapeutic situation that they would prefer to avoid. One thing is certain: the Gestalt orientation to team building should not be used except by practitioners trained in this method.

TECHNIQUES AND EXERCISES USED IN TEAM BUILDING

A number of techniques and exercises are used in team building to facilitate team performance and to address specific problematic issues. These are useful and powerful ways to structure the team's activities and energies in order to achieve understanding of the issues and to take corrective actions. Before using these techniques, a careful diagnosis should be made to ensure that the technique is appropriate. Team-building sessions often include many of these techniques and exercises.

Role Analysis Technique

The role analysis technique (RAT)* intervention is designed to clarify role expectations and obligations of team members to improve team effectiveness. In organizations individuals fill different specialized roles in which they manifest certain behaviors. This division of labor and function facilitates organization performance. Often, however, the role incumbent may not have a clear idea of the behaviors ex-

---

*Our colleague Charles Hosford suggests the more euphonic label role analysis process (RAP) for this procedure.

pected of him or her by others and, equally often, what others can do to help the incumbent fulfill the role is not understood. Ishwar Dayal and John M. Thomas developed a technique for clarifying the roles of the top management of a new organization in India.[23] This technique is particularly applicable for new teams, but it may also be helpful in established teams where role ambiguity or confusion exists. The intervention is predicated on the belief that consensual determination of role requirements for team members, consisting of a joint building of the requirements by all concerned, leads to more mutually satisfactory and productive behavior. Dayal and Thomas call the activity the *role analysis technique.*

In a structured series of steps, role incumbents, in conjunction with team members, define and delineate role requirements. The role being defined is called the *focal role.* In a new organization, it may be desirable to conduct a role analysis for each of the major roles.

The first step consists of an analysis of the focal role initiated by the focal role individual. The role, its place in the organization, the rationale for its existence, and its place in achieving overall organization goals are examined along with the specific duties of the office. The specific duties and behaviors are listed on a chalkboard and are discussed by the entire team. Behaviors are added and deleted until the group and the role incumbent are satisfied that they have defined the role completely.

The second step examines the focal role incumbent's expectations of others. The incumbent lists his or her expectations of the other roles in the group that most affect the incumbent's own role performance, and these expectations are discussed, modified, added to, and agreed upon by the entire group.

The third step consists of explicating others' expectations and desired behaviors of the focal role, that is, the members of the group describe what they want from and expect from the incumbent in the focal role. These expectations of others are discussed, modified, and agreed upon by the group and the focal role person.

Upon conclusion of this step, the focal role person assumes responsibility for making a written summary of the role as it has been defined; this is called a *role profile* and is derived from the results of the discussions in steps 1 through 3. Dayal and Thomas describe the role profile as follows: "This consists of (a) a set of activities classified as to the prescribed and discretionary elements of the role, (b) the obligation of the role to each role in its set, and (c) the expectations of this role from others in its set. Viewed in toto, this provides a comprehensive understanding of each individual's 'role space.'"[24]

The written role profile is briefly reviewed at the following meeting before another focal role is analyzed. The accepted role profile constitutes the role activities for the focal role person.

This intervention can be a nonthreatening activity with high payoff. Often the mutual demands, expectations, and obligations of interdependent team members have never been publicly examined. Each role incumbent wonders why "those other people" are "not doing what they are supposed to do," while in reality all the incumbents are performing as they think they are supposed to. Collaborative role analysis and definition by the entire work group not only clarifies who is to do what but ensures commitment to the role once it has been clarified.

From our experience, this procedure can be shortened if there is already high visibility and understanding of the current activities of various role incumbents. For example, if one of the problems facing an organization is confusion over the duties of the board of directors and the president or the executive director, the following sequence can be highly productive. This occurred in a workshop setting involving the board, the president, and the key subordinates in one of our team-building sessions.

1. With the board listening, the president and his staff members discuss this question: "If the board were operating in an optimally effective way, what would they be doing?"

2. During this discussion, responses are made visible on a chalkboard or on large newsprint, and disagreements are recorded.

3. After 45 minutes or so, the list is modified on the basis of general consensus of the total group.

4. The procedure is repeated, but this time the president listens while staff and board members discuss the question, "If the president were operating in an optimally effective way, what would he be doing?" Again, responses are made visible during the discussion. The president responds, and then there is an attempt at consensus.

As with the longer technique, this procedure helps to clarify role expectations and obligations and frequently leads to some significant shifts in the whole network of activities of the management group, including the board. For example, we have seen this procedure result in boards shifting their activities almost exclusively to policy determination, pulling away from previously dysfunctional tinkering with day-to-day operating problems, and delegating operations to the president and the staff.

Interdependency Exercise

An interdependency exercise is a useful intervention if team members have expressed a desire to improve cooperation among themselves and among their units. This exercise is also useful for assisting people in getting better acquainted, in surfacing problems that may be latent and not previously examined, and in providing useful information about current challenges being faced in others' areas of responsibility.

The interdependency exercise can be structured as follows, although facilitators can invent other versions. It works well with up to approximately ten people, but can become too cumbersome and time consuming if more than that number are involved. Let's assume the top ten people of an organization or a division of the organization are present.

1. Two straight lines of five persons each are formed with the lines facing each other. Each person is seated facing one other person, but with pairs of people seated far enough apart to minimize distractions. Thus, persons 1, 2, 3, 4, and 5 will be seated facing persons 6, 7, 8, 9, and 10. Person 1 faces person 6; person 2 faces person 7, and so on.

2. Using the assignment sheets for taking notes as shown in Figure 9-2, persons facing each other are instructed to interview each other about the important interdependencies between their two jobs and/or units. Furthermore, they are instructed to interview each other about what seems to be going particu-

Figure 9-2 Interdependency Interviews

(For taking notes: for your use only)

Person being interviewed _____

Unit _____

Please ask these questions:

What/where are the most important interdependencies between our two units (or our two jobs)?

What's going particularly well?

Present or potential snags?

Any action plans or agreement to meet further _____

Tailor the dialogue to fit your circumstances. For example, if there is very little interdependency, learn a few things about the other person's job, etc.

---

larly well in the interdependencies and what present or potential snags are perceived. They are also instructed to make mutual action plans at the end of the interview or to meet further, if desired.

3. At the end of ten minutes, people in one row are asked to shift positions one chair within their row. That is, person 1 moves to where 2 had been sitting, 2 moves to where 3 had been sitting, and so on, and 5 moves from the end of the row to where 1 had been sitting. (Persons 6 to 10 keep their same seats. Only the one row moves.)

4. Once the first round of five interviews is completed, the group takes a break. After the break, the persons in *each row* pair up and interview each other. This requires a series of five more interview periods with one person sitting out each period.

Since there are ten persons involved, each person must interview nine others, for a total of 90 minutes of interviewing. Approximately two hours should be allocated for the total exercise. Participants report that this procedure is tiring, but in many ways exhilarating and extremely productive. Participants report considerable follow-up after the workshop.

Obviously, this exercise requires the participants' cooperation and assumes no serious conflict situations. Serious, intense conflict situations require a different structure and more time.

A shortened version of this same technique can be used in a large group of say, 60 people, if clusters of ten people interview each other, each having a different question. Each cluster has the same assignment and the same questions. For example, in each cluster of ten people, each person 1 through 10 is assigned a different question. Each interviews the five people seated in the opposite row through the procedure of asking people in one row to move over one chair at specified intervals of time. People who move take their question with them.

After the five paired interviews are completed, all of the "experts" about one question are now asked to meet together. Thus, ten new groups are formed by asking all six people who had the same question to meet and share what they found out. That is, persons 1 from each of the six clusters meet together; persons 2 meet together, and so on. These new groups share the data, extract the themes, and report the themes to the total group.* This procedure is a rapid way to gather a great deal of data for diagnostic purposes.

A Role Negotiation Technique

When the causes of team ineffectiveness are based on people's behaviors that they are unwilling to change because it would mean a loss of power or influence to the individual, a technique developed by Roger Harrison called "role negotiation" can often be used to great advantage.[25]

---

*We are indebted to Herman (Hy) Resnick for introducing us to this "phalanx" technique of interviewing. We are uncertain as to its origin.

Role negotiation intervenes directly in the relationships of power, authority, and influence within the group. The change effort is directed at the work relationships among members. It avoids probing into the likes and dislikes of members for one another and their personal feelings about one another.[26]

The technique is basically an imposed structure for controlled negotiations between parties in which each party agrees in writing to change certain behaviors in return for changes in behavior by the other. The behaviors relate to the job. Specifically, I ask you to change some of your behaviors so that I can do my job more effectively; and you ask me to change some of my behaviors so that you can do your job more effectively. Harrison states that the technique rests on one basic assumption: *"Most people prefer a fair negotiated settlement to a state of unresolved conflict, and they are willing to invest some time and make some concessions in order to achieve a solution."*[27]

The role negotiation technique usually takes at least one day to conduct. A two-day session with a follow-up meeting a month later is best. We will outline the steps of the technique as given by Harrison.[28] The first step is *contract setting*. Here the consultant sets the climate and establishes the ground rules: we are looking at work behaviors, not feelings about people; be specific in stating what you want others to *do more of* or do better, to *do less of* or stop doing, or *maintain unchanged;* all expectations and demands must be *written;* no one is to agree to changing any behavior unless there is a quid pro quo in which the other must agree to a change also; the session will consist of individuals negotiating with each other to arrive at a *written contract* of what behaviors each will change.

The next step is *issue diagnosis*. Individuals think about how their *own effectiveness* can be improved if others change their work behaviors. Then each person fills out an Issue Diagnosis Form for every other person in the group. On this form the individual states what he or she would like the other to do more of, do less of, or maintain unchanged. These messages are then exchanged among all members, and the messages received by each person are written on a chalkboard or newsprint for all to see.

The next step is the *influence trade* or negotiation period, in which two individuals discuss the *most important* behavior changes they want from the other and the changes they are willing to make themselves. A quid pro quo is required in this step: each person must give something in order to get something. Often this step is demonstrated by two individuals with the rest of the group watching. Then the group breaks into negotiating pairs. "The negotiation process consists of parties making contingent offers to one another such as "If you do X, I will do Y.' The negotiation ends when all parties are satisfied that they will receive a reasonable return for whatever they are agreeing to give."[29] All agreements are written, with each party having a copy. The agreement may be published for the group to see or may not. The influence trade step is concluded when all the negotiated agreements have been made and written down. It is best to have a follow-up meeting to determine whether the contracts have been honored and to assess the effects of the contracts on effectiveness.

In our view Harrison's role negotiation technique is an effective way of bringing about positive improvement in a situation where power and influence issues are working to maintain an unsatisfactory status quo. We have used this technique successfully with several groups and have found that it is an intervention that leads to improved team functioning. It is based on the fact that frequently individuals must change their work behaviors for the team to become more effective.

The Appreciations and Concerns Exercise

The appreciations and concerns exercise may be appropriate if interview data suggest that one of the deficiencies in the interactions of members of a group is lack of expression of appreciation, and that another deficiency is the avoidance of confronting concerns and irritations. There can be various versions of the appreciations and concerns exercise, but basically it is conducted as follows.

1. The facilitator asks each member of the group to jot down one to three appreciations for each member of the group.

2. Each member is also asked to jot down one or two minor irritations or concerns relative to each person that may be interfering with communications, getting the work done effectively, and so on.

3. Along with the assignment, the facilitator may make some suggestions, such as: "You be the judge of which concerns to raise—will it be helpful to the relationship? To the group? Can the person do anything about it? Would it be better to talk privately with the person? On the positive side, sometimes raising concerns in a team setting can provide an opportunity for others to validate what is being perceived or to provide another perspective. By the way, there will be plenty of time to work things through if there are any misunderstandings."

4. Someone is asked to volunteer to be the first person to listen to members of the group. Each group member mentions both the appreciations and concerns about the volunteer who hears from all of the group members before responding, with the exception that questions of clarification are encouraged after each person mentions his or her items.

5. Each group member listens in turn, either through volunteering to be next or through the simple procedure of rotating clockwise or counterclockwise from the first person.

One variation of this exercise is to have each member of the group put his or her name on the top of a sheet of flip-chart paper, and make two column headings: (1) appreciations, and (2) concerns (or what to do differently or consider, and so on). Sheets are taped to the walls, and with a marking pen each member writes appreciations and concerns on each sheet. Once the writing is finished a volunteer is asked to display his or her sheet and read the items aloud to the group. This version is usually productive, but the first version permits more face-to-face interaction.

In instances in which lack of appreciation is a much more serious deficiency than concerns, focusing solely on appreciations can be a powerful and positive intervention in the life of the group. When the concerns segment is used, a mini-lecture from the facilitator on the nature of constructive feedback is desirable. If there is substantial conflict in the group, a more structured exercise, such as the role negotiation technique, is likely to be more appropriate.

Appreciative Inquiry

An intervention broader than the appreciation and concerns exercise is appreciative inquiry, developed by Frank Barrett and David Cooperrider, and refined by Gervase Bushe. As discussed in Chapter 7, this major intervention is based on the assertion that the organization "is a miracle to be embraced" rather than "a problem to be solved."[30] While interventions have evolved as consultant/researchers have experimented with the approach, basically the central interventions are interviews and then discussions in small groups or organization-wide meetings centering on such core questions as:

1. What have been the peak moments in the life of this organization—"when people felt most alive, most energized, most committed, and most fulfilled in their involvements?"

2. What do staff members value most "about themselves, their tasks, and the organization as a whole?"

3. Where excellence has been demonstrated, "what have been the organizational factors (structures, leadership approaches, systems, values, and so on) that most fostered realization of excellence?"

4. What are the "most significant embryonic possibilities, perhaps latent with the system," that indicate "realistic possibilities for an even better organization?"[31]

Researchers, while generally enthusiastic about the contribution that appreciative inquiry can make in "conditions of intergroup and interpersonal defensiveness," express the caution that this intervention could become "an unwilling accomplice in the dynamic of group flight."[32] One of the important aspects that the approach seems to generate is more attention by the consultant and the client organization to the strengths of the organization and its members.[33]

Responsibility Charting

In work teams decisions are made, tasks are assigned, and individuals and small groups accomplish the tasks. This is easily described on paper, but in reality a decision to have someone do something is somewhat more complex than it appears because there are in fact multiple actors involved in even the simplest task assignment. There is the person who does the work, one or more people who may approve or veto the work, and persons who may "contribute" in some way to the work while not being responsible for it. The issue is, *Who is to do what, with what kind of involvement by others?*

A technique called *responsibility charting* helps to clarify who is responsible for what on various decisions and actions.[34] It is a simple, relevant, and very effective technique for improving team functioning. Richard Beckhard and Reuben Harris explain the technique as follows:

> The first step is to construct a grid; the types of decisions and classes of actions that need to be taken in the total area of work under discussion are listed along the left-hand side of the grid, and the actors who might play some part in decision making on those issues are identified across the top of the grid. . . .
>
> The process, then, is one of assigning a behavior to each of the actors opposite each of the issues. There are four classes of behavior:
>
> 1. *Responsibility* (R)—the responsibility to initiate action to ensure that the decision is carried out. For example, it would be a department head's responsibility (R) to initiate the departmental budget.
>
> 2. *Approval required, or the right to veto* (A-V)—the particular item must be reviewed by the particular role occupant, and this person has the option of either vetoing or approving it.
>
> 3. *Support* (S)—providing logistical support and resources for the particular item.
>
> 4. *Inform* (I)—*must be* informed and, by inference, cannot influence.[35]

A fifth behavior (or nonbehavior) is noninvolvement of a person with the decision; this is indicated on the chart with a dash (—). One type of responsibility chart is in Figure 9-3.

Responsibility charting is usually done in a work team context. Each decision or action is discussed and responsibility is assigned. Next, approval-veto, support, and inform functions are assigned. Beckhard and Harris offer some guidelines for making the technique more effective. First, assign responsibility to only one person. That person initiates and then is responsible and accountable for the action. Second, avoid having too many people with an approval-veto function on an item. That will slow down task accomplishment or will negate it altogether. Third, if one person has approval-veto involvement on most decisions, that person could become a bottleneck for getting things done.

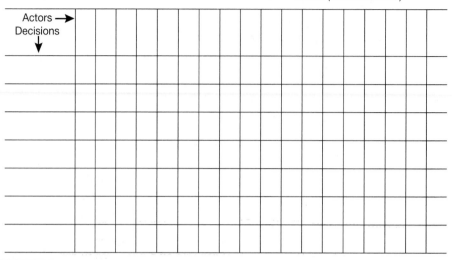

R – Responsibility (initiates)
A–V– Approval (right to veto)
S – Support (put resources against)
I – Inform (to be informed)

Actors →
Decisions ↓

Figure 9–3   Responsibility Chart

Source: Richard Beckhard and Reuben T. Harris, *Organizational Transitions: Managing Complex Change* (Figure 6.1), © 1977 by Addison-Wesley Publishing Company, Inc. Reprinted by permission of the publisher.

Fourth, the support function is critical. A person with a support role has to expend resources or produce something that is then used by the person responsible for the action. This support role and its specific demands must be clarified and clearly assigned. And, finally, the assignment of functions (letters) to persons at times becomes difficult. For example, a person may want A-V on an item, but not really need it; a person may not want S responsibility on an item, but should have it; or two persons each want R on a particular item, but only one can have it.

A responsibility charting session can quickly identify who is to do what on new decisions as well as help to pinpoint reasons why old decisions are not being accomplished as desired. Responsibility charting is a good intervention to use to improve the task performance of a work team.

Visioning

Visioning is a term used for an intervention in which group members in one or more organizational groups develop and/or describe their vision of what they want the organization to be like in the future. The time frame may be anywhere from, say, six months to five years in the future.

The concept of visioning is credited to Ronald Lippitt. According to Weisbord, Lippitt began to tape-record planning meetings in

1949 and found that "people's voices grew softer, more stressed, depressed, as problems were listed and prioritized. You could hear the energy drain away as the lists grew longer."[36] In the 1950s, Lippitt, Ronald Fox, and Eva Schindler-Rainman began referring to "images of potential" rather than to problems as starting points for change, and by the 1970s were involving people in workshops visualizing "preferred futures."[37]

Various visioning techniques are used in team building. Here is an example:

Step 1. On note paper, write down the characteristics you would like to see this organization have one and then two years from now. Use the following categories: (the categories might include products, customer and supplier relationships, human resources practices, leadership style, organizational structure, and so on). You have 90 minutes.

Step 2. Using a marking pen, make the characteristics visible on flipchart paper and display on the wall.

Step 3. Report to the group, and be prepared to answer questions pertaining to clarification. However, no debate is permitted at this point.

Step 4. During a half-hour break, a subgroup of three people extracts the themes from the individual reports and prepares to report them to the total group for discussion.

Here's another example:

Step 1. Each person take a marking pen (and/or yarn, glue, magazines from which to cut pictures, scissors, and so on) and make a collage of what you would like this organization (department, division, and so on) to be two years from now. In an hour (30 minutes, 90 minutes, and so on) be prepared to describe your collage to the group.

Steps 2 and 3. Each person displays and describes his or her collage and the group discusses and extracts the common themes.[38]

Various forms of visioning, or the use of mental imagery or the development of cognitive maps, are extensively used in strategic planning and in future search conferences. Strategic management activities and future search conferences are described in Chapter 12.

 **Force-Field Analysis**

The oldest intervention in the OD practitioner's kit bag is the force-field analysis, a device for *understanding* a problematic situation and *planning corrective actions.* This technique rests on several assumptions: the present state of things (the current condition) is a quasi-stationary equilibrium representing a resultant in a field of opposing forces. A desired future state of affairs (the desired condition) can only be achieved by dislodging the current equilibrium, moving it to the desired state, and stabilizing the equilibrium at that point. To move the equilibrium level from the current to the desired condition the field of forces must be altered—by adding driving forces or by removing restraining forces.

This technique was first proposed by Kurt Lewin in 1947.[39] It is essentially a vector analysis—an analytical tool learned in first-year engineering classes. But the genius of Lewin was to apply the device to social problems, social equilibria, and social change. Lewin proposed that social phenomena—productivity of a factory, morale on a sports team, level of prejudice in a community, and so forth—could best be understood as *processes* being influenced by social forces and events. Furthermore, social phenomena tend to stabilize at equilibrium points because opposing forces come into balance over time.[40] The force-field analysis involves the following steps:

Step 1 Decide upon a problematic situation you are interested in improving, and carefully and completely describe the current condition. What is the status quo? What is the current condition? Why do you want it changed?

Step 2 Carefully and completely describe the desired condition. Where do you want to be? What is the desired state of things?

Step 3 Identify the forces and factors operating in the current force field. Identify the driving forces pushing in the direction of the desired condition; identify the restraining forces pushing away from the desired condition. Identification and specification of the force field should be thorough and exhaustive so that a picture of why things are as they are becomes clear.

Step 4 Examine the forces. Which ones are strong, which are weak? Which forces are susceptible to influence, which are not? Which forces are under your control, which are not? (Important individual forces could themselves be subjected to a force-field analysis in order to understand them better.)

Step 5 Strategies for moving the equilibrium from the current condition to the desired condition are the following: add more driving forces; remove restraining forces; or do both. Lewin advises against simply adding new driving forces because that may increase resistance and tension in the situation. Therefore, in this step select several important, adaptable restraining forces and develop action plans to remove them from the field of forces. As restraining forces are removed, the equilibrium shifts toward the desired condition. New driving forces may also be proposed and action plans developed to implement them.

Step 6 Implement the action plans. This should cause the desired condition to be realized.

Step 7. Describe what actions must be taken to stabilize the equilibrium at the desired condition and implement those actions.

An example of the force-field analysis is shown in Figure 9-4. Assume that the management team of plant X is concerned about excessive turnover and wants to correct that situation. They generate the following force-field analysis:

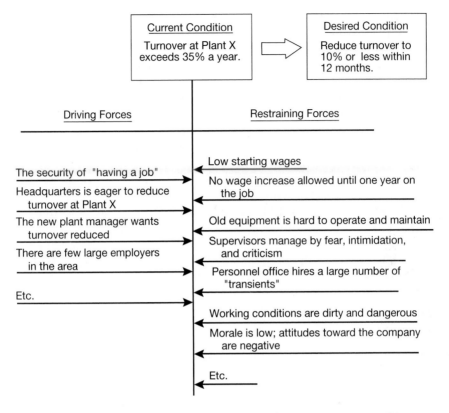

Figure 9-4   Force-field Analysis of a Turnover Problem at Plant X

Mapping the field of forces in this way permits the management team of Plant X to understand the multiple facets of the problem. They would next decide which restraining forces should be removed and develop action plans to initiate those changes.

This technique is excellent for diagnosing change situations. We label it a team intervention (although it is also a tool for individuals) because it can be so powerful and exciting when used by groups. Group analysis typically yields a comprehensive understanding of what is happening to cause the problem and what must be done to correct it.

The force-field analysis is an old and valued friend of the OD practitioner.

A FINAL COMMENT ON TEAMWORK

The reason team-building produces such powerful positive results is because it is an intervention in harmony with the nature of organizations as social systems. Under a system of division of labor, parts of the total organizational task are assigned to teams; and then that team assignment is broken down and assigned to individuals. In most cases individual members of the team are *interdependently related* to each other and must coordinate and integrate individual efforts in order to achieve successful task accomplishment. Conceptualizing the team as the relevant system rather than individuals was the profound insight developed by early OD pioneers such as Blake, Shepard, Mouton, and McGregor: the team is the relevant unit for making individuals more effective. (See Chapter 3 for this history.) The efficacy of team building confirms the validity of that view.

A new conceptualization has evolved in recent years that likewise has validity, efficacy, and implications for practice. That idea is this: on many projects the relevant team (or system) includes persons outside the functional unit; the relevant system is a cross-functional team. The criterion is still the same—identifying those persons who are *interdependently related* in the successful accomplishment of the task. For example, in the development of the new Saturn automobile at General Motors cross-functional teams were used from the outset. Rather than have one functional team (say, design) do its work and then "throw the plans over the wall" to the next functional team (say, production), cross-functional teams provided oversight throughout the entire project.[41] In his book, *Thriving On Chaos*, Tom Peters advocates increasing the use of cross-functional teams so that American industry can compete successfully in today's fast-paced environment.[42] Increasingly, the *relevant system* for making individuals effective and for facilitating task accomplishment includes cross-functional representation.

CONCLUDING COMMENTS

In addition to discussing the nature of effective teams, in this chapter we have examined the major sets of activities that constitute team-building interventions and their rationales. They are at the center of OD activities. However, it is probable that if it were not for the interventions directed to improving intergroup relations (see Chapter 10) or interventions directed to improving the total organization (see Chapters 11 and 12); there would not be such a discipline as OD today; there would instead only be an expanded "small-group" discipline. We want to underscore that while the small group or team is an entry point in most OD strategies, and while ongoing attention to team effectiveness is a sine qua non for successful OD efforts, achieving total organizational improvement is possible only by going beyond the level of the team.

NOTES

1. Wendell L. French, *Human Resources Management*, 3rd ed. (Boston: Houghton Mifflin, 1994), p. 114.
2. Jon R. Katzenbach and Douglas K. Smith, "The Discipline of Teams," *Harvard Business Review*, 71 (March–April 1993), p. 112.

3. Rensis Likert, *New Patterns of Management* (New York: McGraw-Hill, 1961).
4. Douglas McGregor, *The Human Side of Enterprise* (New York: McGraw-Hill, 1960).
5. Carl E. Larson and Frank M. J. LaFasto, *TeamWork* (Newbury Park, CA: Sage Publications, 1990).
6. Glenn M. Parker, *Team Players and Teamwork: The New Competitive Business Strategy* (San Francisco: Jossey-Bass, 1990), p. 33.
7. Jon R. Katzenbach and Douglas K. Smith, *The Wisdom of Teams* (Boston: Harvard Business School Press, 1993), p. 79.
8. From Richard Beckhard, "Optimizing Team-Building Efforts," *Journal of Contemporary Business*, 1, no. 3 (Summer 1972), 23–32.
9. Cecil Bell, Jr. and James Rosenzweig, "Highlights of an Organization Improvement Program in a City Government," in W. L. French, C. H. Bell, Jr., and R. A. Zawacki, eds., *Organization Development Theory, Practice, and Research* (Dallas: Business Publications, 1978).
10. Ibid.
11. William G. Dyer, *Team Building: Issues and Alternatives* (Reading, MA: Addison-Wesley, 1977), p. 41. See also the second edition of Dyer's book published in 1987 by Addison-Wesley. See also W. Brendan Reddy and Kaleel Jamison, *Team Building* (Alexandria, VA: NTL Institute for Applied Behavioral Science; and San Diego: University Associates, 1988). For a detailed description of numerous interventions see J. K. Fordyce and R. Weil, *Managing WITH People: A Manager's Handbook of Organization Development Methods* (Reading, MA: Addison-Wesley, 1971).
12. Edgar H. Schein, *Process Consultation: Its Role in Organization Development* (Reading, MA: Addison-Wesley Publishing Company, 1969; 2nd edition, 1988).
13. Schein, 2nd ed., 1988, vol. I, pp. 193–194.
14. Schein, 1st ed., p. 13.
15. Ibid., pp. 102–103.
16. Ibid., p. 103.
17. Ibid., p. 116.
18. Ibid., p. 116. For more on process consultation, see Jane Moosbruker, "The Consultant as Process Leader," *OD Practitioner*, 21 (March 1989), pp. 10–12.
19. F. Perls, R. Hefferline, and P. Goodman, *Gestalt Therapy* (New York: Julian Press, 1951). See also F. Perls, *Gestalt Therapy Verbatim* (Lafayette, CA: Real People Press, 1969).
20. Robert L. Harman, "Goals of Gestalt Therapy," *Professional Psychology*, (May 1974), pp. 178–184.
21. Stanley M. Herman, "A Gestalt Orientation to Organization Development," in W. Warner Burke, ed., *Contemporary Organization Development: Conceptual Orientations and Interventions* (Washington, DC: NTL Institute for Applied Behavioral Science, 1972), pp. 69–89. This passage is taken from page 70.
22. Stanley M. Herman and Michael Korenich, *Authentic Management: A Gestalt Orientation to Organizations and Their Development* (Reading, MA: Addison-Wesley, 1977).
23. I. Dayal and J. M. Thomas, "Operation KPE: Developing a New Organization," *Journal of Applied Behavioral Science*, 4, no. 4 (1968), 473–506. The present discussion is based on this article.
24. Ibid., p. 488.
25. Roger Harrison, "When Power Conflicts Trigger Team Spirit," *European Business*, (Spring 1972), pp. 27–65.
26. Ibid., p. 58.
27. Ibid., p. 58. [Harrison's emphasis.]
28. These steps are paraphrased from ibid., pp. 59–63.
29. Ibid., p. 63.
30. Frank J. Barrett and David L. Cooperrider, "Generative Metaphor Intervention: A New Approach for Working with Systems Divided by Conflict and Caught in Defensive Perception," *The Journal of Applied Behavioral Science*, 26, no. 2 (1990), 219–239.
31. Based on or inferred from Barrett and Cooperrider, p. 229; and a draft of an

unpublished paper by Gervase R. Bushe, "Advances in Appreciative Inquiry as an Organization Development Technique," (September 1992), pp. 1–7. (Gervase Bushe, Simon Fraser University, Burnaby, British Columbia.)

32. Barrett and Cooperrider, p. 237.

33. Bushe, "Advances in Appreciative Inquiry as an Organization Development Technique," p. 6.

34. See Richard Beckhard and Reuben T. Harris, *Organizational Transitions: Managing Complex Change* (Reading, MA: Addison-Wesley, 1977), pp. 76–82.

35. Ibid., p. 76. See also Richard Beckhard and Wendy Pritchard, *Changing the Essence: The Art of Creating and Leading Fundamental Change in Organizations* (San Francisco: Jossey-Bass Publishers, 1992), pp. 83–84.

36. Marvin R. Weisbord, "Toward Third-Wave Managing and Consulting," *Organizational Dynamics,* 15 (Winter 1987), pp. 20–21.

37. Marvin R. Weisbord, *Productive Workplaces* (San Francisco: Jossey-Bass Publishers, 1987), p. 283.

38. For more on the use of collages, see Fordyce and Weil, *Managing WITH People,* pp. 152–155.

39. Kurt Lewin, "Frontiers in Group Dynamics: Concept, Method, and Reality in Social Science; Social Equilibria and Social Change," *Human Relations,* 1, no. 1 (June 1947), 5–41.

40. See the following articles in *The Planning of Change,* W. G. Bennis, K. D. Benne, and R. Chin, eds., (New York: Holt, Rinehart and Winston, 1964): "The Utility of System Models and Developmental Models for Practitioners" by Robert Chin, pp. 201–214; "Force Field Analysis Applied to a School Situation" by David H. Jenkins, pp. 238–244.

41. Described in the symposium "The Role of OD in General Motors' Saturn Project" at the 1987 Academy of Management Annual Meeting in New Orleans, October 11, 1987.

42. Tom Peters, *Thriving on Chaos* (New York: Alfred A. Knopf, 1988).

10

INTERGROUP AND THIRD-PARTY PEACEMAKING INTERVENTIONS

When there is tension, conflict, or competition among groups, some very predictable things happen: each group sees the other as an "enemy" rather than as a neutral object; each group describes the other in terms of negative stereotypes; interaction and communication between the two groups decrease, cutting off feedback and data input between them; what intergroup communication and interaction does take place is typically distorted and inaccurate; each group begins to prize itself and its products more positively and to denigrate the other group and its products; each group believes and acts as though it can do no wrong and the other group can do no right; under certain circumstances the groups may commit acts of sabotage (of various kinds) against the other group.[1] Most people are aware of the existence of considerable intergroup conflict in organizations, and most people are aware of the patterns of behavior of groups in conflict. But few people know ways to alleviate the conflict to avoid the consequences of the conflict.

Several strategies for reducing intergroup conflict have been identified in the literature. They include a "common enemy" (an outside object or group that both groups dislike, which brings the groups closer together); increasing the interaction and communication among the groups (increased interaction under favorable conditions tends to be associated with increased positive feelings and sentiments); finding a supraordinate goal (a goal that both groups desire to achieve but that neither can achieve without the help of the other); rotating the members of the groups; and instituting some forms of training.[2] Even knowing these strategies for reducing intergroup conflict may not be very help-ful—the questions still remain, How can we *implement* conflict-reducing mechanisms? and How do we *begin?*

The dynamics of conflict and its resolution between *two persons* in organizations are very similar and, therefore, in this chapter we will examine the technology to reduce interpersonal conflict as well as inter-group conflict. These interventions are very important because of the se-rious impact intergroup and interpersonal conflict has on team and orga-nizational functioning and on human satisfactions. In addition, the development of techniques to improve systems larger than single teams has marked a significant step toward being able to improve total sys-tems.

INTERGROUP TEAM-BUILDING INTERVENTIONS

The focus of this team-building group of OD interventions is on improv-ing intergroup relations. The goals of these activities are to increase com-munications and interactions between work-related groups, to reduce the amount of dysfunctional competition, and to replace a parochial in-dependent point of view with an awareness of the necessity for interde-pendence of action calling on the best efforts of both groups. It is not un-common for a significant amount of dysfunctional energy to be spent in competition, misunderstanding, miscommunication, and misperception between groups. Organizational reward structures often encourage such behavior through emphasis on *unit* goal attainment as contrasted with total-organization goal attainment. Organization development methods provide ways of increasing intergroup cooperation and communication, as we see in this series of interventions.

One set of activities developed by Blake, Shepard, and Mouton is widely applicable to situations where relations between groups are strained or overtly hostile.[3] The steps are these:[4]

Step 1. The leaders of the two groups (or the total membership) meet with the consultant and are asked if they think the relations between the two groups can be better and are asked if they are willing to search for mechanisms or procedures that may improve intergroup relations. Their concurrence that they are willing to search for ameliorative mechanisms is all that they are asked to commit themselves to at that time. If they agree to do this, the following ac-tivities take place.

Step 2. The intergroup intervention per se begins now. The two groups meet in separate rooms and build two lists. In one list they give their thoughts, attitudes, feelings, and perceptions of the other group—what the other group is like, what it does that gets in their way, and so on. In the second list the group tries to predict what the other group is saying about them in its list—that is, they try to anticipate what the other group dislikes about them, how the other group sees them and so on. Both groups build these two lists.

Step 3. The two groups come together to share with each other the information on the lists. Group A reads its list of how it sees Group B and what it dislikes about Group B. Group B reads its list of how it sees Group A and what it dislikes about it. The consultant imposes the rule that there will be no discussion of the items on the lists and limits questions to clarifying the meaning of the lists only. Next, Group A reads its list of what it expected Group B would say about it, and Group B reads its list of what it thought Group A would say about it.

Step 4. The two groups return to their separate meeting places and are given two tasks. First, they react to and discuss what they have learned about themselves and the other group. It typically happens that many areas of disagreement and friction are discovered to rest on misperceptions and miscommunication; these are readily resolved through the information sharing of the lists. The differences between the two groups are seen not to be as great as was imagined, and the problems between them are seen to be fewer than imagined. After this discussion, the group is given a second task: to make a list of the priority issues that still need to be resolved between the two groups. The list is generally much smaller than the original list. Each group builds such a list.

Step 5. The two groups come back together and share their lists with each other. After comparing their lists, they then together make one list containing the issues and problems that should be resolved. They set priorities on the items in terms of importance and immediacy. Together they generate action steps for resolving the issues and assign responsibilities for the actions. "Who will do what when" is agreed upon for the most important items. That concludes the intervention.

Step 6. As a follow-up to the intergroup team-building activity, it is desirable to have a meeting of the two groups or their leaders to determine whether the action steps have in fact occurred and to assess how the groups are doing on their action plans. This ensures that the momentum of the intergroup intervention is not lost.

This procedure can also be used with large groups drawn from two very large populations. For example, after an expression of interest by parole officers and police officers in improving mutual understanding and relationships, we spent an evening with the two groups in an exercise called Project Understanding. By coincidence, members of the two groups happened to be attending workshops the same week at the same conference center. We simply divided the two large populations into small groups and paired off these small groups and conducted an exercise almost identical to the sequence given. Tentative action recommendations were posted in the large general session room for informal perusal during a social activity which followed.

A slightly modified version of this procedure is presented by Fordyce and Weil based on their experiences at TRW Systems.[5] In this version, two groups that have decided to work on improving their intergroup relations come together for the intergroup team-building meeting and are separated into two meeting rooms. Each group is assigned the task of building three lists as follows:

1. A "positive feedback" list containing the things the group values and likes about the other group;

2. A "bug" list containing the things the group does not like about the other group;

3. An "empathy" list containing a prediction of what the other group is saying in its list.

The two groups come together, and spokespeople for the groups read their lists. Questions are limited to issues of clarification only; discussion of the items is disallowed.

At this point, instead of breaking into separate groups again, the total group together builds an agenda or a master list of the major problems and unresolved issues between the two groups. The issues are ranked in terms of importance.

Subgroups are formed containing members from each group and are given the task of discussing and working on each item. The subgroups all report back to the total group.

On the basis of the information from the subgroups, the work on the issues that has been going on, and the total information shared by the two groups, the participants now build a list of action steps for improving intergroup relations and commit themselves to carrying out the actions. For each of the action steps, people are assigned specific responsibilities and an overall schedule of completion for the action steps is recorded.

We have found that it is possible to work simultaneously with *three* groups in these kinds of intergroup activities, without the participants (or the consultants) finding the procedure too confusing. For example, in working with the key people in one Indian tribal organization, we requested each of three groups to develop lists about the other two groups plus themselves and to share the results in the total group. More specifically, the tribal council (one of the three groups) was requested to develop the following lists:

I. How the tribal council sees the tribal staff
   A. Things we like about the tribal staff
   B. Concerns we have about the tribal staff
II. What we (the tribal council) predict the tribal staff will say about us
III. How the tribal council sees the Community Action Program (CAP) staff
   A. Things we like about the CAP staff

  B. Concerns we have about the CAP staff

 IV. What we (the tribal council) predict the CAP staff will say about us.

Concurrently, the tribal staff and the CAP staff developed comparable lists reflecting their perceptions of the other two groups and their predictions of what would be said about them.

  These kinds of activities have been found to bring about better intergroup relations. It has empirically been shown time and again, in diverse situations, that in a relatively short time period (say, a day) these structured intergroup activities can result in improved intergroup relations. The intergroup problems and frictions are decreased or resolved, and intergroup communication and interaction are increased.

THIRD-PARTY PEACEMAKING INTERVENTIONS

Third-party interventions into conflict situations have the potential to control (contain) the conflict or resolve it. R. E. Walton has presented a statement of theory and practice for third-party peacemaking interventions that is both important in its own right and important for its role in organization development.[6] His book is directed toward interpersonal conflict—understanding it and intervening in ways to control or resolve the conflict. This intervention technique is somewhat related to intergroup relations described previously but there are many unique aspects to conflict situations involving only two people. In this section, rather than describe specific interventions, we explicate some of the features of the theory presented by Walton.

  A basic feature of third-party intervention is confrontation: the two principals must be willing to confront the fact that conflict exists and that it has consequences for the effectiveness of the two parties involved. The third party must know how, when, and where to utilize confrontation tactics that surface the conflict for examination.

  The third party must be able to diagnose conflict situations, and Walton presents a diagnostic model of interpersonal conflict based on four basic elements: the conflict issues, the precipitating circumstances, the conflict-relevant acts of the principals, and the consequences of the conflict.[7] In addition, conflict is a cyclical process, and the cycles may be benevolent, malevolent, or self-maintaining. For accurate diagnosis it is particularly important to know the source of the conflict. Walton speaks to this issue:

> A major distinction is drawn between substantive and emotional conflict. *Substantive issues* involve disagreements over policies and practices, competitive bids for the same resources, and differing conceptions of roles and role relationships. *Emotional issues* involve nega-

tive feelings between the parties (e. g., anger, distrust, scorn, resentment, fear, rejection).[8]

This distinction is important for the third-party consultant in that substantive issues require problem-solving and bargaining behaviors between the principals, while emotional issues require restructuring perceptions and working through negative feelings.

Intervention tactics for the third party consist of structuring confrontation and dialogue between the principals. Many choice points exist for the consultant. Walton lists the ingredients of productive confrontation:

> 1. mutual positive motivation [both parties are disposed to attempt to resolve the conflict]
> 2. balance in the situational power of the two principals [power parity is most conducive to success]
> 3. synchronization of their confrontation efforts [initiatives and readiness to confront should occur in concert between the two parties]
> 4. appropriate pacing of the differentiation and integration phases of a dialogue [time must be allowed for working through of negative feelings and clarification of ambivalent or positive feelings]
> 5. conditions favoring openness in dialogue [norms supporting openness and reassurance for openness should be structured for the parties]
> 6. reliable communicative signs [making certain each can understand the other]
> 7. optimum tension in the situation [there should be moderate stress on the parties][9]

Most of these ingredients are self-explanatory, but some elaboration may be helpful on the differentiation and integration phases. In the differentiation phase of conflict, the principals clarify the differences that divide them and sort out the negative feelings they have; in the integration phase, the principals seek to clarify their commonalities, the positive feelings or ambivalence that may exist, and the commonality of their goals.

The third party will intervene directly and indirectly in facilitating dialogue between the principals. Examples of direct interventions would be interviewing the principals before a confrontation meeting, helping to set the agenda, attending to the pace of the dialogue, and refereeing the interaction; examples of more subtle interventions of the third party would be setting the meeting on neutral turf, setting time boundaries on the interaction, and the like.

Figure 10-1 shows the steps used by one of your authors in a number of two-person conflict management sessions. These evolved out of experience with Blake, Shepard, and Mouton's intergroup team-building activities, and the conditions and settings were consistent with

Walton's approach to third-party peacemaking interventions as described earlier. These sessions were usually conducted over a total working day in a neutral and comfortable setting, including a totally social lunch, and then were followed up by a two- to three-hour session a month later.

Third-party intervention into interpersonal conflict situations requires a highly skilled professional or a highly skilled layperson who understands the dynamics of conflict. This intervention should not be undertaken by a novice in human and social processes of organizations.

Figure 10-1   Two-Person Conflict Management Sessions

I. The Positives

  A. Jot down, in general terms, what you would like the working relationship to be like (no negatives)

  B. Positive attributes of other person

  C. Share—questions of clarification only—no debate—focus on understanding

II. Sharing of Pain, Resentments

  A. Behaviors of the other person over last 2 to 3 months (or years) that have caused me pain, hurt, anger, embarrassment, resentment (salient incidents)

  B. Share—no debate—check on meaning—you should be able to say it back to other person

  C. Discuss

III. Contracting

  A. (1) It would contribute to my effectiveness if you did the following things *more or better*.

    (2) It would contribute to my effectiveness if you did the following things *less or stopped doing them*.

    (3) It would contribute to my effectiveness if you *continued* doing the following things.

  B. Share—check on meaning

  C. Discussion

  D. Each person writes:

I am willing to	What I need from you if I am to do this effectively
(1)	
(2)	
(3)	
Etc.	

  E. Share

IV. Next action steps (e.g., meet further at a specified time, meet regularly once per _____, etc.)

ORGANIZATION MIRROR INTERVENTIONS

The *organization mirror* is a set of activities in which a particular organizational group, the host group, gets feedback from representatives from several other organizational groups about how it is perceived and regarded. This intervention is designed to improve the relationships between groups and increase the intergroup work effectiveness. It is different from the intergroup team-building intervention in that three or more groups are involved, representatives of other work-related groups typically participate rather than the full membership, and the focus is to assist the host unit that requested the meeting.[10]

The flow of events is as follows: an organizational unit that is experiencing difficulties with units to which it is work related may ask key people from those other units to come to a meeting to provide feedback on how they see the host unit. The consultant often interviews the people attending the meeting before the meeting takes place in order to get a sense of the problems and their magnitude, to prepare the participants, and to answer any questions that the participants may have.

After opening remarks by the manager of the host group, in which he or she sets the climate by stating that the host group genuinely wants to hear how the unit is perceived, the consultant feeds back to the total group information from the interviews. The outsiders "fishbowl" to discuss and explore the data presented by the consultant. (A fishbowl is a group seating and talking configuration in which there is an inner circle of chairs for people who talk and an outside circle of observers and noninteractors.) The fishbowl allows the invited participants to talk about the host unit in a natural, uninterrupted way while the host group members listen and learn. Following this, the host group members fishbowl and talk about what they have heard, ask for any clarification, and generally seek to understand the information they have heard. There may at this point be a general discussion to ensure that everyone understands what is being said, but at this time the participants do not start to work on the problems that have been uncovered.

For actually working on the problems, subgroups composed of both host group members and invited participants are formed. The subgroups are asked to identify the most important changes that need to be made to improve the host unit's effectiveness. After the small groups have identified the key problems, the total group convenes to make a master list to work out specific action plans for bringing about the changes deemed most important. The total group hears a summary report from each subgroup. Action plans are firmed up, people are assigned to tasks, and target dates for completion are agreed upon. This concludes the organization mirror intervention, but a follow-up meeting to assess progress and to review action steps is strongly recommended.

In a short period of time an organizational unit can get the feedback it needs to improve its relations with significant work-related groups. The organization mirror intervention provides this feedback effectively. It is imperative that following the meeting the host group in fact implement the action plans that were developed in the meeting.

PARTNERING

In situations in which two or more organizations are likely to incur unnecessary conflict and cost overruns such as in the owner-contractor relationship in a large construction project, an intervention called *partnering* can be productive for both parties. Partnering is a variation of team building, intergroup team building, and strategic planning having the objective of forming "an effective problem-finding/problem-solving management team composed of personnel from both parties, thus creating a single culture with one set of goals and objectives for the project."[11] Partnering has been used in the private sector—for example, Fluor Daniel and Du Pont—and in military and government construction.[12]

The people from both parties who should be involved are identified by Donald Mosely and colleagues: ". . . Ideally, partnering involves all the functions in the construction project, including engineering and design, site management, and home office support."[13]

In a typical partnering project involving the U.S. Army Corps of Engineers and a contractor, interventions included these steps or events:

1. The Corps of Engineers selected the consultants.

2. A retreat at a neutral site lasting from 21/2 to 41/2 days was scheduled prior to the beginning of construction. Participants included key managers from home offices, site managers from both the Corps and the contractor, and the consultants.

3. The workshop focused on "team building, action research, and planning—including advanced conflict resolution methods, developing a shared vision, and strategic planning with a common set of goals and objectives." Several exercises were used at the beginning to "break the ice" and to demonstrate the utility of group decision making. Lists were developed and shared showing both the "strengths" and "problems" of the Corps and the contractor. Mixed groups comprised of members from both parties selected one or more of the problems to diagnose further, identified and evaluated possible courses of action, and made action recommendations to the total group.

4. At the workshop, mutual commitment to teamwork, equitable problem solving, and open communications was made.

5. A follow-up workshop—this one two days in length—was held three months after construction began.

6. At six months, "on-site data-gathering visits were conducted with follow-up two-day workshops involving all key players."

While partnering did not solve all of the problems that surfaced during the life of the various projects, high success rates have been reported, and participants tended to report "better results than on previous non-partnered projects." As a result, partnering has been used on several other large government projects involving the Air Force, U.S. Navy, and NASA, and their contractors.[14]

CONCLUDING COMMENTS

Intergroup team building, third-party peacemaking, the organization mirror, and partnering are four major interventions that have been developed to improve intergroup and interpersonal relations. They all work; that is, they actually reduce intergroup and interpersonal conflict and improve relationships.

Why these interventions work is not totally understood. But the underlying dynamics that cause these techniques to be efficacious are probably the following:

1. The interactions between the groups are *controlled* and a *structure is imposed to maintain control.* Control is imposed when the groups are asked to build the lists separately, when they are permitted only minimal interaction at the early stages of the interventions, when they are not allowed to argue or defend positions on the lists, and when they are held to a lockstep procedure by the third-party consultant. Even having to build written lists rather than being allowed to talk between groups is a powerful form of control. These controls keep negative feelings and passions in check; any hostile feelings are not allowed to escalate.

2. The interventions are based on data, and the *data are complete and public.* When group A puts down *all* the things about group B that it dislikes, that gives group B a grasp of the scope of the problem issues and permits a *comprehensive understanding* of the differences and problems. Knowing the scope of the issues and having a comprehensive understanding of them is probably a necessary ingredient in making a group (or an individual) move from a defensive posture to a problem-solving stance.

Suppose that group A is telling group B the things it does not like about group B in an ordinary argument situation. Someone introduces item 1. It is argued about, defended, rationalized, and so forth. Probably before there is any resolution on item 1 someone introduces item 2, which triggers a new round of argument and counter-argument and probably no resolution. By the time items 3 and 4 have been tossed into the ring, most of the discussants will be frustrated, angry, and convinced that "*we* were right all along about *them*" and "*they* just don't understand *us*." When the problems are lobbed in like mortar shells, the group feels that it is under attack: its members are continually off balance; they feel their defense is necessary but is not very good, since it is a tactical one only; and they are hindered from building a strategy for defense, much less a strategy for problem solving or change.

Making the data public seems to have its own important dynamic. There is a sense of "Finally, it's all out in the open." Instead of private gripes and complaints, rumors of which may get back to the offending party, now things are public and available to all. For joint problem solving to take place, all the actors who are part of the problem or part of the solution must share the same data. Making the data public is one way of making this happen. Another aspect of public data is that now the problems are clearly identified as specific problems; people now have something to work on—they know what expertise or resources must be brought to bear, and how to start to solve the problems. Furthermore, people are by nature problem solvers—once a specific problem is identified and made public, people just naturally start to "work it."

3. The early stages of these interventions—making lists and sharing them and using the fishbowl technique—lead the participants to *experience feelings of success in dealing with the other group.* Feelings of anxiety, apprehension, and hostility start to give way to feelings of competence and success as the early stages of the interventions produce better communication and understanding than the participants had expected. Nothing succeeds like success, and the early stages are usually perceived as a success experience by both groups. This leads to the optimistic realization that "We *can* work together with those people." Participants are watching for subtle cues of defensiveness, resistance to the data, stubbornness, and the like, and the controlled nature of the process makes most of these unnecessary. This starts building momentum for feelings of competence and success.

4. The *constructive, problem-solving tone* of the meetings, set by the leaders or the consultant, *carries a force of its own.* If people want to be negative, destructive, and defensive, they have to go against the tenor of the meeting. This is increasingly difficult to do if a clear problem-solving climate has been established.

There are no doubt other dynamics of the intergroup and interpersonal interventions, but those just listed indicate some of the reasons why such interventions usually work. The intergroup and interpersonal interventions are an important part of the OD practitioner's repertoire. They require some skill in their execution, but the process itself carries the brunt of the work in making them effective interventions.

NOTES

1. Research evidence for these statements comes from the following sources: M. Sherif and Carolyn Sherif, *Groups in Harmony and Tension* (New York: Harper & Row, 1953); and R. R. Blake and Jane S. Mouton, "Conformity, Resistance, and Conversion," in I. A. Berg and B. M. Bass, eds., *Conformity and Deviation* (New York: Harper & Row, 1961). For a succinct summary of this issue, see E. H. Schein, *Organizational Psychology,* 2nd ed. (Englewood Cliffs, NJ: Prentice-Hall, 1970), Chap. 5.

2. Schein, *Organizational Psychology,* Chap. 5.
3. R. R. Blake, H. A. Shepard, and J. S. Mouton, *Managing Intergroup Conflict in Industry* (Houston: Gulf, 1965).
4. This discussion is based on R. Beckhard, *Organization Development: Strategies and Models* (Reading, MA: Addison-Wesley, 1969), pp. 33–35.
5. This discussion is taken from J. K. Fordyce and R. Weil, *Managing WITH People* (Reading, MA: Addison-Wesley, 1971), pp. 124–30.
6. R. E. Walton, *Interpersonal Peacemaking: Confrontations and Third Party Consultation* (Reading, MA: Addison-Wesley, 1969).
7. Ibid., p. 71.
8. Ibid., p. 73.
9. Ibid. This list is taken from page 94; our interpretation is shown in brackets; Walton's discussion of the list is on pages 94–115. For a newer edition of this work, see Richard E. Walton, *Managing Conflict: Interpersonal Dialogue and Third-Party Roles,* 2nd ed. (Reading, MA: Addison-Wesley Publishing Company, 1987). For a classic statement on interpersonal conflict, see Carl R. Rogers, "Dealing With Psychological Tensions," *Journal of Applied Behavioral Science,* 1 (January-February-March 1965), p. 13.
10. Fordyce and Weil, in *Managing WITH People,* discuss this intervention in detail (pp. 101–105). We believe this technique was developed by the OD practitioners at TRW Systems.
11. Carl Moore, Donald Mosley, and Michelle Slagle, "Partnering: Guidelines for Win-Win Project Management," *Project Management Journal,* 23 (March 1992), p. 18.
12. In addition to the other sources cited, this description of partnering is based on Donald Mosley, Carl Moore, Michelle Slagle, and Daniel Burns, "Partnering in the Construction Industry: Win-Win Strategic Management in Action," *National Productivity Review,* 10 (Summer 1991), pp. 319–325.
13. Ibid., p. 320.
14. Ibid., pp. 320–325. See also Donald C. Mosley, Jeanne Maes, Michelle L. Slagle, and Carl Moore, "An Analysis & Evaluation of a Successful Partnering Project: The Bonneville Navigation Lock," *Organization Development Journal,* 11 (Spring 1993), pp. 57–65.

11

COMPREHENSIVE INTERVENTIONS

In this chapter we examine OD interventions that are comprehensive in terms of the extent to which the total organization is involved and/or the depth of cultural change addressed. Included is a discussion of *"getting the whole system in the room," future search conferences, Beckhard's confrontation meeting, strategic management activities, survey feedback* (linked to *System 4T), Grid OD,* and *Schein's cultural analysis.* We will also discuss *transorganizational development (TD),* a variation of OD that involves several organizations.

"GETTING THE WHOLE SYSTEM IN THE ROOM"

Phrases like "getting the whole system in the room" are appearing with increasing frequency in OD practice.[1] What OD professionals are talking about is the usefulness of getting all of the key actors of a complex organization or system together in a team-building, future-planning kind of session. Future search conferences comprise one version of "getting whole systems in the room," and Beckhard's confrontation meeting is another version. In a sense, partnering, as described in Chapter 10, is in the same mode.

      The rationale for inviting all of the key actors of a complex system to meet together is congruent with systems theory and an extension of the assumptions underlying team building. If you get all of the people with crucial interdependencies together to work on matters of mutual concern, good things can happen. In this case, the system is conceptualized as a total organization or as several organizations in interaction.

"Getting the whole system in one room" has a long and venerable history, including the art and science of conference planning and running large meetings. For example, Burke and Beckhard's book, *Conference Planning*, has essays that go back to the 1940s and that are relevant to today's OD practice.[2] Examples of the "whole system" might be

Managers of all of the functional areas in a business

Representatives of top management, a cross section of employees from all levels, and supplier and customer representatives

All of the librarians in a state or region plus the director and staff of the state library system

Or, the directors of all of the social service agencies in a community.

The latter is an example of the overlap between OD and community development, an overlap that has been apparent since scholar/practitioners like Eva Schindler-Rainman were working with community agencies in the 1950s and 1960s (see Chapter 3).

FUTURE SEARCH CONFERENCES

Marvin Weisbord has written extensively about future search conferences that integrate ideas from Ronald Lippitt, Edward Lindaman, Eric Trist, Fred and Merrelyn Emery, and others. Of particular use were Lippitt's and Lindaman's findings that "when people plan present actions by working backward from what is really desired, they develop energy, enthusiasm, optimism, and high commitment."[3]

Also of particular relevance in the evolution of future search conferences was the experience of Trist and the Emerys in conceptualizing and running conferences for European managers, which included a participative environmental scan and the development of a common vision. In the environmental scan, conference participants described "the network of outside pressures on their organization."[4] (See also the section on visioning, Chapter 9.)

One version of Weisbord's future search conference model consists of the following steps:[5]

1. The consultants (or conference managers) meet with a voluntary committee of four to six potential participants. Many aspects are planned, including the overall focus, who should attend, dates and times, location and meals, group tasks, and so on. The conferences are usually planned to start on

Wednesday evening (with dinner followed by the first working session) and to end on Friday afternoon.

2. Up to 50 or 60 people are invited. Depending on the nature of the focus, the whole system is represented in the conference. This might mean people from all of the functional areas and levels of the organization; persons from all racial, ethnic, sex, and age backgrounds; and might include customers, suppliers, and union leaders. People are asked to bring newspaper and magazine clippings that describe events they believe are influencing and shaping the organization's future.

3. Participants sit at tables of six to eight, with an easel, marking pens, and tape. Depending on the focus and assigned tasks, groupings may vary during the conference, with group membership assigned or based on self-selection. All group output is recorded on easel paper, all ideas are valid, and agreement is not required. The conference is not to solve problems, but to generate awareness, understanding, and mutual support. (Conference members, however, make action recommendations at the end of the workshop.)

4. The conference has four or five segments, each lasting up to a half day. As Weisbord describes it, "Each one requires that people (a) build a data base, (b) look at it together, (c) interpret what they find, and (d) draw conclusions for action."[6]

6. *The first major activity focuses on the past.* Although sitting at a table with others, each person individually is asked to make notes on significant events, milestones, and so on, that they can recall relative to each of the past three decades and from three perspectives: self, company (or town or industry), and society. These individual notes are transferred to sheets on the wall that are organized by topic and by decade.

The group at each table is asked to analyze one theme—self, company, or society—across the three past decades and to extract patterns and meanings. Each table then reports to the total group, and a consultant notes trends. The total conference then interprets "good and bad trends and the direction of movement of each."

7. *The second major activity focuses on present factors*—both external and internal—that are shaping the future of the organization. Relative to the external environment, participants are asked to share their newspaper and magazine clippings with their table group and indicate why they think the article is important. Each group selects priorities from lists that are developed. Next, internal events and trends are surfaced by asking people to generate a list of "prouds" and "sorries" relative to what is currently going on within the organization. People vote for the "proudest prouds" and the "sorriest sorries," and the results are displayed and discussed. The conference managers probe, note key statements, and summarize on flip charts.

8. *The third major activity focuses on the future.* New groups are formed and are given one to two hours to develop a draft of a preferred future scenario. "They are asked to imagine the most desirable, attainable future five years out."[7] Varieties of media are used like colored paper, crayon, scissors, tape, and so on. The groups then report to the total conference.

9. *The fourth major activity focuses on next action steps.* Groups are then asked to reflect on what has been surfaced and discussed, and, depending on the

nature of the groupings, to make three lists of suggested action steps for (a) themselves, (b) their function, and (c) the total organization. Action proposals for functional areas are shared by grouping members of the same department together, and next actions steps are decided. In the meantime, members of top management or the steering committee discuss proposals for the total organization, prioritize themes, and develop action plans. Departmental groups and the top management (or steering committee) then present their action plans to the total conference.

10. Before the conference ends, volunteers agree to document the meeting, communicate with others, and to carry forward the next action steps.

Weisbord's evaluation of such conferences is as follows:

> In my enthusiasm for this mode I don't want to imply that one conference transforms forever, or that no further hard work is needed. I do believe that anyone who has attended one of these events remembers it for a lifetime. The search conference links values and action in real time. It promotes productive workplaces by using more of each person's reality. It joins people who need one another, yet rarely interact, in a new kind of relationship. It stimulates creativity and innovative thinking. It offers a unique third-wave springboard for planning and goal setting. In the last half of the twentieth century few media exist as powerful as this one for raising awareness of who we are, what we are up against, what we want, and how we might work together to get it.[8]

BECKHARD'S CONFRONTATION MEETING

The *confrontation meeting*, developed by Richard Beckhard, is a one-day meeting of the entire management of an organization in which they take a reading of their own organizational health.[9] In a series of activities, the management group generates information about its major problems, analyzes the underlying causes, develops action plans to correct the problems, and sets a schedule for completed remedial work. This intervention is an important one in organization development; it is a quick, simple, and reliable way in which to generate data about an organization and to set action plans for organizational improvement. Beckhard says of the confrontation meeting:

> Experience shows that it is appropriate where
> There is a need for the total management group to examine its own workings.
> Very limited time is available for the activity.
> Top management wishes to improve the conditions quickly.
> There is enough cohesion in the top team to ensure follow-up.
> There is real commitment to resolving the issue on the part of top management.

The organization is experiencing, or has recently experienced, some major change.[10]

The steps involved in the confrontation meeting are as follows.[11]

Step 1. Climate Setting (45 to 60 minutes). The top manager introduces the session by stating his or her goals for the meeting, citing the necessity for free and open discussion of issues and problems, and making it clear that individuals will not be punished for what they say. This is generally followed by a statement from the consultant regarding the importance of communication within organizations, the practicability of organization problem solving, and the desirability of addressing and solving organizational problems.

Step 2. Information Collecting (1 hour). Small groups of seven or eight members are formed on the basis of heterogeneity of composition; that is, there is a maximum mixture of people from different functional areas and working situations on each team. The only rule is that bosses and subordinates not be put together on the same team. The top-management group meets as a separate group during this time. The charge to all the groups is as follows:

> Think of yourself as an individual with needs and goals. Also think as a person concerned about the total organization. What are the obstacles, "demotivators," poor procedures or policies, unclear goals, or poor attitudes that exist today? What different conditions, if any, would make the organization more effective and make life in the organization better?[12]

The groups work on this task for an hour and recorder/reporters list the results of the discussion.

Step 3. Information Sharing (1 hour). Reporters from each small group report the group's complete findings to the total group and these are placed on newsprint on the walls. The total list of items is categorized, usually by the meeting leader, into a few major categories that may be based on type of problem (e.g., communications problems), type of relationship (e.g., troubles with top management), or type of area (e.g., problems with the accounting department).

Step 4. Priority Setting and Group Action Planning (1 hour and 15 minutes). This step typically follows a break during which time the items from the lists are duplicated for distribution to everyone. In a 15-minute general session, the meeting leader goes through the list of items and puts a category assignment on each one so that everyone has his or her own copy of the categorized items. Next the participants form into functional, natural work teams reflecting the way they are organized in the organization. Each group is headed by the top manager in the group. The groups are asked to respond to a three-part charge, that is, to do three tasks. First, they are to identify and discuss the issues and problems related to their area, decide on the priorities of these problems, and determine early action steps to remedy the problems that they are prepared to commit themselves (in the total group) to work on. Second, they are asked to identify the problems they think should be the priority issues for top management. Third, they are to determine how they will communicate the results of the confrontation meeting to their subordinates. This completes the confrontation meeting for all the managers except for the top-management group.

Step 5. Immediate Follow-up by Top Team (1 to 3 hours). The top-management team meets after the rest of the participants have left to plan first follow-up action steps and to determine what actions should be taken on the basis of what they have learned during the day. These follow-up action plans are communicated to the rest of the management group within several days.

Step 6. Progress Review (2 hours). A follow-up meeting with the total management group is held four to six weeks later to report progress and to review the actions resulting from the confrontation meeting.

This is the flow of activities for the confrontation meeting. It is an excellent way to get fast results leading toward organization improvement. Beckhard believes that the confrontation meeting provides a quick and accurate means for diagnosing organizational health, promotes constructive problem identification and problem solving, enhances upward communication within the organization, and increases involvement and commitment to action on the part of the entire managerial group.[13] We agree with his assessment.

STRATEGIC MANAGEMENT ACTIVITIES

Many OD programs and interventions are directed toward the internal workings of the organization. Interventions such as team building, managing intergroup relations, survey feedback, and conflict resolution are intended to fine tune the organization to make it function better. There has been a growing awareness that this internal focus must be complemented with an external focus if OD is truly to serve the best interests of the organization. In other words, OD must develop outward-looking interventions directed toward environmental analysis and strategic planning to ensure that the organization is in synchrony with its environment.

The field of business policy developed the concept of strategic management, which is defined as the development and implementation of the organization's grand design or overall strategy for relating to its current and future environmental demands. The concept is described by Schendel and Hofer as follows: "There are six major tasks that comprise the strategic management process: (1) goal formulation; (2) environmental analysis; (3) strategy formulation; (4) strategy evaluation; (5) strategy implementation; and (6) strategic control."[14]

Developing organizational goals is the first step; this means defining the mission and purpose of the organization. Next an assessment is made of the constraints and opportunities afforded by the environment. Two environments are relevant: the present environment and the future environment. The present environment can be monitored directly; constraints and opportunities of the future environment must be predicted. Strategic plans, derived from goals and environmental analysis, are then developed, implemented, and monitored for results. It is generally assumed that some dominant coalition of key decision makers in the organization is responsible for the strategic management process.

Several OD interventions directed toward strategic planning have been around for a long time. These include goal-setting activities, Beckhard's Confrontation Meeting, future search conferences, and phases 4, 5, and 6 of Blake and Mouton's Grid OD. In phase 4 of a Grid program, for example, organization members build an ideal strategic corporate model, and in later stages they develop action plans to achieve that model.

Additional OD strategic planning techniques will be described here. One technique, used by our colleague Charles E. Summer who conducts strategic planning activities with organizations, is based on four questions:

1. What is your present strategy?
2. What are the opportunities and threats to that strategy?
3. What are your strengths and weaknesses to meet those threats and opportunities?
4. What kind of future policies must you adopt to avoid the threats and maximize your strengths?[15]

A top-management team will work for six months to a year answering these four questions. Meetings are held every one or two months; extensive data collection and analysis take place between meetings. It can be seen that the first question requires an in-depth analysis of what the organization is currently doing or what it thinks it is doing. The second question directs attention to the external environment and to forces that may affect the organization's ability to compete and remain viable. The third question starts to mesh organizational capabilities with environmental demands. The fourth question addresses the actions and changes needed to allow the organization to operate as desired in the future.

A strategic planning technique developed by Thomas Rogers[16] uses a series of two-day meetings with the top policymakers. After several "warm-up" questions to get everyone focused on long-range patterns within the organization and within the environment, the group addresses the question, What business are we in? The answers are worked into a *mission statement* for the organization. The next step is to identify and analyze the various "domains" or environmental segments that make demands on the organization. Rogers says that "A major premise about domains is that organizations do not exist independently, but in an interactive state with the various bodies they affect and are affected by.

Four basic domains are suppliers, consumers, competition, and regulators."[17] The steps involved in analyzing domains are (1) to identify the various domains, (2) to identify the current demands of the domains, (3) to identify the current responses of the organization to those demands, (4) to predict future domain demands and future organizational responses, and (5) to identify ideal or desired domain demands and ideal responses. Action planning and implementation designed to act on the environment to bring about desired conditions are then initiated.

Open systems planning (OSP) is a technique developed by Charles Krone, G. K. Jayaram, and others[18] to assess the environment in a systematic way. Here the top team develops a number of scenarios. The Present scenario is a description of the expectations and demands of environmental domains and internal groups and subgroups, along with a description of the current response to those demands. The Realistic Future scenario projects what the future demand picture is likely to be and what the future response pattern is likely to be *if the organization makes no adaptive changes*. This extrapolation is likely to highlight impending undesirable events if the organization simply maintains the status quo. Next an Idealistic Future scenario is developed that describes what an ideal or desired demand system would be like and identifies what actions would have to be taken by the organization to cause the desired state to exist. These needed actions are then analyzed for feasibility and costs. Open systems planning thus helps decision makers to move back and forth from present to future and from "what is" to "what should be." These word pictures make salient the need for organizational adaptation and change and lead to action planning and implementation.

Beckhard and Harris propose a seven-step strategic planning process for organizations undergoing major transitions.[19] Their approach assumes organizations are open systems that must respond to multiple demands from multiple sources. The first step in their procedure is to determine the core mission of the organization—its reason for being or purpose. Step two maps the current demand system—what groups and organizations are making what demands on the organization? Step three maps the current response system—what the organization is doing to respond to contemporary demands. Step four maps the demand system that is projected to exist in the future three or four years hence—what the likely future demands will be and from whom, assuming that the organization continues on its current path. Step five asks the executives to identify the *desired* state of affairs they would like to see exist in three or four years. Comparisons between the data generated in steps four and five suggest discrepancies that must be corrected if the desired state is to become reality. Step six consists of planning the necessary actions for achieving the desired state—articulating the specific actions that must be taken to ensure the desired state is achieved. Step seven examines feasibility, cost-effectiveness, and intended and unintended consequences of the action plans generated in step six. Having the top executives and managers of an organization work through this process in a systematic way increases the likelihood that the desired future state will become reality, according to Beckhard and Harris.

David Hanna, in *Designing Organizations for High Performance*, presents two strategic planning models.[20] He calls the first one the organization performance (OP) model, and describes its use as follows: "This is a framework for keeping in perspective five key variables that have an impact on organizational performance. This model is especially useful when one is attempting to understand why the organization's results are what they are (and not better) and to plan changes that will lead to improved results."[21] The five key variables are (1) business situation, (2) business results, (3) business strategy, (4) design elements, and (5) culture. *Business situation* examines "The needs which must be satisfied and the pressures which must be managed." This is an environmental scan. *Business results* examine "What does this organization deliver now?" *Business strategy* examines the organization's purpose, mission, goals, and values. *Design elements* refer to the organizational design elements of tasks, structure, rewards, decision making, information, and people. *Culture* examines "How the organization really operates."[22] Hanna explains how to analyze each element and how to achieve alignment between all five elements. Achieving alignment is the difficult part; his discussion is thorough and valuable.

Hanna calls his second model "the outside-in approach: true open systems designing." Most people engaged in designing high-performance organizations rely on a combination of sociotechnical systems theory (STS) and open systems planning (OSP). These theories work well in most cases, but, in Hanna's view, they are often too internally focused. The outside-in approach begins the redesign process with environmental scanning and incorporates such scanning on an ongoing basis. The demands and expectations of external stakeholder and constituent groups are systematically examined in order to determine what the organization's core tasks and processes should be. This is a valuable strategic management model for OD practitioners.[23]

Organization development practitioners need to become experts in strategic management *processes* and need to have a thorough knowledge of strategic management *content*. Excellent sources for learning about strategic management content are the following: Michael Porter's books, *Competitive Strategy, Competitive Advantage*, and *Competition in Global Industries*, summarize and synthesize the field.[24] Tregoe and Zimmerman's *Top Management Strategy* presents the practical side of strategic planning.[25] These two authors worked with hundreds of top-management teams helping them to develop strategic plans for their organizations. Kenichi Ohmae's book, *The Mind of the Strategist,* is highly recommended.[26] *Strategy Pure and Simple* by Michel Robert is clear and practical.[27] *The Art of the Long View* by Peter Schwartz describes scenario planning, a strategic planning method developed by Royal Dutch Shell Company.[28] *Strategic Planning: Models and Analytic Techniques* by Robert Dyson gives a thorough coverage of different strategic planning techniques.[29]

A number of OD practitioners have realized the necessity for OD to become more actively involved in strategic management issues in organizations. Zand observed that there is considerable separation and often conflict between strategic management people and OD people in organizations.[30] As a result, both strategic planning and implementation suffer. Zand calls for closer cooperation between these two fields which can offer so much to each other. Greiner and Schein challenge OD practitioners to become more involved in the strategic management process—both to improve these activities in organizations and to build a power base for the practitioner.[31] Paul Buller recommends blending OD practices with strategic management to enhance the effectiveness of both disciplines.[32] Buller suggests six areas where OD can assist strategic management as follows: "The six primary activities that promote a better strategic management/OD blend are to: assess and develop the organization's state of readiness for strategic change, facilitate the strategic planning process, implement strategy, create the conditions for successful mergers and acquisitions, manage organizational decline, and develop leadership skills."[33] He explains how specific OD interventions can facilitate these processes. We agree with Buller—these are six strategic areas where OD can and should make valuable contributions to organization leaders.

A thoughtful analysis by Mariann Jelinek and Joseph Litterer describes the importance of strategy in today's turbulent environment with its changing paradigms and shifting demands.[34] They urge OD practitioners to apply OD skills to the strategic management process in order to improve both strategy formulation and implementation. OD skills and methods can be invaluable for organization strategists, *but OD practitioners are not stepping up to the challenge.*

We end this discussion of strategic management with observations from Jelinek and Litterer:

> Managers and organization members need OD skills to help to navigate these difficult shoals. OD must create the bridges, through thoughtful analysis and careful articulation, to join strategic management needs with OD skills. Comprehensive organizational change, change in culture or strategic mission are by definition "strategic," and inseparably intertwined with classic OD skills. This situation presents a major opportunity to OD practitioners.[35]

SURVEY FEEDBACK

An important and widely used intervention for organization development rests on the process of systematically collecting data about the system and feeding back the data for individuals and groups at all levels of
the organization to analyze, interpret the meaning of, and design corrective action steps upon. These activities—which have two major components, the use of a climate or attitude survey and the use of feedback
workshops—are called *survey feedback*. This approach is based on the
Systems 1-4T "management system" to be described later.

An attitude survey, if properly used, can be a powerful tool in
organization improvement. Most surveys are not used in an optimal
way—at the maximum, most give top management some data for changing practices or provide an index against which to compare trends. At
the minimum, they are filed away with little of consequence resulting.
(See Figure 11-1 for a comparison of two approaches to the use of atti-

Figure 11-1   Two Approaches to the Use of Attitude or Climate Surveys

	Traditional Approach	Survey Feedback or OD Approach
Data collected from:	Rank and file, and maybe supervisors	Everyone in the system or subsystem
Data reported to:	Top management, department heads, and perhaps to employees through newspaper	Everyone who participated
Implications of data are worked on by:	Top management (maybe)	Everyone in work teams, with workshops starting at the top (all superiors with their subordinates)
Third-party intervention strategy:	Design and administration of questionnaire, development of a report	Obtaining concurrence on total strategy, design and administration of questionnaire, design of workshops, appropriate interventions in workshops
Action planning done by:	Top management only	Teams at all levels
Probable extent of change and improvement:	Low	High

tude surveys—the traditional approach and the survey feedback approach.)

Research at the Institute for Social Research at the University of Michigan indicates that if the survey is to be optimally useful, the following steps must occur.[36]

Step 1. Organization members at the top of the hierarchy are involved in the preliminary planning.

Step 2. Data are collected from all organization members.

Step 3. Data are fed back to the top executive team and then down through the hierarchy in functional teams. Mann refers to this as an "interlocking chain of conferences."[37]

Step 4. Each superior presides at a meeting with his or her subordinates in which the data are discussed and in which (a) subordinates are asked to help interpret the data, (b) plans are made for making constructive changes, and (c) plans are made for the introduction of the data at the next lower level.

Step 5. Most feedback meetings include a consultant who has helped prepare the superior for the meeting and who serves as a resource person.

The conclusions regarding the usefulness of survey feedback grew out of a four-year program with a large organization. In the first phase, data were gathered from some 8,000 employees throughout the company (1948). Comparable data were gathered two years later (1950) from the eight accounting departments, involving 800 employees and 78 supervisors. In this second phase, four of the eight departments carried on feedback activities as described earlier; two departments served as control groups with nothing further done after one all-department meeting; and two departments were eliminated from the design because of changes in key personnel. Two years later (1952), another survey was made and the researchers found that "more significant positive changes occurred in employee attitudes and perceptions in the four experimental departments than in the two control departments."[38] In particular, important changes occurred relative to how employees felt about "(1) the kind of work they do (job interest, importance, and level of responsibility); (2) their supervisor (ability to handle people, give recognition, direct their work, and represent them in handling complaints); (3) their progress in the company; and (4) their group's ability to get the job done."[39]

From our experience, feedback workshops take on many of the characteristics of team-building sessions but are less likely to deal with interpersonal matters. However, they frequently focus on leadership style or on matters pertaining to cooperation and teamwork. For example, the following two items were included in a questionnaire used by one of the authors:

Management sidesteps
or evades things that
bother people on the
job

Strongly agree	Agree	Undecided	Disagree	Strongly disagree

There is good cooperation
and teamwork in my work
group

Strongly agree	Agree	Undecided	Disagree	Strongly disagree

In this questionnaire, items were included pertaining to "Organizational Climate," "Pay and Benefits," "Relations with Other Units," "Communications," "Supervisor/Employee Relations," "Performance Counseling," "My Job," "Pressure of Work," "Management by Objectives," "Opportunities for Personal Growth and Advancement," and "Training."

This kind of attitude or climate survey, coupled with a series of workshops involving work teams at successively lower levels of the organization, can be used to create action plans and change across a wide range of variables in the social, structural, goal, and task subsystems of an organization. We think this approach has exciting possibilities because, in the words of Baumgartel (also quoted in Chapter 3), *"it deals with the system of human relationships as a whole . . . and it deals with each manager, supervisor, and employee in the context of his own job, his own problems, and his own work relationships."*[40] This is the thrust that permeates most OD activities and is one of the dimensions that differentiates OD from traditional interventions in organizations.

A closer look at some of the underlying dynamics of survey feedback reveals why it works. The survey feedback technique is essentially a procedure for giving objective data about the system's functioning to the system members so that they can change or improve selected aspects of the system. The objective data are obtained by a survey; working with the data to improve the organization is done in feedback sessions.

Frank Neff states that for organization improvement (change) to take place, three things must happen. First, the work group must *accept the data as valid*. Often people are defensive and resistant to data about their own organization. This must be overcome. Second, the work group must *accept responsibility* for the part they play in the problems identified. The leader plays a very important role in this regard—he or she should "model" behaviors indicating that the problem is "owned" by the leader and the group. Third, the work group must commit itself to *solving problems;* that is, its members must commit themselves to doing something about the problems. In summary, the work group must accept the data from the survey as valid, must accept responsibility for the problems identified, and must start solving the problems.[41]

Bowers and Franklin state that the rationale for survey feedback, or what they also call "survey-guided development," is based on a model that views people as rational, cognitive, information processing individuals. Furthermore, when there are differences between a person's perceptions, these differences act as sources of motivation. New information leads to new perceptions that may be in conflict with old perceptions. In this way, new information becomes a force for changing perceptions and actions. Another basic assumption of survey-guided development is that human behavior is goal-seeking or goal-oriented. Bowers and Franklin describe how the goal-seeking process works:

> at least four elements are involved: (1) a model, (2) a goal, (3) an activity, and (4) feedback. The model is a mental picture of the surrounding world, including not only structural properties, but cause-and-effect relations. It is built by the person(s) from past accumulations of information, stored in memory. From the workings of the model and from the modeling process which he employs, alternative possible future states are generated, of which one is selected as a *goal*. At this point what is called the "goal selection system" ends and what is known as the "control system" *per se* begins. *Activities* are initiated to attain the goal, and *feedback*, which comes by some route from the person's environment, is used to compare, confirm, adjust, and correct responses by signaling departures from what was expected.[42]

A well-designed survey helps organization members to develop valid models of how organizations work and also provides information (feedback) about progress toward the goal.

Survey feedback has been shown to be an effective change technique in OD. In a longitudinal study evaluating the effects of different change techniques in 23 different organizations, survey feedback was found to be the most effective change strategy when compared with interpersonal process consultation, task process consultation, and laboratory training.[43] These results may be somewhat misleading, however, in that the survey feedback programs may have been more comprehensive than the other programs and the positive results may reflect the superiority of more comprehensive programs compared with less comprehensive ones. On the other hand, survey feedback is a cost-effective means of implementing a comprehensive program, thus making it a highly desirable change technique.

SYSTEMS 1-4T

Survey feedback is based on a conceptual scheme and an integrated package of measurements that Rensis Likert and colleagues called Systems 1-4 (and later 1-4T). This management typology is based largely on measures pertaining to leadership, organizational climate, and job satisfaction. Using a 105-item questionnaire, called the *Survey of Organizations*, as well as shorter forms, Likert found that organizations were markedly different in terms of these characteristics. (See Figure 11-2 for the categories of items in the *Survey*.) Further, the *Survey* could be used to track changes over time.

Figure 11-3 shows the profile of perceptions of the top 52 managers at two time periods in a plant run by a successful plant manager. The latest measures show the prevailing management system to be

Figure 11-2 Dimensions of the Survey of Organizations Questionnaire

Source: James C. Taylor and David G. Bowers, *Survey of Organizations: A Machine-Scored Standardized Questionnaire Instrument,* Institute for Social Research (Ann Arbor, MI: University of Michigan, 1972), pp. 3–4. © 1972. Reprinted by permission.

Leadership

1. Managerial support
2. Managerial goal emphasis
3. Managerial work facilitation
4. Managerial interaction facilitation
5. Peer support
6. Peer goal-emphasis
7. Peer work facilitation
8. Peer interaction facilitation

Organizational Climate

9. Communication with company
10. Motivation
11. Decision-making
12. Control within company
13. Coordination between departments
14. General management

Satisfaction

15. Satisfaction with company
16. Satisfaction with supervisor
17. Satisfaction with job
18. Satisfaction with pay
19. Satisfaction with work group

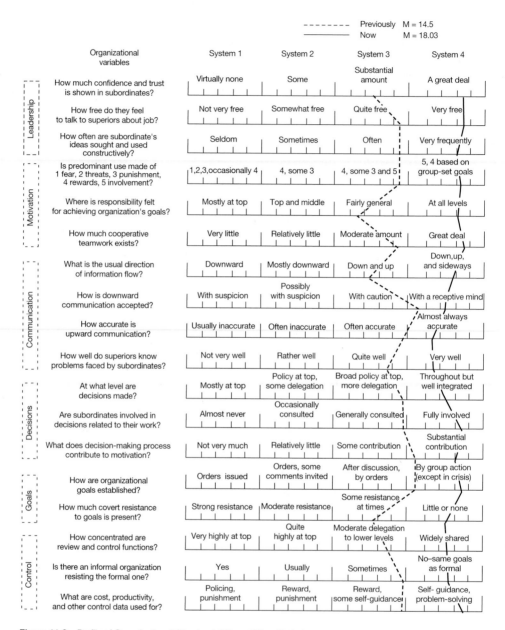

Figure 11-3 Profile of Organizational Climate at Different Time Periods

Source: Rensis Likert and Jane Gibson Likert, *New Ways of Managing Conflict* (New York: McGraw-Hill, 1976), p. 75. © Reprinted with permission.

System 4. In his earlier writings, Likert called System 1 "exploitive authoritative," System 2 "benevolent authoritative," System 3 "consultative," and System 4 "participative group." In later works only the

Systems 1-4 terms were used, probably because of the heavily evaluative connotations of the other terms.

Some would argue that the terminology of some of the scales is also too value laden. This argument suggests that the wording of the scales might be inducing respondents, if asked, to indicate that they would prefer the climate to shift toward the right-hand side of the scale. This is one of the reasons why organization development approaches feature thorough group discussions, unit by unit, with all of those who participated in the survey centered on what the patterns of responses mean and what the implications might be.

In the Likert model, each type of organization (Systems 1–4) is seen as having internally consistent characteristics of which organizational climate is a major part. A description of each type of system follows. (This discussion is based on the questionnaires in Likert and Likert,[44] Likert,[45] Likert,[46] and Bowers.[47])

In the System 1 type of organization. control, goal setting, and decision making are concentrated at the top. There is practically no seeking of subordinates' ideas, and subordinates are not involved in decisions related to their work. In general, little or no confidence is shown in subordinates. Extensive use is made of threats, punishment, and fear. Cost and productivity data are used for policing and punishment. Communication is largely downward. There is little lateral communication and upward communication is minimal and frequently distorted. Mistrust, hostility, and dissatisfaction are extensive, and there is considerable resistance in the informal system to the directives of the formal organization. Teamwork is essentially nonexistent. Motivation, except at the top, is low.

System 2 is slightly more participative. In this system, control and direction and decision making are perceived as largely concentrated at the top but there is some delegating of decision making relative to implementing policies; some comment is invited about organizational goals. Subordinates' ideas are sometimes sought and subordinates are occasionally consulted before decisions are made about their work. Communication is mostly downward, there is some lateral communication; and upward communication is frequently filtered for superiors. Some confidence is shown in subordinates, but it tends to be of a condescending nature. Extensive use is made of monetary awards; some use is made of threats and punishment, but there is generally less fear than in System 1. Cost and productivity data are used for rewards and punishments. There is sometimes considerable hostility in the organization, but at times favorable attitudes do exist. Generally, there is substantial dissatisfaction with, and considerable covert resistance to, the formal system. Little teamwork exists. Motivation is relatively low, but higher than in System 1.

System 3 is significantly more participative than Systems 1 and

2. Broad policy is decided at the top, but there is substantial delegation of decision making down through the organization. Goals are formulated at the top after consultation. There is moderate delegation of review and control activities. Subordinates' ideas are usually sought, and subordinates are generally consulted about decisions related to their work. Substantial confidence is shown in subordinates. Communication tends to be both downward and upward without much distortion; lateral communication is common and encouraged. Extensive use is made of involvement and rewards as motivating forces, and little use is made of fear. Cost and productivity data and other controls are used for rewards and some self-guidance. There is little hostility, and attitudes are generally favorable; most individuals feel responsible for the overall welfare of the organization. Resistance in the informal system is generally low. Teamwork exists in moderate amounts.

System 4 is the most participative and is highly group-process oriented. As viewed by organization members, goals are established through participation and many decisions are made by consensus. Group interaction is facilitated by superiors who are the linking pins between work groups and by task force members from various relevant units. Subordinates' ideas are sought as a matter of course and they are fully involved in decisions related to their work. A high level of confidence is shown in subordinates. Communication flow is downward, upward, and lateral, and there is little distortion. No use is made of coercion or fear, and high motivation is based on extensive involvement, group goals, and compensation systems developed through participation. Cost, productivity, and other control data are used for self-guidance and problem solving. Attitudes are generally quite favorable. People at all levels feel responsible for achieving the organization's goals and there is little or no covert resistance to unit goals and policies. Teamwork is evident throughout the organization.

When variables such as "the levels of performance goals" and the "level of technical competence" are added to the typology and these scores are high, Likert and Likert refer to this condition as *System 4T*, the *T* standing for "total model."[48] (We believe these additions are extremely important in terms of organizational effectiveness. In a way, these dimensions are a reminder of the overriding importance of *both* the social system and the technological system and their interrelationships.)

Each of the Systems 1–4 works, although there is considerable evidence to show that System 1 organizations usually pay a heavy price in terms of employee resistance of all kinds and in low morale and commitment. (To extend the concept to nations, it is quite obvious that the former Soviet Union was a System 1 on a massive scale, and equally obvious that it was a massive failure.) Furthermore, there is a good deal of research indicating that, over the long term, high scores on organizational climate and other dimensions of the *Survey* questionnaire described earlier tend to be associated with organizational profitability and excellent labor relations.[49] In general, and increasingly, managers and employees alike have the expectation that organizations can profitably shift toward Systems 3 or 4 (or 4T). Organization development approaches, including survey feedback, are ways of getting there.

GRID ORGANIZATION DEVELOPMENT

A thoroughgoing and systematic organization development program, designed by Robert R. Blake and Jane S. Mouton, is *Grid Organization Development*.[50] In a six-phase program lasting about three to five years, an organization can move systematically from the stage of examining managerial behavior and style to the development and implementation of an "ideal strategic corporate model." The program utilizes a considerable number of instruments, enabling individuals and groups to assess their own strengths and weaknesses; it focuses on skills, knowledge, and processes necessary for effectiveness at the individual, group, intergroup, and total-organization levels. The organizational program is conducted by internal members who have been pretrained in Grid concepts.

Basic to the Grid OD program are the concepts and methods of the Managerial Grid, also developed by Blake and Mouton, a two-dimensional schematic for examining and improving the managerial practices of individual managers. One dimension underlying this diagnostic questionnaire is "concern for people"; the other dimension is "concern for production." The most effective managers are those who score high on both of these dimensions—a 9,9 position. A 9,9 management style is described as follows: "Work accomplishment is from committed people; interdependence through a 'common stake' in organization purpose leads to relationships of trust and respect."[51]

The relation between the Managerial Grid diagnostic questionnaire and Grid OD is explained by Blake and Mouton: "The single most significant premise on which Grid Organization Development rests is that the 9,9 way of doing business is acknowledged universally by managers as the soundest way to manage to achieve excellence."[52] As used in the Grid OD process, the Managerial Grid questionnaire becomes one vehicle for individuals and groups to examine and explore their styles and modify prevailing practices.

Behavioral science concepts and rigorous business logic are combined in the Grid OD program's six phases. These phases are described as follows.[53]

Prephase 1. Before an organization (usually a business corporation) begins a Grid organization development program, selected key managers who will later be instructors in the organization attend a Grid Seminar. In this week-long experience-based laboratory, managers learn about Grid concepts, assess their own styles using the Managerial Grid questionnaire and the two-dimensional schematic, develop team action skills, learn problem-solving and critiquing skills, work at improved communication skills, and learn to analyze the culture of a team and of an organization. Learning takes place through the use of instruments, study team projects which are judged for adequacy, critiquing of individual and team performance, and conceptual inputs.

After several managers have gone to a Grid Seminar, some might go on to advanced Grid courses or for further exposure to the Grid OD approach. At a Grid OD Seminar, participants are taught the materials involved in phases 2 to 6. They learn both what the Grid OD program is all about and how to conduct it in their own company.

Another advanced course is the Instructor Development Seminar, in which participants actually learn to conduct an in-company phase 1 Grid Seminar. Training these managers in the various seminars accomplishes two things: the managers learn how to conduct a Grid OD program in their own organization, and they can also evaluate the Grid approach to determine whether or not they think it is a good idea for their organization to embark on such a course of action.

If, at this point, the company decides to implement a Grid organization development program, it might conduct a *pilot* phase 1 program for volunteer managers. If the result of this is a "go" signal, then phase 1 begins.

Phase 1: The Managerial Grid. In this phase, a Grid Seminar, conducted by in-company managers, is given to all the managers of the organization. The focus of the training is similar to that just described: attention is given to assessing an individual's managerial styles; problem-solving, critiquing, and communication skills are practiced; the skills of synergistic teamwork are learned and practiced. In this phase, managers learn to become 9,9 managers.

Phase 2: Teamwork Development. The focus of this phase is work teams in the organization. The goal is *perfecting* teamwork in the organization through analysis of team culture, traditions, and the like and also developing skills in planning, setting objectives, and problem solving. Additional aspects of this phase include feedback given to each manager about his or her individual and team behavior; this critique allows the manager to understand how others see his or her strengths and weaknesses in the team's working.

Working on teamwork is done in the context of actual work problems. The problems and issues dealt with are the real ones of the team. In this process of phase 2, individuals learn how to study and manage the culture of their work teams.

Phase 3: Intergroup Development.   The focus of this phase is intergroup relations, and the goal of this phase is to move groups from their ineffective, often win-lose *actual* ways of relating between groups toward an *ideal* model of intergroup relations. The dynamics of intergroup cooperation and competition are explored. Each group separately analyzes what an ideal relationship would be like; these are shared between groups. Action steps to move toward the ideal are developed and assigned to individuals. The phase thus includes building operational plans for moving the two groups from their actual state to an ideal state of intergroup relations.

The phase consists of teams convening, in twos, to work on the issues stated above. Not all teams would pair with all others; only teams that have particularly important interface relationships do so. Often only selected members of the teams take part in the exercises and activities. These are the people who have close working relations with the other team.

Phase 4: Developing an Ideal Strategic Corporate Model.   In this phase the focus shifts to corporate strategic planning, with the goals being to learn the concepts and the skills of corporate logic necessary to achieve corporate excellence. The top-management group engages in the strategy planning activities of this phase, although their plans and ideas are tested, evaluated, and critiqued in conjunction with other corporate members. The charge to the top-management group is to design an ideal strategic corporate model that would define what the corporation would be like if it were truly excellent. Fact-finding, technical inputs and so on may be contributed from all persons in the organization.

Using the comparisons of ideal corporate logic versus real corporate logic, the top-management team is better able to recognize what aspects of the culture must be changed to achieve excellence.

In a process that may take up to a year, the top executives build the ideal strategic corporate model *for their particular organization.* This is the model used in the next phase.

Phase 5: Implementing the Ideal Strategic Model.   In several different steps, the organization seeks to implement the model of corporate excellence developed in phase 4. To execute the conversion to the ideal strategic model, the organization must be reorganized. Logical components of the corporation are designated (these might be profit centers, geographical locations, product lines, etc.). Each component appoints a planning team whose job is to examine every phase of the component's operation to see how the business may be moved more in line with the ideal model. Every concept of the ideal strategic corporate model is studied by the planning team for its implications for the component. In addition, a phase 5 coordinator is appointed to act as a resource to the planning teams.

The planning teams thus conduct "conversion studies" to see how the components must change to fit the ideal strategic corporate model. An additional planning team is formed and is given the charge of designing a headquarters that would operate effectively and yet keep overhead to a minimum. After the planning and assessment steps are completed, conversion of the organization to the ideal condition is implemented.

Phase 6: Systematic Critique.   In this phase the results of the Grid OD program, from prephase 1 to postphase 5, are measured. Systematic critiquing, measuring, and evaluating lead to knowledge of what progress has been made, what barriers still exist and must be overcome, and what new opportunities have developed that may be exploited. This phase is begun after phase 5 is going well and is beginning to convert the organization well along toward the ideal model. Taking stock of where the corporation has been, how far it has come, and where it currently is thus represents a "new beginning" from which to continue striving toward corporate excellence.

Grid organization development is an approach to organization improvement that is complete and systematic and difficult. Does it work? Blake, Mouton, Barnes, and Greiner evaluated the results of a Grid OD program conducted in a large plant that was part of a very large multiplant company. The 800 managers and staff personnel of the 4,000-person work force at the plant were all given training in the Managerial Grid and Grid OD concepts. Significant organizational improvements showed up on such "bottom-line" measures as greater profits, lower costs, and less waste.[54] Managers themselves, when asked about their own effectiveness and that of their corporation, likewise declared that changes for the better had resulted from the program.

SCHEIN'S CULTURAL ANALYSIS

A particularly deep and difficult intervention is Edgar Schein's *cultural analysis*. This intervention is complex, probes deeply into the organization, and is not for every OD consultant nor for every client organization. Indeed, as Schein says,

> If someone says "We want to do a cultural analysis," I spend quite a bit of time probing why, what for, and where we are going with it. . . . Sometimes it will in fact lead to a workshop dealing with culture, but that same set of questions may lead to some other form of consultation or counseling.[55]

Basically, when Schein and clients agree that the intervention is appropriate, the flow is as follows. We will use Schein's words to describe the process.

Once the purpose is established I would suggest to the immediate clients that they consider bringing together groupings of managers and/or employees to discuss the culture concept and to begin to identify some of their own assumptions. When such a group is assembled, I give a short lecture on the distinction between artifacts, espoused values, and underlying assumptions, followed by an invitation to the group to start brainstorming on what they see as the artifacts of their organization. If there are newcomers in the organization they are often a good group to begin with.

As various artifacts such as the architecture, the office layout, the mode of dress, the perquisites and status symbols, etc. are identified, I write them down on flip charts and fill the walls with them. Within an hour or less the group participants will begin to see some of the values that lie behind the artifacts and these are now also written down for common observation. As this process proceeds, the outsider should begin to push for some of the underlying assumptions by noting areas of consistency and areas of inconsistency. Sometimes the best way to get at an underlying assumption is to note where espoused values are out of line with observed artifacts. The outsider can also offer hypotheses at this point to further stimulate the group's efforts to identify assumptions and begin to help the group to classify them if they fall into clusters or form a pattern.

The next step in the intervention is typically to send the participants off in smaller groups with the task of further identifying assumptions and then classifying them into two categories: 1) those cultural assumptions that will aid us in getting to our goals; and 2) those cultural assumptions that will hinder us in getting to our goals. This self-diagnosis is then reported back to the total group and analyzed with the help of the outside consultant to determine what steps might be appropriate.

In this discussion it is crucial that the consultant help the group to focus on the helpful parts of the culture, and help the group to recognize what the consequences are of saying that they want to change those parts of the culture that they may view as non helpful. But all of this only makes sense in the context of some strategic or tactical goals that the group is pursuing. Doing a cultural analysis for its own sake is at best boring and at worst dangerous.[56]

Schein goes on to note that the client system "is fully involved in owning both the diagnosis and the interventions." He further emphasizes that the role of the OD consultant is to provide the conceptual framework for the analysis and to "manage the process."[57]

TRANSORGANIZATIONAL DEVELOPMENT

When consultants get "the whole system in the room" and that system is conceptualized as involving several organizations (for example, in connection with some future search conferences, Weisbord talks about getting customers, suppliers, and union leaders together with organizational members), we can begin to sense some of the complexities of *transorganizational development*. Thomas Cummings has provided one of the best descriptions of this form of OD, which he says is "not simply an extension of OD, but constitutes a distinct level of practice commensurate with the dynamics emerging at this higher level of social system."[58]

Transorganizational development (TD) is seen by Cummings to be an important form of organizational change process for transorganizational systems (TSs). TSs are comprised of business alliances, consortia, or "network alliances" formed for such purposes as coordinating services to the public, conducting joint research and development, exchanging technology, or gaining access to worldwide markets. Linkages among members are "loosely coupled" or indirect. Power and leadership are dispersed rather than hierarchical, and there may be wide fluctuations in commitment to the collaboration over time.[59]

Cummings sees three phases in typical TD practice:

Phase 1: Potential Member Organizations Are Identified. TD practitioners assist early members in forming a steering committee, establishing criteria for membership, and perhaps serving as brokers to introduce potential partners to each other.

Phase 2: Member Organizations Are Convened. Representatives from member organizations are brought together, sometimes in a search conference, to assess the desirability and feasibility of creating a TS. These conferences permit members to share perceptions and ideas and to negotiate equitable benefits, and to develop action plans.

Phase 3: The TS Is Organized. Once common purposes and sufficient motivation have been generated, TD practitioners help members create the roles, structures. and mechanisms needed to coordinate the collaborative efforts of TS members.[60]

Practitioners need to play more of an activist role than is traditionally seen in OD. Furthermore, practitioners need to maintain a neutral role and not be seen as being aligned with particular member organizations or people.[61]

CONCLUDING COMMENTS

Comprehensive OD interventions are very much alive and visible in contemporary OD practice. Some, like Beckhard's confrontation meeting and strategic management activities, involve all of top management or, in the case of smaller organizations, the entire management group. (The confrontation meeting is also applicable to all of the employees of very small organizations.) Others, like future search conferences, tend to involve a wide spectrum of organizational members and can involve others beyond the immediate organization. Some, like survey feedback, based on Systems 1-4T theory, are designed to involve all members of an organization or of a relatively autonomous subdivision of an organization. One intervention, Schein's cultural analysis, is a fairly deep intervention in the organization's basic culture.

Transorganizational development (TD), aimed at assisting organizations in forming and developing alliances, has many similarities to the planning and conducting of future search conferences. However, TD requires practitioners to take on a more activist, brokerage role and to give considerable assistance and leadership in developing appropriate structures for communications and decision making. (The applicability to internal problems of nations and to international alliance development will be apparent to the reader, but this exploration is beyond the scope of this volume.) Some interventions involve "getting the whole system in the room," a feature that a number of comprehensive interventions have in common, including future search conferences, transorganizational development, partnering, and the confrontation meeting.

Like all OD interventions, these comprehensive interventions must involve a collaborative effort between the client organization and the consultant(s) in both diagnosis and intervention. To be successful, they must fit the realities being experienced by the client system and must engage the cooperation and goodwill of client system members.

NOTES

1. See, for example, Marvin Weisbord, "Toward Third-Wave Managing and Consulting." *Organizational Dynamics,* 15 (Winter 1987), p. 9.
2. W. Warner Burke and Richard Beckhard, *Conference Planning,* 2nd ed. (San Diego: University Associates, 1970).
3. Marvin R. Weisbord, *Productive Workplaces* (San Francisco: Jossey-Bass Publishers, 1987), p. 283.
4. Ibid., p. 282.
5. From Weisbord, *Productive Workplaces*, pp. 284–292.
6. Ibid., p. 289.
7. Ibid., p. 291.
8. Ibid., p. 295.
9. Richard Beckhard, "The Confrontation Meeting," *Harvard Business Review,* 45 (March–April 1967), pp. 149–155.
10. Ibid., p. 150.
11. This discussion represents paraphrasing, ibid., p. 154.
12. Ibid., p. 154.
13 Ibid., p. 153.
14. Dan E. Schendel and Charles W. Hofer, eds., *Strategic Management* (Boston: Little, Brown, 1979), p. 14.

15. Charles E. Summer, *Strategic Behavior in Business and Government* (Boston: Little, Brown, 1980), Chap. 10.

16. Thomas H. Rogers, "Strategic Planning: A Major OD Intervention," in *American Society for Training and Development*, ASTD Publications, 1981, pp. 50–55.

17. Ibid., p. 52.

18. See Charles Krone, "Open Systems Redesign," in John Adams, ed., *Theory and Management in Organization Development: An Evolutionary Process* (Roslyn, VA: NTL Institute, 1974); and G. K. Jayaram, "Open Systems Planning," in W. G. Bennis, K. D. Benne, R. Chin, and K. Cory, eds., *The Planning of Change*, 3rd ed. (New York: Holt, Rinehart and Winston, 1976), pp. 275–283. This discussion is based primarily on Jayaram's article.

19. R. Beckhard and R. T. Harris, *Organizational Transitions: Managing Complex Change*, (Reading, MA: Addison-Wesley, 1977). See also the 2nd edition, 1987.

20. David P. Hanna, *Designing Organizations for High Performance* (Reading, MA: Addison-Wesley Publishing Company, 1988).

21. Ibid., pp. 40–41.

22. Ibid., from Chapter 2.

23. Ibid., from Chapter 4.

24. Michael Porter, *Competitive Strategy* (New York: The Free Press, 1980), *Competitive Advantage* (New York: The Free Press, 1985), and *Competition in Global Industries* (Boston: Harvard Business School Press, 1986).

25. B. B. Tregoe and J. W. Zimmerman, *Top Management Strategy* (New York: Simon and Schuster, 1980).

26. Kenichi Ohmae, *The Mind of the Strategist* (New York: Penguin Books, 1982).

27. Michel Robert, *Strategy Pure and Simple* (New York: McGraw-Hill, Inc., 1993).

28. Peter Schwartz, *The Art of the Long View* (New York: Doubleday Publishing Co., 1991).

29. Robert G. Dyson, *Strategic Planning: Models and Analytic Techniques* (Chichester, West Sussex, England: John Wiley and Sons, Ltd., 1990).

30. Dale E. Zand, "Organization Development and Strategic Management," *OD Newsletter* (Winter 1984), pp. 1, 6–7.

31. Larry E. Greiner and Virginia E. Schein, "A Revisionist Look at Power and OD," *The Industrial-Organizational Psychologist*, 25, no. 2 (1988), 59–61.

32. Paul F. Buller, "For Successful Strategic Change: Blend OD Practices with Strategic Management," *Organizational Dynamics*, 16 (1988), pp. 42–55.

33. Ibid., p. 43.

34. Mariann Jelinek and Joseph A. Litterer, "Why OD Must Become Strategic," from R. W. Woodman and W. A. Pasmore, eds., *Research in Organizational Change and Development*, vol. 2 (Greenwich, CT: JAI Press, 1988), pp. 135–162.

35. Ibid., pp. 159–160.

36. Floyd C. Mann, "Studying and Creating Change," in W. G. Bennis, K. D. Benne, and R. Chin, eds., *The Planning of Change* (New York: Holt, Rinehart and Winston, 1961), pp. 605–613.

37. Ibid., p. 609.

38. Ibid., p. 611.

39. Ibid., p. 611.

40. Howard Baumgartel, "Using Employee Questionnaire Results for Improving Organizations: The Survey 'Feedback' Experiment," *Kansas Business Review*, 12 (December 1959), p. 6. [Baumgartel's emphasis.]

41. Frank W. Neff, "Survey Research: A Tool for Problem Diagnosis and Improvement in Organizations," in A. W. Gouldner and S. M. Miller, eds., *Applied Sociology* (New York: Free Press, 1966), pp. 23–38.

42. David G. Bowers and Jerome L. Franklin, "Survey-Guided Development: Using Human Resources Measurement in Organizational Change," *Journal of Contemporary Business*, 1, no. 3 (Summer 1972), 43–55. This passage is taken from page 48.

43. David G. Bowers, "OD Techniques and Their Results in 23 Organizations: The Michigan ICL Study," *Journal of Applied Behavioral Science,* 9, no. 1 (1973), 21–43.

44. Rensis and Jane Gibson Likert, *New Ways of Managing Conflict* (New York: McGraw-Hill, 1976), pp. 21–32.

45. Rensis Likert, *The Human Organization: Its Management and Value* (New York: McGraw-Hill, 1967), pp. 3–10.

46. Rensis Likert, *New Patterns of Management* (New York: McGraw-Hill, 1961), pp. 223–233.

47. David G. Bowers, *Systems of Organization* (Ann Arbor, MI: University of Michigan Press, 1976), pp. 101–107.

48. Likert and Likert, *New Ways of Managing Conflict,* pp. 49–50.

49. Ibid., pp. 71–98.

50. Robert R. Blake, Jane Srygley Mouton, and Anne Adams McCanse, *Change by Design* (Reading, MA: Addison-Wesley, 1989), pp. 116–216; R. R. Blake and J. S. Mouton, *The Managerial Grid* (Houston: Gulf Publishing, 1964); and *The New Managerial Grid* (Houston: Gulf Publishing, 1978).

51. R. R. Blake and J. S. Mouton, *Building a Dynamic Corporation Through Grid Organization Development* (Reading, MA: Addison-Wesley, 1969), p. 61.

52. Ibid., p. 63.

53. This discussion is based on ibid., pp. 76–109.

54. R. R. Blake, J. S. Mouton, L. B. Barnes, and L. E. Greiner, "Breakthrough in Organization Development," *Harvard Business Review,* 42 (November–December 1964), pp. 133–155.

55. Fred Luthans, "Conversation with Edgar H. Schein," *Organizational Dynamics,* 17 (Spring 1989), p. 73.

56. Edgar H. Schein, "Organization Development and the Study of Organizational Culture," *Academy of Management OD Newsletter* (Summer 1990), pp. 4–5. Used by permission.

57. Ibid., p. 5. For a more detailed description of the process, see Edgar H. Schein, *Organizational Culture and Leadership,* 2nd ed. (Jossey-Bass Publishers, 1992). For more on organizational culture, see Ralph H. Kilmann, Mary J. Saxton, Roy Serpa and Associates, *Gaining Control of the Corporate Culture* (San Francisco: Jossey-Bass Publishers, 1985); and J. Steven Ott, *The Organizational Culture Perspective* (Pacific Grove, CA: Brooks/Cole Publishing Company, 1989).

58. Thomas G. Cummings, "Transorganizational Development," *Academy of Management OD Newsletter* (Summer 1989), p. 9.

59. Ibid., pp. 8–9.

60. Ibid., pp. 9–10.

61. Ibid., p. 10. See also Thomas G. Cummings and Christopher G. Worley, *Organization Development and Change,* 5th ed. (Minneapolis/St. Paul: West Publishing Company, 1993); and Jerry I. Porras and Peter J. Robertson, "Organization Development: Theory, Practice, and Research," in Marvin D. Dunnette and Leaetta M. Hough, *Handbook of Industrial and Organizational Psychology,* 2nd ed., vol. 3 (Palo Alto, CA: Consulting Psychologists Press, 1992), pp. 719–822.

12

STRUCTURAL INTERVENTIONS

In this chapter we will examine what we call *structural interventions*, sometimes called *technostructural interventions*, a shorthand term for a broad class of interventions or change efforts aimed at improving organizational effectiveness through changes in the task, structural, technological, and goal processes in the organization. This class of interventions includes changes in how the overall work of the organization is divided into units, who reports to whom, methods of control, the spatial arrangements of equipment and people, work flow arrangements, and changes in communication and influence practices.

In particular, we want to examine the structural interventions that are commonly labeled *OD*: sociotechnical systems (STS), self-managed teams, work redesign, management by objectives (MBO), quality circles, quality of work life projects (QWL), parallel learning structures (or collateral organizations), physical settings, and total quality management (TQM). (We also want to examine reengineering, an intervention modality that is usually not considered OD but, nevertheless, needs to be understood by OD practitioners and clients.)

Most of these structural interventions seek a joint optimization of the social and technological systems of organizations. Applications are properly called *OD* to the extent that the latter is true: there is use of the participant action research model, and there are other characteristics congruent with how OD has been described in earlier chapters. We would hope the *OD label* would *not* be applied whenever structural interventions are carried out without attention to the social system or to humanistic values.

Finally, we want to look briefly at the concept of large-scale systems change. In this connection, we also want to examine organization transformation, or second-order change, which usually involves a variety of OD interventions over a relatively long time period.

SOCIOTECHNICAL SYSTEMS (STS)

The term *sociotechnical systems* (or STS) is largely associated with experiments that emerged under the auspices of the Tavistock Institute in Great Britain or have stemmed from the Tavistock approach. In recent years, additional institutions, such as the University of Southern California, have been associated with STS innovations. These efforts have generally attempted to create a better "fit" among the technology, structure, and social interaction of a particular production unit in a mine, factory, or office.

As described by Cummings and Worley, STS theory has two basic premises. One is that "effective work systems must jointly optimize the relationship between their social and technical parts." The second premise is that "such systems must effectively manage the boundary separating and relating them to the environment" in such a way that there are effective exchanges with the environment along with protection from external disruptions. Furthermore, the implementation of STS is seen as "highly participative" involving all of the relevant stakeholders, including employees, engineers, staff experts, and managers.[1]

As indicated in Chapter 5, STS projects tend to feature the formation of autonomous work groups (the terms *self-managing* or *self-managed* are now more frequently used), the grouping of core tasks so that a team has a major unit of the total work to be accomplished, the training of group members in multiple skills, delegation to the work group of many aspects of how the work gets done, and the availability of a great deal of information and feedback to work groups for the self-regulation of productivity and quality. The theory suggests that effectiveness, efficiency, and morale will be enhanced, and this is generally confirmed by numerous studies that have been carried out over the years.

One of the earliest studies was in British coal mining where the consultant-researchers found that by reintroducing a team approach to mining coal, broadening job scope, and providing team pay incentives, a number of benefits resulted, including improved productivity, safety, and morale.[2] An experiment in India in a textile weaving mill also utilized increased job scope and autonomous work groups with beneficial consequences.[3] Other experiments and research have appeared with increasing frequency around the world, particularly in Norway and Sweden[4] and the United States.

Part of the heritage of these experiments was the emergence of *work restructuring* projects such as at the Volvo plants in Sweden, and the General Foods pet-food plant in Topeka, Kansas. Common characteristics have been the use of autonomous work teams, participative decision making, considerable team autonomy in planning and controlling production and in screening new team members, and pay geared to the number of tasks mastered by each team member ("skill-based pay").[5] These experiments have sometimes overlapped with programs that have been called quality of work life (QWL) projects.

Other organizations where self-managed teams have been used extensively include Digital, Frito-Lay, General Electric, Hewlett-Packard, Honeywell, Pepsi-Cola, the Oregon Department of Transportation, the San Diego Zoo, and many smaller organizations.[6] Lawler has followed up on a number of plants using self-managed teams, including the General Foods plant, and concludes that "virtually every plant has thrived and continues to be managed in a very participative way."[7]

SELF-MANAGED TEAMS: PROBLEMS IN IMPLEMENTATION

Several problems are typically encountered in moving toward the use of self-managed teams. The first problem is what to do with the first-line supervisors who are no longer needed as supervisors. Some can assume new responsibilities as coordinators or coaches; some can rejoin the work group, but many will no longer be needed. Another problem is that the managers (or coordinators) that are now one level above the teams will likely oversee the activities of several teams, and their roles will change to emphasize planning, expediting, and coordinating. These managers will need considerable training to acquire skills in group leadership and the ability to delegate to the teams. Furthermore, team members will need to develop new skills in running and participating in team meetings, as well as in planning, quality control, budgeting, and so forth. Frequently, all team members learn all of the technical tasks performed by the team.[8]

OD interventions such as team-building activities are relevant to sociotechnical systems design and the development of self-managed teams. Furthermore, these activities need to be ongoing because, as Lawler puts it, well-run plants using self-managed teams "run the risk of becoming stagnant and complacent." He suggests the development of "an ongoing organizational assessment capability that constantly surfaces issues of organizational effectiveness and renewal."[9]

WORK REDESIGN

Richard Hackman and Greg Oldham have provided an OD approach to work redesign based on a theoretical model of what job characteristics lead to the psychological states that produce what they call "high internal work motivation." Their approach has OD characteristics in the extensive use of diagnosis, participation, and feedback, and particularly in applications to the redesign of group work where extensive use of the facilitator role in team development is recommended. Their model is shown in Figure 12-1.

Hackman and Oldham recommend that organizations analyze jobs using the five core job characteristics shown in Figure 12-1 and then re-design jobs to maximize worker motivation. The five core job characteristics are skill variety, task identity, task significance, autonomy, and feedback from the job. The first three are related to "experienced meaningfulness of the work." Job autonomy is related to "experienced responsibility for the

Figure 12-1   The Complete Job Characteristics Model

Source: J. Richard Hackman and Greg R. Oldham, *Work Redesign* (Figure 4.6), p. 90. © 1980 Addison-Wesley Publishing Company, Inc. Reprinted with permission of the publisher.

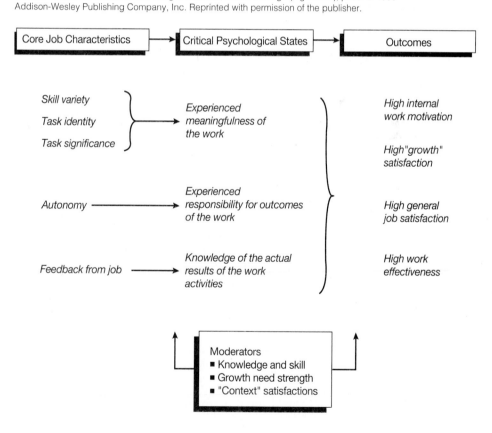

outcomes of the work." Feedback from the job is related to the psychological state of "knowledge of the results of the work activities." The expected outcomes, in turn, are high work motivation, high satisfaction with the job and with one's growth on the job, and high work effectiveness.[10]

As noted at the bottom of Figure 12-1, some factors can minimize or moderate these outcomes. One factor is knowledge and skill. Deficiencies in either can lead to less than desirable performance and a sense of failure. Another moderating factor is the strength of a person's need to learn and develop. If this need is low, the presence of the core job characteristics is less likely to lead to high motivation and job satisfaction. A third factor is satisfaction with the context of the job. Dissatisfaction with such matters as pay, job security, coworkers, or supervision is likely to minimize the otherwise favorable consequences of designing more complex and challenging jobs.[11]

The same authors extend their concepts to the redesign of the work of teams, self-managed teams, in particular. In this context they describe an approach in which an outside agent such as a consultant or manager helps group members develop and monitor their own performance norms:

> When a work group is being formed, the person responsible for designing the group might meet with group members to discuss explicitly how they want to develop their performance strategies. Merely talking through this issue may foster a climate in which strategic questions can be openly discussed—both when initial norms about strategy are developed and in the future when circumstances change. In effect, the manager or consultant would be helping members develop a *general* norm that encourages open and self-conscious discussion of *specific* norms about how group members work together on the task.[12]

Hackman and Oldham offer both an endorsement and a caution about self-managed teams:

> Self-managing work teams are a powerful social invention. In a moderately supportive organizational context they can prompt significant alterations in how work gets done and how the organization itself is managed. But if the people or the managerial climate and style of the organization are clearly unsympathetic to a group design for work, the potential benefits of such groups are unlikely to be realized.[13]

MBO AND APPRAISAL

To be congruent with the OD effort, goal-setting and performance review processes should have a team thrust and should be both participative and transactional. By *participative and transactional* we mean that in goal setting, subordinates should have meaningful ways to provide inputs; and in reviewing performance, a collaborative examination of the major significant forces in the situation needs to be made, including the superior's and the team's impact on the subordinate's performance, not just an appraisal of the subordinate's performance. In their more congruent forms, MBO programs evolve from a collaborative organization diagnosis and are systems of joint target setting and performance review designed to increase a focus on objectives and to increase the frequency of problem-solving discussions between supervisors and subordinates and within work teams. In their least congruent forms, MBO programs are unilateral, autocratic mechanisms designed to force compliance with a superior's directives and, in the process, reinforce a one-on-one leadership mode.

Our hunch is that many MBO programs are imposed by line managers or promoted by personnel/human resources departments without much diagnosis of the problem to be solved. If there is some diagnosis, we suspect it is a diagnosis made by a very few people. Furthermore, our impression is that most MBO programs do not use a team approach, that they do not provide for sufficient acknowledgment of the interdependency between jobs, and that rather than helping examine team culture, they tend to intensify dysfunctional competition within teams.[14]

If an MBO effort is to avoid some of these deficiencies, and if it is to avoid being punitive or overly constraining, we think it should include such ingredients as the following. We call this "Collaborative Management by Objectives" or CMBO:[15]

1. A collaborative diagnosis of organizational problems, from which it is concluded that a collaborative MBO effort would be functional.

2. Increased skills in interpersonal communications and group processes. (This will be crucial to the team aspects of this approach.)

3. Real subordinate participation, in team configurations, in setting goals.

4. A team approach to reviewing individual and group targets and their achievement.

5. Ongoing individual and team problem-solving discussions with superiors.

6. A continuous helping relationship within teams and in superior-subordinate relationships. (This will not occur quickly; a win-win climate that says "Let's try to help each other succeed" needs to emerge.)

7. Attention to personal and career goals in a real effort to make these complementary to organizational goals.

There is some research evidence to support arguments for some of these ingredients. Research at General Electric, for example, found that criticism by the superior tended to produce defensiveness and impaired performance, that goal setting and mutual goal setting between superior and subordinate were associated with improved performance, and that coaching needed to be a day-to-day activity.[16] A follow-up study at General Electric found that appraisals went better in a climate promoting trust, openness, support, and development.[17] Research in a public utility also found the organizational climate dimension of support to be a critical factor in the perceived success of MBO efforts.[18]

Likert and Fisher describe a participative, team approach to MBO in use in a retail division of a consumer products organization and in an automobile plant. They report impressive increases in contribution to corporate profits in the retail sales division and substantially increased productivity and reduced scrap and rejects in the automobile plant. They call the approach Management by Group Objectives (MBGO).[19]

QUALITY CIRCLES

The quality circle concept is a form of group problem solving and goal setting with a primary focus on maintaining and enhancing product quality. Quality circles have been extensively used in Japan since the introduction of quality control techniques there in the 1950s and 1960s by Edwards Deming, Joseph Juran, and A. W. Feigenbaum.[20] It is reported that Kaoru Ishikawa of Tokyo University integrated these techniques with the theories of American behavioral scientists such as Maslow, McGregor, and Herzberg, and thus, the quality circle was born.[21]

The Lockheed Missile and Space Company appears to be the first American firm to study the emerging Japanese approach and to implement an extensive program.[22] By 1985 it was estimated that over 90 percent of the *Fortune* 500 companies were utilizing quality circles, including such firms as Honeywell, Digital Equipment, TRW, and Westinghouse.[23]

Quality circles consist of a group of seven to ten employees from a unit (or across units) who have volunteered to meet together regularly to analyze and make proposals about product quality and other problems. Recommendations are forwarded to a coordinating or steering committee; meetings are typically held once a week for an hour on company time. Sometimes the meetings are chaired by a supervisor, and sometimes are chaired by an employee elected from the group. Leaders are encouraged to create a high degree of participation within the group.

Prior to the formation of quality circles, those supervisors who have volunteered to participate are trained by quality control experts and facilitators in such matters as quality control concepts, including the necessary statistical tools, in leading participative group discussions, and in group dynamics and communications skills. In turn, the supervisors, with the help of facilitators, train those subordinates who volunteer to participate. The facilitators also help each circle in its linking with other groups and with the overall coordinating committee. Groups are encouraged to use experts from within the organization when their specialities are relevant and are frequently authorized by management to make changes without higher authority whenever feasible. Once or twice a year, a member of higher management meets with each group.[24]

Favorable results have generally been reported in the popular and technical media. In the first three years of Lockheed's experimentation with the process, the company was reported to have saved six dollars for every one it spent on the process, and defects in manufacturing declined by two-thirds. Morale and job satisfaction among participants were reported to have increased.[25] At Nippon Kokon K.K., where thousands of employees are involved in quality control circles, savings were reported of some $86 million in one year, stemming from suggestions emerging from the groups.[26]

A 1990 study of 313 organizations found 52 percent evaluated their quality circle programs as successful, 36 percent were undecided, and 12 percent reported that they were unsuccessful.[27]

Favorable results have also been reported through the use of cross-functional (or multi-functional) quality circle teams at such organizations as Ford and IBM. The latter has an extensive program using "Process Improvement Teams" whose members are drawn from multiple functions.[28]

QUALITY OF WORK LIFE PROJECTS

The term *quality of work life (QWL)* has been applied to a wide variety of organizational improvement efforts. The common elements seem to be, as Goodman indicates, an "attempt to restructure multiple dimensions of the organization" and to "institute a mechanism which introduces and sustains changes over time."[29] Aspects of the change mechanism are usually an increase in participation by employees in shop floor decisions and an increase in problem solving between the union and management.

At some General Motors plants, QWL projects have included some of the following features:

> Voluntary involvement on the part of employees
> Union agreement with the process and participation in it
> Assurance of no loss of jobs as a result of the programs
> Training of employees in team problem solving

The use of quality circles where employees discuss problems affecting the performance of the plant and the work environment

Work team participation in forecasting, work planning, and team leader and team member selection

Regular plant and team meetings to discuss such matters as quality, safety, customer orders, and schedules

Encouragement of skill development and job rotation within work teams

Skill training

Responsiveness to employee concerns[30]

While the specifics vary from one QWL project to another, both within a given organization and between organizations, several features tend to be common. These features include union involvement; a focus on work teams; problem-solving sessions by work teams in which the agenda may include productivity, quality, and safety problems; autonomy in planning work; the availability of skill training; and increased responsiveness to employees by supervision.

Although many of these QWL projects have had at least modest success, frequently there have been difficulties in sustaining or expanding the process beyond a few years. Some of the reasons, according to Goodman, include changes in union leadership, expectations that were too high, efforts aimed at production and clerical levels with insufficient attention to changes at the managerial and professional levels, and too little attention to long-term financial rewards for the participants.[31] Major resistance from supervisors has frequently occurred when top management has paid insufficient attention to issues of job security and role definition for people at this level.[32]

PARALLEL LEARNING STRUCTURES

As discussed in Chapter 5, in their most basic forms, parallel learning structures generally consist of a steering committee and a number of working groups that study what changes are needed in the organization, make recommendations for improvement, and then monitor the resulting change efforts. Use is made of the facilitator role, data gathering, data feedback, and process consultation. As described by Gervase Bushe and A. B. Shani, these parallel organizations, or collateral organizations as described by Dale Zand, are essentially microcosms of the total organization and are set up in tandem with the ongoing activities of the organization.

As viewed by Zand, the collateral organization is created to deal with "ill-structured" (i.e., complex, nonroutine, future-oriented) problems that have high priority and that are systemwide, involving more than one unit. A deliberate effort is made to develop a set of norms different from those in the formal system. In particular, "careful questioning and analysis of goals, assumptions, methods, alternatives, and criteria for evaluation" are encouraged.[33] Bushe and Shani also emphasize the importance of the creation of different norms and culture within the parallel or collateral organization. In particular, they say "What's important is that people act in a way that promotes learning and adaptation."[34]

Also as indicated in Chapter 5, the parallel learning structure has been extensively used across a wide array of change programs. These have included quality of work life (QWL) programs, sociotechnical systems (STS) work redesign efforts, open systems planning programs, and the coordination of employee involvement teams.

PHYSICAL SETTINGS AND OD

Some consultants have been active in working with clients and in conceptualizing about how to make physical settings congruent with OD assumptions and the OD process. A notable example of this thrust is Steele's work. To Steele, physical settings are an important part of organization culture that work groups should learn to diagnose and manage, and about which top management needs input in designing plants and buildings.

Steele cites many instances in which physical settings were found to interfere with effective group and organizational functioning. For example,

A personnel director promoted to senior vice-president, a position inheriting the incredible, mandatory practice of having a secretary share the same office (which was supposed to signal high status), with the resulting lack of privacy and typewriter noise, adversely affecting the executive's ability to hold spontaneous meetings with employees

An executive group wanting to rearrange an office setting to increase interaction and rapport, but locked into status considerations relative to the larger and corner offices

A factory management encouraging group decision making, yet providing no space for more than six people to meet at one time

Classroom and lecture hall arrangement in universities reinforcing a teacher-dominated and low-peer-interaction climate[35]

Many OD consultants have long given considerable attention to the physical arrangements for team-building sessions, and Steele reinforces this approach by urging facilitators to include the dimension of physical arrangements in their "process consultation" interventions.[36] Steele describes a rating process he uses to examine things such as desks, lights, or machines, patterns of elements such as the arrangement of chairs, and sociological factors such as norms about the use of physical settings.[37]

While architecture and interior arrangements and design are not OD per se, both the approach used by Steele, which includes a strong emphasis on participative diagnosis, and the outcomes, which tend to meet client needs (e.g., enhancing team efforts when needed and privacy when needed) are highly congruent with OD. Steele's work is a notable example of some of the creative integrations that have occurred between OD and other consultancy modes.

TOTAL QUALITY MANAGEMENT (TQM)

Total quality management (TQM), sometimes called continuous quality improvement, is a combination of a number of organization improvement techniques and approaches, including the use of quality circles, statistical quality control, statistical process control, self-managed teams and task forces, and extensive use of employee participation. Much of the impetus for TQM has come from a growing awareness by American executives of the critical need for American corporations to compete on a global scale. In particular, it has become obvious that it is necessary to compete with the Japanese who have had great success in managing quality.

The following features tend to characterize TQM. This list is largely based on total quality conferences held in the United States and abroad by the Conference Board and on a special issue of *Business Week* entitled *The Quality Imperative*.[38]

Primary emphasis on customers. The development of an organizational culture in which employees at all levels, including the CEO, give paramount treatment to customer needs and expectations.

Daily operational use of the concept of internal customers. Emphasis on the concept that work flow and internal interdependencies require that organizational members treat each other as valued customers across functional lines as well as within units.

An emphasis on measurement using both statistical quality control and statistical process control techniques. Statistical quality control is a method of measuring and analyzing deviations in manufactured products; statistical process control is a method of analyzing deviations in manufacturing processes.

Competitive benchmarking. Continuous rating of the company's products and practices against the world's best firms, including other organizations in other industries.

Continuous search for sources of defects with a goal of eliminating them entirely. The Japanese call this *Kaizen.*

Participative management. This includes extensive delegation and involvement and a coaching, supportive leadership style.

An emphasis on teams and teamwork. Typically this includes self-managed teams. Cross-functional and multilevel task forces are also used extensively.

A major emphasis on continuous training. This means learning new and better ways of doing things and adding new skills. In many organizations it is reinforced by changes in the reward system, for example, the introduction of skill-based or knowledge-based pay.

Top-management support on an ongoing basis. This requires a long-term perspective and a long-term commitment on the part of top management.

Some version of total quality management is being used in virtually all types of organizations, for example, electronics, semiconductors, basic metals, chemicals, automobiles, software development, railroads, airlines, insurance, and retail sales. Organizations as diverse as hospitals and Navy aircraft carriers have become involved.

Some of the problems experienced by companies attempting to implement TQM are common to many organization improvement efforts which require a major change in the culture of the organization. For example, there can be initial union resistance, as experienced at the Inland Steel Bar Company, particularly when there has been a history of adversarial relations. As another example, first-line and middle managers may be threatened by the need to delegate extensive responsibility to self-managed teams and/or task forces and may resist shifting to more of a coaching and supporting role. Furthermore, as is the case in all major organization improvement efforts, new ways of doing things will not compensate for having an inappropriate corporate strategy.[39]

Although numerous TQM efforts have not been successful due to problems such as the ones mentioned previously, many companies have achieved considerable success. At the request of Congress, the U.S. General Accounting Office assessed the impact of TQM programs in companies selected from among the highest-scoring applicants for the Malcolm Baldrige National Quality Award. This award is established under a law named for a former secretary of commerce, and is designed to recognize companies that have successfully implemented total quality management systems. The GAO reported the following results:

> Companies that adopted quality management practices experienced an overall improvement in corporate performance. In nearly all cases, companies . . . achieved better employee relations, higher productivity, greater customer satisfaction, increased market share, and greater profitability.[40]

The GAO further found that total quality management is relevant for small companies as well as large ones. The GAO reported that sufficient time needs to be allowed for gains to appear—on the average, companies required two and one-half years to improve their performance. Thus, TQM requires a long-term perspective; it is a long-term, continuous process.[41]

In a study examining both TQM and employee involvement programs, Lawler, Mohrman, and Ledford found that the greatest success was achieved when organizations pursued both simultaneously. They conclude:

> Total quality may have provided the business focus that was missing in some of the early employee involvement programs. . . . The good news is that, for the most part, the practices utilized in total quality management and employee involvement appear to be complementary. The use of total quality practices appears to bolster the impact of employee involvement, particularly on business outcomes. This is much more likely if employee involvement and total quality are managed in an integrated way than if they are managed as separate programs.[42]

Because of the emphasis in successful applications on creating an organizational culture that features extensive participation, an emphasis on teams and teamwork, cooperation between teams and units, the generation of valid data,[43] and continuous learning, TQM appears to be highly congruent with OD approaches and values. Indeed, Dan Ciampa states that a major aspect of TQM is derived from OD:

> The people side of Total Quality is a direct descendant of Organization Development. To truly understand TQ and to be able to make it a reality, one must be expert in creating change on the people side of the organizational excellence equation. The values on which OD is based, its dedication to human learning, its elements of adult education and management training are all necessary parts of a true, successful TQ effort.[44]

Although there is this historical connection, many TQM practitioners would probably not consider themselves to be involved in organization development, the improvement strategy based on behavioral science described in this book. At this point the two fields are relatively independent of each other. There is great potential for synergy between TQM and OD, however, as indicated by the Lawler et al. research just mentioned and the book on total quality by Dan Ciampa.

REENGINEERING

Recently, considerable interest has been generated in reengineering, which has emerged hard on the heels of the burgeoning total quality management (TQM) movement. Authors Hammer and Champy define reengineering as "the fundamental rethinking and radical redesign of business processes to achieve dramatic improvements in critical, contemporary measures of performance, such as cost, quality, service, and speed."[45] They do not see reengineering as appropriate for making incremental improvements of, say, 10 percent in costs or customer service, but as appropriate for making "quantum leaps in performance."[46]

According to Hammer and Champy, reengineering focuses on visualizing and streamlining any or all "business processes" in the organization, which they define as a "collection of activities that takes one or more kinds of input and creates an output that is of value to the customer."[47] They provide numerous examples of business processes, such as "order fulfillment, which takes an order as its input and results in delivery of the ordered goods."[48] Reengineering seeks to make such processes more efficient by combining, eliminating, or restructuring activities without regard to present hierarchical or control procedures.

While we see focusing on processes as extraordinarily important (see Chapter 5 and our writings going back to 1963),[49] and reengineering may indeed be required in many organizations, it appears to us to be a massive application of industrial engineering. Reengineering, as presently conceptualized, at least by Hammer and Champy, does not appear to pay much attention to the social system of organizations relative to change processes and the redesign of work. (However, one of Hammer and Champy's clients gave considerable attention to social system factors as shown in the transcripts of conversations with the authors. See the following reference to DRG.) In contrast, sociotechnical systems emerged out of the realization that the interdependence and "fit" of the technical and social systems of organizations were extremely important.

Reengineering, as seen by Hammer and Champy, is clearly a top-down program that assumes neither an upward flow of involvement nor that consensus decision making will work to accomplish dramatic changes.[50] They argue that people lower down in the organization do not have sufficient perspective to visualize the changes that are needed. They do point out that it is important to pay attention to the "company's human resource and organizational infrastructure,"[51] but they say little beyond that. However, they do write two or three pages about people's "values and beliefs," and focus on rewarding behavior that exhibits the appropriate values pertaining to customers, teamwork, and ownership of problems.[52] Furthermore, they see the role of the manager changing from being a boss to that of a coach,[53] which is consistent with the experience of organizations that move toward self-managed teams.

Reengineering, then, seems largely incongruent with OD processes in some major ways, particularly with respect to the minimal participation that is recommended. But it also appears to have some congruency in terms of certain hoped-for outcomes, such as effective teamwork and the changing role of the supervisor. Where, if any place in a reengineering effort, might OD make a contribution? Or, to pose the question differently, how might OD and reengineering become congruent?

First, if top management has bought into reengineering, OD and human resources people can argue for making the process as humane as possible, including an early facing up to the options open if people are displaced from their jobs. Reduction through attrition? Retraining? Transfer? Early retirement incentives? Carefully designed outplacement programs? Recall rights? How much notice? And so forth. Capital Holding Corporation, a Louisville, Kentucky, financial services company which participated in a major reengineering program in its Commonwealth group of life insurance companies, was able to transfer most of the displaced Commonwealth employees to jobs in other divisions that were adding employees. However, in most instances, reengineering has resulted in large layoffs.[54]

Second, those who advocate OD-type values and processes can look for avenues for meaningful involvement of employees at all levels in any reengineering effort. We are less pessimistic than Hammer and Champy relative to the ability of people at lower and middle levels of the organization to see the broad picture. The experience of one of their clients is also less pessimistic. As reported by a senior vice president of DRG, a marketing insurance company also owned by Capital Holding Corporation, DRG involved numerous people at various levels before reengineering various company processes. For example, DRG used a multilevel, cross-functional team as well as focus groups to attempt to understand the norms and underlying assumptions that were governing the company's present operations.[55] Furthermore, other authors such as Robert Janson write about a form of reengineering that can involve everyone in the organization.[56]

Third, people with OD skills can help emerging new teams to be more effective than they otherwise might be. Effective teams of various kinds would seem to be important for successful implementation of reengineering. For example, Hammer and Champy recommend the formation of "reengineering teams" who focus on a particular process and its redesign and implementation.[57] Then there is a "steering committee," a policy-making group of senior managers. Also, and extremely crucial, it seems to us, is the effectiveness of the various "process teams" that emerge to replace functional departments.[58] OD has much to contribute to the formation and development of effective teams.

Fourth, OD knowledge about how to design and implement parallel structures discussed earlier is relevant to reengineering. It would seem that the steering committee and process team structure described earlier lend themselves to the use of facilitators, action research, and process consultation.

Reengineering raises a major ethical issue for OD and human resource management (HRM) and development professionals if it results in large layoffs. What kind of recommendations should OD and HRM professionals make about assisting with the problem of large-scale dislocations of people? According to *The Wall Street Journal*,

> So far, the potential magnitude of the re-engineering movement and the productivity boom it could spawn have escaped the attention of Washington policy makers and even most economists who specialize in productivity trends. No one has a fix on the likely political and social ramifications of re-engineering, but some estimates call for it to wipe out as many as 25 million jobs. . ."[59]

We are not suggesting that OD practitioners and OD clients become twenty-first century Luddites in resisting technological change. We are suggesting that reengineering and other forms of corporate restructuring that can produce massive layoffs be balanced by management philosophy and government policies that mitigate the human and social consequences of rapid downsizing. Some of the options are downsizing through attrition, hiring freezes, retraining, temporary work sharing, early retirement inducements, comprehensive outplacement programs, and the like.

LARGE-SCALE SYSTEMS CHANGE AND ORGANIZATIONAL TRANSFORMATION

Any of the interventions described in earlier chapters and in this chapter could be part of a large-scale systems change effort. Typically, when OD approaches are used in large-scale change efforts, multiple types of OD interventions are utilized.

By *large-scale systems change* we mean organizational change that is massive in terms of the number of organizational units involved, the number of people affected, the number of organizational subsystems altered, and/or the depth of the cultural change involved. For example, a major restructuring with objectives including a reduction in hierarchical levels from eight to four and shifting to a more participative leadership style might involve every unit of the organization, affect the responsibilities of every employee at every level, and would require changes in such aspects as work flow, reporting relationships, job descriptions and titles, compensation, and training programs.

Figure 12-2 portrays some of the differences between evolutionary, incremental or mid-range, and large-scale systems change.[60] Included in the latter is what Levy and Merry call "second-order change," that is, ". . . a multidimensional, multi-level, qualitative, discontinuous, radical organizational change involving a paradigmatic

	EVOLUTIONARY CHANGE	*INCREMENTAL OR MID-RANGE CHANGE*	*LARGE-SCALE SYSTEMS CHANGE*
Problem solving	*Business as usual.* Some employee and supervisory training of a technical nature that enhances job performance.	*OD helps with participative problem solving.* Several units, beginning with top management, hold periodic retreats to take a reading on strengths and problem areas—largely the technological and task aspects of their units—and to make action plans. Task forces are utilized.	*Technological/structural approaches.* Organization engages in massive reengineering program to speed up product development and customer service. Or Organization, in an efficiency move, merges several divisions, sells two, eliminates two layers of management, lays off ten percent of the workforce.
Problem solving plus cultural change	*Business as usual plus modest shift in culture.* Some managers and employees, in addition to technical training, attend various seminars and courses. Individual managers begin to shift toward a more participative, open, supportive leadership style.	*OD begins to have a significant impact on organizational culture.* Units holding retreats include a collaborative look at functional and dysfuctional consequences of technological/task aspects plus leadership, group process, teamwork, and conflict management aspects. Process matters begin to be a legitimate part of any meeting agenda.	*Organizational transformation including OD.* Organization reconceptualizes the nature of its business and engages in a comprehensive TQM effort, including extensive use of survey feedback, team building, and organization mirror techniques. Or Organization reconceptualizes the nature of its business, reduces management levels, uses multiple OD interventions, including the collateral organization, team building, survey feedback, task forces, and intensive leadership training.

Figure 12-2 Examples of Different Types and Degrees of Organizational Change

shift." Their use of the term *second-order change* is essentially synonymous with "organization transformation."[61]

Organizational transformation, or second-order change, usually requires a multiplicity of interventions and takes place over a fairly long period of time. For example, the five-year organizational transformation process at British Airways, as reported by Goodstein and Burke, included the following:

- Replacement of the top-management team
- Redefining the nature of the business from transportation to service

- Diagonal task forces to plan changes
- A reduction in hierarchical levels
- Substantial downsizing of the work force, including middle management, without layoffs
- Team building (off site), including role clarification and negotiation
- Process consultation
- Modifying the budget process
- Top-management commitment and involvement
- Personnel staff trained to be internal consultants
- Peer support groups
- Performance-based compensation and profit sharing
- Experiential training programs for senior and middle managers including feedback on managerial behavior
- Open communications
- Continuous data-based feedback on work group and organizational climate and management practices
- A new appraisal system emphasizing both behavior and performance
- Continuous use of task forces[62]

The reader will note that a wide variety of interventions were utilized in this large-scale systems change program.

SUMMARY OF THE CHARACTERISTICS OF SELECTED STRUCTURAL INTERVENTIONS

The following summarizes some of the differences and similarities as well as the overlap between sociotechnical systems (STS), self-managed teams, work redesign, MBO, quality circles, quality of work life (QWL) programs, parallel or collateral structures, physical settings, total quality management (TQM), reengineering, and large-scale systems change:

1. *Sociological systems (STS) theory* says that it is important to jointly optimize the social and technological systems of organizations. Furthermore,

(a) the boundary between the organization and its environment should be managed in such a way that there are effective exchanges, but protection from external disruptions,

(b) the implementation of STS should be highly participative, and

(c) the creation and development of self-managed teams is an important factor in STS implementation (Cummings and Worley; Trist, Higgin, Murray, and Pollock and others).

2. The creation of *self-managed teams* involves

(a) providing teams with a grouping of tasks that comprises a major unit of the total work to be performed;

(b) training group members in multiple skills, including team-effectiveness skills;

(c) delegating to the team many aspects of how the work gets done;

(d) providing a great deal of information and feedback for self-regulation of quality and productivity;

(e) solving the problem of dislocation of first-line supervisors; and

(f) reconceptualizing the role of managers with emphasis on coaching, expediting, and coordinating (Walton, Lawler and others).

3. *Work redesign theory* suggests that

(a) motivation and performance can be enhanced through re-designing jobs to heighten skill variety, task identity, task significance, autonomy, and feedback from the job;

(b) the concept can be extended to the creation of self-managed teams; and

(c) third-party assistance in the development and monitoring of group norms can be useful (Hackman and Oldham).

4. *Traditional MBO theory* assumes there is a need for systematic goal setting linking the goals of superiors to subordinates and that

(a) objectives or targets should be stated in quantitative terms whenever possible,

(b) goal setting and appraisal should be one-on-one dialogues between superior and subordinate. However, additional conceptualization and experience indicate that

(c) MBO can vary on an autocratic-participative continuum and that

(d) MBO can feature a participative team approach (French and Hollmann, Likert and Fisher).

5. *Quality circles*, at least the participative, problem-solving versions, are based on the assumptions that many, if not most, employees are willing to work collaboratively in group settings—both natural work teams and cross-functional teams—on problems of product quality and system effectiveness, and that they can learn to effectively utilize both technical and process consultants, providing they are

(a) trained in quality-control concepts and the relevant measuring techniques, and are

(b) trained in group dynamics, team leadership, and interpersonal communication skills.

6. *Quality of work life (QWL) programs* vary in content but frequently include restructuring of several dimensions of the organization, including

(a) increased problem solving between management and the union;

(b) increased participation by teams of employees in shop floor decisions pertaining to production flow, quality control, and safety; and

(c) skill development through technical skill training, job rotation, and training in team problem solving (Fuller, Carrigan, Bluestone, Goodman, Lawler, Ledford, Walton and others).

7. *Parallel learning structures (or collateral organizations)* are organizations established within ongoing organizations and having the following features:

(a) a mandate to deal with complex, nonroutine, future-oriented problems and/or to coordinate large-scale systems change;

(b) the creation of different norms and culture, to enhance creative problem solving and to create a model organization from which the organization can learn (Zand, Bushe and Shani).

8. *Physical settings or arrangements* can be the focus of interventions that can utilize and be highly congruent with OD techniques and assumptions (Steele).

9. *Total quality management (TQM) programs* are combinations of a number of approaches, including

(a) a high emphasis on customers, including internal customers;

(b) the use of statistical quality control and statistical process control techniques;

(c) competitive benchmarking;

(d) participative management;

(e) an emphasis on teams and teamwork; and

(f) an emphasis on continuous training (Peters and Peters, Ciampa, Sashkin and others).

10. *Reengineering* as currently conceptualized (Hammer and Champy)

(a) focuses almost exclusively on streamlining "business processes," and

(b) appears to pay little attention to the human-social system. However, it appears theoretically possible for reengineering programs to utilize OD approaches in which

(c) there is extensive use of collateral organizations, and

(d) organizational members are extensively involved and adequately protected.

11. *Large-scale systems change (including organizational transformation) with an extensive OD thrust* typically requires a multiplicity of interventions over an extended time period, including

(a) a reconceptualization of the nature of the business;

(b) the use of a parallel learning structure;

(c) a reduction in hierarchical levels;

(d) team building and development, including the use of cross-functional teams;

(e) survey feedback;

(f) extensive use of task forces; and

(g) intensive leadership training (Nadler, Ackerman, Porras and Silvers, Cummings and Worley, Weisbord and others).

NOTES

1. Thomas G. Cummings and Christopher G. Worley, *Organization Development and Change*, 5th ed. (Minneapolis/St. Paul: West Publishing Company, 1993), pp. 353–354.
2. E. L. Trist, G. W. Higgin, H. Murray, and A. B. Pollock, *Organizational Choice* (London: Tavistock, 1965).

3. A. K. Rice, "Productivity and Social Organization in an Indian Weaving Shed: An Examination of Some Aspects of the Socio-Technical System of an Experimental Automatic Loom Shed," *Human Relations*, 6 (1953), pp. 297–329.

4. See, for example, E. Thorsrud, "Socio-Technical Approach to Job Design and Organizational Development," *Management International Review*, 8 (1968), pp. 120–131. See also Calvin Pava, "Designing Managerial and Professional Work for High Performance: A Sociotechnical Approach," *National Productivity Review*, 2 (Spring 1983), pp. 126–135; and Calvin Pava, "Redesigning Sociotechnical Systems Design: Concepts and Methods for the 1990s," *The Journal of Applied Behavioral Science*, 22, no. 3 (1986), 201–221.

5. Richard E. Walton, "From Hawthorne to Topeka and Kalmar," in E. L. Cass and Frederick G. Zimmer, eds., *Man and Work in Society* (New York: Van Nostrand Reinhold, 1975), pp. 116–129. See also William A. Pasmore, "Overcoming the Roadblocks in Work-Restructuring Efforts," *Organizational Dynamics*, 10 (Spring 1982), pp. 54–67; and Berth Jonsson and Alden Lake, "Volvo: A Report," *Human Resource Management*, 24 (Winter 1985), pp. 455–465.

6. David Barry, "Managing the Bossless Team: Lessons in Distributed Leadership," *Organizational Dynamics*, 20 (Summer 1991), p. 31; Oregon Department of Transportation, Region 4, and Gossard-Pyron Associates, *Self-Directed Maintenance Crews: Results of a Two Year Pilot Program* (January 1993), 92 pages; *Fortune*, October 17, 1992, p. 113; and Jana Schilder, "Work Teams Boost Productivity," *Personnel Journal*, 71 (February 1992), pp. 67–71.

7. Edward E. Lawler III, "The New Plant Revolution Revisited," *Organizational Dynamics*, 19 (Autumn 1990), p. 10.

8. For more on problems in the use of self-managed teams, see Tom Peters, *Thriving on Chaos* (New York: Alfred A. Knopf, 1988), pp. 299–300; and Tony Kulisch and David K. Banner, "Self-managed Work Teams: An Update," *Leadership & Organization Development Journal*, 14, no. 2 (1993), 25–29.

9. Lawler, "The New Plant Revolution," p. 11. For more on sociotechnical systems design and self-managed teams, see Abraham B. Shani and Ord Elliott, "Sociotechnical System Design in Transition," in Walter Sikes, Allan B. Drexler, and Jack Gant, eds. *The Emerging Practice of Organization Development* (Alexandria,VA: NTL Institute and San Diego: Universlty Associates, 1989), pp. 187–198; and Louis E. Davis, "Guides to the Design and Redesign of Organizations," in Robert Tannenbaum, Newton Margulies, and Fred Massarik and Associates, *Human Systems Development* (San Francisco: Jossey-Bass Publishers, 1985), pp. 143–166.

10. J. Richard Hackman and Greg R. Oldham, *Work Redesign* (Reading, MA: Addison-Wesley Publishing Company, 1980), pp. 77–83.

11. Ibid., pp. 82–88.

12. Ibid., p. 181.

13. Ibid., p. 184.

14. For a description of a federal government MBO program "laid on from the top" and the consequent resistance and token use, see Edward J. Ryan, Jr., "Federal Government MBO: Another Managerial Fad?" *MSU Business Topics*, 21 (Autumn 1976), pp. 35–43. For more on some of the basic faults in many MBO efforts, see Harry Levinson, "Management by Whose Objectives?" *Harvard Business Review*, 48 (July–August 1970), pp. 125–134.

15. See Wendell French and Robert Hollmann, "Management by Objectives: The Team Approach," *California Management Review*, 17 (Spring 1975), pp. 13–22. A workshop participant has suggested we call this "COMBO." See also Wendell L. French and John A. Drexler, Jr., "A Team Approach to MBO," *Leadership & Organization Development Journal*, 5, no. 5 (1984), 22–26.

16. H. H. Meyer, E. Kay, and J. R. P. French, Jr., "Split Roles in Performance Appraisal," *Harvard Business Review*, 43 (January–February 1965), pp. 124–139.

17. Edward E. Lawler III, Alan M. Mohrman, Jr., and Susan M. Resnick, "Performance Appraisal Revisited," *Organizational Dynamics*, 13 (Summer 1984), pp. 20–35.

18. Robert W. Hollmann, "Supportive Organization Climate and Managerial Assessment of MBO Effectiveness," *Academy of Management Journal*, 19 (December 1976), pp. 560–576.

19. Rensis Likert and M. Scott Fisher, "MBGO: Putting Some Team Spirit into MBO," *Personnel*, 54 (January–February 1977), pp. 40–47. Actually, Likert had done some research on such an approach in the mid-1960s but had not called it a form of MBO. See Rensis Likert's discussion of "a group method of sales supervision" in his *The Human Organization: Its Management and Value* (New York: McGraw-Hill, 1967), pp. 55–71.

20. Peter F. Drucker, "Learning from Foreign Management," *The Wall Street Journal*, June 4, 1980, p. 20.

21. Donald L. Dewar, *Quality Circle Member Manual* (Red Bluff, CA: Quality Circle Institute, 1980), p. iii.

22. Robert E. Cole, "Made in Japan—Quality-Control Circles," *Across the Board*, 16 (November 1979), pp. 72–78.

23. Edward E. Lawler III and Susan A. Mohrman, "Quality Circles After the Fad," *Harvard Business Review*, 63 (January–February 1985), pp. 65–71.

24. Based on interviews and observations at Lockheed Shipbuilding; Robert E. Cole and Dennis S. Tachiki, "Forging Institutional Links: Making Quality Circles Work in the U.S." *National Productivity Review*, 3 (Autumn 1984), pp. 417–429; and Mary Zippo, "Productivity and Morale Sagging? Try the Quality Circle Approach," *Personnel*, 57 (May–June 1980), pp. 43–45.

25. Cole, "Made in Japan," p. 76.

26. "Quality Control Circles Pay Off Big," *Industry Week*, October 29, 1979, p. 17.

27. Edward E. Lawler III, Susan A. Mohrman, and Gerald E. Ledford, Jr., *Employee Involvement and Total Quality Management* (San Francisco: Jossey-Bass Publishers, 1992), p. 57.

28. Tom Peters, *Thriving on Chaos* (New York: Alfred A. Knopf, 1988), p. 85. For some of the potential problems with quality circles, see Gregory P. Shea, "Quality Circles: The Danger of Bottled Change," *Sloan Management Review*, 27 (Spring 1986), pp. 33–46; Donald D. White and David A. Bednar, "Locating Problems with Quality Circles," *National Productivity Review*, 4 (Winter 1984–85), pp. 45–52; and Edward E. Lawler III and Susan A. Mohrman, "Quality Circles: After the Honeymoon," *Organizational Dynamics*, 14 (Spring 1987), pp. 42–55.

29. Paul S. Goodman, "Quality of Work Life Projects in the 1980s," *Labor Law Journal*, 31 (August 1980), p. 487. See also Louis E. Davis, "Guides to the Design and Redesign of Organizations," in Robert Tannenbaum, Newton Margulies, Fred Massarik and Associates, *Human Systems Development* (San Francisco: Jossey-Bass Publishers, 1985), pp. 143–166.

30. Stephen H. Fuller, "How Quality-of-Worklife Projects Work for General Motors," *Monthly Labor Review*, 103 (July 1980), pp. 37–39; Irving Bluestone, "How Quality-of-Worklife Projects Work for the United Auto Workers" *Monthly Labor Review*, 103 (July 1980), pp. 39–41; and Patricia M. Carrigan, "Up from the Ashes," *OD Practitioner*, 18 (March 1986), pp. 1–6. See also Edward M. Glaser and Paul A. Nelson, "A Quality of Worklife Improvement Effort at Five Mental Health Facilities," *OD Practitioner*, 19 (March 1987), pp. 1–6.

31. Goodman, "Quality of Work Life Projects in the 1980s," pp. 387–494. See also Edward E. Lawler III and Gerald E. Ledford, Jr., "Productivity and the Quality of Work Life," *National Productivity Review*, 1 (Winter 1981–82), pp. 23–36. For further discussion of QWL projects, see Louis E. Davis and Albert B. Cherns, eds., *The Quality of Working Life*, vol. II (New York: The Free Press, 1975); Richard E. Walton, "Work Innovations at Topeka: After Six Years," *Journal of Applied Behavioral Science*, 13, no. 3 (1977), 422–433; and Richard E. Walton, "Work Innovations in the United States," *Harvard Business Review*, 57 (July–August 1979), pp. 88–98.

32. See Janice A. Klein, "Why Supervisors Resist Employee Involvement," *Harvard Business Review,* 62 (September–October 1984), pp. 87–95. See also Robert T. Golembiewski and Ben-Chu Sun, "Positive-Findings Bias in QWL Studies: Rigor and Outcomes in a Large Sample," *Journal of the Academy of Management,* 16, no. 3 (1990), 665–674.

33. This discussion is based on Dale Zand, "Collateral Organization: A New Change Strategy," *Journal of Applied Behavioral Science,* 10, no. 1 (1974), 63–89. See also Dale E. Zand, *Information, Organization, and Power* (New York: McGraw-Hill, 1981), Chap. 4; and Barry A. Stein and Rosabeth Moss Kanter, "Building the Parallel Organization: Creating Mechanisms for Permanent Quality of Work Life," *The Journal of Applied Behavioral Science,* 16 (July–September 1980), pp. 371–386. See also Abraham B. Shani and Bruce J. Eberhardt, "Parallel Organization in a Health Care Institution," *Group & Organization Studies,* 12 (June 1987), pp. 147–173.

34. Gervase R. Bushe and A. B. (Rami) Shani, *Parallel Learning Structures* (Reading, MA: Addison-Wesley Publishing Company, 1991), p. 10.

35. Fred I. Steele, *Physical Settings and Organization Development* (Reading, MA: Addison-Wesley, 1973), pp. 101–107.

36. Ibid., p. 131.

37. Ibid., pp 97–98. See also Jerry I. Porras and Peter J. Robertson, "Organization Development: Theory, Practice, and Research," in Marvin D. Dunnette and L. M. Hough, *Handbook of Industrial & Organizational Psychology,* 2nd ed. (Palto Alto, CA: Consulting Psychologists Press, 1992), pp. 773–774, 775–779.

38. Barbara H. Peters and Jim L. Peters, *Total Quality Management,* The Conference Board Report No. 963, 1991, 63 pages; and *Business Week* special issue "The Quality Imperative," October 25, 1991, 216 pages.

39. See also Jack Steele, "Implementing Total Quality Management for Long- and Short-Term Bottom-Line Results," *National Productivity Review* 12 (Summer 1993), pp. 425–441; and Dan Ciampa, *Total Quality* (Reading, MA: Addison-Wesley Publishing Company, 1992).

40. United States General Accounting Office, *Management Practices: U.S. Companies Improving Performance Through Quality Efforts,* National Security and International Affairs Division (May 1991), p. 2.

41. Ibid., p. 4.

42. Lawler, Mohrman, and Ledford, *Employee Involvement and Total Quality Management,* p. 120.

43. Marshall Sashkin emphasizes the dimension of valid data in his paper distributed at a Bowling Green State University Master of Organization Development program in April 1992: "TQM Implications for OD," pp. 4–5.

44. Dan Ciampa, *Total Quality,* p. 33. For more on the cultural dimensions of TQM, see Marshall Sashkin and Kenneth J. Kiser, *Total Quality Management* (Seabrook, MD: Ducochon Press, 1991), Chapters 4 and 5.

45. Michael Hammer and James Champy, *Reengineering the Corporation: A Manifesto for Business Revolution* (New York: HarperCollins Publishers, 1993), p. 32.

46. Ibid.

47. Ibid., p. 35.

48. Ibid.

49. Wendell L. French, "Processes vis-à-vis Systems: Toward a Model of the Enterprise and Administration," *Academy of Management Journal,* 6 (March 1963), pp. 46–58.

50. Hammer and Champy, pp. 206–208.

51. Ibid., p. 192.

52. Ibid., pp. 72–78.

53. Ibid., p. 76.

54. *The Wall Street Journal,* March 16, 1993, pp. A1, A12.

55. Hammer and Champy, p. 186.

56. Robert Janson, "How Reengineering Transforms Organizations to Satisfy Customers," *National Productivity Review,* 12 (Winter 1992/93), pp. 45–53.

57. Hammer and Champy, p. 102.

58. Ibid., p. 65.

59. *The Wall Street Journal*, March 16, 1993, p. A1.

60. This conceptualizing of different types of change has been influenced by a number of authors and sources, including David A. Nadler, "Organizational Frame Bending: Principles for Managing Reorientation," *Academy of Management EXECUTIVE*, 3 (August 1989), pp. 194–204; Linda Ackerman, "Development, Transition or Transformation: The Question of Change in Organizations," *OD Practitioner*, 18 (December 1986), pp. 1–8; Marvin R. Weisbord, "Toward Third-Wave Managing and Consulting," *Organizational Dynamics*, 15 (Winter 1987), pp. 5–25; Jerry I. Porras and Robert C. Silvers, "Organization Development and Transformation," *Annual Review of Psychology*, 42 (1991), pp. 51–78; and Thomas G. Cummings and Christopher G. Worley, *Organization Development and Change*, 5th ed. (Minneapolis/St. Paul: West Publishing Company, 1993), pp. 520–523.

61. Amir Levy and Uri Merry, *Organizational Transformation* (New York: Praeger Publishers, 1986), p. 5.

62. Leonard D. Goodstein and W. Warner Burke, "Creating Successful Organizational Change," *Organizational Dynamics*, 19 (Spring 1991), pp. 5–17.

13

TRAINING EXPERIENCES

A number of training or educational experiences aimed at individuals have utility in the successful evolution of an OD effort. These OD interventions can be complementary and reinforcing adjuncts to the OD process. There are many different kinds of seminars and workshops, of course, including those of a technical nature such as budgeting, statistical process control, and long-range planning that can be of assistance to individuals, depending upon their experiences to date and the problems being faced by the organization. But we want to highlight several that focus on the human and social processes of organizations, especially those that are of relevance to leadership, interpersonal and group skills, and to career development.

In particular, we want to focus on *T-groups, behavior modeling,* and *life and career planning,* including the use of *career anchors.* T-group training (sometimes called sensitivity training), which is the educational and social invention giving rise to the laboratory training movement, typically yields important learnings about the self, interpersonal relations, group dynamics, and leadership. Behavior modeling is a training technique designed to increase effectiveness in problematic interpersonal situations. Life- and career-planning workshops are less process oriented than the other educational activities in this chapter and emphasize individuals examining their career and life plans and then usually discussing their analyses and plans in small groups.

T-GROUPS

Early in the OD movement, T-groups were sometimes used with intact work teams, but such use has largely given way to team building. The latter has a much more diagnostic, problem-solving, and organizational focus. Nevertheless, as an educational experience for the individual, the T-group has high relevance for developing skills of importance in the unfolding of an OD effort and for personal growth and development.

A T-group is an essentially unstructured, agendaless group session for about 10 to 12 members and a professional "trainer" who acts as catalyst and facilitator for the group. The data for discussion are the data provided by the interaction of the group members as they strive to create a viable society for themselves. Actions, reactions, interactions, and the concomitant feelings accompanying all of these are the data for the group. The group typically meets for three days up to two weeks. Conceptual material relating to interpersonal relations, individual personality theory, and group dynamics is a part of the program. But the main learning vehicle is the group experience.

Learnings derived from the T-group vary for different individuals, but they are usually described as learning to be more competent in interpersonal relationships, learning more about oneself as a person, learning how others react to one's behavior, and learning about the dynamics of group formation and group norms and group growth. Benne, Bradford, and Ronald Lippitt list the goals of the laboratory method as follows:

1. One hoped-for outcome for the participant is increased awareness of and sensitivity to emotional reactions and expression in himself and in others. . . .

2. Another desired objective is greater ability to perceive and to learn from the consequences of his actions through attention to feelings, his own and others'. Emphasis is placed on the development of sensitivity to cues furnished by the behavior of others and ability to utilize "feedback" in understanding his own behaviors.

3. The staff also attempts to stimulate the clarification and development of personal values and goals consonant with a democratic and scientific approach to problems and personal decision and action. . . .

4. Another objective is the development of concepts and theoretical insights which will serve as tools in linking personal values, goals, and intentions to actions consistent with these inner factors and with the requirements of the situation. . . . One important source of valid concepts is the findings and methodologies of the behavioral sciences. . . .

5. All laboratory programs foster the achievement of behavioral effectiveness in transactions with one's environment. . . . The learning of concepts, the setting of goals, the clarification of values, and even the achievement

of valid insight into self, are sometimes far ahead of the development of the performance skills necessary to expression in actual social transactions. For this reason laboratory programs normally focus on the development of behavioral skills to support better integration of intentions and actions.[1]

The T-group is a powerful learning laboratory where individuals gain insights into the meaning and consequences of their own behavior, the meaning and consequences of others' behaviors, and the dynamics and processes of group behavior. These insights are coupled with growth of skills in diagnosing and taking more effective interpersonal and group action. Thus, the T-group can give individuals the basic skills necessary for more competent action taking in the organization.

Uses of T-groups relative to OD are varied, but they are particularly appropriate to introduce key members of the organization to group and interpersonal process issues and for enhancing basic skills relevant to group and interpersonal dynamics. The most frequently used T-group format is the "stranger" lab composed of people from a variety of organizations. To illustrate, a one-week T-group experience might involve three trainers and 30 to 36 participants, all strangers to each other at the beginning of the lab. Another format involves several clusters of two or three persons from the same organizations, with people who know each other assigned to different T-groups. (The Oregon Leadership Institute, for example, encourages this arrangement.)

Our impression from discussions with Warner Burke of Teachers College, Columbia University, Craig Lundberg of Cornell, and others is that a significant number of long-time, senior OD consultant-scholars see the need for more encouragement of managers and OD practitioners to attend T-group experiences. A quote from Marvin Weisbord, in the context of commenting on research on the positive and negative uses of power and authority in self-managing groups, tends to support this. He states, "This confirms for me that the T-group, which put these issues in stark relief, is an important *learning* structure."[2] Peter Vaill says, "I think that sensitivity training is the most original and powerful contribution that the applied behavioral sciences have made to civilized culture."[3] We agree and believe that T-group learnings provide numerous insights and skills of importance to successful OD efforts and to effective organizational functioning.

BEHAVIOR MODELING

Behavior modeling is a training technique designed to improve interpersonal competence. It is not an OD intervention per se, but we believe it should be added to the OD practitioner's repertoire because it is such an effective tool, and because problems with interpersonal relations are common in organizations. For improving interpersonal skills, behavior modeling is an important training option.

Based on Albert Bandura's Social Learning Theory and utilizing procedures developed by Goldstein and Sorcher, behavior modeling has been shown to be an excellent way to make first-line supervisors more effective (Latham and Saari) and to improve organizational performance (Porras et al.).[4] The basic premise of Social Learning Theory is that for persons to engage successfully in a behavior, they (1) must perceive a link between the behavior and certain outcomes; (2) must desire those outcomes (called positive valence); and (3) must believe they can do it (called self-efficacy).[5] For example, many first-line supervisors find it difficult to discipline employees. To learn this behavior they must see a link between successful disciplining and desired outcomes (like favorable recognition from superiors or less hassle from subordinates) and must come to believe they can do it. This latter belief can be instilled by viewing a model similar to them being successful, by discovering the specific behavioral skills that led to success, and by practicing the skills until they too are proficient. This is the methodology of behavior modeling.

A simple problem-solving model underlies most behavior modeling training. Porras and Singh describe it as follows:

> The problem-solving approach, a rather straightforward one consisting of three phases—problem identification, problem-solving, and implementation, consisted of five behavioral skills:
>
> 1. Behavior description. The ability to describe behavior of self or others in specific concrete terms and to avoid generalizations or inferences drawn from observed behaviors.
>
> 2. Justification. The ability to clearly explain the impact of an observed behavior on the individual, the observer, or the organization.
>
> 3. Active listening. The ability to accurately reflect both content and feelings of another's communication.
>
> 4. Participative problem-solving. The ability to involve another, meaningfully and appropriately, in the process of solving a work-related problem.
>
> 5. Positive reinforcement. The ability to compliment another in a sincere and authentic manner.[6]

The steps involved in behavior modeling are simple. First determine the most pressing problems facing a target group, say, first-line supervisors. These usually consist of such issues as counseling the poor performer, correcting absenteeism, encouraging the average performer, correcting unsafe work behavior, and so forth. Training modules for each of about ten problems are developed, the core of which are videotapes showing a person (model) correctly handling the situation. The specific behaviors exhibited by the model that cause success are highlighted as "learning points"—typically these are the behavioral skills mentioned by Porras and Singh. Weekly training sessions of four hours each are scheduled for each module for groups of approximately ten participants.

At the training sessions the problem situation is announced and briefly discussed. Participants then observe a videotape in which the model (who looks similar to them) successfully solves the problem by enacting specific behavioral skills. The trainees discuss the behavioral skills and then *role play the situation* receiving *feedback from the group and the trainer* on their performances. Role playing continues until each participant successfully masters all the specific skills. Participants then commit to practicing the new skills on the job in the coming week. At the beginning of the next session participants report on how their new skills worked on the job. If necessary, additional practice is held to ensure mastery of the skills. Then a new problem is addressed, the model is observed on videotape, and role playing and feedback occur until all participants learn how to solve the new problem.

Behavior modeling works; it teaches the skills and behaviors needed to deal with interpersonal problems. It should be in the practitioner's kit bag.

LIFE AND CAREER PLANNING

A number of approaches exist to help the individual think through and analyze his or her life and career trajectory. This information is often used in workshop or other educational settings in the context of small-group discussions and some theory input. We will focus primarily on some contributions of Edgar Schein, Herbert Shepard, and Jack Fordyce and Raymond Weil.

Career Anchors

Edgar Schein has provided the concept of *career anchors*, which are useful individually and in voluntary group discussions in career-development workshops. Based on a longitudinal study of MIT Sloan School alumni, Schein hypothesized five basic career anchors. He defines the career anchor as "the pattern of self-perceived talents, motives, and values" which serves "to guide, constrain, stabilize, and integrate the person's career" and which tends to "remain stable throughout the person's career. . . ."[7]

The five career anchors are as follows:

Technical/functional competence: The entire career is organized around a particular set of technical or functional skills which the person is good at and values, leading to a self-concept of remaining in an occupation that would continue to provide challenging work around those particular skills wherever they were. . . .

Managerial competence: The entire career is organized around climbing an organizational ladder to achieve a position of responsibility in general management in which decisions and their consequences could be clearly related by the individual to his own efforts in analyzing problems, dealing with people, and making difficult decisions in uncertain conditions. . . .

Creativity: The entire career is organized around some kind of entrepreneurial effort which would permit the individual to create a new service or product, to invent something, or to build his or her own business. . . .

Security or stability: The entire career is organized around the location of an organizational niche that would guarantee continued employment, a stable future, and the ability to provide comfortably for the family through achieving a measure of financial independence.

Autonomy: The entire career is organized around finding an occupation such as teaching, consulting, writing, running a store, or something equivalent which permits the individual to determine his own hours, lifestyle, and working patterns. . . .[8]

In his book, *Career Dynamics,* Schein provides a "self-analysis form," a questionnaire which a person can use to provide information to help determine his or her own career anchor.[9]

Life Goals Exercise

One series of life- and career-planning exercises is shown in the outline that follows. Herbert A. Shepard is generally acknowledged as the author and originator of these exercises.

I. First phase
   A. Draw a straight horizontal line from left to right to represent your life span. The length should represent the totality of your experience and future expectations.
   B. Indicate where you are now.
   C. Prepare a life inventory of important "happenings" for you, including the following:
      1. Any peak experiences you have had.
      2. Things which you do well.
      3. Things which you do poorly.
      4. Things you would like to stop doing.
      5. Things you would like to learn to do well.
      6. Peak experiences you would like to have.
      7. Values (e.g., power, money, etc.) you want to achieve.
      8. Things you would like to start doing now.

D. Discussions in subgroups.
II. Second phase
    A. Take 20 minutes to write your own obituary.
    B. Form pairs. Take 20 minutes to write a eulogy for your partner.
    C. Discussions in subgroups.[10]

The Collage and the Letters

As another example, the outline of activities suggested by Fordyce and Weil has the following steps.[11] First, individuals working in small groups are asked to make a "collage"—a symbolic representation of their lives constructed out of art materials, old magazines and news-papers, and the like; these are posted on the walls for later discussion. Second, individuals write two letters, the instructions for which are as follows:

> Now imagine that you have died ten years from now. Write a letter from one of your best friends to another good friend, telling about you and your life. What do you *want* him to be able to say about you? Next, imagine you have been killed in an auto accident next week. Now write a similar letter. What would he be likely to say about you?[12]

At this point, the group discusses the collages and letters of each individual, giving the individual the chance to get feedback from the rest of the group about their reactions and also allowing the group to learn more about each other.

This third set of public sharing serves to prepare the members for the next step, consisting of building a "life inventory," similar to the "life goals exercise" discussed earlier. After the preparation of the life inventory, each individual prepares a career inventory by writing answers to questions like the following: What facets of work (my career up to this point) do I like most, least? What do I think are my best skills, abilities, and talents that I bring to the work situation? What kinds of rewards do I seek from my job—money, status, recognition, being a part of a team? What new career areas do I want to pursue? What new skills do I need to develop for the new career areas? These inventories are shared and discussed within the group. As a final step, individuals set down a plan of action steps for achieving the goals they have identified.

Life- and career-planning activities may take one day, an entire week, or, when spread out a few hours at a time, several weeks. These activities involve generating data about oneself, analyzing the data both individually and in groups, and formulating clear goals and action plans for achieving them. These activities tend to be very meaningful for organization members who volunteer for the experience. The activities are particularly helpful for those who feel they are on "dead center," who are contemplating a career change, or who have seldom been introspective about their own lifestyle and career pattern.

SUMMARY

In this chapter we have examined several types of training/educational experiences relevant to OD, such as T-groups, behavior modeling, and life and career planning. All can provide significant developmental experiences for organizational members.

NOTES

1. K. D. Benne, L. P. Bradford, and R. Lippitt, "The Laboratory Method," in L. P. Bradford, J. R. Gibb, and K. D. Benne, eds., *T-Group Theory and Laboratory Method* (New York: John Wiley, 1964), pp. 15–44. This quotation, pp. 16–17.
2. Marvin R. Weisbord, *Productive Workplaces* (San Francisco: Jossey-Bass Publishers, 1987), pp. 334–335.
3. Peter B. Vaill, "Integrating the Diverse Directions of the Behavioral Sciences," in Robert Tannenbaum, Newton Margulies, Fred Massarik and Associates, *Human Systems Development* (San Francisco: Jossey-Bass Publishers, 1985), p. 558.
4. See Albert Bandura, *Social Learning Theory* (Englewood Cliffs, NJ: Prentice-Hall, 1977); A. P. Goldstein and M. Sorcher, *Changing Supervisor Behavior* (New York: Pergamon, 1974); G. P. Latham and L. M. Saari, "Application of Social-Learning Theory to Training Supervisors Through Behavioral Modeling," *Journal of Applied Psychology*, 64 (1979), pp. 239–246; and J. I. Porras, K. Hargis, K. J. Patterson, D. C. Maxfield, N. Roberts, and R. J. Bies, "Modeling-Based Organizational Development: A Longitudinal Assessment," *The Journal of Applied Behavioral Science*, 18, no. 4 (1982), 433–446.
5. Bandura, ibid.
6. J. I. Porras and J. V. Singh, "Alpha, Beta, and Gamma Change in Modeling-Based Organization Development," *Journal of Occupational Behavior*, 7 (1986), pp. 9–23. This quotation is from page 11.
7. Edgar H. Schein, *Career Dynamics: Matching Individual and Organizational Needs* (Reading, MA: Addison-Wesley Publishing Company, 1978), pp. 126–127.
8. Edgar H. Schein, *Occupational Psychology*, 3rd ed. (Englewood Cliffs, NJ: Prentice-Hall, Inc., 1980), pp. 83–84.
9. Schein, *Career Dynamics*, pp. 257–262. See also Edgar H. Schein, "Individuals and Careers," in Jay W. Lorsch, ed., *Handbook of Organizational Behavior* (Englewood Cliffs, NJ: Prentice Hall, 1987), pp. 155–171.
10. These are representative of the life-planning exercises that have been used in NTL Institute programs for the training of OD practitioners. See also Gordon Lippitt, "Developing Life Plans," *Training and Development Journal* (May 1970), pp. 2–7.
11. Based on discussions in J. K. Fordyce and R. Weil, *Managing WITH People* (Reading, MA: Addison-Wesley, 1971), pp. 109–113.
12. Ibid., p. 131.

14

ISSUES IN CONSULTANT-CLIENT RELATIONSHIPS

A number of interrelated issues can arise in consultant-client relationships in OD activities, and they need to be managed appropriately if adverse effects are to be avoided. These issues tend to center on the following important areas:

Entry and contracting
Defining the client system
Trust
The nature of the consultant's expertise
Diagnosis and appropriate interventions
The depth of interventions
On being absorbed by the culture
The consultant as a model
The consultant team as a microcosm
Action research and the OD process
Client dependency and terminating the relationship
Ethical standards in OD
Implications of OD for the client

There are no simple prescriptions for resolving dilemmas or problems in these aspects of OD, but we do have some notions about managing these areas.

ENTRY AND CONTRACTING

An initial discussion that can lead to an OD consulting contract can occur in various ways, but typically events evolve something like this. There is a telephone call: An executive has some concerns about his or her organization and the consultant has been recommended as someone who could help. After a brief description of some of the problems and a discussion of the extent to which the consultant's expertise is a reasonable fit for the situation, an agreement is made to pursue the matter over a meal or through an appointment at the executive's office.

During the face-to-face meeting, the consultant explores with the potential client some of the deeper aspects of the presenting problem. If "communications between managers aren't as thorough and as cordial as they ought to be," the consultant asks for examples to get a better fix on the nature of the problem and its dynamics. Almost inevitably there are several interrelated problems. Or if the potential client says, "I want to move to self-managed teams in Plant B," the rationale and objectives for such a program are explored.

Furthermore, in the first meeting, the consultant and the client probably begin to sort out what group would be the logical starting point for an OD intervention. For example, in a particular manufacturing organization it might be important to focus on the top-management team of eight people; or, in a city government it might appear prudent to include the top 20 key people which would involve the city manager, assistant city managers, and all of the department heads. Considerable thought must be given to exactly who is to be included—and thus who is to be excluded—in the first interventions. The exclusion of key people, in particular, can be a serious mistake.

If the problems appear to lend themselves to OD interventions, the consultant describes how he or she usually proceeds in such circumstances. For example, the consultant might say: "If I were to undertake this assignment, here's how I would probably want to proceed. First, I would like to get the cooperation of the top-management group to set aside, say, two and one-half days for an off-site workshop and to participate in interviews in preparation for that workshop. I would then like to have individual interviews with the entire group, ask each what's going well with the top-management team, what the problems are, and what they would like things to be like. I would then extract the themes from the interviews. These themes would be reported to the group at the workshop and the problem areas would become the agenda for our work together."

All kinds of nuances can arise in this discussion. In addition to problems of who can and who should attend a workshop, there are matters of when and where it could be held, whether or not the management group can be away from their offices for the desired period, whether or not the top person is to be briefed about interview themes prior to the workshop, the extent of confidentiality of the interviews, and so on. An overriding dimension in this preliminary discussion is the extent of mutual confidence and trust that begins to develop between consultant and client.

Among the ground rules Marvin Weisbord has for his consulting relationships are the following:

> Any information I collect and present will be anonymous. I will never attach names to anything people tell me. However, in certain situations (e.g., team building) I don't *want* confidential information, meaning anything which you are unwilling for other team members to know, even anonymously. . . .
>
> All data belongs to the people who supply it. I will never give or show it to anyone without their permission.[1]

If both parties agree, this becomes part of the overall psychological contract between consultant and client.

The more formal compensation aspects of the intitial contract are also important and need to be clarified for the peace of mind of both client and consultant. One course of action is to have an oral agreement for an hourly or daily fee, with no charge for a brief telephone discussion, and usually no charge for a longer first exploration. Thereafter, there might be a bill sent monthly for time spent, or there might be an agreement for a bill to be submitted for the total agreed-upon price for the particular project.

Contracting, in both a psychological and financial sense, occurs over and over in OD consulting. Again, drawing on Weisbord and focusing on the psychological contract:

> Contracting, like the seasons, is repetitive and continually renewable. If I have a long-term contract (e.g., four days a month for a year) I also have a separate contract for each meeting, which I present on a flipsheet and discuss at the outset. If I have a contract with a boss to help him build his team, I need to extend it to the team before we go to work. . . .
>
> In short, I'm never finished contracting. Each client meeting requires that I reexamine the contract. Does it cover everybody I'm working with? Is it clear what we're doing now? And why?[2]

DEFINING THE CLIENT SYSTEM

The question of who the client is quickly becomes an important issue in consultant-client relationships. (We will usually refer to the consultant in the singular, but the points we want to make also tend to apply to consultant teams. Similarly, the initial client may be an individual or a management team.) We think a viable model is one in which, in the initial contact, a single manager is the client, but as trust and confidence develop between the key client and the consultant, both begin to view the manager and his or her subordinate team as the client, and then the manager's total organization as the client. Ideally, this begins to occur in the first interview. Thus the health and vitality of the various organizational subsystems, as well as the effectiveness and growth of all individual members of the client system, clearly become the consultant's concern.

Another viable model is one in which a small, top-management team (for example, the CEO, vice president of human resources, and another vice president) comprises the initial client group. Still another model of who the client might be is a steering committee comprised of representatives from different levels and functional areas. In this case, if the CEO is not a member, the consultant will need to be sensitive to who represents the CEO, or, in short, who represents the power structure. The whole process will be impotent if a steering committee is not free to act in the absence of the CEO.

Warner Burke presents a provocative, perhaps even more useful, view of who the client is: ". . . I have come to think of my client as the relationship and/or interface between individuals and units within and related to the system. . . . This in-between-ness is the main subject of my consulting."[3]

He then goes on to remind us that Chris Argyris, in his book *Intervention Theory and Method*, favored terms like *intervenor* and *interventionist* over terms like *consultant* or *change agent*. Further, Argyris defined intervention as follows: "To intervene is to enter into an ongoing system of relationships, to come between or among persons, groups, or objects for the purpose of helping them."[4]

Thus, to Burke and Argyris, who the client is has more to do with interactions, interrelationships, and interfaces than to specific persons or units. This is a tremendously useful concept.

THE TRUST ISSUE

A good deal of the interaction in early contacts between client and consultant is implicitly related to developing a relationship of mutual trust. For example, the key client may be fearful that things will get out of hand with an outsider intervening in the system—that the organization will be overwhelmed with petty complaints or that people will be encouraged to criticize their superiors. Subordinates may be concerned that they will be manipulated toward their superiors' goals with little attention given to their own. These kinds of concerns mean that the consultant will need to earn trust in these and other areas and that high trust will not be immediate.

Similarly, the consultant's trust of the client may be starting at neutral. The consultant will be trying to understand the client's motives and will want to surface any that are partly hidden. For example, if the client has hopes that a team-building session will punish an inadequately performing subordinate, the consultant and the client will need to reassess the purposes of team building and examine whether that activity is the appropriate context for confronting the matter. On a positive note, the client may see OD as a means of increasing both the client's and the subordinates' effectiveness, plus having hopes that a successful OD effort may bring considerable recognition from superiors. Surfacing such motives and examining their implications for effective behavior will enhance trust between the consultant and the client and will help to assure the eventual success of OD activities.

Trust and resistance problems also center on what we call the "good guy–bad guy syndrome." Internal or external OD consultants, through their enthusiasm for an exciting technology, may signal that they perceive themselves as the carriers of the message, that is, that they are "good guys," and implicitly that others are not, or at least are backward. This obviously creates all sorts of trust and resistance problems. People usually want to work collaboratively with others in the pursuit of common ends—but people tend to resist being pushed around, or put down, under whatever banner. No one likes being put in the "bad guy" role, and we mistrust and resent those who seem to be doing that to us. This can be a trap not only for the consultant but also for the overly enthusiastic line manager.

Confidentiality must be maintained if trust is to be maintained, as implied in Weisbord's ground rules for contracting. Even unintentional errors can be disastrous to the consultant-client relationship. Gavin gives an illustration in which notes made by consultants on the leadership and communication styles of managers were inadvertently duplicated and circulated to participants along with notes on workshop themes and action steps. The consultants had been asked to do the latter; the notes on the managers' styles had been intended to be used by the facilitators in private counseling sessions with individual managers. As Gavin reports it, "By the time these notes had been circulated, any semblance of trust in the consultants had been destroyed."[5] We will have more to say about trust later.

THE NATURE OF THE CONSULTANT'S EXPERTISE

Partly because of the unfamiliarity with organization development methods, clients frequently try to put the consultant in the role of the expert on substantive content, such as on personnel policy or business strategy. *We believe it is possible, and desirable, for the OD consultant to be an expert in the sense of being competent to present a range of options open to the client,* but any extensive reliance on the traditional mode of consulting, that is, giving substantive advice, will tend to negate the OD consultant's effectiveness. The OD consultant needs to resist the temptation of playing the content expert and will need to clarify his or her role with the client when this becomes an issue. However, we think the OD consultant should be prepared to describe in broad outline what the organization might look like if it were to go very far with an OD effort.

Moving into the expert or advocate role—or as Schein says, the "purchase of expertise role" or the "doctor-patient model"[6] frequently stems from an overriding desire to please the client. The consultant wishes to maintain the relationship for a variety of reasons—professional, financial, or self-esteem—and naturally wants to be perceived as competent. The consultant, therefore, gets trapped into preparing reports or giving substantive advice, which if more than minimal, will reduce his or her effectiveness.

There are at least four good reasons why the OD consultant should largely stay out of the expert role. The first is that a major objective of an OD effort is to help the client system to develop its own resources. The expert role creates a kind of dependency that typically does not lead to internal skill development.

The second reason is that the expert role almost inevitably requires the consultant to defend his or her recommendations. With reference to an initial exploratory meeting, Schein mentions the danger of being "seduced into a selling role" and states that under such conditions "we are no longer exploring the problem."[7] In short, finding oneself in the expert role and defending one's advice tends to negate a collaborative, developmental approach to improving organizational processes.

A third reason for largely avoiding the expert role has to do with trust. As shown in Table 14-1, one criterion for resolving whether to provide confidential reports or advice to top management is how such an intervention would affect various client groups in the organization and the consultant's relationship with them. The OD consultant's role is a tenuous one at best. Any impression that the consultant is making recommendations inimical to members of client groups puts the consultant in the role of an adversary. For example, the disclosure that the consultant has made a secret recommendation that the number of divisions and vice presidents be reduced from 16 to 8 is likely to be met with widespread alarm and immediate distrust of the consultant. The question will also immediately arise, What else is the consultant up to that we don't know about? Thus, making recommendations to the top is quite different from confronting the top-management group with the data that three-fourths of the members of the top team believe that the organization has serious problems, partly stemming from too many divisions. In the one instance, the consultant is the expert; in the other instance, the consult-

Table 14-1 Is a Given Intervention Compatible with the OD Facilitator Role? Ideas to Consider

INTERVENTION	TO OR FOR CEO OR UNIT LEADER	TO OR FOR CLIENT TEAM
Confidential report of advice on qualifications of job incumbents	No.	No.
Confidential report or advice on structure of organization or unit	No.	Usually not; at stake is the trust of the various team members. One question for resolving the issue would be, Who would be hurt?
Technical report or advice in some area of the consultant's expertise, e.g., computer applications, or a wage and salary survey, or training in statistical process control	Usually not. One consideration would be, What would this "purchase of expertise" mode of consulting do to the client's expectations about my role?	Usually not. One consideration would be, What would this "purchase of expertise" mode of consulting do to the client's expectations about my role?
Describing various options open to the client and the implications of those options	Yes and no. Depends on whether the intervention is seen as perspective enlarging or prescriptive for the CEO or other key client, whether the client and consultant are open with others about the request, and whether considerable trust has been earned.	Yes, providing that the intervention is seen as perspective enlarging and not as prescriptive.
Advice on OD strategy	Yes, if it is overall organizational strategy and if shared with top team and more broadly in the organization. Yes, if it is strategy for team, providing that it is shared with team.	Yes, if it is strategy for team. Yes, if it is broad organization strategy providing that advice is shared widely in the organization.
Advice on intervention, e.g., when and how a team-building session should be conducted	Yes, providing that advice is shared with team.	Yes.
Data feedback to CEO or unit leader from interviews or questionnaires	Yes, if it is data about the leader. Yes, if it is a team or organizational data and others have concurred in the strategy of the top person having a preliminary briefing. No, if the understanding was that the data would be fed back to the team first.	Yes, if it is data about the team. No, if it is data about other teams, unless data have been aggregated to present overall organization averages, ranges, etc., and there has been wide concurrence on the strategy.
Guidance or moderating of a team-building session	Yes, if it is with concurrence of team.	Yes, if it is with concurrence of team.
Process consultation or coaching on individual behavior or style	Yes, if it is requested.	Yes, if it is requested.

ant is helping the top team to be more expert in surfacing data and diagnosing the state of the system.

A fourth reason has to do with expectations. If the consultant goes very far in the direction of being an expert on substance in contrast to process, the client is likely to expect more and more substantive recommendations, thus negating the OD consultant's central mission which is to help with process.

There are exceptions to these reasons, some of which we describe in Table 14-1. For example, it is usually desirable and necessary to give advice on the design of a workshop or the design of a questionnaire. Such advice is usually quite facilitating, providing that the consultant is open to modifications of his or her suggestions by members of the client system. As Schein states it,

> The process consultant should not withhold his expertise on matters of the learning process itself; but he should be very careful not to confuse being an expert on *how to help an organization to learn* with being an expert on the *actual management problems* which the organization is trying to solve.[8]

In other words, the OD consultant should act in the expert role on the *process* used but not on the *task*.

Another exception consists of providing a range of options open to the client. For example, if there are issues about how a unit or organization should be structured in terms of which functions should be grouped together or who should report to whom, it can be helpful for the OD consultant to present some optional forms and to discuss the possible implications of each. However, such an intervention should ordinarily be presented in a team situation so as not to be misinterpreted, must be timely in terms of its relevance and acceptability, and should be essentially perspective-enlarging in contrast to prescriptive. *We believe that the more extensive the OD consultant's knowledge of management and organization, the more effective the OD consultant can be. But there is a difference between being essentially a facilitator-educator and being essentially an advice-giver.* Even the presenting of options can be overdone. If the consultant's ideas become the focal point for prolonged discussion and debate, the consultant has clearly shifted away from the facilitator role. Obviously, this is not an either/or matter; it is a matter of degree and emphasis.

DIAGNOSIS AND APPROPRIATE INTERVENTIONS

Another pitfall for the consultant is the temptation to apply an intervention technique which he or she particularly likes and which has produced good results in the past, but may not square with a careful diagnosis of the immediate situation. For example, giving subgroups an assignment to describe "what is going well in our weekly department head meetings" and "what is preventing the meetings from being as effective as we'd like" might be more on target and more timely than launching into the role analysis technique with the boss's role as the focus of discussion. It might be too soon; that is, there might be too much defensiveness on the part of the boss and too much apprehension on the part of subordinates for a productive discussion to take place. As Herbert Shepard has said, the consultant should "start where the system is."[9]

We think a consultant should do what he or she can do, but the intervention should be appropriate to the diagnosis. This requires an intensive look at the data, for example, the themes from interviews. The wider the range of interventions with which the consultant is familiar, of course, the more options the consultant can consider. The more the consultant's expertise and experience, the less agonizing is likely to be required in selecting or designing appropriate interventions.

DEPTH OF INTERVENTION

A major aspect of selecting appropriate interventions is the matter of *depth of intervention*. In Roger Harrison's terms, depth of intervention can be assessed using the concepts of accessibility and individuality. By *accessibility* Harrison means the degree to which the data are more or less public versus being hidden or private and the ease with which the intervention skills can be learned. By *individuality* is meant the closeness to the person's perceptions of self and the degree to which the effects of an intervention are in the individual in contrast to the organization.[10] We are assuming that the closer one moves on this continuum to the sense of self, the more the inherent processes have to do with emotions, values, and hidden matters and, consequently, the more potent they are to do either good or harm. It requires a careful diagnosis to determine that these interventions are appropriate and relevant. If they are inappropriate, they may be destructive or, at a minimum, unacceptable to the client or the client system.

To minimize these risks, Harrison suggests two criteria for determining the appropriate depth of intervention:

> First to *intervene at a level no deeper than that required to produce enduring solutions to the problems at hand;* and, second, to *intervene at a level no deeper than that at which the energy and resources of the client can be committed to problem solving and to change.*[11]

To Harrison, these criteria require that the consultant proceed no faster or deeper than the legitimation obtained from the client system culture and that he or she stay at the level of consciously felt needs.[12] We believe these are sound guidelines.

Harrison does recognize, however, and we agree, that the change agent is continuously confronted by the dilemma of whether to "lead and push, or to collaborate and follow."[13] Harrison's orientation is to the latter, but we are inclined to be slightly less conservative. We think that, to be effective, the consultant needs occasionally but prudently to take minor risks in the direction of leading and pushing, but these risks should not be quantum jumps. As the consultant develops expertise in diagnosis and in making interventions, the risks that are run are mainly the risks of a rejected suggestion. We do, however, agree with the essence of what Harrison is suggesting and agree with his criteria.

Another way of viewing depth of intervention might be to think about the performance of units by descending order of systems and subsystems. Data about the behavior and performance of the total organization are perhaps the most accessible and the least personal and perhaps create the least personal anxiety and defensiveness. Performance and behavior data about *me* in an organization are perhaps the least accessible and the most personal. The consultant, then, needs to have the skills to intervene effectively down through these progressively smaller systems—frequently simultaneously—according to whether the issue is

How well are we performing as a total organization?
How well are we doing as a large unit?
How well are we doing as a team?
How well are you and I working together?
How well are you doing?
How well am I doing?

The concept of depth of intervention, viewed either in this way or in terms of a continuum of the formal system, informal system, and self, suggests that the consultant needs an extensive repertoire of conceptual models, intervention techniques, and sensitivities to be able to be helpful at various levels. The consultant's awareness of his or her own capabilities and limitations, of course, is extremely important.

ON BEING ABSORBED BY THE CULTURE

One of the many mistakes one can make in the change-agent role is to let oneself be seduced into joining the culture of the client organization. While one needs to join the culture enough to participate in and enjoy the functional aspects of the prevailing culture—an example would be good-natured bantering when it is clear to everyone that such bantering is in fun and means inclusion and liking—participating in the organization's pathology will neutralize the consultant's effectiveness.

One of us recalls an experience in which the most critical issue to surface in preliminary interviews with members of a professional staff group—we'll call it an engineering organization—was who would be the new manager. The current manager's promotion was to take effect in a few weeks, and he was anxious that the group members provide some input on the selection of his successor as well as that they tidy up a number of unresolved communications and administrative matters. One obvious candidate for the promotion was a senior engineer who was highly respected for his professional competency—clearly an engineer's engineer. However, younger members of the staff privately expressed fears to the consultant that the senior engineer would be too authoritarian if he assumed the manager's role, and they did not want to lose his accessibility as professional mentor. On the other hand they had strong concerns that they would seriously hurt the man's feelings by openly confronting the issue of his style and that he might resign if the matter were confronted. As a result, the consultant team acquiesced in not feeding back to the group the issue most troubling them. In effect, everyone but the senior engineer conspired to protect him, to pretend that he was a strong candidate for promotion, and to postpone the decision. As a result, the group was partly paralyzed for weeks. The immediate effect of the team-building session was one of frustration for all of the participants. In retrospect, the consultant's view is that the client system could probably have worked through the matter and that the senior engineer would have proved to be the strongest and most adaptable there that day, including the consultants.

The dilemma created when a client subgroup describes an issue to the consultant but says, "We won't deal with it and we won't let you surface it in the total group," is a troublesome one. One way out of the dilemma may be to discuss the likely consequences of not dealing with the issue. One consequence may be that the recipient of unclear communication develops a kind of paranoia from the confusing or distorted signals he or she is receiving. Another consequence is that a norm may be implicitly created that says *all* negative interpersonal feedback is off limits, which has the deeper consequence that the entire group is denied data about problem areas that could be constructively worked on. Another consequence might be that the group is denied the capability of sharing much positive feedback for fear that such sharing could spill over into qualifying statements that begin to get into negative areas. Confronting the subgroup with the dilemma and outlining the consequences of inaction, then, may be much more constructive than succumbing to the pressures of the culture:

Reddin provides us with a delightful account of another instance of the consultant's being absorbed by the culture.

> The chairman of a 10,000 employee subsidiary of a British industrial giant invited me to dinner with his board at their country house

> training centre. It was an epic meal and the vintage port flowed. The conversation was witty and I had to lean on my limited classical education to keep up with the literary allusions. In preparation for an MBO conference I had in fact recently re-read Thucydides' *History of the Peloponnesian War* and this gave me some good lines. My first error was accepting the first invitation and then my next was visiting in similar circumstances yet again. It was a superb, if unconscious, seduction job by the client. My relationship to this client became intellectual witty companion. My attempts to change it were met with incredulity.[14]

Although Reddin did not elaborate, the implication is that once the consultant became the "intellectual witty companion," the chairman resisted any efforts to be guided, along with the board members, toward examining the functional and dysfunctional aspects of the culture of the organization. Perhaps the only course of action open to the consultant, once he realized he had been absorbed by the culture, would have been to express openly his feelings and concerns about the situation to the chairman. Such an intervention might or might not have shifted the relationship more toward an OD consultant-key client mode. This is another illustration in which being absorbed by the culture of the client organization immobilized the change agent.

Internal change agents may be even more susceptible to absorption by the prevailing organizational culture than are external change agents. As long as they work with people and units that have considerable "political distance" from their own unit, their objectivity may not be any more vulnerable than that of a consultant from the outside. On the other hand, if their own unit (whether they are specialists who are part of a human resources or an OD unit or have a home base in some line department) is somehow engaged in maneuvering for resources or power in competition with their client, they may inadvertently be drawn into the politics of the situation. Rather than helping to surface the dynamics of dysfunctional rivalry under appropriate circumstances, the change agents may become part of the problem, thus helping to submerge an issue or contributing to tactics incompatible with the helping role and thereby alienating the client or potential clients.

THE CONSULTANT AS A MODEL

Another important issue is whether change agents are willing and able to practice what they preach. In the area of feelings, for example, the consultant may be advocating a more open system in which feelings are considered legitimate and their expression important to effective problem solving and at the same time suppressing his or her own feelings about what is happening in the client system. In particular, this can be a frequent problem for the less-experienced practitioner, and it usually has an impact on this person's feeling of competency: "If only I had said. . . ." The more one learns to be in touch with one's own feelings, the more spontaneous one can be and the greater the options open for interventions. (This is one reason why we recommend extensive T-group experience for OD consultants.) However, the client system is not the appropriate ground for working out any problems the consultant may be currently experiencing. On the other hand, being too aloof emotionally will tend to minimize the possibilities of helping the client.

As another example of modeling behavior, the OD consultant needs to give out clear messages—that is, the consultant's words and apparent feelings needs to be congruent. The consultant also needs to check on meanings, to suggest optional methods of solving problems, to encourage and support, to give feedback in constructive ways and to accept feedback, to help formulate issues, and to provide a spirit of inquiry. We are not suggesting that the OD consultant must be a paragon of virtue; rather, we are suggesting that to maximize one's effectiveness, it is necessary continuously to practice and develop the effective behaviors one wishes to instill in the client system.

THE CONSULTANT TEAM AS A MICROCOSM

The consultant-key client viewed as a team, or consultants working as a team, can profitably be viewed as a microcosm of the organization they are trying to create. In the first place, the consultant team must set an example of an effective unit if the team is to enhance its credibility. Second, practitioners need the effectiveness that comes from continuous growth and renewal processes. And third, the quality of the interrelationships within the consulting team carries over directly into the quality of their diagnosis, their intervention designs, and their interventions. To be more explicit about the last point, unresolved and growing conflict between two consultants can paralyze an intervention. Or simple lack of attention to team maintenance matters can produce morale problems that reduce spontaneity and creativity in planning sessions or in interacting with the client system.

ACTION RESEARCH AND THE OD PROCESS

A related issue is whether the OD process itself will be subject to the ongoing action research being experienced by the client system. The issue of congruency is, of course, important, but the viability of the OD effort and the effectiveness of the consultants may be at stake. Unless there are feedback loops relative to various interventions and stages in the OD process, the change agents and the organization will not learn how to make the future OD interventions more effective.

Feedback loops do not necessarily have to be complicated. Simple questionnaires or interviews can be very helpful. As an illustration, we recall having lunch with the key people who had been involved in a problem-solving workshop, and upon asking several questions about how things were going "back at the shop," we found that problems had emerged centering on who had been invited to attend the workshop and who had not. This feedback, at a minimum, has caused us to pay even more attention to prework and to helping workshop participants plan how to share effectively what has occurred with those not attending.

THE DEPENDENCY ISSUE AND TERMINATING THE RELATIONSHIP

If the consultant is in the business of enhancing the client system's abilities in problem solving and renewal, then the consultant is in the business of assisting the client to internalize skills and insights rather than to create a prolonged dependency relationship. This tends not to be much of an issue, however, if the consultant and the client work out the expert versus facilitator issue described earlier and if the consultant subscribes to the notion that OD should be a shared technology. The facilitator role, we believe, creates less dependency and more client growth than the traditional consulting modes, and the notion of a shared technology leads to rapid learning on the part of the client.

The latter notion is congruent with Argyris's admonition that if the consultant intervention is to be helpful in an ongoing sense, it is imperative for the client to have "free, informed choice."[15] And to have this free choice, it is necessary for the client to have a cognitive map of the overall process.[16] Thus the consultant will have to be quite open about such matters as the objectives of the various interventions that are made and about the sequence of planned events. The OD consultant should continuously be part educator as he or she intervenes in the system.

An issue of personal importance to the consultant is the dilemma of working to increase the resourcefulness of the client versus wanting to remain involved, to feel needed, and to feel competent. We think there is a satisfactory solution to this dilemma. A good case can be made, we believe, for a gradual reduction in external consultant use as an OD effort reaches maturity. In a large organization, one or more key consultants may be retained in an ongoing relationship, but with less frequent use. If the consultants are constantly developing their skills, they can continue to make innovative contributions. Furthermore, they can serve as a link with outside resources such as universities and research programs, and more important, they can serve to help keep the OD effort at the highest possible professional and ethical level. Their skills and insights should serve as a standard against which to compare the activities of internal change agents. Some of the most innovative and successful OD efforts on the world scene, in our judgment, have maintained some planned level of external consultant use.

Another dimension of the issue arises, however, when the consultant senses that his or her assistance is no longer needed or could be greatly reduced. For the client's good, to avoid wasting the consultant's own professional resources, and to be congruent, the consultant should confront the issue.

A particularly troublesome dilemma occurs when the use of the consultant, in the judgment of the consultant, is declining more rapidly than progress on the OD effort seems to warrant. It would be easy to say that here, too, the consultant should raise the matter with the client, and undoubtedly this should occur even if there are risks in appearing self-serving, but we wish more were known about the dynamics of OD efforts' losing their momentum. Such additional knowledge would help consultants and clients to assess more objectively the extent of need for consultant assistance, how to improve the skills of the consultant and the client in managing the OD effort, and how to rejuvenate the OD effort if rejuvenation is warranted.

Tannenbaum believes that many OD programs taper off because there has not been enough attention to helping people and units let go of matters that need to be laid to rest, to die. He believes that in a real sense, facilitators should be able to assist in a mourning process, but to be of help, facilitators must be able to confront their own tendencies to want to hang on and their own vulnerability.

> My hunch is that after we get beyond those attitudes and behaviors most individuals and groups are relatively willing to alter, we then begin challenging the more central fixities that define individuals and organizational units at their cores. Holding on at this level becomes crucial. Yet we keep working on processes that focus on *change*, and do *not* do very much about facilitating mourning and the dying process—helping units let go.[17]

We also suspect that OD efforts frequently flounder because of internal power struggles that have not been sensed early enough by the consultant or understood well enough for anyone to intervene constructively. For example, some relatively powerful person or group may be fearful of losing status or influence and may be mobilizing support for the status quo through such tactics as distorting information or discrediting whoever is seen as the threat. The threat may be the practitioner or the OD effort or the threat may be wholly unrelated to the OD process. But if people in the organization get caught up in the political power maneuvering, the OD effort may be immobilized. While not much is known about these occurrences as they relate to OD efforts, it would seem that these situations, if sensed, need to be surfaced and confronted head on. Such shadowy struggles are usually dysfunctional whether or not there is an OD effort under way, and the remedy may need to be a prompt description of reality by the chief executive officer. While a long-term OD effort should replace most such covert maneuvering with an open, working through of issues, these situations can and do occur while an OD effort is under way.

Sometimes the organization may simply be temporarily overloaded by externally imposed crises occupying the attention of key people. Under such conditions, the best strategy may be one of reducing or suspending the more formalized OD interventions and letting people carry on with their enhanced skills and then returning to the more formalized aspects at a later date. If more were known about the dynamics of these and the other circumstances we have described, the resolution of the problem of what to do when the OD effort seems to be running out of steam might take directions other than reducing or terminating the involvement of the change agent.

ETHICAL STANDARDS IN OD

Much of this chapter and, indeed, much of what has preceded in other chapters, can be viewed in terms of ethical issues in OD practice, that is, in terms of enhancement versus violation of basic values and/or in terms of help versus harm to persons. Louis White and Kevin Wooten see five categories of ethical dilemmas in organization development practice stemming from the actions of either the consultant or client or both. The types of ethical dilemmas they see are: (1) misrepresentation and collusion; (2) misuse of data; (3) manipulation and coercion; (4) value and goal conflicts; and (5) technical ineptness.[18]

We will draw on and modify their categories to suggest what we see as some of the more serious areas for potential ethics violations in OD consulting. Some of these areas apply not only to OD consulting, but to management consulting in general. The illustrations are ours and are only hypothetical.

Misrepresentation of the Consultant's Skills. An obvious area for unethical behavior would be to distort or misrepresent one's background, training, competencies, or experience in vita sheets, advertising, or conversation. A subtle form of misrepresentation would be to let the client assume one has certain skills when one does not.

Professional/Technical Ineptness.   The potential for unethical behavior stemming from lack of expertise is pervasive in OD. To give one example using Harrison's concept of depth of intervention, it would seem to be unethical to ask people in a team-building session to provide mutual feedback about leadership style when neither preliminary interviews nor the client group has indicated a readiness or a willingness to do so. Another example would be as follows: A preliminary diagnosis suggests the appropriateness of a feedback intervention, but the consultant has no experience from which to draw in order to design a constructive feedback exercise. The consultant goes ahead anyway. It would be unethical for the consultant to plow ahead without some coaching by a more experienced colleague. (This may be a situation that calls for the "shadow consultant," the consultant to a single individual, in this case another consultant.[19]) Thus, we have hypothesized two violations of ethical standards: (1) using an intervention that has a low probability of being helpful (and may be harmful in this circumstance), and (2) using an intervention that exceeds one's expertise.

Misuse of Data.   Again, the possibilities for unethical behavior in the form of data misuse on the part of either the client or the consultant are abundant. This is why confidentiality is so important in OD efforts. (See Weisbord's ground rules for contracting earlier in the chapter.) Data can be used to punish or otherwise harm persons or groups. An obvious example would be a consultant's disclosure to the boss of who provided information about the boss's dysfunctional behavior. Another example would be showing climate survey results from Department A to the head of Department B if this had not been authorized.

Serious distortions of the data would also be unethical. Let's imagine a scenario in which the consultant interviews the top 20 members of management and finds several department heads are angry about the behaviors of fellow department head Z and the practices in Z's department. Further, Z is hostile and uncooperative with the consultant in the data-gathering interview. The consultant is now angry but is not conscious of the extent of the anger. When the consultant feeds back the themes from the interviews to the group, his or her anger takes the form of overstating and overemphasizing the dysfunctional aspects of Z's unit. (In an ironic twist, the group might turn on the consultant and defend Z. As a colleague of ours says, "Never attack the 'worst' member of the group—the group will reject you."[20])

Collusion.   An example of collusion would be the consultant agreeing with the key client to schedule a team-building workshop when it is known that department head Z will be on vacation. (This is hardly the way to deal with the problems created by Z, is likely to create reduced trust in the consultant and the key client, Z's boss, and is likely to intensify Z's dysfunctional behavior.) Another example illustrating the power that a consultant with expertise in group dynamics can wield for good or harm is the consultant colluding with other members of the group to set up a feedback situation in which Z's deficiencies will be all too apparent, particularly to Z's boss. Instead of creating a situation in which everyone, including Z, has a chance of improving performance, this collusion is aimed at Z's undoing. (We've picked on Z enough; if he or she is this much of a problem, Z's performance should be confronted head on by the boss, outside of the team-building setting, and preferably well in advance. If OD interventions are perceived as methods for "getting" anyone, the OD process is doomed to failure.)

      Coercion.   It is unethical to force organizational members into settings where they are, in effect, required to disclose information about themselves or their units which they prefer to keep private. The creation of a T-group with unwilling participants would be an example.

      A troublesome dilemma occurs in the case of a manager and most of his or her subordinates who want to go off-site for a problem-solving workshop but one or two members are strongly resisting. If friendly persuasion and addressing the concerns of the individual(s)—not painful arm-twisting—do not solve the matter, perhaps a reasonable option is for the manager to indicate that nonparticipation is acceptable, and that there will be no recriminations, but it should be understood that the group will go ahead and try to reach consensus on action plans for unit improvement without their input.

      Promising Unrealistic Outcomes.   Obviously, this is unethical and counterproductive. The temptation to make promises in order to gain a client contract can be great, but the consequences can be reduced credibility of the consultant and the OD field, and the reduced credibility of the key client within his or her organization.

      Thus, the values underlying ethical OD practice are honesty; openness; voluntarism; integrity; confidentiality; the development of people; and the development of consultant expertise, high standards, and self-awareness.

IMPLICATIONS OF OD FOR THE CLIENT

An OD effort has some fundamental implications for the chief executive officer and top managers of an organization, and we believe that these implications need to be shared and understood at the outset. We reach the following conclusions when we ask ourselves, What is top management buying into in participating in and supporting an OD effort?

Basically, *OD interventions* as we have described them, *are a conscious effort on the part of top management*

1. *To enlarge the data base for making management decisions.* In particular, the expertise, perceptions and sentiments of team members throughout the organization are more extensively considered than heretofore.

2. *To expand the influence processes.* The OD process tends to further a process of mutual influence; managers and subordinates alike tend to be influential in ways they have not experienced previously.

3. *To capitalize on the strengths of the informal system and to make the formal and the informal system more congruent.* A great deal of information that has previously been suppressed within individuals or within the informal system (e.g., appreciations, frustrations, hurts, opinions about how to do things more effectively, fears) begins to be surfaced and dealt with. Energies spent suppressing matters can now be rechanneled into cooperative effort.

4. *To become more responsive.* Management must now respond to data that have been submerged and must begin to move in the direction of personal, team, and organizational effectiveness suggested by the data.

5. *To legitimatize conflict as an area of collaborative management.* Rather than using win-lose, smoothing, or withdrawal modes of conflict resolution, the mode gradually becomes one of confronting the underlying basis for the conflict and working the problem through to a successful resolution.[21]

6. *To examine its own leadership style and ways of managing.* We do not think an OD effort can be viable long if the top-management team (the CEO plus subordinate team or the top team of an essentially autonomous unit) does not actively participate in the effort. The top team inevitably is a powerful determinant of organizational culture. OD is not a televised game being played for viewing by top management; members of top management are the key players.

7. *To legitimatize and encourage the collaborative management of team, interteam, and organization cultures.* This is largely the essence of OD.

We think that these items largely describe the underlying implications for top management and that the OD consultant needs to be clear about them from the very beginning and to help the top-management group be clear about them as the process unfolds.[22]

SUMMARY

Numerous issues regarding the client-consultant relationship need to be addressed and managed in a successful OD effort. These issues have to do with establishing the initial contract, identifying who is the client, establishing trust, clarifying the role of the consultant, determining the appropriate depth of intervention, examining the consequences of being absorbed by the organization's culture, viewing the consultant and consulting teams as models, applying action research to OD, terminating the relationship, and ethical standards. These issues have important implications for practitioners, top management, and the organization.

NOTES

1. Marvin Weisbord, "The Organization Development Contract," *Organization Development Practitioner*, 5, no. 2 (1973), 1–4.
2. Ibid.
3. W. Warner Burke, *Organization Development*, 2nd ed. (Reading, MA: Addison-Wesley Publishing Company, 1994), p. 86.
4. Chris Argyris, *Intervention Theory and Method: A Behavioral Science View* (Reading, MA: Addison-Wesley Publishing Company, 1970), p. 15.
5. James F. Gavin, "Survey Feedback: The Feedback of Science and Practice," *Group & Organization Studies*, 9 (March 1984), p. 46. For more on trust, see Dale E. Zand, *Information, Organization, and Power* (New York: McGraw-Hill, 1981), pp. 37–55.
6. Edgar H. Schein, *Process Consultation, Vol. I: Its Role in Organization Development*, 2nd ed. (Reading, MA: Addison-Wesley Publishing Company, 1988), pp. 5–11.
7. Edgar H. Schein, *Process Consultation: Its Role in Organization Development* (Reading, MA: Addison-Wesley, 1969), p. 82.
8. Ibid., p. 120.
9. Herbert A. Shepard, "Rules of Thumb for Change Agents," *OD Practitioner*, 17 (December 1985), p. 2. Shepard calls this the "Empathy Rule."
10. This discussion is based on Roger Harrison's essay, "Choosing the Depth of Organizational Intervention," *Journal of Applied Behavioral Science*, 6 (April–June 1970), pp. 181–202.
11. Ibid., p. 201. [Harrison's emphasis.]
12. Ibid., pp. 198–199.
13. Ibid., p. 202.
14. W. J. Reddin, "My Errors in OD," paper presented to the Organization Development Division at the Academy of Management 36th Annual Meeting, Kansas City, Missouri, August 13, 1976, p. 3.
15. Chris Argyris, *Intervention Theory and Method* (Reading, MA: Addison-Wesley, 1970), p. 17.
16. See Chris Argyris, *Management and Organizational Development: The Path from XA to YB* (New York: McGraw-Hill, 1971), pp. 58, 108, 137, for a discussion of the importance of "maps."
17. Robert Tannenbaum, "Some Matters of Life and Death," *OD Practitioner*, 8 (February 1976), p. 5. See also Robert Tannenbaum and Robert W. Hanna, "Holding On, Letting Go, and Moving On," in Robert Tannenbaum, Newton Margulies, Fred Massarik and Associates, *Human Systems Development* (San Francisco: Jossey-Bass Publishers, 1985), pp. 95–121.
18. Louis P. White and Kevin C. Wooten, "Ethical Dilemmas in Various Stages of Organizational Development," *Academy of Management Review*, 8 (October 1983), pp. 690–697.
19. Mikki Ritvo and Ronald Lippitt, "Shadow Consulting: An Emerging Role," in Walter Sikes, Allan Drexler, and Jack Gant, *The Emerging Practice of Organization Development* (Alexandria, VA: NTL Institute, 1989), pp. 219–224.
20. Conversation with Charles Hosford (Summer 1993).
21. Blake and Mouton refer to "confrontation," "forcing," "smoothing," "compromise," and "withdrawal" as the different modes of conflict resolution. See Robert Blake and Jane Mouton, *The Managerial Grid* (Houston: Gulf, 1964), pp. 30, 67, 93, 94, 122, 123, 163.

22. For more on the implications of OD for behavior changes in the client system, see Jerry I. Porras and Susan J. Hoffer, "Common Behavior Changes in Successful Organization Development Efforts," *The Journal of Applied Behavioral Science*, 22, no. 4 (1986), 477–494. For more on consultant-client relationships see Diane McKinney Kellogg, "Contrasting Successful and Unsuccessful OD Consultation Relationships," *Group & Organization Studies*, 9 (June 1984), pp. 151–176.

15

SYSTEM RAMIFICATIONS

Systems theory and a great deal of accumulated experience by OD practitioners tell us that an extensive ripple effect occurs as OD interventions begin to occur in an organization. This may be an understatement because some of the ramifications in the total organizational system can be far-reaching. The ramifications we will mention can be major challenges; all must be attended to if an OD effort is to succeed for the long term.

HUMAN RESOURCES LEADERSHIP AND INVOLVEMENT

Because OD efforts and human resources policies and practices inevitably are interdependent, we will first comment on the role of the human resources (HR) or personnel department. Most, if not all, of the areas of system ramifications we will touch on in this chapter are areas of concern for the senior HR executive and for HR departments. OD efforts have implications for staffing, rewards, training and development, labor relations, and other broad HR processes.

It should be noted that OD directors and practitioners typically report to the senior HR executive. Furthermore, in some organizations, many HR professionals are expected to have or develop expertise as OD practitioners. This has been the case, for example, at British Airways[1] and at TRW Space & Electronics Group (see Chapter 3).

RESISTANCE TO CHANGE

The reasons for resistance to change are many and vary with the circumstances, but whenever there is a perceived possibility of loss of position or status, of inequitable treatment, or the loss of the use of present competencies, there is the strong likelihood that resistance to change will emerge. An obvious implication is that management should reassure people as clearly as possible about those areas in which there is no need for concern and in those areas in which there will likely be benefits, along with establishing realistic expectations about the pains and challenges that will occur. There is no substitute, of course, for experiential discovery by organizational members that they can successfully accommodate to change processes and that things are getting better.

We believe that most OD efforts result in enhanced morale, improved communications, more mutual influence, and improved organizational effectiveness. However, if decisions have already been made that major restructuring will occur and that there will be extensive sacrifice and pain associated with the change effort, it should be made clear that the sacrifice and pain will be shared across the organization and at all levels. Conversely, if there are to be extensive positive outcomes, policies for sharing in the gains should be clearly articulated. (We will say more about rewards later.) In general, OD practitioners have a major role in recommending participative/influence processes that will minimize unneeded resistance, and in urging top management to pay attention to matters of fairness and full communications.

LEADERSHIP AND LEADERSHIP STYLE

To be optimally successful, OD efforts require a kind of leadership that John Kotter distinguishes from management. Both are necessary. Management, to Kotter, involves "organizing and staffing," "planning and budgeting," and "controlling and problem solving." In contrast, leadership involves "establishing direction," including developing a vision and strategies for getting there; "aligning people," including the communication of the desired direction and securing cooperation; and "motivating and inspiring," which Kotter asserts often requires "appealing to very basic, but often untapped, human needs, values, and emotions." Both effective leadership and management are essential, according to Kotter, if organizations are to be successful for the long term. The leadership behaviors that Kotter describes would seem to be particularly crucial to maintaining the momentum of a continuous improvement effort such as OD or a combination of OD with TQM.[2]

This raises the matter of management succession and continuity. Most long-time OD practitioners can cite illustrations of OD efforts that appeared to be highly successful under one CEO, division head, or plant manager, only to wither away under the neglect or misdirection of a successor. For continuity of effort and to avoid the loss of what has been invested in an OD effort, boards of directors and top-management teams must understand and support the OD process and be prepared to select replacement executives who can carry the process forward. This holds true, of course, for other major improvement efforts, including TQM and QWL programs.

It is clear that the dominant leadership style in organizations undergoing a large-scale OD effort must feature or move toward extensive use of employee involvement at all levels. Furthermore, leadership must be of a team and team-process variety. That is, leadership must be conceptualized as a highly interactive, shared process, with members of all teams developing skills in this shared process.

Real, substantive delegation is critical for individual empowerment, and is particularly important as organizations move toward self-managed teams. Skills in consensus decision making are needed, and individuals and teams need to see that they are influencing the course of events.

TRAINING AND THE DEVELOPMENT OF CONSULTATION SKILLS

Training is extremely important for organizational members to develop competencies for the new assignments precipitated by major organizational change. This means that the training department and managers throughout the organization must anticipate and be on top of emerging training needs. And this probably means an increased budgetary allocation.

As implied earlier, the OD process itself suggests the need for some additional kinds of training. For example, managers, supervisors, and teams at all levels will need training in group problem solving, in effective group participation, and in the management of team meetings.

Ideally, selected human resources staff members and line managers are trained to do some OD facilitation work in collaboration with external and internal OD consultants. In larger organizations in particular, cost factors plus the attractiveness that the development of consultation skills holds for some managers and professionals will suggest the desirability of selecting and training additional consultants. The training of internal consultants might include T-group experience, university courses in OD and related subjects, NTL training in consultation skills, an extensive apprenticeship with an experienced professional, and supervised consultation.

In addition, the widespread development of facilitator and consultation skills by organizational members across specialties and hierarchical lines can be a valuable adjunct to the OD process and to the organization's functioning. The more that organizational members in general are helpful to peers, subordinates, and superiors and to customers and suppliers in listening, in examining options, and in running meetings, the more successful both the OD effort and the organization are likely to be.

REWARDS

As Edward Lawler says, effective organizational change efforts must pay attention to the reward system:

> When the pay system is not changed in a timely fashion, it can prevent the institutionalization of the other changes in several ways. It may not reward the behavior which is needed to make the changed systems work. Worse yet, it may even reward behavior that is the antithesis of what is needed to make the changes work.[3]

Both theory and experience suggest that organization improvement processes that depend upon the cooperation, teamwork, creativity, and intensified effort of organizational members must pay attention to the allocation of rewards if the process is to be sustained and if dysfunctional consequences are to be minimized. More specifically, if management, including owners of an enterprise, exhort and empower employees toward higher performance and then reward only themselves, organizational members will respond with cynicism, lowered trust, and decreased loyalty. We are referring, of course, to both financial rewards and recognition.

On the positive side, when OD efforts are supported by ongoing, frequent recognition of individual and team efforts, and by financial rewards consistent with improved organizational goal attainment, the OD effort and organization improvement are likely to be sustained. Various kinds of plantwide productivity gainsharing plans, such as Improshare[4] and the Scanlon Plan,[5] and profit sharing are consistent with the collaborative, team approach inherent in OD.[6] Gainsharing plans such as the Scanlon Plan, in particular, are congruent with OD because the plans themselves feature extensive employee involvement. On the other hand, individual incentive plans, unless accompanied by broader team and organizational rewards, may interfere with the OD process by reinforcing lack of cooperation or dysfunctional competition among individuals and groups.

At a minimum, it would be important to manage the movement of wage and salary scales consistent with the success of the organization, and to inform employees of this. The possibility of temporarily reducing wage and salary levels as one option in a financial crisis produced by external events would also seem more likely in an organization that has been involved in an OD effort for some time.

If an organization moves toward self-managed teams, management and employees will probably want to move in the direction of skills-based or knowledge-based pay for team members. Under this concept, team members are paid in accordance with the number of skills they have mastered. At some of Volvo's plants in Sweden, a bonus scheme is utilized to reward individual skill development as well as the extent of responsibility assumed by teams in such areas as quality control, maintenance. and personnel administration.[7]

FEEDBACK

Since more extensive data gathering, including making legitimate the expression of feelings and attitudes, is an integral part of an OD effort, people will have to learn how to give and manage feedback in such a way that it is helpful and not destructive. This means training in giving and receiving feedback, and it means paying attention to the gamut of feedback systems—all the way from interpersonal kinds of exchanges to subunit production or cost data and to the results of organizationwide attitude surveys.

For example, at the interpersonal level, feedback tends to be the most constructive when such conditions as the following are met:

> It is solicited.
>
> It is fairly immediate after the event.
>
> It is specific.
>
> It is reported in terms of the impact on the person who is providing the feedback.
>
> It is nonjudgmental in that it does not label the recipient "stupid," "worthless," and the like.
>
> It is given when the basic motive is to improve the relationship (in contrast to a desire to punish, belittle, etc.).
>
> It is given in private or in a supportive group atmosphere.
>
> It is given in the spirit of mutual give-and-take.
>
> It is given in the context of sharing appreciations as well as concerns.

At the level of subunit production or cost data, feedback is most helpful if it is reported

> Directly to the manager or team who can take remedial action, in contrast to top management or a staff department

Frequently enough so the manager or team can plan remedial action

Specifically, so that the manager or team can easily identify the problem area (this will usually mean that the using manager or team will need to be involved in designing the reporting system)

In terms of attitude and climate surveys, feedback tends to be the most constructive

When it is sought by the leader and the unit involved

When unit data and aggregate organizational data are reported to the respective manager, but not data specific to other units (direct comparisons with peers tend to be highly threatening at first)

When managers plus their subordinates discuss the dynamics underlying the data with the help of a third party and make action plans

David Nadler emphasizes the importance of *how* feedback is carried out:

> . . . . the way in which the data collection and feedback activities are conducted, the *process* of feedback, is of major importance. Where there has been an effective and active process for using the data, such as frequent meetings, intensive training, or specific structures for using feedback, then positive changes tend to occur. Similarly, the greater the participation by members of the organization in the entire collection-feedback process the more change comes from the data.[8]

STAFFING AND CAREER DEVELOPMENT

Many aspects of the staffing and career development processes, broadly conceived, can be affected by an evolving OD effort, and vice versa. There are implications for selection, orientation and assimilation, transfer and promotion, training and development, and separation.

Selection

In the selection process, for example, there is likely to be an increasing degree of participation by peers in the nomination, evaluation, and selection of candidates. This would be congruent with a broadened level of participation in the organization and with more emphasis on the ability of employees to work interdependently and in team configurations. Training of present employees in effective interviewing of candidates would be important in this evolution. Team member involvement in the selection of both team leaders and new team members is a feature of a number of contemporary work restructuring projects.[9]

Orientation and Assimilation

Substantial attention needs to be paid to the process of introducing new people into the system (sometimes called the "joining up process") if the staffing process is to be congruent with assumptions and values underlying OD efforts. Group methods in orientation and assimilation seem to be particularly useful. Such sessions, under the guidance of a facilitator or a supervisor having skills in group processes, can do much to alleviate dysfunctional anxiety on the part of present members and to help them make plans for quickly incorporating the new person into the team. A group session with the new member—for example, involving introductions, descriptions of what each person is currently working on, concerns of the new person—can also be useful.

Career Development and Progression

If a major thrust of the OD process is to shift organization culture toward more honesty, more openness, more mutual support, and improved personal development, the career and growth aspirations of all organization members must be an area of concern. These are matters of considerable interest to employees at all levels and will tend to become more openly talked about. This will probably mean paying more attention to advancement and transfer opportunites and will require more of a commitment of resources to training and management development. There might also be some commitment of resources to "life-planning" or "career-planning" workshops; many organizations have experimented with such learning laboratories. Technical courses might not be directly related to the OD process but could be important in a systematic program of career development. These experiences, however, will tend to be more highly specific to individual and system needs than is the usual case; that is, more attention will be given to the diagnosis of training and development needs, with less reliance on packaged programs.

Another shift will probably occur. The climate could well shift from suppressing dialogue about the merits of leaving the organization toward openly facing the issue of internal versus external career opportunities. A likely outcome, as indicated earlier, will be more effort to increase opportunities for internal mobility. Ideally, new departments, divisions, or subsidiaries could be spawned through paying attention to the entrepreneurial and career aspirations of organizational members. The removal of arbitrary ceilings on responsibility will probably release a good deal of energy for constructive contributions within the system.

To use terminology sometimes found in labor contracts, "job posting" (i.e., notifying present employees of job vacancies) and "bidding" (i.e., permitting people to apply for these vacancies) are possible outcomes of an OD effort. This would be congruent with the open developmental thrust of OD. Another outcome might be more attention to the development of "career ladders," which are diagrams of routes of promotion and transfer within and across various job specialities. These devices are used to advise employees about career opportunities and to assist management in planning the training required for progression from one job to another.[10] As a result of such devices as job posting, bidding and career ladders, more time and effort is likely to be spent in processing internal requests for transfer and promotion and in developing training opportunities. The net effect on employees, however, is likely to be one of higher morale, better placement, better diagnosis of training needs, and improved skills.

The developmental philosophy inherent in the OD process creates a major dilemma relative to the use of psychological tests for selection purposes, especially in the promotion system. On the one hand, some tests, such as intelligence tests, can have sufficient validity in specific circumstances to warrant their use as one additional source of relevant data. On the other hand, tests can leave the candidate feeling subject to mysterious or arbitrary criteria or locked into his or her own personal characteristics which are not subject to modification.

The "assessment center" concept may provide some leads toward solving the testing dilemma. Briefly, companies using assessment centers typically give the candidate, usually a nonsupervisory person interested in promotion, an extensive battery of tests and involve the candidate in an interview and group discussions and other group situations. Trained line managers, who have been observing, then make rankings of the relative performance of the candidates. In general, it has been found that assessment centers increase the proportion of successful to unsuccessful supervisors and higher managers and are useful in identifying management potential among minority and women employees.[11]

The ingredients that can shift the assessment center process from being strictly a matter of selection to one that is developmental are the dialogue that communicates the results to the candidate and the developmental opportunities that are subsequently provided. For example, if the assessment center highlights some deficiencies in group discussion, a center staff member can provide some feedback (ideally, requested by the candidate), and the organization may provide opportunities for developing additional skill. Then, too, the whole process permitting candidates to apply for the assessment center experience and selecting some candidates for promotion tends to create an element of openness and mobility in the system which might not otherwise be there. This is not to say that the use of an assessment center is always constructive. The lack of an effective feedback and discussion process can produce suspicion and hostility. Further, there will be great resentment if the process is perceived as forever cutting someone off from promotional opportunities. Some experimentation has occurred—apparently successful—in dispensing with the selection aspects of assessment centers and focusing solely on using the process as a developmental tool. In this case, no report is given to higher management.[12]

Group input in the selection of formal leaders would also be congruent with the thrust of an OD effort. Although such an approach, like a number of others we have mentioned, can and does occur outside of OD efforts, it would be inconsistent with the OD process not to consider the feelings and perceptions of group members in these important decisions. There may be instances when it would be appropriate to delegate to a group the selection of a new leader.

Layoffs and Other Crises

In an era of downsizings and employee layoffs, it would seem incongruous with OD approaches not to take every possible avenue for minimizing the trauma on individuals and for assisting them in coping with what is frequently both an individual and a family crisis. Indeed, OD has played a major role in tempering the impact of layoffs for many years. For example, during an aerospace industry downturn of more than 20 years ago, one high-tech firm, having had an OD effort for a number of years, used facilitators and group methods in assisting those being laid off to enable them to overcome their disappointment and anxiety and to make plans for a job search. Although there was no legal requirement do do so at that time, those being laid off were notified weeks ahead of the layoff date, but overall the performance of those affected did not deteriorate. The company also made great efforts to place those employees with other organizations. (Most laid-off employees subsequently returned when business picked up again.) OD techniques were also used to help groups face up to the realities of the situation, to decrease distortions in perception, and to make plans to cope with the cutback.[13] Ideally, the OD process assists top management in examining a wide range of options to consider in a budgetary crisis.

OD interventions can also assist organization members, and thus the organization, in other crises as well. Hurricane, flood, or earthquake disasters, the death of a top executive, a serious fire or explosion, or a potential plant closure are all examples of crises in which OD facilitators can assist in helping individuals deal with shock and in avoiding the kind of organizational paralysis that can otherwise occur.

ORGANIZATIONAL JUSTICE

A shift in team and organizational culture toward more openness and toward more mutual concern should, in large part, facilitate the airing of felt injustices. From our experience, this does occur—and in a more natural and less threatening way. Grievances tend to be raised when they occur and are worked out quickly. (This phenomenon plus others that tend to stem from OD efforts, from our observations, seemingly improves mental health. We see OD as a way of improving mental health in an organization; many of its practices and underlying concepts are congruent with theory and clinical experience in counseling psychology, family therapy, some aspects of psychiatry, and community mental health programs.)

We are not recommending doing away with formalized appeal procedures, however, or what we call *organizational due process*. We have defined the latter as consisting of "established procedures for handling complaints and grievances, protection against punitive action for using such established procedures, and careful, systematic, and thorough review of the substance of complaints and grievance."[14] We believe a formalized appeal system may be needed to protect individuals from gross anomalies in an organization's culture. For example, what if a norm begins to develop that says it is taboo ever to question the usefulness of any part of the OD effort? Or that subordinates should always be "open" no matter what the consequences might be, but that superiors may have hidden agendas? Or that talking about seniority is off limits even though employees feel deeply that length of service is a significant investment to be taken into account in job retention? Such an environment needs a formal appeal system. It is clearly consistent for a system that values openness to retain mechanisms that tend to protect openness.

LABOR RELATIONS

In unionized settings, joint efforts on the part of management and union leadership to move toward a problem-solving, mutual-reward kind of bargaining relationship would be congruent with the general philosophy and thrust of OD. Richard Walton and Robert McKersie's description of "integrative bargaining" and the Federal Mediation and Conciliation Service's "relations by objectives (RBO)" encompass this approach.[15] Productivity bargaining and agreements under quality of work life (QWL) programs are two forms of integrative bargaining.

National Labor Relations Board decisions have created some confusion as to the status of employee involvement programs and the use of problem-solving teams, but it is unlikely that OD efforts will be affected, providing certain guidelines are followed. Some background: In the 1992 *Electromation* case, the NLRB ruled that "action committees" established by the Electromation Company were illegal under the Wagner Act. It was held that the company dominated the teams and discussed areas reserved for collective bargaining such as work rules and wages.[16]

In 1993, in a case involving Du Pont's Chambers Works plant and the plant's Chemical Workers Association, the NLRB ordered Du Pont to disband several committees that had been formed to deal with recreation and safety issues.[17]

A likely consequence of these decisions will be a major effort in Congress to amend the National Labor Relations Act toward supporting employee involvement efforts. Furthermore, Labor Secretary Robert Reich has repeatedly stated that he would seek legislation in support of worker-management teams if the actions of the NLRB served to stifle them.[18] In addition, President Clinton's nominee to the board stated late in 1993 that he firmly backed labor-management teams.[19]

Meanwhile, some guidelines written by a former NLRB member may suffice. These were written after an administrative law judge had ruled in the Electromation case and before the full NLRB had ruled:

Participation in such groups as action teams, improvement teams, quality circles, and the like, should be strictly voluntary.

Committees should focus on such areas as improving productivity and product/customer service quality or supplier relations.

Meetings should not be held that appear to be negotiations between management and labor over the terms and conditions of employment.

Committees should not be formed when the company is facing a union organizing campaign.[20]

MONETARY COSTS AND SKILL DEMANDS

The use of external and internal third parties in the role of practitioners, the use of off-site workshops, and additional training programs are obviously going to cost money. If an organization development effort is successful, however, there must be commitment to the notion that the development of the total organization, including the development of human resources and the social system, is a continuous process worthy of an ongoing investment.

In addition, the costs in terms of effort and skill demands should not be ignored. In some ways, the environment we have been describing is more difficult and demanding than that found in more traditional organizational cultures. Team members, for example, no longer find it comfortable to let the formal leader carry the total responsibility for decision making, or find it convenient to blame others when things go wrong. The newer culture is likely to include a commitment to examine all of the forces bearing on a problem or challenge, including one's own impact. Thus, while the newer culture may be, and usually is, more exciting and rewarding, it is likely to be more difficult and challenging as well.

CONCLUDING COMMENTS

A sustained, successful organization development effort will have extensive ramifications throughout the system. Attention will need to be paid to the role of the human resources department and staff, to managing resistance to change, to leadership style throughout the organization, to training including training in consultation skills, to the reward system, to the kinds and quality of feedback systems, to many aspects of staffing and career development, to managing crises, to systems of organizational justice, and to labor relations and labor law. Monetary and time costs will be significant, and demands for improved performance will be ongoing. But the culture and climate and, hopefully, more tangible rewards as well are likely to be much more exciting and satisfying to participants.

NOTES

1. Leonard D. Goodstein and W. Warner Burke, "Creating Successful Organizational Change," *Organizational Dynamics*, 19 (Spring 1991), p. 13.
2. John P. Kotter, *A Force for Change: How Leadership Differs From Management* (New York: The Free Press, 1990), pp. 4–5.
3. Edward E. Lawler III, *Pay and Organization Development* (Reading, MA: Addison-Wesley Publishing Company, 1981), pp. 205–206.
4. Brian E. Graham-Moore and Timothy L. Ross, *Productivity Gainsharing: How Employee Incentive Programs Can Improve Business Performance* (Englewood Cliffs, NJ: Prentice-Hall, 1983), pp. 23–24.
5. See Michael Schuster, "The Scanlon Plan: A Longitudinal Analysis," *Journal of Applied Behavioral Science*, 20, no. 1 (1984), 23–38.
6. See Elizabeth M. Doherty, Walter R. Nord, and Jerry L. Adams, "Gainsharing and Organization Development: A Productive Synergy," *Journal of Applied Psychology*, 25, no. 3 (1989), 209–229; and Edward E. Lawler III, *Pay and Organization Development* (Reading, MA: Addison-Wesley Publishing Company, 1981), Chapter 9.
7. Berth Jonsson and Alden G. Lank, "Volvo: A Report on the Workshop on Production Technology and Quality of Work Life," *Human Resource Management*, 24 (Winter 1985), pp. 461–463.
8. David A. Nadler, *Feedback and Organization Development: Using Data-Based Methods* (Reading, MA: Addison-Wesley Publishing Company, 1977), p. 170.
9. Stephen H. Fuller, "How Quality-of-Worklife Projects Work for General Motors," *Monthly Labor Review*, 103 (July 1980), pp. 37–39; and Irving Bluestone, "How Quality of Worklife Projects Work for the United Auto Workers," *Monthly Labor Review*, 103 (July 1980), pp. 39–41.
10. See Robert W. Goddard, "Lateral Moves Enhance Careers," *HR Magazine*, 35 (December 1990), pp. 69–74.
11. James R. Huck and Douglas W. Bray, "Management Assessment Center Evaluations and Subsequent Performance of White and Black Females," *Personnel Psychology*, 29 (Spring 1976), p. 13; and Robert B. Finkle, "Managerial Assessment Centers," in Marvin D. Dunnette, ed., *Handbook of Industrial and Organizational Psychology* (Chicago: Rand McNally, 1976), pp. 861–888.
12. Louis Olivas, "Using Assessment Centers for Individual and Organization Development," *Personnel*, 57 (May–June 1980), pp. 63–67.
13. For a discussion of the use of OD facilitators in layoff situations, see Sheldon Davis and

Herbert Shepard, "Organization Development in Good Times and Bad," *Journal of Contemporary Business,* 1 (Summer 1972), pp. 65–73. See also Leonard Greenhalgh, "Maintaining Organizational Effectiveness During Organizational Retrenchment," *Journal of Applied Behavioral Science,* 18, no. 2 (1982), 155–170; and Susan A. Mohrman and Allan M. Mohrman, Jr., "Employee Involvement in Declining Organizations," *Human Resource Management,* 22 (Winter 1983), pp. 445–466.

14. Wendell L. French, *Human Resources Management,* 3rd ed. (Boston: Houghton Mifflin Company, 1994), p. 509.

15. Richard E. Walton and Robert B. McKersie, *A Behavioral Theory of Labor Negotiations* (New York: McGraw-Hill, 1965), pp. 4–6; and David A. Gray, Anthony V. Sinogropi, and Paula Ann Hughes, "From Conflict to Cooperation: A Joint Union-Management Goal-Setting and Problem-Solving Program," *Proceedings of the Thirty-Fourth Annual Meeting,* Industrial Relations Research Association Series (December 1981), pp. 26–32.

16. *The New York Times,* December 18, 1992, p. A 15; and *The Wall Street Journal,* December 18, 1992, p. A 12.

17. *The Wall Street Journal,* June 7, 1993, pp. A 2, A 14; and *The Wall Street Journal,* June 9, 1993, p. A 14.

18. Ibid.

19. *The Wall Street Journal,* October 4, 1993, p. A5B.

20. Larry Reynolds, "Old NLRB Rule Could Jeapordize Quality Programs," *HR Focus,* 68 (December 1991), pp. 1–2.

16

POWER, POLITICS, AND ORGANIZATION DEVELOPMENT

Power and politics are indisputable facts of social and organizational life that must be understood if one wishes to be effective in organizations. In this chapter the concepts of power and politics are examined in relation to organization development. The OD practitioner needs both awareness (knowledge) and behavioral competence (skill) in the arenas of organizational power and politics. As Warner Burke observes: "Organization development signifies change, and *for change to occur in an organization, power must be exercised.*"[1]

Organization development has been criticized in the past for not taking account of power in organizations.[2] That criticism was essentially correct for many years although it is less valid today. Recent years have seen a sizable outpouring of theory and research on power and politics,[3] and OD practitioners have attempted to derive implications and applications for the field of OD.[4] But we are still in the early stages of knowing how power and organization development should be related. One goal of this chapter is to advance our understanding of the role of power in OD and the role of OD in a power setting.[5]

POWER DEFINED AND EXPLORED

Let us examine several representative definitions of power.

"Power is the intentional influence over the beliefs, emotions, and behaviors of people. Potential power is the capacity to do so, but kinetic power is the act of doing so. . . . One person exerts power over another to the degree that he is able to exact compliance as desired."[6]

"A has power over B to the extent that he can get B to do something that B would otherwise not do."[7]

Power is "the ability of those who possess power to bring about the outcomes they desire."[8]

"Power is defined in this book simply as the capacity to effect (or affect) organizational outcomes. The French word 'pouvoir' stands for both the noun 'power' and the verb 'to be able.' To have power is to be able to get desired things done, to effect outcomes—actions and the decisions that precede them."[9]

Analysis of these definitions shows some common elements: effectance—getting one's way; the necessity of social interaction between two or more parties; the act or ability of influencing others; and outcomes favoring one party over the other. We therefore define interpersonal power as *the ability to get one's way in a social situation.*

The phenomenon of power is ubiquitous. Without influence (power) there would be no cooperation and no society. Without leadership (power) in medical, political, technological, financial, spiritual, and organizational activities, humankind would not have the standard of living it does today. Without leadership (power) directed toward warfare, confiscation, and repression, humankind would not have much of the misery it does today. Power-in-action may take many forms, both positive and negative. Leading, influencing, selling, persuading—these are examples of positive uses of power. Crushing, forcing, hurting, coercing—these are examples of negative uses of power. Power per se is probably neither good nor bad although Lord Acton observed that "power tends to corrupt; absolute power corrupts absolutely." A moment's reflection, however, suggests that many problems with power stem from some of the goals of persons with power and some of the means they use, not the possession of power as such.

Two Faces of Power

This discussion is based on the important distinction articulated by David McClelland who identified "two faces of power"—positive and negative.[10] McClelland observed that while power has a negative connotation for most people, it is through the use of power that things get done in the world. According to him, the negative face of power is characterized by a primitive, unsocialized need to have dominance over submissive others. The positive face of power is characterized by a socialized need to initiate, influence, and lead. This positive face of power is intended to enable others to reach their goals *as well as* let the person exercising power reach his or her goals. The negative face of power seeks domination and control of others; the positive face of power seeks to empower self and others. It seems to us that this is a good insight into the concept of power.

In most organizations the positive face of power is much more prevalent than the negative face of power. Patchen found in organizational decision making that coercive tactics were "noticeable chiefly by their absence" and problem solving and consensus seeking were much more prevalent.[11] The positive and negative faces of power appear to be what Roberts calls "collective power" and "competitive power" respectively. Her research in four organizations showed both kinds of power being exercised, with collective power being the predominant mode.[12]

THEORIES ABOUT THE SOURCES OF SOCIAL POWER

Power exists in virtually all social situations. It is especially salient in coordinated activities such as those found in organizations. In fact, for organizations to function, the authority or power dimension must be clarified and agreed upon in a more or less formal way.

How do some people come to possess power? How is power generated, bestowed, or acquired? In this section we will examine four different views about who gets power and how: Emerson's "power-dependence theory," French and Raven's "bases of social power," a "strategic-contingency model of power" by Salancik and Pfeffer, and Mintzberg's observations concerning the genesis of power in organizations.

Power-dependence theory states that power is inherent in any social relationship in which one person is dependent upon another. The sociologist Richard Emerson states that "the dependence of Actor A upon Actor B is (1) directly proportional to A's motivational investment in the goals mediated by B, and (2) inversely proportional to the availability of those goals to A outside of the A-B relation."[13] In other words, if a person has something we want badly and we cannot get it any place else, that person has power over us. The components of this theory are *a social relation* between two parties, *resources* (commodities, goals, rewards), *that are controlled* by one party, *and desired* by the other party.

Power-dependence theory is related to a broader framework of social interaction called *social exchange theory* which posits that what goes on between persons in interaction is an exchange of social commodities: love, hate, respect, power, influence, information, praise, blame, attraction, rejection, and so forth. We enter into and continue in exchange relationships when what we receive from others is equivalent to or in excess of what we must give to others. When the net balance for us is positive, we will continue the exchange relationship; when the net balance for us is negative, we will terminate or alter the relationship. Social interaction represents an exchange of social goods and services. Viewed in this light, giving someone power over us is the commodity we exchange when we are dependent on that particular person for something we want.

Closely related to these ideas is the classic statement by John R. P. French and Bertram Raven on "the bases of social power."[14] These authors suggested five sources, or bases, of social power as follows:

1. *Reward power*—power based on the ability of the powerholder to reward another, that is, to give something valued by the other.

2. *Coercive power*—power based on the ability of the powerholder to punish another, that is, to give something negatively valued by the other.

3. *Legitimate power*—power based on the fact that everyone believes that the powerholder has a legitimate right to exert influence and that the power-receiver has a legitimate obligation to accept the influence.

4. *Referent power*—power based on the power-receiver having an identification with (attraction to, or feeling of oneness with) the powerholder.

5. *Expert power*—power based on the powerholder possessing expert knowledge or expertise that is needed by the other. *Informational power* is a form of expert power where the powerholder possesses important facts or information needed by the other.

It can be seen that power belongs to the person who has control over or mediates desired commodities. Exchange theory and power-dependence theory are quite compatible with the bases of social power proposed by French and Raven.

The strategic-contingency model of power asserts that power in organizations accrues to organizational subunits (individuals, units, or departments) that are most important for coping with and solving the most critical problems of the organization.[15] These critical problems are generally "uncertainties" posed by the environment. This theory, like the ones discussed previously, supports the notion that those who have something highly valued by others—in this case, the special expertise most needed for the organization's survival—have power.

Once power is gained, Salancik and Pfeffer suggest how it is then used: "Power is used by subunits, indeed, used by all who have it, to enhance their own survival through control of scarce critical resources, through the placement of allies in key positions, and through the definition of organizational problems and policies."[16] These authors view organizational power as a good thing, for power in the hands of the critical problem solvers helps the organization cope with the various realities it faces.

Henry Mintzberg has developed a theory of organizational power drawn from the organization theory literature and his own creative synthesis abilities.[17] This theory, "is built on the premise that organizational behavior is a power game in which various players, called *influencers*, seek to control the organization's decisions and actions."[18] The three basic conditions for the exercise of power are (1) some source or basis of power, coupled with (2) the expenditure of energy in a (3) politically skillful way when necessary. There are five possible bases of power according to Mintzberg: first, control of a resource; second, control of a technical skill; and, third, control of a body of knowledge. All of these must be critical to the organization. The fourth basis of power is legal prerogatives—being given exclusive rights or privileges to impose choices. And a fifth basis of power is access to those who have power based on the first four bases.[19] In addition to a base of power the influencer must have the "will" to use it and the "skill" to use it.

There are many potential influencers in and around an organization such as the board of directors, the managers, the top executives, the employees, the unions, suppliers, customers, regulators, and so forth. The important aspects of the theory for our purposes here are that the sources of power derive from possession of a commodity valued and desired by others, that power-in-action requires will and skill, and that the organization is the setting or context for the exercise of power.

In summary, these four views of the sources of power are remarkably similar—power stems from possession of or mediation of desired resources. The resources may vary from ability to reward and punish, being in control of critical skills, knowledge, or information, being able to solve critical problems or exigencies, or anything that creates dependence of one actor or set of actors on another.

ORGANIZATIONAL POLITICS DEFINED AND EXPLORED

Let us now examine the concept of politics in organizations. Several representative definitions of politics are the following:

> Harold Lasswell defined politics simply as: the study of who gets what, when, and how.[20]
>
> Organizational politics involve those activities taken within organizations to acquire, develop and use power and other resources to obtain one's preferred outcomes in a situation in which there is uncertainty or dissensus about choices.[21]
>
> Organizational politics involve intentional acts of influence to enhance or protect the self-interest of individuals or groups.[22]
>
> Organizational politics is the management of influence to obtain ends not sanctioned by the organization or to obtain ends through non-sanctioned influence means.[23]

> We view *politics* as a subset of power, treating it . . . as *informal power,* illegitimate in nature. Likewise we also treat authority as a subset of power, but in this sense, *formal* power, the power vested in office, the capacity to get things done by virtue of the position held.[24]

Analysis of these definitions suggests that the concepts of power and politics are very similar. Both relate to getting one's way—effectance. Both relate to pursuit of self-interest and overcoming the resistance of others. For our purposes, organizational politics is power-in-action in organizations; it is engaging in activities to get one's way in an organizational setting.

One important feature in these definitions should be examined further. The first three definitions treat politics as a neutral set of activities: the last two definitions view politics as illegitimate or unsanctioned activities. We are inclined to consider politics as neither good nor bad per se and believe that *politics, like power, has two faces.*

Organizational politics can have a positive and a negative face. The negative face is characterized by *extreme* pursuit of self-interest; unsocialized needs to dominate others; a tendency to view most situations in win-lose terms—what I win, you must lose—rather than win-win terms; and predominant use of the tactics of fighting such as secrecy, surprise, holding hidden agendas, withholding information, deceiving. The positive face of politics is characterized by a *balanced* pursuit of self-interest and interest in the welfare of others; viewing situations in win-win terms as much as possible; engaging in open problem solving and then moving to action and influencing; a relative absence of the tactics of fighting; and a socialized need to lead, initiate, and influence others.

Pursuit of unsanctioned organizational goals or the use of unsanctioned organizational means might be examples of the negative face of politics. Illegitimate uses of authority, information, or resources might also be examples of the negative face of politics. But a positive face of politics is shown whenever "hard decisions" must be made, are made, and most organizational members feel good about what was decided and how it was decided. In this regard, Jeffrey Pfeffer argues that politics are *necessary* if organizations are to function effectively and efficiently. This concept of the two faces of politics handles the two sides of the phenomenon that we all see in our common experience. Some organizations reflect a mostly positive face of politics and other organizations reflect a mostly negative face of politics.

Organizational politics tend to be associated with the decision making, resource allocation, and conflict resolution processes in organizations. These are the key decision points; these are the areas where actors win and lose; these are where the "goods" are distributed and the goals are decided. In fact, one gains a quick understanding of the overall "political climate" of an organization by studying its methods of resource allocation, conflict resolution, and choosing among alternative means and goals.

Organizations often display modal patterns in the way their decision making, resource allocation, and conflict resolution processes operate. Patterns identified in the organization theory literature include the bureaucratic, rational, and political models.[25] In a bureaucratic mode, decisions are made on the basis of rules, procedures, traditions, and historical precedents. In a rational mode, decisions are made on the basis of rational problem solving: goals are identified and agreed upon; situations are analyzed objectively in relation to goals; alternative action plans are generated and evaluated; and certain alternatives are chosen and implemented. In a political mode decisions are made on the basis of perceived self-interest by coalitions jockeying for dominance, influence, or resource control. Most organizations exhibit all these modes in the conduct of their business. Some organizations exhibit one predominant mode. It is important to realize that a predominantly political orientation is only one of several possibilities.

FRAMEWORKS FOR ANALYZING POWER AND POLITICS

Two conceptual models will provide a picture of the component parts of situations involving organizational power and politics. The first is taken from Pfeffer's book, *Power in Organizations*. The second is derived from the

Figure 16-1 A Model of the Conditions Producing the Use of Power and Politics in Organizational Decision Making

Source: Jeffery Pfeffer, *Power in Organizations* (Marshfield, MA: Pitman Publishing, Inc., 1981), p. 69. Used by permission.

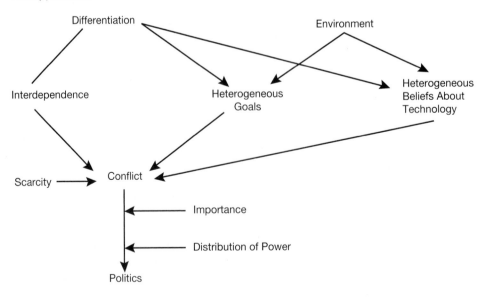

literature on game theory. A useful model of the antecedents and conditions for power is shown in Figure 16-1.

In this diagram, political activities are seen to be the outcome of a number of conditions. When these conditions exist, power and politics result. According to Pfeffer, the environment of the organization imposes demands and constraints that will be accommodated to in the form of "means" and "ends"—that is, what the organization does and how the organization gets its job done. Ends are the goals pursued by the organization. Often heterogeneous or incompatible goals are sought by different members of the organization. Likewise, different or incompatible ways to accomplish the goals may be sought by different members of the organization. Preferences for different means to the goals is what is meant by the term "heterogeneous beliefs about technology." Differentiation refers to the fact that division of labor in organizations causes the creation of many subgroups, which in turn produces different world views, different subgroup goals, and "tunnel vision" of subgroup members.

The three primary conditions giving rise to conflict are scarcity (there are not enough desired resources to allow all parties to have all they want), interdependence (the parties are related to each other in such a way that the distribution of resources affects everyone in some way), and incompatible goals and/or means to goals. When these conditions exist, conflict is a probable result. And when conflict exists, power and political behavior are a likely result if two additional features are present. As Pfeffer states:

> Together the conditions of scarcity, interdependence, and heterogeneous goals and beliefs about technology produce conflict. Whether that conflict eventuates in politics, the use of power in organizational settings depends upon two other conditions. The first condition is the importance of the decision issue or the resource. In the case of our example, the resource was very important—necessary for survival. In situations in which the decision may be perceived as less critical, power and politics may not be employed to resolve the decision because the issue is too trivial to merit the investment of political resources and effort. The second condition is the distribution of power. Political activity, bargaining, and coalition formation occur primarily when power is dispersed. When power is highly centralized, the centralized authority makes decisions using its own rules and values. The political contests that sometimes occur in organizations take place only because there is some dispersion of power and authority in the social system.[26]

It is possible to increase or decrease the amount of political activity in organizations by manipulating the conditions of power shown in the model. For example, if resource scarcity were replaced by resource abundance, conflict would be reduced and politics would be reduced. If organizational actors were made less interdependent (for instance, through the use of profit centers and other structural arrangements), conflict and power would be reduced. Likewise, increased consensus about goals and means and more centralized power would reduce conflict and, hence, reduce political activity. The model suggests the factors that can be changed if less political activity is desired.

A second model is taken from the game theory literature. The conditions giving rise to cooperation and competition and to the use of power have been studied extensively by economists and behavioral scientists in an attempt to understand wars, strikes, and arguments as well as collective cooperation and altruism.[27] Several concepts have been identified that provide a framework for understanding power and politics. Some of these concepts are conflict, the payoff matrix, the nature of interdependent relationships, and integrative and distributive bargaining.

In game theory, conflict is viewed as a critical condition leading to power and political behavior. There can be *conflict of interest* in which different parties prefer different goals. There can be *conflict or competition for scarce resources* where different parties want the same resources but both parties cannot possess them.

Thus conflict arises because of the real or perceived nature of the *payoff matrix*, the way in which the goods and services sought by two or more parties are to be distributed. Some payoff matrices promote cooperation and minimal power use; other payoff matrices promote competition, conflict, and maximal power use. Understanding the nature of the payoff matrix is the key to understanding conflict, which in turn is the key to understanding most political behavior. An outside observer who wants to analyze a particular situation for its potential for organizational power and politics thus would want to know answers to the following questions:

> What is the commodity or issue that is under decision?
> How important is the commodity or issue?
> What are the possible payoffs that are available?
> What are the likely payoffs?
> Can all parties get their desires, or must one party win and one party lose?

These questions lead to another concept involved in power and politics—the nature of the relationship between the parties. Two parties in interdependent interaction can have one of three possible relationships based on the nature of the payoff matrix: *purely competitive* (a win-lose or zero-sum situation in which what one party wins the other party loses and the total payoffs always sum to zero), *purely cooperative* (a situation in which both parties have completely compatible interests but must engage in communication or coordination in order to receive their payoffs), and *mixed or mixed motive* (a situation in which both a push to compete and a push to cooperate are inherent in the payoffs).[28] Power and politics will predominate in the purely competitive, win-lose situation. Power should be absent from the purely cooperative, win-win situation; here the appropriate behaviors are communication, coordination, and cooperation. Power may or may not prevail in the mixed-motive situation; here each party needs the other to transact an exchange, yet each party is seeking to maximize its own gains. In the mixed-motive situation too much competition may cause both parties to lose; yet "too little" competition by one party may allow the other to gain a significant advantage.

Mixed-motive relationships are prominent in many social and organizational settings. In fact, many everyday situations are mixed-motive in nature. Examples are found in labor-management relations, the relations between two peers both of whom are working for a promotion that only one can obtain, and relations among members of a sports team all of whom want the team to win but each of whom wants to be the "star." Mixed-motive situations thus contain a push and a potential for both cooperation and competition, and which of these occurs depends on the behaviors of the two parties. But the important thing to realize is that to cooperate effectively and to compete effectively require quite different kinds of behaviors. Cooperation usually requires problem solving; competition usually requires power-oriented action.

This brings us to the concepts of integrative and distributive bargaining proposed by Walton and McKersie.[29] They studied labor-management bargaining situations and concluded that for best results for both parties the bargaining process should be conceptualized as a two-phase process: (1) a problem-solving, collaborative phase in which the total joint payoffs are maximized, and (2) a bargaining phase in which the payoffs are divided between the parties. In the first phase, called integrative bargaining, the parties try to identify the areas of mutual concern, search for alternative courses of action, and identify the largest joint sum of values possible. This is a cooperative, problem-solving phase. In the second phase, called distributive bargaining, the parties are in a conflict situation. Here each party tries to establish norms and procedures that will help to maximize its gains while trying to keep the gains of the other party to a minimum. Integrative bargaining calls for problem solving, honesty, open communication, and mutual exploration of all ideas. Distributive bargaining calls for secrecy, suspicion, deception, and not accepting the ideas of the other party. By separating bargaining into these two phases, better solutions can be achieved for both parties involved in the bargaining.

These concepts from game theory are applicable to understanding political processes in organizations. The sources of conflict are competition for scarce resources and conflict over incompatible goals and means to goals. A key factor is the nature of the payoffs to all parties—what they stand to win or lose. Positive outcomes for both parties can often be enhanced through a two-phase bargaining process in which integrative bargaining precedes distributive bargaining.

THE ROLE OF POWER AND POLITICS
IN THE PRACTICE OF OD

A number of ideas concerning power and politics have been discussed. In this section we shall attempt to integrate those concepts with organization development and offer advice to the OD practitioner for dealing with the political realities found in organizations.

The Nature of Organization Development
in Relation to Power and Politics

Organization development was founded on the belief that using behavioral science methods to increase collaborative problem solving would increase both organizational effectiveness and individual well-being. This belief gave rise to the field and is the guiding premise behind its technology. To increase collaborative problem solving is to increase the positive face of power and decrease the negative face of power. Thus from its inception OD addressed issues of power and politics in that it proposed that collaboration, cooperation, and joint problem solving are better ways to get things done in organizations than relying solely on bargaining and politics. The nature of OD in relation to power and politics can be inferred from several sources—its strategy of change, its interventions, its values, and the role of the OD practitioner.

Organization development is a particular approach that rests heavily on behavioral science interventions, systematic joint problem solving, and collaborative management of the organization's culture and processes. As such, OD programs implement normative-reeducative and empirical-rational strategies of change, not a power-coercive strategy, to use the framework of Robert Chin and Kenneth Benne.[30] The normative-reeducative strategy of change focuses on norms, culture, processes, and prevailing attitudes and belief systems. Change occurs by changing the matrix of norms and beliefs, usually through education and reeducation. The empirical-rational strategy of change seeks out facts and information in an attempt to find "better" ways to do things. Change using this strategy occurs by discovering these better ways and then adopting them. The power-coercive strategy of change focuses on gaining and using power and on developing enforcement methods. Change occurs when people with more power force their preferences on people with less power and exact compliance. OD practitioners advocate normative-reeducative and empirical-rational strategies of change and OD interventions are designed to implement these strategies. In addition, OD values legitimate these two strategies. Organization development thus has a distinct bias toward a normative-reeducative strategy of change and against a power strategy.

Examining OD interventions demonstrates that problem solving and collaboration are emphasized while power and politics are deemphasized. Virtually all OD interventions promote problem solving, not politics, as a preferred way to get things accomplished. OD interventions are designed to increase problem solving, collaboration, cooperation, fact-finding, and effective pursuit of goals while decreasing reliance on the negative faces of power and politics. We know of no OD interventions designed to increase coercion or unilateral power. For example, OD interventions typically generate valid, public data about the organization's culture, processes, strengths, and weaknesses. Valid, public data are indispensable for problem solving but anathema for organizational politics. OD interventions do not deny or attempt to abolish the reality of power in organizations, rather, they enhance the positive face of power thereby making the negative face of power less prevalent and/or necessary. Given the nature of OD interventions, it can be seen that not only is organization development not a power/political intervention strategy, it is instead a rational problem solving approach that is incompatible with extreme power-oriented situations.

OD values are consistent with the positive face of power but not with the negative face of power. Values such as trust, openness, collaboration, individual dignity, and promoting individual and organizational competence are part of the foundation of organization development. These values are congruent with rational problem solving and incongruent with extremely political modes of operating. "Power equalization" has long been described as one of the values of organization development, and that is correct. But emphasis on power equalization stems from two beliefs: first, problem solving is usually superior to power coercion as a way to find solutions to problematic situations; second, power equalization, being one aspect of the positive face of power, *increases* the amount of power available to organization members, and by so doing adds power to the organization.

The role of the OD practitioner is that of a facilitator, catalyst, problem solver, and educator. The practitioner is not a political activist or power broker. According to Chris Argyris, the "interventionist" has three primary tasks: (1) to generate valid useful information, (2) to promote free, informed choice, and (3) to help promote the client's internal commitment to the choices made.[31] The practitioner works to strengthen skills and knowledge in the organization. But organization members are free to accept or reject the practitioner, his or her program, and his or her values, methods, and expertise. The OD consultant, like all consultants, is providing a service that the organization is free to "buy" or "not buy." The facilitator or educator role is incompatible with a political activist role because cooperation requires one set of behaviors and competition requires a different set of behaviors, as was seen earlier in this chapter. Cobb and Margulies caution that OD practitioners can get into trouble if they move from a facilitator role to a political role.[32] We believe that is true.

In summary, organization development represents an approach and method to enable organization members to *go beyond* the negative face of power and politics. This is a major strength of OD, and it is derived from the strategy of change employed, the technology of OD, and the values and roles of OD practitioners.

Operating in a Political Environment

General observations will be presented followed by some rules of thumb for the OD practitioner.

First, organization development practitioners operate from a potentially strong power base that may be used to advantage. Using the framework of French and Raven, the OD consultant possesses power from the following bases: legitimate power (the OD program and consultant are authorized by the organization's decision makers); expert power (the consultant possesses expert knowledge); informational power (the consultant has a wealth of information about the strengths and weaknesses of the organization); and possibly referent power (others may identify with and be attracted to the consultant). These sources of influence produce a substantial power base that will enhance the likelihood of success. Michael Beer has identified additional means by which an OD group can gain and wield power in organizations:[33]

1. *Competence.* Demonstrated competence is the most important source of power, acceptability, and ability to gain organizational support.

2. *Political access and sensitivity.* Cultivate and nurture multiple relationships with key power figures in the organization. This will ensure timely information and multiple sources of support.

3. *Sponsorship.* "Organization development groups will gain power to the extent that they have sponsorship, preferably multiple sponsorship, in powerful places."[34] This maxim has been recognized for years under the heading of "get top-level support for the program."

4. *Stature and credibility.* This item is related to point 1. Beer notes that power accrues to those who have been successful and effective. Successful efforts lead to credibility and stature. Early successes in the OD program help promote this reputation. Usefulness to key managers of the organization helps promote this reputation.

5. *Resource management.* Power accrues to those who control re-

sources—in this case, the resources of OD expertise and ability to help organizational subunits solve their pressing problems.

6. *Group support.* If the OD group is strong internally, it will be strong externally. If the OD group is cohesive and free of internal dissention, it will gain more power.

Paying attention to these sources of power will enhance the likelihood of success of OD programs.

Second, the models presented in this discussion suggest ways the OD practitioner can help organization members reduce the negative face of power. Creation of slack resources, replacing tight coupling of interdependent relationships with more loose coupling, gaining agreement on goals and means for goal accomplishment, centralizing some decision making, and addressing mixed-motive situations in two phases as indicated by integrative and distributive bargaining—all these processes have been demonstrated to reduce the negative consequences of intense power and politics. The OD practitioner can help implement these conditions in the organization thereby modifying the political climate.

Third, the concept of the positive and negative faces of power and politics suggests where the practitioner is likely to be more effective and less effective. We believe that OD programs are likely to be unsuccessful in organizations with high negative faces of politics and power: the OD program will likely be used as a pawn in the power struggles of the organization, and the OD practitioner can become a logical scapegoat when conditions require a "sacrifice." On the other hand, OD programs are likely to be highly effective in organizations with positive faces of power and politics: the practitioner helps organization members to build multiple power bases in the organization (more power to everyone); he or she promotes collaborative problem solving, which leads to better decisions being made; and the practitioner teaches organization members how to manage mixed-motive situations to ensure the best outcomes.

Fourth, the OD practitioner is encouraged to learn as much as possible about bargaining, negotiations, the nature of power and politics, the strategy and tactics of influence, and the characteristics and behaviors of powerholders. This knowledge is not for the purpose of becoming a political activist but rather to understand better those organizational dynamics where power is an important factor. This knowledge will make the OD practitioner a more competent actor in the organization and a more effective consultant in helping organization members solve their problems and take advantage of opportunities.

Fifth, the OD practitioner realizes that power stems from possessing a commodity valued by others. If the OD program indeed improves individual and organizational functioning; if the OD practitioner has indeed learned his or her craft well, then a valuable commodity has been produced that will be welcomed by the organization powerholders.

What advice is available for OD practitioners who want to operate more effectively in a political environment? Several rules of thumb are implied by the fact that power accrues to persons who control valued resources or commodities.

Rule One.   Become a desired commodity, both as a person and as a professional. Becoming a desired commodity as a person means being interpersonally competent and trustworthy. OD practitioners are likely to have high interpersonal competence by virtue of their training, experience, and expertise. Skills such as listening, communicating, problem solving, coaching, counseling, and showing appreciation for the strengths of others are components of interpersonal competence. Good OD practitioners will have learned and practiced these skills. Being trustworthy means being reliable, dependable, and honest in dealing with others. These skills and traits are highly valued in social exchanges; persons who possess them become desired commodities and accrue power.
Making oneself a desired commodity as a professional is related to the issues of competence, stature, and credibility mentioned above by Beer. Good OD consultants are experts on people, organizations, and change. Such expertise is a rare and valuable commodity. Becoming an expert on people, organizations, and change requires hard work, learning the craft of organization development, continuously learning from experience, gaining exposure to a wide variety of problematic situations, and lots of practice. OD practitioners who get results, help solve longstanding problems, help create successes for organization members, and give credit for success to others become desired commodities and gain power. Such expertise is especially valued in today's rapidly changing world because it is critical for organizational survival.

Rule Two.   Make the OD program itself a desired commodity. OD programs become desired commodities when they are instruments that allow individuals and organizations to reach their goals. OD programs should be results-oriented and goal-oriented. Another way the OD program becomes a desired commodity is by focusing on important issues, those issues vital to the organization's success. In this regard, Greiner and Schein challenge OD practitioners to become more involved in the strategic management process.[35] They state:

> We argue that a "new OD" must emerge to help the power structure change not only itself but the strategic alignment of the firm with its environment. OD can, if properly devised, provide a more effective process than political bargaining for assisting the dominant coalition to address pressing strategic issues. In essence, OD must enter the arena that has long been sacred ground to the power elite—the strat-

egy of the company, its structure for delivering on it, the positions that key leaders will hold in the structure, and the manner in which they will lead.[36]

We agree with Greiner and Schein on the need for OD practitioners to extend their activities to include strategic management issues and senior executives. We also agree that OD methods are superior to political bargaining. If the OD program itself is to become a desired commodity, it must be instrumental in addressing and resolving crucial issues.

Rule Three. Make the OD program a valued commodity for multiple powerful people in the organization. When the OD program serves the needs of top executives it gains an aura of respect and protection that sets it above most political entanglements. Although the program should be of value to persons at all levels of the organizational hierarchy, paying special attention to the needs of top executives is a useful rule of thumb. Again the issue is goal achievement—helping people realize their important goals. The powerholders can be expected to reciprocate with endorsement, support, and protection of the OD program. Being of value to multiple powerholders rather than a single one both increases support and protection and reduces the likelihood that the program will become the target of political activities.

Rule Four. Create win-win solutions. The nature of organizations and the nature of organization development suggest this rule. Organizations are social systems in which members have both a history and a future of interacting together. Effective conflict management techniques are required in organizations to enhance stable, constructive social relationships. Many OD interventions are specifically designed to promote win-win solutions in conflict situations. OD professionals who are skilled in conflict management techniques and OD programs that encompass conflict resolution activities become valued commodities.

The preceding rules of thumb describe ways to increase or solidify one's power base. The following rules describe ways to avoid becoming involved in one's own or in others' political struggles. Each is derived from the general principle: Mind your own business.

Rule Five. Mind your own business which is to help someone else solve his or her major problems. Sometimes OD practitioners overlook the fact that they are hired by others, usually managers, to help them achieve *their* goals and solve *their* problems. The OD consultant is successful to the extent that the manager is successful; the OD consultant is competent to the extent that the manager's goals are met through collaboration between consultant and key client. OD consultants are not hired to instill OD values in an organization, or to cause the widespread use of participative management, or to "do good and expunge evil" (as defined by the consultant). Instead, OD consultants have a formal or informal contractual agreement with managers to help them do what they are trying to do—better. The role of the OD consultant is to help others upon request. Beer and Walton argue that field or organization development should move from being practitioner-centered to being manager-centered.[37] That is sound advice. *The OD program belongs to the manager, not the OD consultant.* A valuable byproduct of this fact is that if the program runs into political turbulence, the manager will defend it, probably vigorously.

Rule Six. Mind your own business which is to be an expert on process, not content. Organizational politics revolve around decisions: Should we seek Goal A or Goal B? Should we use Means X or Means Y? Should we promote Mary or John? The proper role of OD consultants is to help decision makers by providing them with good decision-making *processes,* not by getting involved in the answers. The processes used are the business of the OD consultant, the answers chosen are not. Abiding by this rule keeps the consultant from becoming entangled in politics, while at the same time increases his or her usefulness to the organization's powerholders. The principle is simple but powerful: know your legitimate business and stick to it.

Rule Seven. Mind your own business because to do otherwise is to invite political trouble. A subtle phenomenon is involved here: when people engage in illegitimate behavior, such behavior is often interpreted as politically motivated thereby thrusting the actors into political battles. Illegitimate behavior encroaches on others' legitimate "turf," which arouses defensive and protective actions. Illegitimate behavior reduces predictability, causing others to try to exert greater control over the situation. We believe the legitimate role of the OD practitioner is that of facilitator, catalyst, problem solver, and educator, not power activist or power broker.[38]

More rules of thumb could be articulated, but these give the flavor of the issues that must be considered when operating in a political environment. Attention to these rules can save OD practitioners time and energy that can be more profitably invested in the OD program.

ACQUIRING AND USING POWER SKILLS

We have stated that the OD practitioner is neither power activist nor power broker. But that does not mean practitioners must be naive or incompetent in the political arena. Earlier we stated that the OD practitioner is encouraged to learn as much as possible about bargaining, negotiations, the nature of power and politics, the strategy and tactics of influence, and the characteristics and behaviors of powerholders. The purpose of this section is to contribute to that learning; specifically, we examine how to acquire and use skills to increase the positive face of power in organizations.

A recent book by Larry Greiner and Virginia Schein, *Power and Organization Development: Mobilizing Power to Implement Change,* provides a comprehensive look at power and OD.[39] The authors argue that OD values of trust, cooperation, and collaboration can not only coexist with a "pluralistic/political" model of organizations, but can make those organizations more humane and effective. The pluralistic/political model assumes that organizations contain self-interested groups seeking their own goals. The thrust of the book is that ". . . power and OD are not incompatible if used constructively and responsibly."[40] This is an appealing thesis. Here is how it is to be obtained:

> The effective combination of OD and power represents, for us, taking the *high road* to organization improvement. It begins by adhering to the valuable roots of OD where an educational process is used to encourage people to collaborate in making decisions that affect their own destiny. But as we will attempt to show in this book, OD goes on to incorporate modern approaches to power by (1) building its own power base so that it has access to those in power, (2) utilizing power strategies that are open and above-board for influencing key powerholders to accept the use of OD, (3) providing a facilitative process for these powerholders to address critical substantive issues that proves more creative and efficient than political bargaining, (4) assisting the power structure to confront and transform itself so that change can be more lasting, and (5) upholding the concerns and interests of those with less power who are affected by these changes.
>
> The *low road* represents vested political interest groups who, if left only to power and deception without OD, can destroy organizations by failing to tap human potential. Ironically, the *low road* also includes not only traditional champions of power who think that manipulation and political games are the essence of success, but those OD chameleons who sell out to power. [41]

Careful reflection on this quotation reveals that Greiner and Schein are breaking new ground on the topic of power and OD. In essence, they are saying, *use OD values and methods to show the powerholders better ways to wield power in organizations for the good of the entire organization.* These are valuable, new insights for the field of OD.

The authors proceed to show how to achieve the five goals listed earlier through examples, research, theorizing, and a large case study. For example, they discuss methods for increasing one's power base. They also discuss different power strategies and identify three sets of successful power strategies. Figure 16-2 shows the three most successful power strategies and how they relate to individual power bases.

Individual Power Bases	Strategies for Success
Knowledge • Expertise • Information • Tradition	*Playing It Straight* • Use data to convince • Focus on target group • Be persistent
Others' Support • Political access • Staff support	*Using Social Networks* • Alliances and coalitions • Deal with decision maker • Contacts for information
Personality • Charisma • Reputation • Professional credibility	*Going Around Formal System* • Work around roadblocks • (Don't) use organization rules

Figure 16-2   Power Base and Power Strategy Connection

Source: Larry E. Greiner and Virginia E. Schein, *Power and Organization Development* (Table 4–5), p. 52. © 1988 by Addison-Wesley Publishing Company, Inc. Reprinted by permission of the publisher.

As shown in the figure, individual power derives from knowledge, others' support, and personality characteristics. Three successful power strategies are "playing it straight," "using social networks," and "going around the formal system." OD practitioners have typically pursued a "playing it straight" strategy as their sole means of exerting power. The authors propose adding the "using social networks" strategy (which is currently underutilized) to their repertoires, thereby greatly expanding practitioner influence. This is done by participating in alliances and coalitions, dealing directly with powerholders and decision makers, and using contacts for information. Networking is increasingly recognized as a potent, viable, yet legitimate means of acquiring power in the organizational behavior literature. Greiner and Schein have now added it to the OD literature. "Going around the formal system" is a high-risk strategy, usually not recommended.

An interesting chapter on diagnosing power focuses on understanding the power relationships between seven sets of significant actors: the consultant and sponsor, the sponsor and other key executives, key executives to each other, consultant to key executives, top executives to higher authority, key executives to the organization, and organizational units to each other. Say, for example, that the power relationship between the consultant and sponsor is high, effective, and conducive to working well together. But the power diagnosis shows that the sponsor's power relationships with the other key executives are low. Given this situation, the sponsor may not be able to persuade the other executives to support the OD program. Greiner and Schein advise practitioners to conduct an early and thorough power diagnosis, and *they show how to do it* by describing where to look, what to look for, and what questions to ask. This represents a new dimension in the OD literature.

Finally, the authors propose a four-stage model in which the OD process is used to help the power elite transform the organization in ways beneficial for all concerned. The four stages are:

> **Phase I.** Consolidating Power to Prepare for Change
> **Phase II.** Focusing Power on Strategic Consensus
> **Phase III.** Aligning Power with Structure and People
> **Phase IV.** Releasing Power through Leadership and Collaboration[42]

These stages are the *means* the OD consultant uses to "take the high road" mentioned in the previous quotation—build a power base, influence key powerholders to accept the use of OD, then utilize a facilitative OD process in which the powerholders work on strategic business issues by developing a corporate strategy using consensus decision making. This will cause the power structure to realize that collaborative power is preferable to manipulation and deception, which in turn will protect the interests of all concerned, even those of little power. This practical, how-to book on power and organization development is well worth studying. The authors have presented the beginning of a theory of power and OD; we expect other investigators to build on their foundation.

We conclude this chapter by examining a model of power and influence proposed by David Whetten and Kim Cameron in *Developing Management Skills*.[43] The book is designed to increase managerial skills—developing self-awareness, problem solving, conflict management, motivating others, gaining power and influence, and so forth. Their model is shown in Figure 16-3.

As can be seen, a person's power comes from two main sources, personal power and position power. Personal power, in turn, arises from expertise, personal attraction, effort, and legitimacy. (Legitimacy refers to abiding by and promoting the values of the organization.) Position power derives from five sources: *Centrality* refers to access to information in a communication network; *criticality* refers to how important or critical one's job is; *flexibility* refers to the amount of discretion in the job; *visibility* refers to how much one's work is seen by influential people; and *relevance* refers to how important one's task is in relation to organizational priorities.[44]

The authors write about the importance of networking as follows:

> One of the most important ways of gaining power in an organization is by establishing a broad network of task and interpersonal relationships. . . . Networks are critical to effective performance for one compelling reason: Except for routine jobs, no one has the necessary information and resources to accomplish what's expected of them.

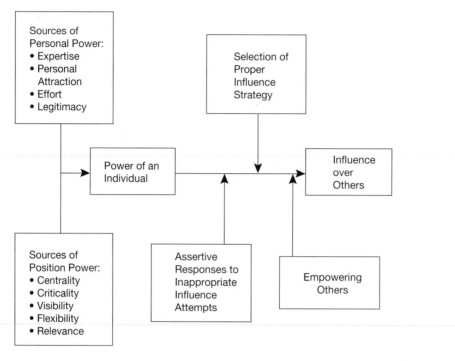

Figure 16-3 Model of Power and Influence

Source: From *Developing Management Skills*, 2nd ed., p. 309, by David A. Whetton and Kim S. Cameron. Copyright © 1991 by HarperCollins Publishers Inc. Reprinted by permission of HarperCollins Publishers.

Indeed, one investigation of the determinants of effective management performance concluded that a key factor distinguishing high and low performers was the ability to establish informal relationships via networks.[45]

Networking is used to increase both personal power and position power. Having power is one thing; actually using it to get things done is another, according to these authors. Power-in-use is called *influence*. They write: "Influence entails actually securing the consent of others to work with you in accomplishing an objective." And, "Power is converted into influence when the target individual consents to behave according to the desires of the power holder."[46] As shown in Figure 16-3, three things are involved in converting power into influence: resisting other people's inappropriate influence attempts, selecting the proper influence strategy, and empowering others. Three influence strategies are described—reason, reciprocity, and retribution. *Reason* refers to persuasion by facts, *reciprocity* refers to exchange of favors, and *retribution* refers to coercion and threats. Usually reason is the preferred strategy, and reciprocity can be useful when reason fails. Retribution is not recommended except in unusual cases. Whetton and Cameron suggest several means of resisting others' influence attempts such as confrontation and using countervailing power. Methods for empowering others are the following: (1) involve subordinates in the assignment of work, (2) provide a positive, collaborative work environment, (3) reward and encourage others in visible and personal ways, (4) express confidence, (5) foster initiative and responsibility, and (6) build on success.[47]

We think this model and the explanation of it by Whetton and Cameron provide useful information for OD practitioners. It complements the work of Greiner and Schein, and it offers practical insights for acquiring and using power in organizations. Power and politics are inherently complex ingredients of OD programs, but the work of these two sets of authors increases our understanding of this vital arena.

CONCLUDING COMMENTS

In this chapter we have examined the concepts of power and politics with the goals of understanding the phenomena and deriving implications for OD practitioners. Power and politics are similar in nature, arise from known conditions, and are amenable to positive control. Suggestions for using power to operate effectively in organizations were given that may help practitioners avoid the perils and pitfalls of power that "go with the territory" of organizational change.

NOTES

1. W. Warner Burke, *Organization Development: Principles and Practices* (Boston: Little, Brown and Co., 1982), p. 127.
2. See George Strauss, "Organization Development," in Robert Dubin, ed., *Handbook of Work, Organization, and Society* (Chicago: Rand McNally, 1976), pp. 617–685; Robert L. Kahn, "Organizational Development: Some Problems and Proposals," *Journal of Applied Behavioral Science*, 10, no. 4 (1974), 485–502; Warren G. Bennis, *Organization Development: Its Nature, Origins, and Prospects* (Reading, MA: Addison-Wesley, 1969), pp. 78–79; and Wendell L. French and Cecil H. Bell, Jr., *Organization Development*, 2nd ed. (Englewood Cliffs, NJ: Prentice-Hall, 1978), Chap. 20.
3. Important contributions to management and organization thought are Jeffrey Pfeffer, *Power in Organizations* (Marshfield, MA: Pitman, 1981); Henry Mintzberg, *Power In and Around Organizations* (Englewood Cliffs, NJ: Prentice-Hall, 1983); Kenneth Thomas, "Conflict and Conflict Management," in Marvin D. Dunnette, ed., *Handbook of Industrial and Organizational Psychology* (Chicago: Rand McNally, 1976), pp. 889–935; and John P. Kotter, "Power, Success, and Organizational Effectiveness," *Organizational Dynamics* (March–April 1976), pp. 27–40.
4. Important contributions to the OD literature are Anthony T. Cobb and Newton Margulies, "Organization Development: A Political Perspective," *Academy of Management Review* (January 1981), pp. 49–59; Virginia E. Schein, "Political Strategies for Implementing Organizational Change," *Group and Organization Studies*, 2 (1977), pp.

42–48; Andrew Pettigrew, "Towards a Political Theory of Organizational Intervention," *Human Relations*, 28, no. 3 (1979), 191–208; and Burke, *Organization Development*, Chapter 7.

5. This chapter draws on material from our book of readings in OD, W. L. French, C. H. Bell, Jr., and R. A. Zawacki, eds., *Organization Development: Theory, Practice, Research* (Burr Ridge, IL: Irwin, 1994), Part V.

6. R. G. H. Siu, *The Craft of Power* (New York: John Wiley, 1979), p. 31.

7. R. A. Dahl, "The Concept of Power," *Behavioral Science* (1957), pp. 202–203.

8. Gerald Salancik and Jeffrey Pfeffer, "Who Gets Power—And How They Hold on to It: A Strategic-Contingency Model of Power," *Organizational Dynamics*, 5 (1977), p. 3.

9. Mintzberg, *Power In and Around Organizations*, p. 4. [Mintzberg's emphasis.]

10. David C. McClelland, "The Two Faces of Power," *Journal of International Affairs*, 24, no. I (1970), 29–47.

11. M. Patchen, "The Locus and Bases of Influence in Organization Decisions," *Organization Behavior and Human Performance*, 11 (1974), pp. 195–221. This quotation is from p. 216.

12. Nancy C. Roberts, "Organizational Power Styles: Collective and Competitive Power Under Varying Organizational Conditions," *Journal of Applied Behavioral Science*, 22, no. 4 (1986), 443–458. Roberts has developed a Power Styles Inventory that measures five different influence styles: directive, impression management, transactional, consensual, and charismatic. See N. C. Roberts, *Organizational Power Styles: Their Determinants and Consequences*, unpublished doctoral dissertation, Stanford University, 1983.

13. Richard M. Emerson, "Power-Dependence Relations," *American Sociological Review*, 27 (1962), pp. 31–40. This quotation is from page 32.

14. John R. P. French, Jr. and Bertram Raven, "The Bases of Social Power," in Dorwin Cartwright, ed., *Studies in Social Power* (Ann Arbor: Institute for Social Research of the University of Michigan, 1959), pp. 150–167.

15. This discussion is taken from Salancik and Pfeffer, "Who Gets Power—And How They Hold on to It." An earlier treatment of this view is "A Strategic Contingencies Theory of Intraorganizational Power," by D. J. Hickson, C. R. Hinings, C. A. Lee, R. E. Schneck, and J. M. Pennings, in *Administrative Science Quarterly*, 16, no. 2 (June 1971), 216–229.

16. Salancik and Pfeffer, "Who Gets Power," p. 3.

17. Mintzberg, *Power In and Around Organizations*. This book is an important contribution to the concept of power in general and organizational power in particular.

18. Ibid., p. 22.

19. This discussion is taken from ibid., Chap. 3, especially pp. 24–26.

20. Harold Lasswell, *Politics: Who Gets What, When, How* (New York: McGraw-Hill, 1936).

21. Pfeffer, *Power in Organizations*, p. 7.

22. Robert W. Allen, Dan L. Madison, Lyman W. Porter, Patricia A. Renwick, and Bronston T. Mayes, "Organizational Politics: Tactics and Characteristics of Its Actors," *California Management Review*, 22 (1979), p. 77.

23. Bronston T. Mayes and Robert W. Allen, "Toward a Definition of Organizational Politics," *The Academy of Management Review*, 2, no. 4 (October 1977), 676.

24. Mintzberg, *Power In and Around Organizations*, p. 5.

25. Pfeffer, *Power in Organizations*, Chapter 1. See also Jay M. Shafritz and J. Steven Ott, eds., *Classics of Organization Theory*, 2nd ed. (Chicago, IL: The Dorsey Press, 1987).

26. Pfeffer, *Power in Organizations*, pp. 69–70.

27. See, for example, J. Von Neumann and O. Morgenstern, *Theory of Games and Economic Behavior* (Princeton: NJ: Princeton University Press, 1947); R. D. Luce and H. Raiffa, *Games and Decisions: Introduction and Critical Survey* (New York: John Wiley, 1957); T. C. Schelling, *The Strategy of Conflict* (Cambridge, MA: Harvard University Press, 1960); and J. W. Thibaut and H. H. Kelley, *The Social Psychology of Groups* (New York: John Wiley, 1959).

28. Schelling, *The Strategy of Conflict*.

29. R. E. Walton and R. B. McKersie, *A Behavioral Theory of Labor Negotiations* (New York: McGraw-Hill, 1965).
30. Robert Chin and Kenneth D. Benne, "General Strategies for Effecting Change in Human Systems," in Warren G. Bennis, Kenneth D. Benne, Robert Chin, and Kenneth E. Corey, eds., *The Planning of Change*, 3rd ed. (New York: Holt, Rinehart and Winston, 1976).
31. Chris Argyris, *Intervention Theory and Method: A Behavioral Science View* (Reading, MA: Addison-Wesley, 1970), pp. 17–20.
32. Cobb and Margulies, "Organization Development: A Political Perspective," *Academy of Management Review,* 6 (January 1981), pp. 50–59.
33. Michael Beer, *Organization Change and Development: A Systems View* (Santa Monica, CA: Goodyear, 1980), pp. 258–261.
34. Ibid., p. 259.
35. Larry E. Greiner and Virginia E. Schein, "A Revisionist Look at Power and OD," *The Industrial-Organizational Psychologist,* 25, no. 2 (1988), 59–61.
36. Ibid., p. 60.
37. Michael Beer and Anna E. Walton, "Organization Change and Development," *Annual Review of Psychology,* 38 (1987), pp. 339–67.
38. A growing number of authors assert that OD practitioners should be political activists and/or powerbrokers. We disagree. For this other point of view, see: R. G. Harrison and D. C. Pitt, "Organizational Development: A Missing Political Dimension?" (pp. 65–85), and P. Reason, "Is Organization Development Possible in Power Cultures?" (pp. 185–202), both from the book *Power, Politics, and Organizations* edited by A. Kakabadse and C. Parker (Chichester: John Wiley and Sons, Ltd., 1984). See also W. R. Nord, "The Failure of Current Applied Behavioral Science—A Marxian Perspective," *Journal of Applied Behavioral Science,* 10 (1974), pp. 557–578; Andrew Pettigrew, "Toward a Political Theory of Organizational Intervention"; Virginia Schein, "Political Strategies for Implementing Organizational Change"; and N. Margulies and A. P. Raia, "The Politics of Organization Development," *Training and Development Journal,* 38 (1984), pp. 20–23.
39. Larry E. Greiner and Virginia E. Schein, *Power and Organization Development: Mobilizing Power to Implement Change* (Reading, MA: Addison-Wesley Publishing Company, 1988).
40. Ibid., p. 7.
41. Ibid., p. 7.
42. Ibid., p. 96.
43. David A. Whetten and Kim S. Cameron, *Developing Management Skills*, 2nd ed. (New York: HarperCollins Publishers, Inc., 1991). See pp. 272–333.
44. Ibid., pp. 290–297.
45. Ibid., p. 290.
46. Ibid., p. 297.
47. Ibid., pp. 307–308.

17

RESEARCH ON ORGANIZATION DEVELOPMENT

The aims of this chapter are to describe the problems inherent in conducting research on OD, to show the substantial progress that has been made in improving research in the field, and to summarize the results of studies conducted on OD and OD processes. The conclusions of the chapter are these: (1) Organization development works, that is, it produces organizational improvement and individual development. (2) There is good evidence to support the preceding statement. (3) An explanation of why OD works is not available at this time primarily because explanatory theories are too rudimentary.

Evaluating OD programs is complicated and difficult. Teasing out the effects of specific interventions or a package of interventions is an inherently formidable task because field research of this nature is prone to confounding from many sources. Let's look at some of the problems involved in research on OD.

ASSESSING THE EFFECTS OF OD: SOME ISSUES AND PROBLEMS

Organization development is a prescription for a process of planned change in organizations that includes concepts, techniques, and interventions. The desired outcomes of organization development are to make the organization and its members and work groups more effective while also making the organization a better place to satisfy human needs. The OD process, then, utilizes various techniques to bring about improvement or change in various target groups—individuals, groups, and the total organization. Viewed from a research perspective, two questions arise: Does OD in fact bring about or cause these desired effects? and If we observe these desired effects in an organization engaged in an OD program, can we attribute the effects to the OD program? Unambiguous answers to these questions can come only from careful, controlled, empirical research.

In research terminology the OD program could be called the independent variable (IV), or the treatment, or "cause." It is presumed to cause variation in the dependent variable (DV), or "effect." The independent variable is manipulated (by being either present or absent), and this causes changes on the dependent variable (in this case, increased effectiveness). If we let the independent variable be X and the dependent variable be Y, then the relation between the two is stated as "X leads to Y"; "X is a determining condition of Y"; or "X causes Y." In research on organization development we are interested in determining whether or not OD (X) causes or leads to greater effectiveness of individuals, groups, and organizations (Y). Parenthetically, Pate, Nielsen, and Bacon suggest, and we agree, that it may be incorrect to conceptualize OD or an OD program as an independent variable; rather it is a treatment whereby the independent variable is manipulated.[1]

> Some researchers regarded OD itself to be an independent variable. However, in our view, OD does not generally constitute the independent variable, but is only instrumental in its manipulation. For example, one might expect introduction of participative decision making (OD intervention) to facilitate worker awareness of the rationale for organizational actions (independent variable), which in turn may increase support for and commitment to those actions (dependent variable).[2]

It is not really known in most cases what "causes" the effects of an OD intervention; it is only known that something within the overall activities caused some changes. In the strictest sense, the cause is the independent variable, and since that is usually not identified in OD research, we will loosely refer to the OD intervention or program as a "treatment" that *contains* some independent variables having an impact on dependent variables of interest.

Problems with Definitions and Concepts

One of the first problems in research on organization development is that X and Y are not precise terms. There are endless variations of "OD." A program can consist of many activities or only one or two activities, yet it would be referred to as OD. A program can be a one-shot intervention or a multiyear intervention and be called OD. A program can include a particular intervention—say, intergroup team building—or not include it and be called OD. And some programs we would not label OD are called OD. Thus there is no unitary treatment known as OD, and research on OD is therefore not on OD per se but rather on a specific set of treatment activities.

Robert Kahn has criticized the field of OD for its lack of precise meaning as follows:

> *Organizational development* is not a concept, at least not in the scientific sense of the word: it is not precisely defined; it is not reducible to specific, uniform, observable behaviors; it does not have a prescribed and verifiable place in a network of logically related concepts, a theory.[3]

We agree with this assessment and believe that lack of precision in definitions has slowed the development of research on the OD process.

Furthermore, the Y, improved effectiveness, is not a precise term. Is it to mean greater efficiency? Greater productivity? Greater profits? More positive attitudes? Is it to mean improvements in individual functioning, group functioning, the functioning of most of the organization, or the functioning of all of the organization? And how much "better" must the improvement be over the status quo to be called improvement? Answers to these questions are generally not found in the research literature. Thus, improved organizational effectiveness is treated in a variety of ways in research on OD; it is a global term that refers to many different outcomes.

The major means of overcoming the problem of imprecision in definitions is to be more specific in defining X's and Y's. This is done by giving operational definitions to the terms. An *operational definition* is a statement of the specific operations or activities involved in both implementing the treatment and measuring the effects or results.[4] We must also move from describing global treatments and global effects to describing independent and dependent variables—cause-effect linkages.

Problems with Internal Validity

A second problem in research on OD is that of demonstrating that the X of interest, some OD activities, in fact caused the variation in Y and not some other known or unknown X. This is the problem of internal validity. *"Internal validity* is the basic minimum without which any experiment is uninterpretable: Did in fact the experimental treatments make a difference in this specific experimental instance?"[5] This is a problem in all field research and evaluation research: there is simply so much going on in the real-world situation that it is difficult to pinpoint what is causing the changes that occur. The key to overcoming or at least attenuating this problem lies in the research design—the structure of the research effort from start to finish. The research must be so executed that *rival explanations* for the changes in the dependent variables can be systematically discounted. For example, if simultaneously with an OD program everyone in the organization received a substantial salary increase, and if we were measuring the effects of the program on attitudes toward work and the organization, then any positive shift in attitudes could be caused by the OD program, by the salary raise, or by some other unknown factor or factors.

Campbell and Stanley have suggested a number of designs that overcome threats to internal validity.[6] In addition, when conditions do not permit true experimental designs, they suggest ways to build "quasi-experimental" designs that will rule out rival explanations for the changes found. The research designs used in OD are getting better in terms of controlling threats to internal validity: in a review of 37 research studies on OD, Pate, Nielsen, and Bacon found that experimental or quasi-experimental designs were used in 29 of them; in a review of OD research from 1964 to 1974, White and Mitchell found that experimental or quasi-experimental designs were used in only 12 (out of 44) studies.[7] Porras and Berg reviewed 160 organizational change studies conducted between 1959 and mid-1975. Of these, 35 reflected OD interventions that were carefully executed and carefully evaluated. Analysis of the 35 studies showed that 77 percent used quasi-experimental designs and 49 percent used comparison groups.[8]

Several design features enhance internal validity. One of the best methods is to have comparison or control groups that receive no treatment but are measured on the dependent variables. If changes occur in the experimental groups that receive the treatment but no changes occur in the control groups, this is evidence for the treatment's causing the observed effects. It is of course imperative that there be pretreatment and posttreatment measures to register any changes. Posttreatment measures only are of limited value, since one can never know whether the treatment led to the results observed or whether the results would have been there without the treatment. "Time-series" designs offer a compromise between control groups and no control groups. In a time-series design, multiple measures are made on the experimental group over time. If changes in the measures occur after the treatments, this is some support for the hypothesis that the treatment caused the changes.

Norman Berkowitz discussed the problems inherent in research on OD and proposed an elaborate time series design.[9] He further suggests that an excessive concern for internal validity in OD research as reflected in trying to use truly experimental designs rather than quasi-experimental designs may be inappropriate at this stage of the research efforts. Finally, random assignment of units (individuals, groups, or organizations) to experimental and control groups is a way of controlling for rival explanations for why the change occurred and controlling for extraneous variables. But random assignment is often difficult to achieve in field research. Organizations involved in OD self-select themselves to engage in such programs and would probably be unwilling to be placed in a "no-treatment" control group for research purposes. Furthermore, an organization hostile to OD is in the "no-treatment" group for very definite reasons. With self-selection it is never possible to know that any changes that occurred were due to the treatment and not to some other unknown factors.

Problems with External Validity

A third problem in research on OD is that of external validity, *"External validity* asks the question of *generalizability:* To what populations, settings, treatment variables, and measurement variables can this effect be generalized?"[10] This question of generalizability to other settings and circumstances is always an important one and will probably become even more important in the future. Organization development is being applied in an ever-increasing number of settings,[11] and what "works" in one setting may not work in another. For example, organization development techniques are effective in middle-class suburban schools, but are they also effective in ghetto urban schools? Organization development techniques have been shown to increase productivity in private sector business organizations; can they do the same in a federal bureaucracy? It is likely that some techniques or treatments will be found to be situation specific, while others will be more universally applicable.

Problems with Lack of Theory

Another problem is that OD research is not theory-guided research; in fact, there is essentially no comprehensive theory to explain the process of planned change in organizations. Kerlinger defines *theory* as *"a set of interrelated constructs (concepts), definitions, and propositions that present a systematic view of phenomena by specifying relations among variables, with the purpose of explaining and predicting the phenomena."*[12] Without a theory of organization development, the relations among variables and the variables themselves are unknown. Organization development researchers are forced to fall back on a strategy of measuring the effects of global treatments (not independent variables) on a potpourri of dependent variables—things that should *probably* be affected by the intervention.

Theory-guided research is more efficient, more precise, and more definitive. With theory, researchers know what to look for and where to look for it in their research efforts. Research either confirms or does not confirm the theory; if the theory is disconfirmed, it is modified and new avenues for further research are indicated. The first major step in building theory in OD is the identification and specification of independent and dependent variables that explain the phenomena. Next the relations among these variables are specified with increasing precision. These will be the major chores of OD practitioners, researchers, and theoreticians in the future.

Significant progress is being made, however, in the development of theory and the identification and specification of relevant independent and dependent variables. Alderfer has coalesced a number of disparate ideas relating to planned organizational change into a coherent theory with research implications;[13] Argyris has proposed a general theory of intervention in human systems based on his experience and research;[14] Blake and Mouton have developed a theory and classification scheme for the consultation process;[15] and Vaill has discussed some of the unique requirements for building a "practice theory"—a theory applicable to applied change problems.[16] Bowers, Franklin, and Pecorella have developed a taxonomy that starts to clarify some of the variables involved in organizational improvement strategies by focusing on both the problems the intervention is designed to rectify and the interventions themselves.[17]

In their review of research on OD, White and Mitchell propose a classification system based on facet theory for independent and dependent variables found in OD interventions.[18] These authors identify three underlying dimensions or facets of OD interventions and the effects of OD interventions: (1) a target or recipient of change, (2) a specific content area of change, and (3) the context or relationships that are supposed to change. The first facet, *target of change,* consists of three elements—the individual, the subgroup, and the total organization. The *content area of change* facet consists of four elements: conceptual, behavioral, procedural, and structural. The *context of change* facet consists of five elements: intrapersonal, interpersonal, intragroup, intergroup, and organizational.[19] Almost all OD interventions and their desired effects can be specified on these three facets and the twelve elements. For example, a team-building intervention would have as a target the subgroup, the content area of change would be either conceptual or behavioral, and the relationships of change would be either interpersonal or intragroup. With such a classification system in mind, researchers can design their data collection methods better and can start to test for the effects of various interventions on the different facets and elements. This will lead to research based on specified hypothesized relations among variables instead of a "shotgun" approach in which numerous measures are made on variables to "see if anything happened."

Dunn and Swierczek applied a refined content analysis technique (called "retrospective case analysis") to 67 successful and unsuccessful change efforts, many of them case studies, in an attempt to test whether certain hypothesized relations about what causes success would hold up.[20] They examined 11 hypotheses that appear in the literature. These hypotheses consist of such statements as "Change efforts in economic organizations will be more successful than will change efforts in other types of organizations"—not supported by the data—and "Change efforts directed at the total organization will be more successful than will change efforts directed at lower levels"—also not supported by the evidence. Three hypotheses received moderate support as marking successful versus unsuccessful change efforts: first, change efforts in which the mode of intervention is *collaborative* as opposed to other intervention modes tend to be more successful; second, change efforts in which the change agent has a *participative orientation* versus other orientations tend to be more successful; and, third, change efforts employing standardized strategies that involve *high levels of participation* will be more successful than those that involve low levels of participation.[21] This effort toward building a theory of organizational change processes "grounded" or based on empirical research is a laudable one. Benefits derive both from discovering which hypotheses are supported and from discovering which hypotheses are not supported. These hypotheses specify relations among variables that can form the basis for a theory of organization change and development.

Problems with Measuring Attitude Change

Research on organization development often involves administering preintervention and postintervention attitude questionnaires and observing pre- and postintervention differences on the attitude scores. If responses become more favorable, that is taken as evidence that the intervention helped to produce positive attitude change. If responses stay the same or become less favorable, that is taken as evidence that the intervention had no effect or had a negative effect. In an important article in 1976 Golembiewski, Billingsley, and Yeager suggested that three different kinds of change can occur between the pre- and postmeasures. They labeled these alpha, beta, and gamma change.[22] Alpha change is real or true change; your attitude is more positive or negative after the intervention and the questionnaires accurately reflect that. Beta change is change based on scale recalibration; you view the scale intervals differently after the intervention—for example, a "5" on a 10-point scale of "trust in my group" has taken on a different meaning for you. Gamma change is change based on a reconceptualization or redefinition of the concept being measured; you now view the concept itself in a totally different way.

The problem identified by Golembiewski and his colleagues appears to be valid. What is a researcher to do? Fortunately, researchers such as Armenakis and Zmud,[23] Randolph,[24] and Terborg, Howard, and

Maxwell[25] have developed methods to *measure* the three types of change if and when they occur. OD research must be carefully planned to identify these changes, but the methods for doing so are available.

For example, Porras and others conducted a behavior modeling OD program in plywood mills. The program produced many positive changes. Were they real? Porras and Singh[26] examined the results and found that true (alpha) change occurred as well as some scale recalibration (beta) change; no gamma change was found.

The implications for practitioners and researchers are that additional care and planning must go into research on OD that involves measuring attitude changes.

Problems with "Normal Science"

There is a controversy within organization development regarding the best ways to conduct research on action programs. Specifically, an increasing number of theorists and researchers are rejecting "normal science" with its requirements of replication, control groups, random assignment to treatment conditions, specifying single cause-and-effect linkages, and so forth in favor of less rigorous but richer "action research."

Earlier we noted Argyris's call for "action science" (a form of action research) as a more effective means for studying complex social change than normal science.[27] Other authors are calling attention to the need for other research methods for OD. Blumberg and Pringle show how the use of control groups in the Rushton Coal Mine experiment distorted the data and even forced the termination of the experiment.[28] Bullock and Svyantek argue the case that it is logically impossible to use random strategies of selection and assignment to study the OD process itself.[29] They say that OD *techniques* can be evaluated using random strategies, but not organization development itself because it is by nature collaborative and diagnosis-based—that is, what one does depends on each specific situation's needs. Bullock and Svyantek state:

> No one has ever suggested that a rigorous OD researcher randomly select organizations from across the country—including, for example, volunteer organizations, work organizations, political organizations, health service organizations—then randomly assign them to OD interventions (the local Boy Scout troop to management by objectives, General Motors to team building, the Ku Klux Klan to T groups, the nursing home to career planning) designed to fundamentally change the organizations as social systems, and with that change to alter the lives and careers of individuals. Yet we continue to evaluate OD research as if such an action were reasonable.[30]

Bullock and Bullock report an experiment involving two kinds of data feedback to an organization, " pure science" and "science-action."[31]

Minimal change and usefulness resulted from the pure science feedback approach (giving a one-inch thick book of statistics tables to decision makers); extensive change, problem solving, and energy resulted from the science-action approach in which the scientist acted also as a change agent/OD facilitator.

Beer and Walton criticize the methods of current OD research on four counts.[32] First, the research attempts to identify causation of a single intervention while overlooking the systemic nature of organizations. Clearly other internal and external forces are operating during OD programs. Second, the research is not sufficiently longitudinal to capture long term change or to identify nonpermanent change. Third, the research is "flat"; it does not describe in enough detail the intervention and the context. And finally, the research does not fit the needs of its users. Beer and Walton conclude: "What we are recommending is a return to the action research traditions of OD with full participation of the client in the research but with much longer time frames and the inclusion of rich descriptions of context and system dynamics.[33]

Conclusion

We have discussed six major problems confronting research on OD: imprecision of definitions and conceptualizations concerning OD research, problems with internal and external validity, the lack of supporting theory to guide research, problems with measuring attitude change, and problems with using normal science methods to study OD programs. These do not appear to be insurmountable problems at this time, although they continue to plague research efforts.

The future of OD research will no doubt see the movement from evaluation and validation studies (the does-it-work-and-can-we-demonstrate-that-it-does stage) to a theory-building and hypothesis-testing stage that will signify a more mature level of research. Friedlander and Brown indicate some of the challenges of the future for OD research:

> If the practice and theory of OD is to merge into a broader field of planned change, what role will research play in this transformation? We believe that research will either play a far more crucial role in the advancement of this field, or become an increasingly irrelevant appendage to it. Thus far it has utilized its techniques primarily for evaluation and validation, and its current techniques are well adapted to this. Thus far it has chosen to play a relatively uninvolved and distant role in the change-practice situation. Thus far it has focused on producing data for research needs rather than practice needs. As a result, we have theory from an external research perspective only. We have generally failed to produce a theory of change which emerges from the change process itself. We need a way of enriching our understanding and our action synergistically rather than at one

or the other's expense—to become a science in which knowledge-getting and knowledge-giving are an integrated process, and one that is valuable to all parties involved. We believe that a theory of planned change must be a theory of practice, which emerges from practice data and is of the practice situation, not merely about it.[34]

POSITIVE DEVELOPMENTS IN RESEARCH ON OD

Some advances in the area of research on organization development have already been cited, namely, increasing use of experimental and quasi-experimental research designs that really permit us to know what the treatment effects are and increasing attention to the formulation of theory and testable hypotheses. These advances augur well for the future of OD research.

Another positive feature is the increasing incidence of longitudinal studies on the effects of OD. In the review article by Pate, Nielsen, and Bacon, 18 of the 37 studies examined are longitudinal research efforts.[35] Although these authors end their review with a plea for *more* systematic, longitudinal research, it is a good sign that such studies are becoming more prevalent. Longitudinal research allows both short- and long-term effects of OD interventions to be noted; it permits the use of tighter research designs; and it allows for the differential effects of different interventions to be discovered. Development of theory will go hand in hand with the emergence of more longitudinal research on OD.

Several longitudinal research efforts of a *programmatic nature* exist. The Institute for Survey Research of the University of Michigan has been engaged for many years in gathering data on a variety of organizations.[36] These data serve as a repository for measuring the effects of a variety of factors impacting on the organizations including planned change programs.[37] Another long-range programmatic research effort directed specifically at measuring the effects of organizational improvement programs is the Quality of Work Life program located at the University of Michigan.[38] This program, under the direction of professor Edward E. Lawler III, now at the University of Southern California, is monitoring and evaluating a number of quality of work life (QWL) projects initiated in the mid- and late-1970s. The results look promising: significant gains in productivity and job satisfaction have occurred in several (but by no means all) of the projects.[39]

Advances in measurement techniques and valid measurement instruments have also contributed to better research on OD. Alderfer reviewed the OD research from the 1974-1976 period and noted several advances along these lines:

there have been significant research developments in OD during the time covered by this review. More rigorous research designs have been employed to evaluate interventions; both positive and negative outcomes have been observed. There is clear evidence that better measuring instruments are being developed, and greater understanding of measurement errors is being obtained.[40]

Research and verified theory can advance only as fast as the measurement capabilities of a scientific field. Therefore, these improvements in measurement techniques are important developments.

In a critique of the OD research literature, Nancy Roberts and Jerry Porras find reasons for cautious optimism. They note that substantial progress is being made in four major areas: progress in operationalizing the concept of change, progress in improving measurement processes and also measurement procedures, and progress in developing appropriate statistical and analytical models.[41]

Furthermore, there is an increased awareness among practitioners and clients of the value and usefulness of research on OD. In part this may be due to a "coming of age" of OD and research on OD. But credit is also due to the numerous excellent reviews and critiques of OD research that have appeared in the professional journals and a number of books. Friedlander and Brown,[42] Alderfer,[43] Faucheux, Amado, and Laurent,[44] Beer and Walton,[45] and Porras and Silvers[46] have written careful comprehensive reviews and critiques of OD research for the 1974, 1977, 1982, 1987, and 1991 editions, respectively, of the *Annual Review of Psychology*. Michael Beer,[47] George Strauss,[48] and Jerry Porras and Peter Robertson[49] have told the broad story of OD in three important handbooks. White and Mitchell,[50] Pate, Nielsen, and Bacon,[51] Porras and Berg,[52] and Golembiewski, Proehl, and Sink[53] reviewed the research on OD and offered helpful suggestions for improving it. All these contributions have played a role in emphasizing the need for competent research on OD and have additionally raised the level of sophistication regarding research.

Marshall Sashkin and Warner Burke reviewed the state of OD research in 1987 and discovered positive trends.[54] One positive development is the use of "meta analysis" to evaluate OD studies (we discuss this topic later). Regarding the *quality* of OD research they report it has been improving consistently with each decade, as indicated by greater methodological rigor and better measurement. Regarding the *true effects* of OD interventions, they state: "There is little doubt that, when applied properly, OD has substantial positive effects in terms of performance measures."[55] Sashkin and Burke draw these conclusions:

> OD research has, by the mid-1980s, shed quite a bit of light on the effects and effectiveness of OD. We are also in the position of understanding far more clearly than ever the key research problems in OD.

Solutions are another matter. Although few today are willing to argue that OD has no real effects, there remains considerable uncertainty over how properly to measure these effects. And it may well be that effective OD is actually inconsistent with rigorous research, as some have argued. . . .[56]

Their last sentence relates to the question of using normal science versus action research to evaluate OD programs. All in all, the Sashkin and Burke review reflects positively on the state of research on OD.

Figure 17-1 Factors Constituting the Organizational Work Setting

Source: Jerry I. Porras and Peter J. Robertson. "Organizational Development: Theory, Practice and Research," p. 729. Modified and reproduced by special permission of the Publisher, Consulting Psychologists Press, Inc., Palo Alto, CA 94303, from *Handbook of Industrial and Organizational Psychology, 2nd ed., Vol. 3,* by M. D. Dunnette and L. M. Hough (eds). Copyright 1992 by Consulting Psychologists Press, Inc. All rights reserved. Further reproduction is prohibited without the Publisher's written consent.

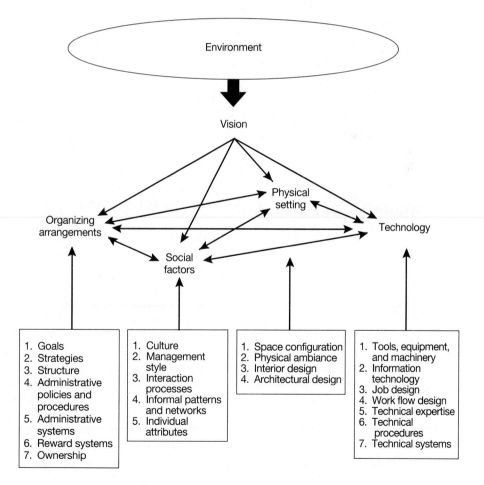

Porras and Silvers reviewed published OD research from 1985 through 1989 and report advances in research methods and research results.[57] Positive developments are better theories, improved study designs, improved measurement, better statistical methods, and good use of meta-analytical techniques. They notice a shift away from research on social factors such as interpersonal relations, management, values, norms, and so on, toward research on organizing arrangements such as organization structure, strategies, administrative systems, and so on. This shift represents a move toward examining organizational-level issues, that is, a look at how *systems* change as a result of OD efforts. This review reflects generally good news about OD research.

In a comprehensive review, Porras and Robertson examine the effects of different OD and human resource interventions on individual and organizational performance.[58] In addition, they test a theory of planned change. This work merits a closer look.

In a discussion earlier on stream analysis, we stated that Porras and his associates focus on the *work setting* as the primary source of individual behavior. Furthermore, change occurs when individuals start to behave differently. This is the foundation of the theory. Figure 17-1 shows the four categories of variables included in the work setting: organizing arrangements (OA), social factors (SF), physical setting (PS), and technology (T).

Porras and Robertson write: "The process of intervening into organizational systems, creating changes in organizational components that will in turn result in changes in the work behaviors of organizational members, constitutes the primary activity of organizational development."[59] For these authors, OD interventions impact the variables comprising the work setting; this in turn leads to changes in individual behaviors which lead to organizational performance and individual development, the desired outcomes of OD programs. Figure 17-2 shows Porras and Robertson's overall model of organization development.

In this model, the environment places constraints and opportunities on the organization, which serve as inputs for the leaders to formulate a vision. "Vision is the force that guides the organization, for both the short and long term. Organizational vision is a complex concept comprised of four distinct, yet interdependent parts: (a) the core values and beliefs of the organization, (b) the organization's enduring purpose, (c) a highly compelling mission, and (d) the vivid description that brings the mission to life. . . ."[60]

The work setting provides *information and cues* to members regarding what to think and how to act. Other organizational members also provide such information and cues. The result is individual cognitions (beliefs and attitudes) about how to behave which determine on-the-job behavior. We think this is a promising model for OD.

Next Porras and Robertson related or "mapped" various OD interventions to organization variables; for example, team building

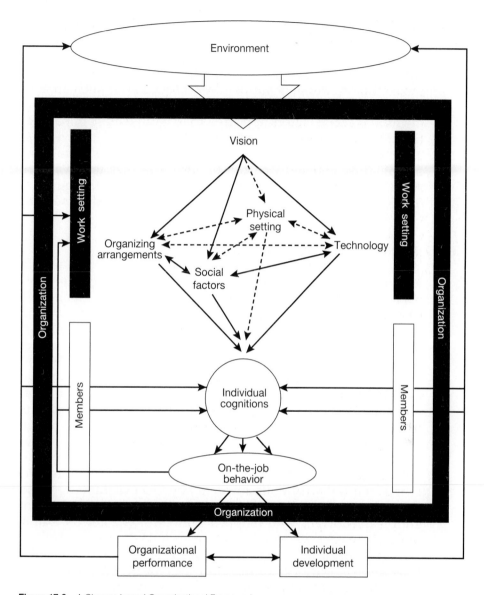

Figure 17-2 A Change-based Organizational Framework

Source: Jerry I. Porras and Peter J. Robertson, "Organizational Development: Theory, Practice, and Research," p. 738. Modified and reproduced by special permission of the Publisher, Consulting Psychologists Press, Inc., Palo Alto, CA 94303, from *Handbook of Industrial and Organizational Psychology, 2nd ed., Vol. 3,* by M. D. Dunnette and L. M. Hough (eds). Copyright 1992 by Consulting Psychologists Press, Inc. All rights reserved. Further reproduction is prohibited without the Publisher's written consent.

should impact social factors, parallel learning structures and quality circles should impact organizing arrangements. Then research studies of different interventions were examined to see if they: (1) changed the work setting, which (2) changed individual cognitions, which (3) changed on-the-job behaviors, which (4) led to outcomes of organizational performance and individual development. Sixty-three research studies were used to test the model. The results were complicated and mixed, but moderately supportive, especially for such an ambitious undertaking. For example, interventions related to organizing arrangements and social factors appeared to have a positive impact on organizational performance, as expected.

We have presented this model and discussion to show how theory building and research can be used together to advance the understanding of the OD process. This example, and the others cited here, demonstrate that significant advances are being made in research on OD.

DOES OD WORK? A REVIEW OF REVIEWS

We conclude this chapter by looking at the results of numerous research studies on OD as summarized in literature reviews. Such reviews give a broad overview of the state of the field. In addition, we examine several studies using meta-analysis, a statistical technique that measures the effects of OD interventions on dependent variables such as performance and satisfaction.

Several excellent literature reviews attest to the efficacy of organization development to bring about desired and intended changes. These surveys of OD research and practice cover a broad range of programs conducted over several decades. Such summaries are valuable for providing a perspective of the field. Several conclusions may be drawn from these reports: first, the preponderance of OD programs produce positive results; second, some OD interventions are more effective than others; third, the variables impacted by OD programs are becoming better understood; and, fourth, the actual causal mechanisms of OD programs are not yet well mapped and clarified. Let us examine briefly some of the reviews.

Porras and Berg[61] screened 160 studies and reduced the total to a set of 35 studies exhibiting clear organization development interventions that were evaluated by rigorous research standards. They found that 308 different variables were measured in the 35 studies; these variables were classified into "outcome" variables and "process" variables. Outcome variables are such typical performance measures as profitability, productivity, and turnover, and individual performance measures such as job satisfaction and job understanding. Process variables are such things as goal emphasis, decision making, influence, and human interaction variables such as openness.

In terms of results, Porras and Berg found the following. Outcome variables were measured in 22 studies, and in 51 percent of the cases substantial positive changes occurred. Analyses were made at the level of the individual, leader, group, and organization with changes being found at all levels. Of interest to us is the authors' comment: "At the organizational level, economic performance improved over 50 percent of the times it was measured (in seven of nine projects)."[62]

Regarding process variables, overall 46 percent of the process variables showed positive changes. It was also found that different interventions produced different results: the Managerial Grid had the greatest impact on outcome variables followed by task-oriented laboratory training and survey feedback. The use of multiple intervention approaches was associated with greater positive change. In addition, either relatively short (four to six months) or relatively long (25 or more months) programs seemed to be associated with the greatest amount of change.

Margulies, Wright, and Scholl[63] analyzed 30 studies and found positive results in over 70 percent of them. Dunn and Swierczek[64] examined 67 cases and found positive gains almost 70 percent of the time. John Nicholas assessed the impact of a variety of OD interventions on *hard criteria* such as costs, profits, and quantity and quality of production in 65 studies.[65] Positive outcomes were found in about half of these cases.

Katzell and Guzzo reviewed 207 field experiments using 11 psychological approaches to improving employee productivity and found gains were reported in 87 percent of the studies. The time frame was from 1971 to 1981 and the interventions included such activities as sociotechnical systems redesign, goal setting, training and instruction, appraisal and feedback, and the like.[66]

Golembiewski, Proehl, and Sink report on an extensive review of the OD literature.[67] They found 574 cases of OD applications occurring from 1945 to mid-1980, with 47 percent of these cases being public sector applications and 53 percent being business or private sector programs. A "global estimate of efficacy" was made by examining each case and assigning it to one of four evaluative categories in which the intervention had (1) highly positive and intended effects, (2) definite balance of positive and intended effects, (3) no appreciable effects, and (4) negative effects. The results were favorable: over 80 percent of the cases showed either highly positive or a definite balance of positive outcomes. On the other hand, only 8 percent of the applications showed negative effects. Additional analyses showed that improvements were found at the individual, leader, group, and total organization levels.

Finally, a massive review of some 800 work improvement efforts by Barry Macy (cited in Sashkin and Burke) shows "generally positive conclusions with respect to both performance and worker satisfaction."[68] Taken together, these literature reviews strongly support the conclusion that OD programs produce positive changes at the organizational and individual levels.

Meta-Analysis

One of the most exciting innovations in the research field is meta-analysis, a set of statistical methods developed by Glass, McGaw, and Smith and by Hunter, Schmidt, and Jackson, to assess treatment effects over a set of studies.[69] Meta-analysis uses quantitative data gathered from single studies, cumulates the data across many studies, and estimates the true effects of treatments on dependent variables. In essence this technique allows investigators to assess the impact of an intervention by using the results from a number of studies, not just a single study. It is a very powerful method for evaluating the effects and effectiveness of OD interventions.

Guzzo, Jette, and Katzell conducted a meta-analysis on the 207 studies included in the literature review by Katzell and Guzzo mentioned earlier.[70] The meta-analysis revealed that the interventions (sociotechnical systems redesign, goal setting, training, and so on), on average, raised worker productivity by one-half standard deviation, a very substantial gain indeed. These authors conclude their article as follows: *"Behavioral science techniques for increasing worker productivity are, on the whole, effective.* For industrial and organizational psychologists, that should be great news!"[71]

A meta-analysis by Neuman, Edwards, and Raju examined 126 empirical studies using a variety of OD interventions for their effects on satisfaction and other attitudes, such as attitudes toward the job, others, and the organization.[72] The results are complex, but they show that OD interventions have a positive and significant effect on attitudes. Specifically, OD programs using multiple interventions cause greater positive effects than programs using only a single intervention. Human process interventions such as team building and laboratory training appear to be most effective for producing positive attitudinal changes, and technostructural interventions have a lesser impact on attitudes.

A meta-analysis by Robertson, Roberts, and Porras based on 52 research studies confirmed the efficacy of OD interventions to produce positive change.[73] This study examined the effects of OD interventions and also tested the model shown in Figure 17-2. Interventions were classified into five kinds relating to organizing arrangements, social factors, technology, physical setting, and multifaceted (or multiple interventions). Dependent measures were classified into seven kinds—organizing arrangements, social factors, technology, physical setting, individual behavior, organizational performance, and individual development.

The results are complex but supportive. For example, the effects of all interventions on all dependent measures were significant and positive. Likewise, the effects of social factors interventions, multifaceted interventions, and organizing arrangements interventions on all dependent measures were positive and significant. Physical settings interventions had a significant negative effect, and technology interventions showed mixed effects. An interesting discovery was that the interventions produced greater significant changes in individual behavior and individual development measures than organizational performance measures. This study supports the usefulness of the Porras and Robertson model and also demonstrates that OD interventions produce significant, positive changes.

Paul Spector examined the effects of interventions that increase autonomy and participation on performance and attitudes.[74] Increased autonomy and participation should lead to a sense of greater "perceived control" by employees. Using 101 samples from 88 studies, he found the following: "For all studies combined, it was found that high levels of perceived control was associated with high levels of job satisfaction (overall and individual facets), commitment, involvement, performance and motivation, and low levels of physical symptoms, emotional distress, role stress, absenteeism, intent to turnover, and turnover."[75] This is good news for OD because most OD interventions are designed to increase participation and autonomy.

Sociotechnical systems (STS) interventions are a very important part of the OD field. These efforts aim to optimize the technical and social systems of organizations in order to increase both productivity and the quality of life. A thorough review of STS research studies by Pasmore, Francis, Haldeman, and Shani showed that STS interventions increase productivity in 87 percent of the cases, a very positive finding.[76] Rafik Beekun conducted a meta-analysis of 17 sociotechnical studies to estimate their effects on productivity and "escape behavior" (absenteeism, turnover, and tardiness).[77] The results show that STS interventions significantly increase productivity and decrease escape behavior, as expected. A number of moderator variables (such as technological changes, change in pay systems, and the number of people involved in the program) were found to impact program effectiveness. In general, programs that utilized autonomous work groups (versus semiautonomous or nonautonomous work groups) showed higher gains in productivity; programs that included an increase in pay showed higher gains in productivity; and STS programs in countries other than the United States showed higher gains in productivity than programs in the United States. Decreases in escape behaviors like absenteeism and turnover were greater in programs that used nonautonomous work groups and that did not change the pay system. These are complicated, but valuable results because they (1) show STS programs produce desired effects, and (2) identify ways to improve future STS interventions.

A meta-analysis of gainsharing case studies by Bullock and Tubbs examined the ingredients of successful gainsharing programs.[78]

Gainsharing is a compensation program in which employees generate ideas for productivity increases and cost-cutting methods and share in the financial benefits that result. Gainsharing is considered by many to be an OD intervention with potential to increase organizational performance and individual satisfaction directly—profits and paychecks both go up. Case studies are in-depth analyses of the effects of an intervention at one organization; from a research standpoint they are often criticized because they are limited to a sample size of only one.

Bullock and Tubbs gathered data from 33 case studies of gainsharing programs spanning 50 years, coded the data to make them amenable to meta-analysis, and tested hypotheses derived from a model predicting gainsharing success. The meta-analysis was designed to discover the factors in gainsharing programs that contributed to success, not to discover the effects of gainsharing per se. The authors found the following features associated with successful gainsharing programs: employee involvement in designing the plan, the use of outside practitioners, the presence of formal structures to facilitate involvement and generation of ideas, employee favorability toward the plan, and participative management style. This study is important for several reasons: It provides good information on how to increase success in gainsharing programs; it demonstrates a new use for meta-analysis methods; and it shows that case studies can be used to generate robust research results.

To summarize, the results from these various meta-analyses argue strongly that OD interventions are powerful methods for improving organizational performance. A variety of interventions was found to be efficacious in a variety of settings and situations. Meta-analysis has proved to be a useful research tool for understanding the effects of OD interventions.

CONCLUDING COMMENTS

This overview of problems, positive developments, and results for research on organization development substantiates the valuable contribution OD makes to organizations and the people in them. OD practitioners have always had "faith" in the power of OD; "faith-plus-data" is even more reassuring.

NOTES

1. Larry E. Pate, Warren R. Nielsen, and Paula C. Bacon, "Advances in Research on Organization Development: Toward a Beginning," in Robert L. Taylor, Michael J. O'Connell, Robert A. Zawacki, and D. D. Warrick, eds., *Academy of Management Proceedings '76*, Proceedings of the 36th Annual Meeting of the Academy of Management, Kansas City, Missouri, August 11–14, 1976, pp. 389–394.

2. Ibid., pp. 389 and 392.
3. Robert L. Kahn, "Organizational Development: Some Problems and Proposals," *Journal of Applied Behavioral Science*, 10, no. 4 (1974), 485–502. Kahn also criticized the research on OD as being mostly case studies, a condition that was more true then than now.
4. See, for example, Fred N. Kerlinger, *Foundations of Behavioral Research*, 2nd ed. (New York: Holt, Rinehart and Winston, 1973).
5. Donald T. Campbell and Julian C. Stanley, *Experimental and Quasi-Experimental Designs for Research* (Chicago: Rand McNally, 1963), p. 5.
6. Ibid. This little book is generally considered to be one of the best expositions of research designs available.
7. Pate, Nielsen, and Bacon, "Advances in Research on Organization Development"; and Sam E. White and Terence R. Mitchell, "Organization Development: A Review of Research Content and Research Design," *Academy of Management Review*, 1 (April 1976), pp. 57–73.
8. Jerry I. Porras and P. O. Berg, "The Impact of Organization Development," *The Academy of Management Review*, 3, no. 2 (April 1978), 249–266.
9. Norman Berkowitz, "Audiences and Their Implications for Evaluation Research," *Journal of Applied Behavioral Science*, 5, no. 3 (1969), 411–428.
10. Campbell and Stanley, *Experimental and Quasi-Experimental Designs*, p. 5.
11. Clayton P. Alderfer, "Organization Development," in *Annual Review of Psychology*, 28 (1977), pp. 197–223.
12. Kerlinger, *Foundations of Behavioral Research*, p. 9. Italics in the original.
13. Clayton P. Alderfer, "Change Processes in Organizations," in Marvin D. Dunnette, ed., *Handbook of Industrial and Organizational Psychology* (Chicago: Rand McNally, 1976), pp. 1591–1638.
14. Chris Argyris, *Intervention Theory and Method: A Behavioral Science View* (Reading, MA: Addison-Wesley, 1970).
15. Robert R. Blake and Jane Srygley Mouton, *Consultation* (Reading, MA: Addison-Wesley, 1976).
16. Peter B. Vaill, "Practice Theories in Organization Development," in J. D. Adams, ed., *New Technologies in Organization Development* (La Jolla, CA: University Associates, 1974), pp. 71–84.
17. J. G. Bowers, J. L. Franklin, and P. A. Pecorella, "Matching Problems, Precursors, and Interventions in OD: A Systemic Approach," *Journal of Applied Behavioral Science*, 11 (1975), pp. 391–410.
18. White and Mitchell, "Organization Development." For a discussion of facet theory, see L. Guttman, "An Outline of Some New Methodology for Social Research," *Public Opinion Quarterly*, 18 (1955), pp. 395–404.
19. See White and Mitchell, "Organization Development," pp. 59–66, for this discussion.
20. William N. Dunn and Frederic W. Swierczek, "Planned Organizational Change: Toward Grounded Theory," *Journal of Applied Behavioral Science*, 13, no. 2 (1977), 135–157.
21. Ibid., p. 149.
22. R. J. Golembiewski, K. Billingsley, and S. Yeager, "Measuring Change and Persistence in Human Affairs: Types of Change Generated by OD Designs," *The Journal of Applied Behavioral Science*, 12 (1976), pp. 133–157.
23. A. A. Armenakis and R. W. Zmud, "Interpreting the Measurement of Change in Organizational Research," *Personnel Psychology*, 32 (1979), pp. 709–723.
24. A. Randolph, "Planned Organizational Change and Its Measurement," *Personnel Psychology*, 35 (1982), pp. 117–139.
25. J. A. Terborg, G. S. Howard, and S. E. Maxwell, "Evaluating Planning Organizational Change: A Method for Assessing Alpha, Beta, and Gamma Change," *Academy of Management Review*, 5 (1980), pp. 109–121.

26. J. I. Porras and J. V. Singh, "Alpha, Beta, and Gamma Change in Modeling-Based Organization Development," *Journal of Occupational Behavior*, 7 (1986), pp. 9–24.

27. C. Argyris, R. Putnam, and D. M. Smith, *Action Science* (San Francisco: Jossey-Bass, 1985).

28. M. Blumberg and C. D. Pringle, "How Control Groups Can Cause Loss of Control in Action Research: The Case of Rushton Coal Mine," *The Journal of Applied Behavioral Science*, 19 (1983), pp. 409–425.

29. R. J. Bullock and D. J. Svyantek, "The Impossibility of Using Random Strategies to Study the Organization Development Process," *The Journal of Applied Behavioral Science*, 23 (1987), pp. 255–262.

30. Ibid., p. 260.

31. R. J. Bullock and Patti F. Bullock, "Pure Science Versus Science-Action Models of Data Feedback: A Field Experiment," *Group and Organization Studies*, 9 (March 1984), pp. 7–27.

32. Michael Beer and Anna Elise Walton, "Organization Change and Development," *Annual Review of Psychology*, 38 (1987), pp. 339–367.

33. Ibid., p. 344.

34. Frank Friedlander and L. Dave Brown, "Organization Development," in *Annual Review of Psychology*, 25 (1974), p. 336.

35. Pate, Nielsen, and Bacon, "Advances in Research in Organization Development," pp. 390–391.

36. J. Taylor and D. G. Bowers, *The Survey of Organizations: A Machine-Scored Standardized Questionnaire Instrument* (Ann Arbor, MI: Institute for Social Research, 1972).

37. See, for example, David G. Bowers, "OD Techniques and Their Results in 23 Organizations: The Michigan ICL Study," *Journal of Applied Behavioral Science*, 9, no. 1 (1973), 21–43.

38. See, for example, the *Michigan Organizational Assessment Package Program Report II* (Ann Arbor, MI: Survey Research Center, August 1975). This program is partially sponsored by the National Center for Productivity and the Quality of Working Life, an independent agency of the federal government.

39. Edward E. Lawler III and Gerald E. Ledford, Jr., "Productivity and the Quality of Work Life," *National Productivity Review*, 1, no. 1 (Winter 1981–1982), 23–36; and G. E. Ledford, Jr. and E. E. Lawler III, "Quality of Work Life Programs, Coordination, and Productivity," *Journal of Contemporary Business*, 11, no. 2 (1982), 93–106. This issue of the *Journal of Contemporary Business* is devoted to addressing behavioral science strategies for organizational improvement and is worthwhile reading.

40. Alderfer, "Organization Development," p. 219.

41. Nancy C. Roberts and Jerry I. Porras, "Progress in Organization Development Research," *Group and Organization Studies*, 7, no. 1 (March 1982), 91–116.

42. Friedlander and Brown, "Organization Development."

43. Alderfer, "Organization Development."

44. Claude Faucheux, Gilles Amada, and Andre Laurent, "Organizational Development and Change," *Annual Review of Psychology*, 33 (1982), pp. 343–370.

45. Beer and Walton, "Organization Change and Development."

46. Jerry I. Porras and Robert C. Silvers, "Organization Development and Transformation," in *Annual Review of Psychology*, 42 (1991), pp. 51–78.

47. Michael Beer, "The Technology of Organization Development," Dunnette, ed., *Handbook of Industrial and Organizational Psychology*, pp. 937–993.

48. George Strauss, "Organization Development," in Robert Dublin, ed., *Handbook of Work, Organization, and Society* (Chicago: Rand McNally, 1976), pp. 617–685.

49. Jerry I. Porras and Peter J. Robertson, "Organizational Development: Theory, Practice, and Research," in Marvin D. Dunnette and Leaetta M. Hough, eds., *Handbook of Industrial and Organizational Psychology*, 2nd ed., vol. 3 (Palo Alto, CA: Consulting Psychologists Press, 1992), pp. 719–822.

50. White and Mitchell, "Organization Development."
51. Pate, Nielsen, and Bacon, "Advances in Research on Organization Development." In addition, a model for evaluation of OD programs has been proposed by John M. Nicholas, "A Systems Analysis Approach for Planning Evaluations of OD Interventions," in Robert L. Taylor, Michael J. O'Connell, Robert A. Zawacki, and D. D. Warrick, eds., *Academy of Mangement Proceedings '77*, Proceedings of the 37th annual meeting of the Academy of Management at Orlando, Florida, August 14–17, 1977, pp. 358–362.
52. Porras and Berg, "The Impact of Organization Development," pp. 249–266.
53. Robert T. Golembiewski, Carl W. Proehl, Jr., and David Sink, "Estimating the Success of OD Applications," *Training and Development Journal*, 36, no. 4 (April 1982), 86–95.
54. Marshall Sashkin and W. Warner Burke, "Organization Development in the 1980s," *Journal of Management*, 13, no. 2 (1987), 393–417.
55. Ibid., p. 403.
56. Ibid., p. 405.
57. Porras and Silvers, "Organization Development and Transformation."
58. Porras and Robertson, "Organizational Development: Theory, Practice, and Research."
59. Ibid., p. 740.
60. Ibid., p. 735.
61. Porras and Berg, "The Impact of Organization Development."
62. Ibid., p. 256.
63. Newton Margulies, Penny L. Wright, and Richard W. Scholl, "Organization Development Techniques: Their Impact on Change," *Group and Organization Studies*, 2, no. 4 (December 1977), 449.
64. Dunn and Swierczek, "Planned Organizational Change."
65. John M. Nicholas, "The Comparative Impact of Organization Development Interventions on Hard Criteria Measures," *Academy of Management Review*, 7, no. 4 (October 1982), 531–541.
66. R. A. Katzell and R. A. Guzzo, "Psychological Approaches to Productivity Improvement," *American Psychologist* (April 1983), pp. 468–472.
67. Golembiewski, Proehl, and Sink, "Estimating the Success of OD Applications."
68 Barry A. Macy, "An Assessment of United States Improvement and Productivity Efforts: 1970–1985." Paper presented at the National Academy of Management meetings, Chicago, August 1986. Cited from p. 403 in Sashkin and Burke, "Organization Development in the 1980s."
69. G. V. Glass, V. McGaw, and M. L. Smith, *Meta-Analysis in Social Research* (Beverly Hills, CA: Sage Publishing, 1982). Also J. F. Hunter, F. L. Schmidt, and G. B. Jackson, *Meta-Analysis: Cumulating Research Findings Across Studies* (Beverly Hills, CA: Sage Publishing, 1982).
70. R. A. Guzzo, R. D. Jette, and R. A. Katzell, "The Effects of Psychologically Based Intervention Programs on Worker Productivity: A Meta-Analysis," *Personnel Psychology*, 38 (1985), pp. 275–291.
71. Ibid., p. 287.
72. G. A. Neuman, J. E. Edwards, and N. S. Raju, "Organizational Development Interventions: A Meta-Analysis of Their Effects on Satisfaction and Other Attitudes," *Personnel Psychology*, 42 (1989), pp. 461–489.
73. P. J. Robertson, D. R. Roberts, and J. I. Porras, "A Meta-Analytic Review of the Impact of Planned Organizational Change Interventions," in J. L. Wall and L. R. Jauch, eds., *Best Papers Proceeding*, Fifty-Second Annual Meeting, Academy of Management, Las Vegas, Nevada, August 9–12, 1992.
74. P. E. Spector, "Perceived Control by Employees: A Meta-Analysis of Studies Concerning Autonomy and Participation at Work," *Human Relations*, 39, no. 11 (1986), 1005–1016.
75. Ibid., p. 1005.

76. W. Pasmore, C. Francis, J. Haldeman, and A. Shani, "Sociotechnical Systems: A North American Reflection on Empirical Studies in the Seventies," *Human Relations*, 35 (1982), pp. 1179–1204.

77. R. I. Beekun, "Assessing the Effectiveness of Sociotechnical Interventions: Antidote or Fad?" *Human Relations*, 42, no. 10 (October 1989), 877–897.

78. R. J. Bullock and M. E. Tubbs, "A Case Meta-Analysis of Gainsharing Plans as Organization Development Interventions," *The Journal of Applied Behavioral Science* , 26, no. 3 (1990), 383–404.

18

THE FUTURE AND OD

No one is omniscient about the future, but our look at OD history and present practice can help develop a picture of what might lie ahead. And what lies ahead is exciting, rewarding, and full of challenges.

THE CHANGING ENVIRONMENT

The environment in which organizations operate is increasingly turbulent in an era of global, national, and regional commercial competitiveness. But paradoxically that competition is part of a rapidly shifting melange of competitiveness and interdependencies. Alliances, consortia, mergers, and acquisitions are all common. Production and communications technology are changing at an exponential rate. Furthermore, dislocation of people through downsizing and restructuring is rampant. Simultaneously, there is a profusion of business startups. Yesterday's strategies are not likely to work in tomorrow's workplaces.

It seems clear that in large part the old organizational paradigm is dying. It doesn't work well in this emerging environment. Top-down, autocratically directed, rigidly hierarchical, fear-generating organizations are giving way to something new. The new paradigm proclaims that the most innovative and successful organizations will be those that derive their strength and vitality from adaptable, committed team players at all levels and from all specialties, not from the omniscience of the hierarchy.[1] Increasingly, organizations will be flatter, with smaller central staffs and with more real delegation to small groups and units. High-performance organizations focusing on the customer and continuous quality improvement and placing high value on human resources, diversity, and high-performance teams will be the norm.[2]

OD will be a major player in assisting organizations to shift to and sustain this new paradigm and to help invent even more effective paradigms in the future. The future of OD is bright, but only if the field continues to evolve. Here are some opinions about that evolution and some of the contingencies that must be faced.

FUNDAMENTAL STRENGTHS OF OD

The central strength of OD is that the processes about which we have written in this book are fundamentally sound. These processes include: careful tuning in to the perceptions and feelings of people; creating relatively safe conditions for surfacing these data; involving people in diagnosing the strengths and weaknesses of their organizations and making action plans for improvement; focusing on team and other interdependent configurations; redesigning work so that it is more meaningful and motivating; explicitly training people toward a participative, open, team leadership mode; and using qualified third parties. These and other characteristics of OD have created a powerful and durable process for organization improvement.

A second fundamental strength has to do with the political, governmental milieu. OD is highly compatible with democratic governmental structures and processes which are well established in many parts of the world and emerging elsewhere. Indeed, OD approaches promote and help sustain democratic processes.

Third, OD practice has been expanding in the last two or three decades to create a blending of attention to people-oriented processes with attention to the design of the human-technical system. More and more there has been a melding of what Frank Friedlander and L. Dave Brown in the 1970s were calling "human-processual" and "technostructural" approaches.[3] To illustrate, this blending can be seen in the increasing use of parallel or collateral organizations in large-scale change projects, many of which involve extensive technological changes. It is also evident in the extensive use of employee involvement in sociotechnical systems (STS) programs, and in the use of OD practitioners in the training and development of self-managed teams.

Fourth, there is a crying need almost everywhere for assistance in getting the right people together to talk constructively about important organizational matters, and for developing processes for making things better. It is clear that the OD field has an enormous and vital role to play in the foreseeable future.

OD won't go away; it can't go away. If it did, it would be reinvented under a new label. We believe that OD can only become stronger and more effective through evolving theory, research, and practice.

OD'S FUTURE

How large a role and how constructive a role OD will play in the drama that is unfolding depend upon a number of interrelated conditions. While most of the conditions we see are generally favorable to OD, there are also countertrends and/or uncertainties. These contingencies have to do with leadership and values, knowledge about OD, OD training, the interdisciplinary nature of OD, diffusion of technique, integrative practice, rediscovering history, and recording the present.

Leadership and Values

For OD to flourish it is important that top management—CEOs, boards of directors, top executives, including the human resources executive—and OD consultants place high value on strong individual, team, and organizational performance coupled with people-oriented values. As O'Toole says, there may be no necessary correlation, but management can *choose* to try to create organizations that have both profitability and humanistic/developmental objectives.[4] It seems that there is an almost schizophrenic situation in the United States, with some top managements highly attentive and committed to this duality of objectives, and others concerned only with the bottom line and/or the price of stock. As George Strauss says, some executives have a "slash and burn" mentality.[5] Most OD consultants, as we have seen in Chapter 4, have strong orientations toward organizational effectiveness coupled with democratic and humanistic values.

Richard Hackman and Greg Oldham in 1980 saw contemporary organizations at a "fork in the road," with a choice between traveling down one of two routes. On Route One, jobs will be fitted to people, with accountable and responsible individuals and teams having considerable autonomy, where organizations will be viewed "as places where people grow and learn new things." Furthermore, "questions of employee motivation and satisfaction will be considered explicitly when new technologies and work practices are invented and engineered. . . ." On Route Two, "technological and engineering considerations will dominate decision making about how jobs are designed. . . .Work performance and organizational productivity will be closely monitored and controlled by managers. . . ." Furthermore, "desired on-the-job behavior will be elicited and maintained by extensive and sophisticated use of extrinsic rewards." They add, pointedly, that on Route Two "most organizations will sponsor programs to help people adapt to life at work, including sophisticated procedures for assisting employees and their families in dealing with alcohol and drug abuse problems." When their book was published, Hackman and Oldham believed that many organizations were moving vigorously down Route Two, which was clearly troubling to them.[6] Hopefully, more and more organizations are going down Route One today. But the point is that there is a fork in the road, and management makes a choice in many large and small decisions, often inadvertently, about which way to travel.

The OD process will take root and flourish in direct proportion to the prevalence of the dual set of values that O'Toole talks about, or the extent top executives decide to travel Route One, as described by Hackman and Oldham. These are value decisions, but must be coupled with strong leadership skills. By strong leadership skills we are referring to Kotter's notions of "establishing direction," "aligning people," and "motivating and inspiring."[7]

Knowledge about OD

Top-management groups are likely to utilize OD to the extent that they are aware of and understand the process involved. While the extent of this knowledge is undoubtedly widespread, we suspect that much of it is constrained by lack of an experiential feel for what the process is like. University courses, workshops sponsored by consultants and consulting firms, laboratory training, books and articles—these and other methods contribute to the information available to managers and executives. Descriptions and explanations by subordinates and by consultants probably play a large part.

Our sense is that news accounts frequently short-change the OD field. Although not every article or news story about a successful employee involvement or participative improvement program can go into detail about the origins of that particular effort, our "wish list" includes more reporting about the major components of improvement programs and how they started. By major components we mean aspects such as a third party teaming up with an executive, the data-gathering methods used, the formation of particular kinds of teams, and so on. We suspect that many of the successful employee involvement efforts reported by the media have OD people and processes and OD-oriented executives as unsung, behind-the-scenes leaders and movers. Perhaps this is part of the "marginality" of OD consultants.[8] Overall, we see the need for more detailed, published case studies of OD efforts—including successes and failures—and the use of OD processes in conjunction with other improvement strategies.

OD Training

The quality of OD training in the United States appears to be high if one looks at the curricula of university programs, NTL's array of training experiences, the training offerings of various consulting and training organizations, and the attention paid to OD matters in conferences of the OD Network, the Academy of Management, the American Society for Training and Development, and other national and international organizations.

T-group experiences warrant special attention. T-groups seem to have given way to some extent to other experiential methods, which may be a mixed bag. As Vaill states it, these other experiential methods, more and more

> ... began to be used to prove something to the learner, rather than as methods and settings within which the learner could do the experimenting that the original philosophy of laboratory education declared to be so important. . . .
>
> What was most significant of all about sensitivity training . . . had been largely lost in subsequent developments. The core belief of laboratory education is no longer apparent in the experiential education community. . . .[9]

We would argue that in the future there will be a need for more availability of T-group training—as a training intervention, not as an organizational intervention—particularly for both aspiring OD practitioners and managers. And we should not overlook the utility of T-group training for any or all organizational members, including first-line supervisors.

Accreditation and peer review of OD skill competency has languished. For a few years there was an implied accreditation of some well-selected professionals through NTL Institute associate status, and then that approach was shifted to accreditation through Certified Consultants International. But the latter organization did not have the support it needed and closed shop, although some regional professional-development groups remained after the national organization closed its doors. Clients, of course, can be encouraged to look at and inquire about credentials and competency. Certainly the attainment of a masters degree or doctorate with an OD concentration, or the completion of an OD track with NTL Institute are examples of credentials that suggest in-depth training.

Interdisciplinary Nature of OD

OD's future, to a significant extent, is related to other disciplines. Historically, as we saw in Chapter 3, OD has been a highly interdisciplinary, eclectic field. It has been built from theory, research, and practice in social psychology, adult education, community development, general systems theory, family group therapy, anthropology, philosophy, counseling, psychiatry, general management, social work, human resources management, large conference management, and other fields.

Are scholars and practitioners looking hard at these early contributing fields to see what else is emerging that might be useful? Are there other bodies of knowledge that should be tracked? Surely there is much to be learned from such fields as international diplomacy, dispute mediation (including divorce mediation), arbitration, and architecture. Historically, there has been some reciprocal influence between these fields and OD. Undoubtedly there should be more.

Diffusion of Technique

OD techniques and approaches have been widely disseminated in society, at least on the American and Canadian scene, and in many parts of Europe, Asia, Australia, New Zealand, Latin America, and elsewhere. In large measure this is a positive development because it demonstrates that OD processes are being widely perceived as having considerable value. It is also a compliment to the professionals of the field, including OD trainers, researchers, and writers.

However, at least two problems may be lurking around the edges of this wide dissemination of technique. One problem is that techniques may be used without sufficient understanding of their theoretical, research, and/or historical foundations. The consequences may be misapplication and, in turn, unnecessary cynicism and resistance on the part of clients.

The other problem is the possibility of a gradual diffusion of the OD field across other specialities, with the resultant loss of some of its integration of values, theory, research, history, and practice. This is not a problem of semantics but a potential problem of loss of focus— OD's central values, what to teach, what to learn, and how to communicate the basics and the subtleties of the field. If OD becomes anything or everything, then what is it?

By now, people in all kinds of disciplines and occupations have been exposed to OD training and/or to OD interventions. Accountants, engineers, psychiatrists, teachers, nurses, lawyers, physicians, computer specialists, managers and employees in government and in social service agencies, military personnel, contractors, flight crews—the list could go on and on—have been exposed to OD concepts and/or experiences. This is generally all to the good. But is there a danger that some people are practicing or utilizing OD without understanding, for example, the importance of appropriate, collaborative diagnoses with the client system and careful selection of suitable interventions? Is there a danger of OD techniques being used to manipulate people toward nondisclosed, solely self-serving ends? The answer to both is "probably." Perhaps solutions lie in the availability of and support for quality training and research in OD and in the careful selection of consultants. Another partial solution may involve widespread understanding of the OD process, so that participants themselves act as a check on misdirected or ill-considered efforts. The less mystery and the more openness and understanding about OD, the better.

Integrative Practice

It would be a challenge, indeed, for any one person to develop skills in all of the interventions we have described in this book, plus acquiring skills in other specialities as well. Yet, there is a major need, in the United States at least, to couple OD skills with the growing number of broad structural interventions, and to do further conceptualizing and research about such integrations. We refer to total quality management (TQM), quality of work life (QWL), and reengineering programs, in particular. The emphasis on teams in TQM and QWL makes OD a natural partner in these efforts. The lack of emphasis on participative approaches in reengineering efforts makes OD-practitioner involvement less likely, but not less necessary. Important conceptualization relative to this integration has occurred. For example, Robert Golembiewski and Ben-Chu Sun and Warner Burke have written about OD and QWL.[10] Dan Ciampa, Marshall Sashkin, Kenneth Kiser, Edward Lawler, Susan Mohrman and Gerald Ledford, and others have made contributions toward the theoretical and applied integration of TQM and OD.[11] This work needs to be extended.

It is desirable for OD practitioners to be as knowledgeable as possible about such structural interventions and these integrations. At the same time, we believe it is essential for experts in the technological aspects of these fields to be knowledgeable about OD. An ideal arrangement may be for OD professionals to join with such experts on consulting teams. This is happening, although just how extensively we do not know. Obviously, this requires that such teams pay considerable attention to their own team building and teamwork.

As an extension of these ideas, there is need for additional conceptualization about large-scale systems change. As Warner Burke says,

> We are on the threshold of a paradigm of the effective management of large-scale organization change. . . . we are beginning to understand much more clearly what the primary levers are for initiating and implementing organization change, levers such as culture, values, key leadership acts (providing a vision and clear sense of direction), the reward system, and management/executive programs.[12]

In short, the OD field is closer to the refinement of such a paradigm, but the journey must continue.

Rediscovering and Recording History

The history of OD is indispensable for retaining and improving effective OD interventions and approaches. For example, as we have discussed, numerous practitioners today are rediscovering the utility, in some circumstances, of "getting the whole system in the room," and are drawing on this history. Knowledge and insight about this goes back at least to the 1950s.[13] As another example, some contemporary practitioners are finding that, for a variety of reasons, a successful change effort in one part of an organization can be suffocated by forces in other parts of the system. Knowledge about this goes back at least to the 1970s and probably earlier.[14] Jyotsna Sanzgiri and Jonathan Gottlieb say that "there will be a resurgence in the need to understand more of what the founders of the field of OD were always interested in: participative structures, decision making based on action research, long-term approaches to management, and processes for organizational renewal and change."[15]

There are portions of OD history that are in danger of being lost forever, although some of these probably get reinvented from time to time. We are convinced that there are hundreds of interventions devised by OD consultants that have been tremendously successful in particular applications, and used perhaps two or three times again when similar circumstances occurred, but never recorded and published. Focusing on the broad, fundamental participant action research process is of overriding importance, but nevertheless intervention techniques are extremely important for the OD professional's "tool kit." We are arguing for "clearinghouse" kinds of publications, similar in approach to what University Associates has used relative to group training techniques. Fordyce and Weil's *Managing WITH People* was a major contribution in the early years of OD. Elaborations about the context in which such techniques could be used, such as provided by Fordyce and Weil's descriptions of "benefits," "limitations," and "operating hints," would be invaluable.[16]

CLOSING COMMENTS

There is enormous opportunity and potential for the OD movement in the future. Organizations throughout the world need the unique help that can be provided by highly trained interventionists using people-oriented, action research approaches. The future of OD is bright, as long as the high-quality, hard work of the past continues, and providing top leaders do not revert to autocratic practices in times of high turbulence or crises.

There is much challenging, difficult work to be done, but also great fun and many rewards in working with people in making their organizations more successful and satisfying.

What is OD all about? OD is really about people helping each other to unleash the human spirit and human capability in the workplace.

NOTES

1. See also Tom Peters, *Liberation Management* (New York: Alfred A. Knopf, 1992), pp. 208–209, 238–239; and A. J. Vogl and David A. Nadler, "It Could Happen to Us," *Across the Board*, 30 (October 1993), pp. 27–32. For more on paradigms, see Joel Arthur Barker, *Future Edge* (New York: William Morrow and Company, 1992).

2. See Walter Kiechel III, "How We Will Work in the Year 2000," *Future*, May 17, 1993, pp. 38–52; Richard A. Melcher, "How Goliaths Can Act Like Davids," in *Business Week* special 1993 issue, *Enterprise: How Entrepreneurs Are Reshaping the Economy and What Big Companies Can Learn;* and Thomas A. Stewart, "The Search for the Organization of Tomorrow," *Fortune*, May 18, 1992, pp. 92–98.

3. Frank Friedlander and L. Dave Brown, "Organization Development," in *Annual Review of Psychology*, 25 (1974), pp. 313–316, 320–321, and 336–341. See also Marshall Sashkin and W. Warner Burke, "Organization Development in the 1980s," *Journal of Management,* 13 (Summer 1987), pp. 395–417; and Michael Beer and Elise Walton, "Developing the Competitive Organization: Interventions and Strategies," *American Psychologist*, 45 (February 1990), p. 160.

4. James O'Toole, "Do Good, Do Well: The Business Enterprise Awards," *California Management Review*, 33 (Spring 1991), p. 21.

5. George Strauss, "President's Column," *Industrial Relations Research Association Series Newsletter*, 35 (September 1993), p. 2.

6. J. Richard Hackman and Greg R. Oldham, *Work Redesign* (Reading, MA: Addison-Wesley Publishing Company, 1980), pp. 260–266.

7. John P. Kotter, *A Force for Change: How Leadership Differs from Management* (New York: The Free Press, 1990), p. 7.

8. See Thomas G. Cummings and Christopher G. Worley, *Organization Development and Change*, 5th ed. (Minneapolis/St. Paul: West Publishing Company, 1993), p. 33.

9. Peter B. Vaill, "Integrating the Diverse Directions of the Behavioral Sciences," in Robert Tannenbaum, Newton Margulies, Fred Massarik and Associates, *Human Systems Development* (San Francisco: Jossey-Bass Publishers, 1985), pp. 560–561.

10. Robert T. Golembiewski and Ben-Chu Sun, "Positive-Findings Bias in QWL Studies," *Journal of Management*, 16 (September 1990), 667; and W. Warner Burke, *Organization Development* (Boston: Little, Brown and Company, 1982), p. 323.

11. Dan Ciampa, *Total Quality* (Reading, MA: Addison-Wesley Publishing Company, 1992); Marshall Sashkin and Kenneth J. Kiser, *Total Quality Management* (Seabrook, MD: Ducochon Press, 1991); Marshall Sashkin and Kenneth J. Kiser, "What Is Total Quality Management and How Does It Relate to OD?" *Academy of Management ODC Newsletter* (Winter 1992), pp. 16–19; and Edward E. Lawler III, Susan Albers Mohrman, and Gerald E. Ledford, Jr., *Employee Involvement and Total Quality Management* (San Francisco: Jossey-Bass Publishers, 1992).

12. W. Warner Burke, *Organization Development* (Reading, MA: Addison-Wesley Publishing Company, 1994), p. 200.

13. See Marvin R. Weisbord, *Productive Workplaces* (San Francisco: Jossey-Bass Publishers, 1987), p. 283.

14. See Paul S. Goodman, *Assessing Organizational Change* (New York: John Wiley, 1979).
15. Jyotsna Sanzgiri and Jonathan Gottlieb, "Philosophic and Pragmatic Influences on the Practice of Organization Development, 1950–2000," *Organizational Dynamics*, 21 (Autumn 1992), p. 64.
18. Jack K. Fordyce and Raymond Weil, *Managing WITH People: A Manager's Handbook of Organization Development Methods* (Reading, MA: Addison-Wesley Publishing Company, 1971).

AUTHOR INDEX

SUBJECT INDEX